Autodesk Official Training Guide

Essentials

M000166574

AutoCAD®

2010

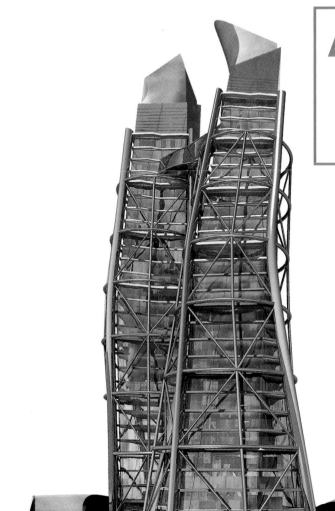

Learning **AutoCAD**® 2010

Using hands-on exercises, learn the features, commands, and techniques for creating, editing, and printing drawings with AutoCAD® 2010 and AutoCAD LT® 2010 software.

Autodesk Certification Preparation

Autodesk®

Published by: Autodesk, Inc.
111 McInnis Parkway
San Rafael, CA 94903, USA

Acknowledgments

The Autodesk Learning team wishes to thank everyone who participated in the development of this project, with special acknowledgement to the authoring contributions and subject matter expertise of Ron Myers and CrWare, LP.

CrWare, LP began publishing courseware for Autodesk® Inventor® in 2001. Since that time, the company has grown to include full-time curriculum developers, subject matter experts, technical writers, and graphics specialists, each with a unique set of industry experiences and talents that enables CrWare to create content that is both accurate and relevant to meeting the learning needs of its readers and customers.

The company's Founder and General Partner, Ron Myers, has been using Autodesk® products since 1989. During that time, Ron Myers worked in all disciplines of drafting and design, until 1996 when he began a career as an Applications Engineer, Instructor, and Author. Ron Myers has been creating courseware and other training material for Autodesk since 1996 and has written and created training material for AutoCAD®, Autodesk Inventor, AutoCAD® Mechanical, Mechanical Desktop®, and Autodesk® Impression.

Acknowledgements:

Cover Image
Guillermo Melantoni

Other Images
Table of contents, chapter header, and left/right margin images courtesy of Agustin Landa Arquitecto.

Special thanks go out to:

Luke Pauw
Sr. Graphic Designer

Diane Erlich
Sr. Graphic/Production Designer

Daniel Gottlieb
Graphic/Production Designer

Table of Contents

Chapter 05

Chapter 10

Chapter 11

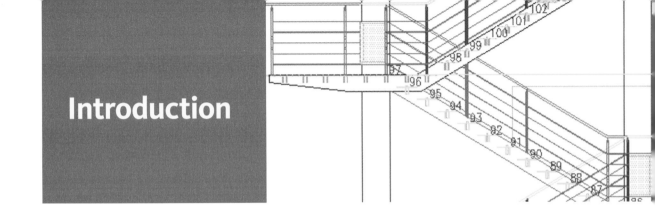

Introduction

Introduction

Welcome to the *Learning AutoCAD 2010 and AutoCAD LT 2010* Autodesk Official Training Guide, a training guide for use in Authorized Training Center (ATC®) locations, corporate training settings, and other classroom settings.

Although this guide is designed for instructor-led courses, you can also use it for self-paced learning. The guide encourages self-learning through the use of the AutoCAD® or AutoCAD LT® Help system.

This introduction covers the following topics:

- Course objectives
- Prerequisites
- Using this guide
- Default installation
- CD contents
- Completing the exercises
- Settings for the exercises
- Installing the exercise data files from the CD
- Imperial and metric datasets
- Notes, tips, and warnings
- Feedback

This guide is complementary to the software documentation. For detailed explanations of features and functionality, refer to the Help in the software.

Course Objectives

After completing this course, you will be able to:

- Navigate the interface, open and close files, and use the Zoom commands to adjust the display of objects on the screen.
- Describe units, function keys, and coordinate systems and create basic objects, using different data input techniques, object snaps, object snap tracking, polar tracking, and PolarSnap.
- Select, modify, and adjust the properties of objects using object grips and the Move, Copy, Rotate, Mirror, and Array commands.
- Create and manage layers and linetypes and obtain geometric information from objects in the drawing.
- Modify objects by changing their size, shape, orientation, or geometric composition using Trim, Extend, Offset, Join, and other commands.
- Create layouts, and create and manipulate viewports on the layouts.

- Create and edit annotation objects using multiline and single line text.
- Create, edit, and manage dimensions and dimension styles.
- Enhance the drawing's visual appearance with hatch patterns and gradient fills.
- Create blocks and reuse them in your drawings using the Insert command, DesignCenter, and tool palettes. Utilize the DesignCenter and tool palettes to insert and create other content in your drawings.
- Create multiple segmented polyline objects, create the smooth curve objects of splines and ellipses, and add tables to your drawings.
- Create and use page setups, and plot your designs from layouts and model space.
- Use drawing templates to simplify the process of creating new drawings that contain all the required dimension styles, text styles, and layers that you would otherwise create manually, each time you create a new drawing.

Prerequisites

This guide is designed for the new user who needs to know the essential commands necessary for professional 2D drawing, design, and drafting using AutoCAD or AutoCAD LT. No previous computer- aided design (CAD) experience is required.

It is recommended that you have a working knowledge of:

- Microsoft® Windows® XP or Microsoft® Vista®.
- Drafting and design experience is a plus.

Using This Guide

The lessons are independent of each other. However, it is recommended that you complete these lessons in the order that they are presented unless you are familiar with the concepts and functionality described in those lessons.

Each chapter contains:

- **Lessons:** Usually two or more lessons in each chapter.
- **Exercises**: Practical, real-world examples for you to practice using the functionality you have just learned. Each exercise contains step-by-step procedures and graphics to help you complete the exercise successfully.

Default Installation

The information in this guide is presented in such a way that it is assumed you have installed AutoCAD or AutoCAD LT using the default installation parameters. You should be using the *2D Drafting & Annotation* workspace as your active workspace throughout the course. You will learn how to do this in Chapter 1.

Completing the Exercises

You can complete the exercise in two ways: using the book or the onscreen version.

- **Using the book:** Follow the step-by-step exercises in the book.
- **Onscreen:** Click the Learning AutoCAD 2010 icon on your desktop, installed from the CD, and follow the step-by-step exercises on screen. The onscreen exercises are the same as those in the book. The onscreen version has the advantage that you can concentrate on the screen without having to glance down at your book.

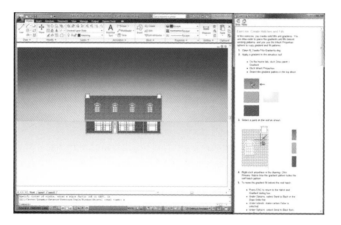

After launching the on-screen exercises, you might need to alter the size of your application window to align both windows.

Settings for the Exercises

Each exercise is written with the assumption that the following Object Snap settings are active. You might need to confirm these settings for each exercise.

Each exercise is written with the assumption that the following status bar options are turned ON. If necessary adjust these options when you open the dataset for each exercise.

Installing the Exercise Data Files

To complete the exercises in this guide, you must download the data files from the following location and install them on your system.

To install the data files for the exercises:

1   Download the zip file from www.sybex.com/go/learningautocad2010.

2   Unzip the file *Setup.exe.*

3   Double-click *Setup.exe* and follow the onscreen instructions to install the files.

4   After the install is complete, you can delete *Setup.exe* from your system (optional).

Unless you specify a different folder, the exercise datasets are installed in the following folder: *C:\Autodesk Learning\AutoCAD 2010\Learning.*

Download a Trial Version of AutoCAD® 2010

This guide was designed for use with AutoCAD® 2010 software. If you do not have AutoCAD 2010 software installed on your system, you can download a trial version.

To download the latest trial version of the AutoCAD 2010 software:

1   Navigate to www.autodesk.com/autocadtrial.

2   Complete the registration and mailing information.

3   Submit the online form to download a free** 30-day trial version.

** This product is subject to the terms and conditions of the end-user license agreement that accompanies the software.

> **Note**
> The datasets and exercises can be used with AutoCAD LT. The location of the files will be the same whether you are using AutoCAD or AutoCAD LT. The name of the shortcut for the online version of the exercises is named Learning AutoCAD 2010, but can also be used with AutoCAD LT 2010.

Imperial and Metric Datasets

For some of the exercises that specify units of measurement, alternative exercise tables are provided. You will see a note stating that imperial and metric versions are available. An example of the file naming convention is as follows:

- Open *i_stair_settings.dwg* (imperial) or *m_stair_settings.dwg* (metric).
  In the exercise steps, you will see either the imperial or metric value as shown in the following example:
- For Length, enter **13'2"**.
- For Length, enter **4038 mm**.
  For exercises with no specific units of measurement, files are provided as shown in the following example:
- Open *c_stair_settings.dwg* (common).
  In the exercise steps, the unitless value is specified as shown in the following example:
- For Length, enter **400**.

Notes, Tips, and Warnings

Throughout this guide, notes, tips, and warnings are called out for special attention.

 Notes contain guidelines, constraints, and other explanatory information.

 Tips provide information to enhance your productivity.

 Warnings provide information about actions that might result in the loss of data, system failures, or other serious consequences.

Feedback

We always welcome feedback on Autodesk Official Training Guides. After completing this course, if you have suggestions for improvements or if you want to report an error in the book or on the CD, please send your comments to *learningtools@autodesk.com*.

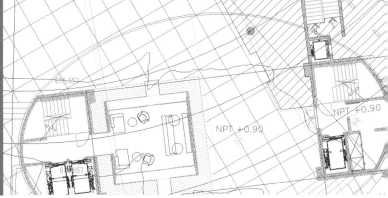

Chapter 01

Taking the AutoCAD Tour

Before you begin to use the software, you need to become familiar with the interface and some of the core functionality and features.

Objectives

After completing this chapter, you will be able to:

- Identify and state the purpose of the main interface elements.

- Open, create, and save drawings.

- Use the Zoom and Pan commands to view different areas of the drawing.

Standard Object Snap and Status Bar Settings
Before completing the exercises in this chapter, refer to the "Settings for the Exercises" section in the Introduction.

Lesson 01 | Navigating the Working Environment

This lesson describes the working environment and the types of interface elements that you must become familiar with if you are to become proficient in the software.

Before you begin creating drawings, you should familiarize yourself with the interface.

After completing this lesson, you will be able to start the application, activate the appropriate workspace, and identify key parts of the interface.

The following image identifies key interface elements:

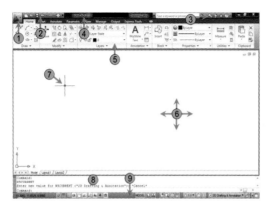

① Application Menu

② Quick Access Toolbar

③ Info Center

④ Title Bar

⑤ Ribbon

⑥ Drawing Area

⑦ Crosshairs

⑧ Command Window

⑨ Status bar

Objectives

After completing this lesson, you will be able to:

- Describe and set the workspace.
- Identify and use keyboard functions.
- Identify key parts of the interface.
- Use the shortcut menu to access commands and options.
- Explain the purpose of AutoCAD-specific interface tools.

Setting the Workspace

Introduction

You launch AutoCAD® in the same way you launch other Windows applications, using one of the following two methods:

- Double-click the AutoCAD 2010 icon on the Windows desktop.
- Click Start > All Programs (or Programs) > Autodesk > AutoCAD 2010 > AutoCAD 2010.

Depending on the options chosen during installation or the status of AutoCAD when it was last closed, you may need to adjust the active workspace.

> **Warning**
> If using AutoCAD LT®, select the icon and start menu options associated with AutoCAD LT.

Workspaces Defined

When you launch the application, the interface elements displayed are only those associated with the active workspace. A workspace is a task-oriented drawing environment oriented in such a way as to provide you with only the tools and interface elements necessary to accomplish the tasks relevant to that environment.

By default, AutoCAD has four workspace configurations:

- 2D Drafting & Annotation
- 3D Modeling
- AutoCAD Classic
- Initial Setup Workspace

Warning
AutoCAD LT has two workspaces, one workspace named *2D Drafting & Annotation*, the other named *AutoCAD LT Classic*.

AutoCAD is shown here with the 2D Drafting & Annotation workspace active.

AutoCAD is shown here with the 3D Modeling workspace active.

AutoCAD is shown here with the AutoCAD Classic workspace active.

After you start the program you can switch to the desired workspace. The application will open with the last workspace used. The Workspace Switching drop-down list is accessed in the lower right corner of the AutoCAD window on the status bar.

Procedure: Setting the 2D Drafting & Annotation Workspace

The following steps give an overview of activating the 2D Drafting & Annotation workspace.

1   Start AutoCAD.

2   Use the default drawing or on the Quick Access toolbar, click New.

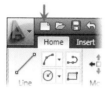

3   Select *acad.dwt* (imperial) or *acadiso.dwt* (metric) as the template file.

4   Click the Workspaces settings icon, located at the bottom right corner of the AutoCAD window. Select 2D Drafting & Annotation.

Procedure: Setting the AutoCAD LT Workspace

The following steps give an overview of activating the AutoCAD LT 2D Drafting &
Annotation workspace.

1   Launch AutoCAD LT.

2   On the Workspaces toolbar, select 2D Drafting and Annotation from the list.

3   Start a new drawing and select *acadlt.dwt* (imperial) or *acadltiso.dwt* (metric) as the
template file.

> **Note**
> The instructions and exercise steps covered in this course are based on the 2D Drafting
> & Annotation workspace. Please activate this workspace if you have not already done so.

Keyboard Input

Using the keyboard is familiar to everyone who works with computers. For much of the work that
you do in AutoCAD you use the keyboard, but you use a few keystrokes more often than others.

Special Keys

You use the following keys most often. These keys have special meaning to the software.

- Use the **ESC** key to cancel all current actions and return to the **Command**: prompt.
- Press the **ENTER** key following all keyboard input. You also complete many
  commands by pressing **ENTER**.
- Pressing the **SPACEBAR** is equivalent to pressing the **ENTER** key and is often easier
  to use.
- Pressing the **SPACEBAR** or **ENTER** at the **Command**: prompt repeats the last
  command used.
- Pressing the **UP** and **DOWN** arrow keys will cycle through previous commands used.
- The **TAB** key is especially useful to navigate in a dialog box. You should use the **TAB**
  key to move from field to field. Be careful not to press **ENTER**.

Function Keys

The use of each of the function keys can be duplicated in other ways with the exception of F2. You
may find that the on-screen equivalents to the function keys are easier and allow you to keep your
eyes on the screen.

Option	Description
F1	Displays Help
F2	Toggles Text Window
F3	Toggles OSNAP
F4	Toggles TABMODE
F5	Toggles ISOPLANE
F6	Toggles UCSDETECT (Not available in AutoCAD LT)
F7	Toggles GRIDMODE
F8	Toggles ORTHOMODE
F9	Toggles SNAPMODE
F10	Toggles Polar Tracking
F11	Toggles Object Snap Tracking
F12	Toggles Dynamic Input

User Interface Layout

There are interface elements common to other Windows applications such as ribbon panels, toolbars, and menus. If you have used other Windows applications, these user interface elements should appear familiar. However, there are interface elements such as the command line and the status bar, which are unique to AutoCAD.

Heads-up Design Defined

Heads-up design is a methodology intended to increase your efficiency while using the software. Whenever you turn your visual focus away from your design to locate a tool, it slows you down. Instead, you should use the most efficient access methods such as Dynamic Input, right-click shortcut menus and the ribbon control panels whenever possible.

Ribbon Defined

The ribbon is a special tool palette associated with each workspace containing only the tools and controls relevant to that workspace. For example, the ribbon for the 2D Drafting & Annotation workspace contains tools relevant to 2D drawing, dimensioning, and annotating, but does not contain tools for 3D geometry creation.

The ribbon supports the heads-up design process because it is space efficient and eliminates the clutter of tool palettes and toolbars. Using the ribbon alone provides you with more space on your screen in the drawing area and enables you to maintain access to the tools and controls you need.

Ribbon Controls

The ribbon is turned on by default when you start the software in either the 2D Drafting & Annotation or the 3D Modeling workspace. The ribbon is organized into a series of tabs. Each tab includes a different set of panels with related commands and controls that may be found on the Classic AutoCAD toolbars and dialog boxes.

You can turn the tabs and associated panels on the ribbon on or off by right-clicking on the ribbon area and selecting Tabs or Panels to select the desired options. You can also turn panel titles on or off by right-clicking the Panel tabs. Additionally, you can save your ribbon configuration.

Each tab on the ribbon has its own set of panels that contain groups of related tools, such as those used for 2D drawing, adding text, or adding dimensions. Some panels can be expanded to display more tools. Likewise some tools can be expanded for more options, such as the Circle tool as indicated by an arrow in the corner of the icon.

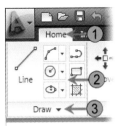

① **Tabs**: Identifies the purpose and name of the control panel.

② **Panels**: Contains groups of related tools associated with the selected tools.

③ **More Tools**: Click and hold the down arrow to display more tools and options in the selected panel.

Add or Remove Tabs

To turn specific tabs on or off, right-click in the ribbon and select Tabs. Choose to display or remove tabs from the ribbon. Tabs currently displayed are indicated with a check mark.

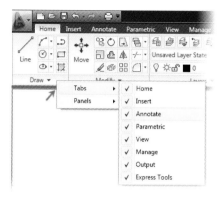

Application Menu

You can use the Application menu to access several key commands such as New, Open, Save, Print, and Close. Most of these commands lead to submenus that give you more detailed options.

Panels

AutoCAD uses ribbon panels as one means to access commands and settings. Similar tools commands are grouped together in panels and can be accessed by clicking the button or icon that indicates the tool's purpose. Each panel consists of a collection of tools that performs related or similar tasks.

When using the 2D Drafting & Annotation workspace, a standard set of panels is displayed on each of the standard set of tabs located on the horizontal ribbon at the top of the AutoCAD drawing area. Notice that when you select a different tab, a different set of panels is displayed.

By default, each panel is docked at the top of the drawing area on the ribbon. You can move the panels away from the docked position to a floating position or drag them back into the ribbon.

Panel Visibility

To turn specific panels on or off, right-click in the ribbon and select Panels. Select to display or remove panels from the ribbon tab. Panels currently displayed are indicated with a check mark, as shown in the illustration on the right.

Panels will appear in the last position (docked or floating) they were in before the panel was removed from the display.

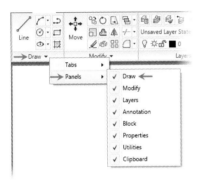

Tip
When you click icons on the ribbon panel, the command is not executed unless the cursor is over the icon when you release the mouse button. If you click the wrong icon, simply drag the cursor away from the button before releasing.

Panel Tools Visibility

Some panels will cascade to reveal additional tools when you select the black arrow in the lower right- hand corner of the panel. You can keep these panels open to display all of the tools by selecting the thumbtack located in the lower left-hand corner of the cascading panel.

Status Bar

The status bar is located at the bottom of the application window.

The left end of the status bar displays the coordinates that show the numerical position of the crosshairs in the drawing. Click this area to turn the coordinate display off or on. In the on position, there are two possibilities. The readout displays the X, Y, and Z values, or the distance and polar angle of the crosshairs as it is moved in the drawing window.

Coordinates Display

To the right of the Coordinates Display, there are buttons that activate features to facilitate drawing construction. Collectively, these features are termed drafting settings.

Drafting Settings

In the middle-right of the status bar are buttons to display the drawing model or the drawing layout views.

MODEL ⊞ ⊠ ▣ ⊡

Model Space and Layout Settings

To the right of the Model Space and Layout buttons are the realtime Pan command and the Zoom command.

Pan and Zoom

Towards the right side of the status bar are the Annotation options for the display of annotative objects such as text and dimensions. When you create annotations with the annotative property selected, the Annotation Scale displayed in the status bar represents the scale in which the new objects are created.

Annotation Settings

About Shortcut Menus

The shortcut menu is context-sensitive. When you right-click in the graphics window, you can use the options presented on the shortcut menu to perform a variety of tasks. Context-sensitive means that the menu will change depending on what you are currently doing in the software. For example, if you are at the command prompt your shortcut menu will have different options available than if you are in the Pline command.

Definition of Shortcut Menu

Shortcut menu options are organized into different areas. The options that are made available to you are based on the current context of your work and will change when you activate the shortcut menu. The following image shows the shortcut menu as it appears when you are creating a polyline.

The top area of the menu offers Enter, Cancel, and Recent Input options.

The middle area of the menu offers options specific to the current command. Notice how the options on the menu match the options on the command line. To use an option for a command, select the option on the shortcut menu. This has the same effect as entering the capital letter(s) of the option on the command line.

The lower area of the menu offers Pan and Zoom functions and access to the QuickCalc command.

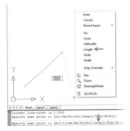

Key Points

- The shortcut menu is context-sensitive, so its options differ depending on the current context of the software, for example, whether you are drawing or editing.
- You can use the shortcut menu as an alternative to entering command options on the command line. This speeds up the design process and is the preferred method for working with suboptions of the active command.

More AutoCAD-Specific Interface Tools

While the software complies with Windows standards for user interface elements, there are some element types that are specific to the application.

The following image shows the command window. Somewhat unique to a graphical windows application, the command window provides another method for the user to interact with the application.

```
Command: e
ERASE
Select objects:
```

Layouts (Drawing Sheets)

Model space (the Model tab) is the area where you create your designs. Layouts (drawing sheets) are for annotation, borders, title blocks, and plotting.

When you design, you should always draw at full scale. The model space environment offers an unlimited amount of space to create your designs. Use layouts to create drawing sheets that represent an area equal to the actual size of the paper.

You can switch between model space and the Layout by selecting the button located in the status bar at the bottom of the AutoCAD window.

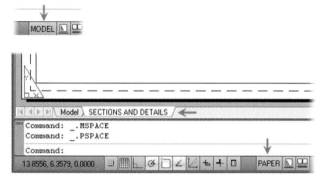

Layer List

The Layer list displays the drawing's layers. Using this list, you can switch the current layer, assign selected objects to a layer, turn layers on and off, freeze layers, and lock layers.

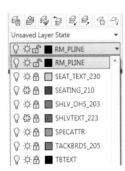

Tool Palettes

Tool palettes simplify the task of adding predefined design content to your drawing.

The tool palettes are a set of overlapping panels contained in a floating window. For easy identification, they are grouped by tabs.

The palettes provide an efficient method for organizing, sharing, and placing area fill patterns and symbols that you use regularly.

You can customize the individual tools on the palettes by setting properties that are specific to the object, such as scale, rotation angle, or a predefined color.

Palettes can also contain custom tools provided by third party developers.

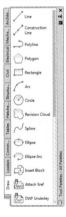

Chapter 1 | Taking the AutoCAD Tour

InfoCenter Defined

The InfoCenter, located to the far right of AutoCAD title bar, consists of the InfoCenter search and access to the Communication Center panel. You can use the InfoCenter search by typing in key words or by typing a question. While there are many locations for which InfoCenter can be configured, the following locations are provided as examples:

- User's Guide
- Command Reference
- New Features Workshop

The InfoCenter is shown in the following illustration.

Communication Center

The Communications Center, accessed through the InfoCenter menu bar, provides real-time notifications, announcements, and news to your desktop. You must be connected to the Internet to take advantage of this feature. The following is a partial list of information sources you can access:

- New Software Updates
- Product Support
- CAD Manager Channel
- RSS Feeds

Access

1. Search for information or help in the configured search locations by entering search keywords, or enter a question in the Help field.

2. Click the search icon to display the search results after entering search keywords. You can browse the results in the Search window.

3. Click the drop-down list to configure InfoCenter. Click Search Settings in the drop-down list to configure InfoCenter search locations and Communication Center settings.

④ Click the key to open Subscription Center.

⑤ Click the satellite dish icon to open Communication Center.

⑥ Click to access a list of favorites.

⑦ Click to access the Help dialog box.

Communication Center Options

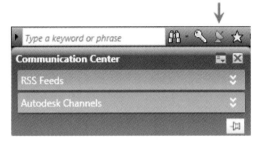

Expand the Communications Center title bar to see all of the configured Autodesk channels.

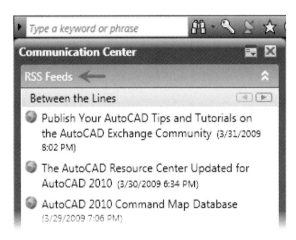

Expand the RSS Feeds title bar to see all of the configured RSS feeds. By default, several RSS feeds are created for you when you install AutoCAD.

Select the Subscription Center button to view all of the configured Subscription Center items, such as product support requests and e-Learning catalogs and lessons (Available to subscription customers only.).

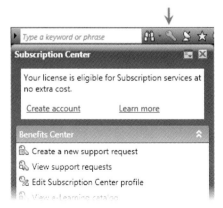

Command Window

The command window is normally located at the bottom of the application window and docked between the drawing area and status bar. Whether you enter a command manually at the command line or click a command tool on a toolbar, all commands are passed through and evaluated by the command line.

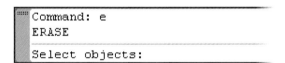

```
Command: e
ERASE
Select objects:
```

It is important that you monitor the activity that occurs in this area. At each stage of the command process, the software either provides you with a series of options to choose from or requires that you input values relevant to that stage of the process.

In normal operation, the command window contains three lines of text. The first two lines list the immediate command history and display the settings or options available within the current command. The bottom line is the command line. You should focus your attention here during the majority of commands.

You type at the cursor position on the command line, that is, the command prompt.

Note: Always press ENTER after you enter values on the command line.

Although the command window is usually docked at the bottom of the drawing window, you can move it freely around the drawing. You can dock it to the edge of the application window or leave it floating over the drawing area. Click and drag the vertical bars to the left of the command window to place it in a floating position over the drawing area.

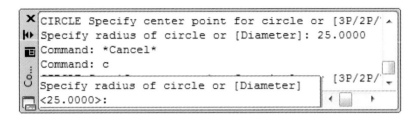

```
X  CIRCLE Specify center point for circle or [3P/2P/
I▶  Specify radius of circle or [Diameter]: 25.0000
    Command: *Cancel*
    Command: c
Co...
    Specify radius of circle or [Diameter]        [3P/2P/
    <25.0000>:
```

Tip

While floating the command window over the drawing area can partially obstruct your view, you may benefit from this configuration because it serves as a reminder to monitor the command window.

Command Sequence

The process of entering command sequences is straightforward but important. To use the software successfully, you must become comfortable with typical command sequences such as the following one for drawing a circle.

- Circle
- Specify center point for circle or [3P/2P/Ttr (tan tan radius)]: **Select a point or enter a coordinate**.
- Specify radius of circle or [Diameter] <25.0000>: **d** (Use a command option).
- Specify diameter of circle <50.0000>: **75** (Enter values when prompted).

If you spend enough time working with the software and paying attention to the command line and other interface elements, you will soon know what information is required without even looking at the command line.

Help Menu

Before you explore the software any further, you should familiarize yourself with the extensive Help documentation provided.

The Help menu provides access to the Help system as well as online resources for Knowledge Base, Training Resources, and the Autodesk User Group International (AUGI). You can also find out more information about and volunteer to participate in the Customer Involvement Program.

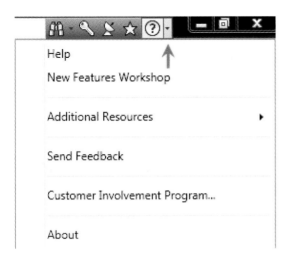

Lesson 02 | Working with Files

This lesson describes how to open, create, and save drawings.

Objectives

After completing this lesson, you will be able to:

- Open drawings, create drawings, and save drawings.

Working with Files

Drawings are created and saved in the DWG drawing file format. To access this data, you must learn how to create a new drawing, save a drawing, and open these file types.

Use the Quick Access toolbar to create, open, and save new drawings.

Open a Drawing

To open a drawing, use the Open command and select the files that you want to open.

Command Access

Open

Command Line: **OPEN**
Application Menu: **File > Open**
Toolbar: **Quick Access**

Open File Dialog Box

> **Note**
> Use standard Windows CTRL+ and SHIFT+ selection methods to select and open multiple files at once.

Create a New Drawing

To create a new drawing, use the New command. Select a template or select Open with no Template (Imperial or Metric). Drawing Templates are drawings that are saved in template format (*.dwt*) and that can contain information such as a title block, layers, text styles, dimension styles, and settings relevant to your specific drawing needs.

Command Access

New

Command Line: **NEW**
Application Menu: **File > New**
Toolbar: **Quick Access**

Select Template Dialog Box

Saving Your Drawings

Use the Save command to save your drawing. The first time you save a drawing, the Save Drawing As dialog box appears. Navigate to the folder where you want to store the drawing, enter a file name, and select Save. To save a drawing with a different name, select Save As.

Command Access

 Save; Save As

Command Line: **SAVE; SAVEAS**
Application Menu: **File > Save; Save As**
Toolbar: **Quick Access**

Save Drawing As Dialog Box

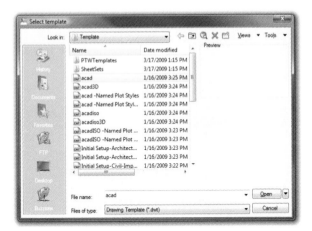

Note

As a new user, you should get in the habit of saving your drawing as soon as you create it and save often as you work on your drawings. This is a habit that can be easily learned and could prove to be very valuable in the event of unexpected system failures. A quick way to save your work is to use the shortcut keys: **CTRL + S**.

Lesson 03 | Displaying Objects

When you use the software, you draw all objects at full scale. Sometimes you need to view the whole drawing, sometimes just smaller details. To assist you in viewing different areas of the drawing, there are a number of zoom and pan tools. You can easily magnify small areas of your drawing to provide a closer view or shift the view to a different or larger part of the drawing. You can save views by name and restore them later.

In this lesson, you explore different methods of using these tools and develop your use of the interface.

Many of the zoom and pan options operate transparently. This means that you can use the options while you are in another command.

After completing this lesson, you will be able to use zoom and pan commands to control the drawing view display, use the wheel mouse to pan and zoom in the drawing, and regenerate the drawing view.

In the following example of a typical drawing, it would be nearly impossible to work on if it were on a sheet of paper that was the size of common computer monitors. Using the display tools, you can magnify any portion of the drawing to fill the available space on your monitor.

Objectives

After completing this lesson, you will be able to:

- Identify tools that control the drawing view display.
- Use the Pan Realtime command to perform real time pan operations in the drawing.
- Use the Zoom Realtime command to perform real time zoom operations in the drawing.
- Use different Zoom commands to control the view magnification.
- Use a wheel mouse to zoom and pan in the drawing.
- Use the Regen command to regenerate the drawing.

Display Tools

Most of the time you will use the wheel on your mouse to zoom in and out of display views in your drawing. Additional zoom tools are located on the Navigate panel in the View tab on the toolbar ribbon.

Command Access

Display Tools

Command Line: **Zoom, Z** or **Pan**
Status Bar: **Pan** or **Zoom**
Ribbon: **View Tab > Navigate Panel > Pan**

> **Note**
> There are additional options for the Zoom command, but they are beyond the scope of this course. See Help for additional command information.

Pan

You can reposition the center of your view on the drawing by using the Pan command. Just like panning with a video camera, panning your drawing changes only the position of your view of the drawing, not the location or magnification of objects in the drawing.

Command Access

Pan

Command Line: **PAN, P**
Ribbon: **View Tab > Navigate Panel > Pan**

Shortcut Menu: **Pan**

When the Pan command is active, the cursor changes to a hand icon as shown above. Click and drag the cursor to pan the drawing view.

Command Options

While in the Pan command you may access other Pan and Zoom options when you right-click in the drawing window to display a shortcut menu.

Option	Description
Exit ✓ Pan Zoom 3D Orbit Zoom Window Zoom Original Zoom Extents	**Exit**: Select to exit the Pan or Zoom Realtime commands. **Zoom**: Select to switch to Zoom Realtime. **3D Orbit**: Select to perform a 3D Orbit of the view. **Zoom Window**: Select to perform a Zoom Window operation and return to the Pan or Zoom Realtime command. **Zoom Original**: Select to return to the view prior to starting the Pan or Zoom Realtime command. **Zoom Extents**: Select to zoom to the drawing extents and return to the Pan or Zoom Realtime command.

Procedure: Panning in Real Time

The following steps outline how to pan dynamically in real time.

1   On the ribbon, click View tab > Navigate panel > Pan.

2   Click and drag the cursor in the direction that you want to pan the drawing view. Release the button when you are in your desired position.

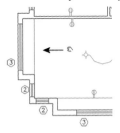

3   Continue to click and drag as required.

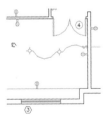

4   Press ESC or ENTER to exit the Pan command.

Panning Considerations

- Panning has the same effect on the drawing as using the horizontal and vertical scroll bars.
- When you pan the drawing, you are not moving geometry, only changing the position from which you view the drawing.

Zoom Realtime

The Zoom command increases or decreases the magnification of the objects displayed in the drawing area. When you zoom out, you see more of the overall drawing. When you zoom in, you magnify parts of your drawing to view them in greater detail.

Just like zooming in and out with a camera, using Zoom does not alter the actual size of the object. It simply changes the relative magnification of objects displayed in the drawing area.

Command Access

 Zoom

Command Line: **Zoom, Z** Press ENTER on the keyboard for Realtime option
Status Bar: **Zoom**

 Zoom

Note: *If the Zoom realtime icon is not readily available, select it from the drop-down list.*

Shortcut Menu: **Zoom**

When the Zoom Realtime command is active, the cursor changes to the icon above. Click and drag the cursor up to increase magnification or down to decrease magnification.

Procedure: Zooming in Real Time

The following steps outline how to zoom dynamically in real time.

1   On the ribbon, click View Tab > Navigate Panel > Zoom drop-down > Realtime. Press ENTER.

2   Click and drag the cursor up to increase magnification.

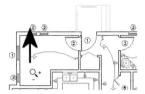

3   Click and drag the cursor down to decrease magnification.

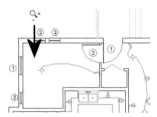

4   Continue to zoom in and out as required.

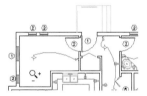

5   Press ESC or ENTER to exit the command.

Zoom Command Options

The Zoom command has multiple options available to customize the Zoom.

Command Access

Following are the most frequently used Zoom command options for viewing different areas of the drawing.

Note: Not all Zoom command options are discussed.

Zoom Command Options

Zoom Window

ZOOM, Z; Pick 2 points to define the window in the drawing area
To use the Zoom Window option, use any method listed above to start the command, click in the drawing to specify the first corner of the window (1), and then click to specify the second corner of the window (2). As a result, the drawing view is magnified and fills the drawing space with the area defined by the zoom window.

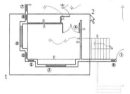

Zoom Extents

Use the Zoom Extents option to zoom to the extents of the drawing, that is, the area of the drawing in which objects are placed. When you zoom to the drawing extents, you magnify the drawing view so that all geometry in the current space (model space or paper space) is visible.
ZOOM, Z; > E then press ENTER

Zoom Previous

Use the Zoom Previous option to return to the previous view.
ZOOM, Z; > P then press ENTER

Wheel Mouse Features

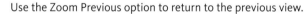

The wheel mouse is a variant of the standard pointing device that is modified with a small wheel between the left and right buttons. You can rotate this wheel in small increments. You can use the wheel to zoom and pan in your drawing without using any commands. When zooming in, the location near your cursor is the focal point of the zoom and thus remains on the screen.

The ZOOMFACTOR system variable controls the incremental change, whether forward or backward. The higher the number of the variable, the greater the zoom.

How to Use the Wheel Mouse

Do this...	Description
Roll the wheel forward	Zoom In
Roll the wheel backward	Zoom Out
Double-click the wheel button	Zoom Extents
Hold down the wheel button and drag the mouse	Pan
Press and hold the SHIFT key and the wheel button and drag the mouse	Constrained Out
Press and hold the CTRL key and the wheel button and drag the mouse	Pan (Joystick)

Tip

In some situations, when using the mouse wheel to pan or zoom, the actions have no effect on the drawing. For example, you might only be able to zoom out to a certain point. When this occurs, you must regenerate the drawing by clicking Regen on the View menu.

Wheel Button Modes

You can set the wheel button to function in two different modes. The value of the MBUTTONPAN system variable controls whether panning is supported.

- If MBUTTONPAN is set to 1, the PAN command is activated when you use the wheel.
- If MBUTTONPAN is set to 0, the Object Snap menu is displayed when you use the wheel.

Regen

Use the Regen command to regenerate all the geometry in the drawing. Use the Regenall command to regenerate all the geometry when there are multiple drawing viewports. When you regenerate the drawing, the screen coordinates for all objects in the drawing are recomputed and the drawing database is reindexed for optimal display performance.

Command Access

Regen

Command Line: **RE, REGEN, REGENALL**

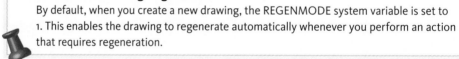

Automatic Drawing Regeneration
By default, when you create a new drawing, the REGENMODE system variable is set to 1. This enables the drawing to regenerate automatically whenever you perform an action that requires regeneration.

Guidelines When Regenerating Large Drawings

- Because regeneration recalculates the screen coordinates for all objects in the drawing, it usually takes longer to regenerate large drawings than smaller ones.
- If you experience performance decreases on larger drawings, consider setting REGENMODE = 0 to prevent automatic regeneration. You can manually regenerate the drawing when you need to.

Exercise | Create Layouts

In this exercise, you open an existing drawing and use the Zoom and Pan tools to view different areas.

The completed exercise

Completing the Exercise

To complete the exercise, follow the steps in this book or in the onscreen exercise. In the onscreen list of chapters and exercises, click *Chapter 1: Taking the AutoCAD Tour.* Click *Exercise: Zoom and Pan in the Drawing.*

1   Open *C_Displaying-Objects.dwg.*

2   On the View Tab, click Navigate Panel > Pan.

3   Alternatively:
    • Right-click anywhere in the drawing area. Click Pan.
    • Click and hold the mouse button and drag to change your view of the drawing.

4   While still panning the drawing, press and hold SHIFT.
    Note: This temporarily restricts the movement of the pan from any direction to orthogonal mode.

5   Right-click anywhere in the drawing. Click Exit to end the Pan command.
    Note: You can also press ESC to end the command.

6   On the status bar, click Zoom. Enter **E** in the command line to select the Extents option. Notice how the view changes.
    Note: If you have a three-button mouse with a scroll wheel, you can double-click the wheel button for the Zoom Extents command.

7   Zoom in real time:

- On the status bar, click Zoom.
- Press ENTER to select real time.
- Click and hold your mouse button and move the cursor up.
- Still holding the mouse button, move the cursor down.
- Notice that as you move the cursor up, the drawing zooms in and as you move the cursor down, it zooms out.
  Note: You can also activate the Zoom Realtime command by rotating the wheel on a wheel mouse. Rotating the wheel away from you zooms in, and rotating toward you zooms out.

8   Zoom to a window:

- On the View tab, click Navigate panel > Zoom drop-down > Window.
- Click two points around the center section of the drawing as shown by the arrows in the following illustration.

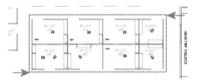

9   Pan to the lower left corner of the drawing.

10   On the View tab, click Navigate panel > Zoom drop-down > Previous. This returns you to the last view of the drawing that you zoomed or panned to.
     Note: Only the last 10 view changes are saved.

11   Close all files. Do not save.

Exercise | Hands-on Tour

In this exercise, you open an existing drawing. You use display commands and explore different areas of the user interface.

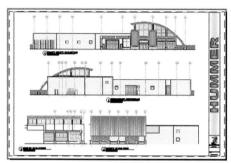

The completed exercise

Completing the Exercise
To complete the exercise, follow the steps in this book or in the onscreen exercise. In the onscreen list of chapters and exercises, click *Chapter 1: Taking the AutoCAD Tour.* Click *Exercise: Hands-On Tour.*

1   Open *C_Hummer-Elevation.dwg.* Because the drawing was last saved with the Color layout view active, the drawing opens to that layout.

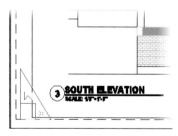

2   On the status bar, click Zoom. Enter **E** and press ENTER to select the Zoom Extents option. The drawing is magnified to fill the screen. If your workstation is equipped with a wheel mouse, double-clicking the roller button also selects Zoom Extents.

3   Use the wheel mouse, if you have it. Position the cursor to the left of the top view and roll the wheel forward then backward. If you do not have a wheel mouse, right-click anywhere in the drawing window and click Zoom. Hold the left button down and drag the mouse up and down. See how the magnification changes.

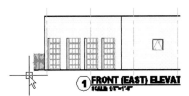

4   On the View tab, click Navigate panel > Zoom drop-down > Extents to view the entire drawing layout.

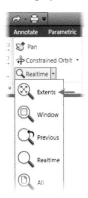

5   Now you switch the drawing view to model space, which is where the geometry for the drawing resides. On the status bar, at the bottom of the AutoCAD window and to the right, click Model.

6   On the View tab, click Navigate panel > Zoom drop-down list > Window. Click near the points indicated in the following illustration to magnify the area defined by the window.

7   On the View tab, click Navigate panel > Zoom drop-down list > Previous. This returns you to the previous view.

8   On the Quick Access toolbar, click Save.

9   In the Application menu, select File > Close.

10   In the Application menu, top right, you see a list of previously opened files for quick access.

Select the *C_Hummer-Elevation* drawing. Notice that it is opened to the last view in which it was saved.

11   On the bottom right of the AutoCAD window, click Layout to activate the color layout. Close the drawing.

12   Now you start a new drawing. On the Quick Access toolbar, click New.

13 In the Select Template dialog box, click the arrow next to Open. Click Open with no Template - Imperial. This opens a blank drawing with basic settings that you can change, such as the units format.

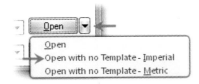

Note: For AutoCAD LT users, click *acadlt.dwt*.

14 Move your cursor near the upper right corner of your drawing area. Observe that the coordinate readout shows a screen size of about 12 x 9 units.

15 Close all files. Do not save.

Chapter Summary

Now that you have been introduced to several core features, you can begin learning how to create geometry.

Having completed this chapter, you can:

- Identify and state the purpose of the main interface elements.
- Open, create, and save drawings.
- Use the Zoom and Pan commands to view different areas of the drawing.

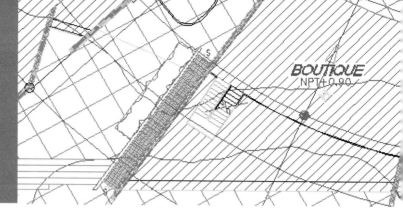

Chapter 02

Create Basic Drawings

Every drawing begins with the creation of basic geometry, objects such as lines, circles, arcs, and rectangles. These objects serve as building blocks for complex drawings and, as a result, you must master the use of the commands that create these objects.

Mastering these commands involves more than just knowing where the command is and how it works. You must also develop an understanding of the underlying coordinate system, and the settings such as object snaps, object snap tracking, and other features that are designed to assist you in creating basic objects.

There is generally more than one way to accomplish a task in the software. After you learn about the commands and features available, you can determine the methods that work best for you.

This chapter, and all subsequent chapters of the book, assume that you will be using the 2D Drafting & Annotations workspace with the toolbar ribbon at the top of the AutoCAD® window. If you are using AutoCAD LT®, while you might see slight interface differences, every attempt has been made to retain the fidelity of the learning experience when using this book.

Objectives

After completing this chapter, you will be able to:

- Identify the default coordinate system and use dynamic input, direct distance, and shortcut menus.

- Use the Line, Circle, Arc, Erase, Rectangle, and Polygon commands to create and erase geometry in the drawing.

- Use object snaps to accurately place and create objects in the drawing.

- Activate and use the Polar Tracking and PolarSnap modes to more accurately create geometry at different angles in the drawing.

- Explain, enable, and use object snap tracking to position geometry in the drawing.

- Use the Unit command to set up the drawing environment.

Lesson 04 | Inputting Data

Every drawing action requires some form of data input. Regardless of the types of geometry you create, you are constantly inputting data in one form or another.

In this lesson, you will learn to input data using the command line, dynamic input, direct distance entry, shortcut menus, and the Cartesian coordinate system. You will use the concepts you learn in this lesson in exercises throughout this course.

After completing this lesson, you will be able to use the command line, explain different types of coordinates, activate and use the Dynamic Input interface, use direct distance to enter values, and use the shortcut menu to access commands and options.

The following image illustrates how to use the Dynamic Input interface to draw a 10 unit line at 30 degrees.

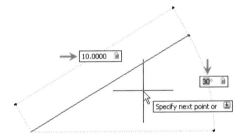

Objectives

After completing this lesson, you will be able to:

- Use the command line to enter commands and command options.
- Explain the difference between a Cartesian and a polar coordinate, and between an absolute and a relative coordinate.
- Activate the dynamic input interface and list key points about using it.
- Create and edit geometry using the dynamic input interface.
- Use direct distance entry to enter distance values.

About the Command Line

There are specific AutoCAD elements such as the ribbon, menus, and other tools that are common to all Microsoft Windows applications. However, the command line interface is unique to AutoCAD.

Most commands have options with which you can control various aspects of how the command is used. You should pay attention to the command line as you work.

Command Line Defined

The command line is the primary place where you communicate with the software. On the command line, you are prompted to input information.

Command Line Options

- Command options appear on the command line. The capitalized letter(s) represents the letter(s) you enter to use that option. You are not required to enter the letter(s) as a capital letter.
- Options for the command appear within [...] brackets. If there is a default option for the command, it appears within <...> brackets. To use the default option, press ENTER.
- Press the F2 key to display the full command window. Each command that you use during your drawing session is saved here. Press F2 again to close the full command window.

The following image shows command line options and a command line default value. In this situation, the user has started the rectangle command, and has entered d for the Dimension option. After pressing ENTER, a default distance of 7.0000 is displayed. If the user does nothing but press ENTER, a value of 7.0000 is used.

```
Specify first corner point or [Chamfer/Elevation/Fillet/Thickne
Specify other corner point or [Area/Dimensions/Rotation]: d ←

Specify length for rectangles <7.0000>: ←
```

Command Line Example

The following image shows a typical command and its options as they are presented on the command line. The last line shows the current status of the command. The previous lines show the command line history.

```
Command:
Command: _pline
Specify start point:
Current line-width is 0.0000
Specify next point or [Arc/Halfwidth/Length/Undo/Width]:
```

About the Coordinate System

Every object you draw is placed in either the world coordinate system (WCS) or a user coordinate system (UCS). When you create 2D geometry, data input is ultimately passed to the software in the form of Cartesian (x,y) or polar coordinates (distance, angle). You can either manually enter these coordinates or infer them by picking a point in the drawing window.

Cartesian Coordinate System

Every object you draw is placed in either the World Coordinate System (WCS) or a User Coordinate System (UCS). When you create 2D geometry, data input is ultimately passed to the software in the form of Cartesian (x,y) or polar coordinates (distance, angle). You can either manually enter these coordinates or infer them by picking a point in the drawing window.

The Cartesian coordinate system is used to determine points in space that are a specified distance from a set of perpendicular axes that intersect at the origin of the system.

In the World Coordinate System, the X axis represents the horizontal direction, the Y axis represents the vertical direction and the origin is located at 0,0. Positive X moves to the right, positive Y moves up, and the Z axis moves in the positive direction directly towards you, the viewer.

Note that for this course we will only be concerned with the X & Y coordinates since we are working in 2D. The Z coordinate will always be zero and need not be specified.

The following image illustrates a line drawn from the origin of the coordinate system 0,0 with its endpoint at the coordinate 4,6.

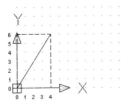

Chapter 2 | Creating Basic Drawings

To specify a Cartesian coordinate, enter the X and Y coordinates and press ENTER. Example: **4,5** where X is equal to the distance from the origin along the X axis and Y is equal to the distance from the origin along the Y axis.

Polar Coordinates

A polar coordinate is a point in the coordinate system that is determined by a distance and an angle.

The following illustration shows a line drawn from the origin of the coordinate system with a length of 7 units and an angle of 45 degrees.

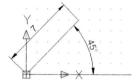

To specify a polar coordinate, type the distance < angle, example **5<45**, where Distance equals the distance traveled from the specified origin point and Angle equals the angle from the X axis.

Polar Angle

The default polar angle is measured counterclockwise from the zero angle position. The default zero angle is in the East compass direction.

The following illustration shows how angles are defined with a polar coordinate. This angle measurement applies to entering coordinates, working with arcs, and rotating objects.

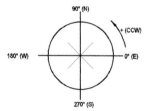

Absolute and Relative Coordinates

When you enter coordinates, they can be in the form of an absolute or a relative coordinate.

- An absolute coordinate represents a specific point in the current coordinate system relative to the origin point (0,0). To enter an absolute coordinate, enter the values as a Cartesian coordinate (x,y) or Polar coordinate (distance angle).

- A relative coordinate is a point located from a previously selected point. To enter a relative coordinate, select your first point, then precede the next coordinate point with the @ symbol. For example **@5<45** would mean 5 units at 45 degrees from the last point selected, and **@3,5** would mean 3 units in the positive X direction and 5 units in the positive Y direction from the last point selected.
  Note that when the Dynamic Input option is selected in the status bar, relativity is automatically assumed.

Entering Coordinates

- You can enter coordinates any time the software is in point acquisition mode, that is, when the command line is prompting you to specify a point or distance.
- Every drawing contains the world coordinate system (WCS). The WCS is identical in every drawing and cannot be altered. For example, an object placed at the absolute coordinate 10,10 would be positioned in the same location in any drawing.
- Unless you specifically define a User Coordinate System, all geometry you create is drawn relative to the WCS.

Tip

The UCS icon displays differently when you are working in the world coordinate system versus a user coordinate system. The UCS icon for the world coordinate system contains a small box at the origin of the X and Y axes.

Absolute and Relative Coordinate Examples

Coordinate	Absolute	Relative
Cartesian coordinate	24,46	@24,46
Polar coordinate	15<45	@15<45

Example of Cartesian Coordinate Input

The following lines could have been drawn using Cartesian or Polar coordinates. Assuming the start point at the red arrow, the command line input for relative Cartesian or Polar coordinates would be as follows:

Point 2: **@4,0** or **@4<0**
Point 3: **@0,2** or **@2<90**
Point 4: **@-1,0** or **@1<180**

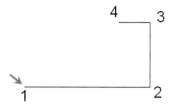

About Dynamic Input

The Dynamic Input interface is a way of entering data dynamically. Rather than entering data on the command line, which is generally positioned at the bottom of the screen, you can use the Dynamic Input interface for heads-up design, entering command information on screen at the cursor location.

Using the Dynamic Input Interface

The Dynamic Input interface is context sensitive based on the current operation. For example, the input and options are different when you are drawing a line than when you are drawing a circle; they also differ based on whether you are creating or editing geometry.

Dynamic Input Interface: Dimensional Input Mode

There are two Dynamic Input interface modes: Dimensional Input and Pointer Input. The following image represents the Dynamic Input interface in Dimensional Input mode. This mode is available when the Dynamic Input option is selected in the status bar and is commonly used for the typical drawing commands such as Line, Circle, and Arc.

Note: Numbers in the following image correspond to the numbers in the list below.

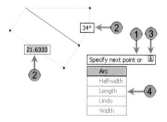

1. Tooltip: Displays instructions for the current step in the command and also reflects the current prompt on the command line.

2. Coordinate, Length, or Angle input fields: Depending on the mode, these fields may vary in value and position. In the image, one field represents the current length of the polyline while the other represents the angle of the cursor. Enter a value to specify an explicit value. Press TAB to cycle between the fields.

3. Down Arrow: Press DOWN ARROW (on the keyboard) to display the Dynamic Input menu. Press UP ARROW to cycle through previously selected coordinates.

4. Dynamic Input Menu: Select an option for the command. Available options vary based on the current context and reflect the options available on the command line.

Dynamic Input Interface—Pointer Input Mode

In the following illustration, the Dynamic Input interface has changed to Pointer Input mode because the values **@ 10 < 45** were entered on the keyboard. In Pointer Input mode, you can enter coordinate information at the pointer as though your focus were on the command line. Use this mode for absolute and relative coordinates. It is also the default mode for commands such as Move, Copy, and Rotate.

Lock icons indicate a value that has been manually entered. To unlock a value, press TAB to enter the input field, press DELETE to clear the value, then press TAB to exit the input field.

The default mode for dynamic input is for relative coordinates, but you can also enter absolute coordinates. To do so, enter a pound sign before the first coordinate, for example, **#2,20**. If you enter **2,20** (without the # sign), the point will be relative to the last selected point. The dynamic input fields adjust to reflect the entry format. In this case, the second field represents the Y coordinate.

Dynamic Input Options

Use the Dynamic Input tab in the Drafting Settings dialog box to change settings related to the Dynamic Input interface.

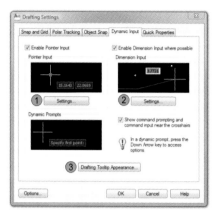

① Click to adjust Pointer Input options.

② Click to adjust Dimensional Input options.

③ Click to adjust appearance-related options for the Dynamic Input tooltips.

Guidelines for Using Dynamic Input

- When you use grips to stretch objects, or when you create new objects, dimensional input displays only acute angles; that is, all angles are displayed as 180 degrees or less. Thus, an angle of 270 degrees is displayed as 90 degrees. Angles that you specify when creating new objects rely on the cursor location to determine the positive angle direction.
- Dynamic Input is not intended to replace the command window. You use both the dynamic interface prompts and the command line in your workflow.
- The Dynamic Input interface is context sensitive.
- When Dynamic Input is on, points that you enter in response to second or next point prompts default to relative.
- Depending on the location of the cursor and the status of other settings such as object snaps, polar tracking, and tooltips, other information may appear on the Dynamic Input interface including object snap tips and command line prompts.

Using the Dynamic Input Interface

You can use the Dynamic Input interface in several ways, but the primary goal of the tool is to let you draw and edit in a heads-up mode, with your focus on the graphics window instead of the command line. Because the Dynamic Input interface is context sensitive, its options and display modes are dependent on the context in which you are working. The following guidelines give an overview of how you can use the Dynamic Input interface during typical drawing and editing tasks.

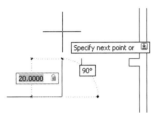

Command Access

Dynamic Input Mode

Command Line: **DYNMODE**
Function Key: **F12**

Procedure: Drawing with Dynamic Input

The following steps give an overview of creating geometry using the Dynamic Input interface and Polar coordinates. Note that because the Dynamic Input display is activated, relativity is assumed and it is not necessary to enter the ampersand symbol (@).

1   Begin a command. The Dynamic Input field displays the command.

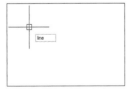

2   After you press ENTER, the interface immediately switches to Point Input mode. The tooltip gives instructions for what is required and the input fields reflect the current *XY* coordinate location of the cursor.

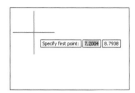

3   The Dynamic Input display prompts you for the next point. Enter a value in the Distance input field and press TAB to lock the distance and activate the Angle input field. Enter a value in the Angle input field and press TAB to lock the angle at o degrees. Click to select the point.

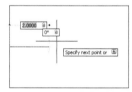

4   Enter another value in the Distance input field and press TAB to lock the distance. Move the cursor to adjust the angle value shown, but note that if you simply click, the angle is rounded up to the nearest whole number as determined in the Units settings. It would be best to enter the angle for accuracy.

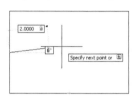

5   Click the final point and press ENTER to complete the line.

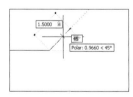

6   Your finished object is shown.

Procedure: Editing with Dynamic Input

The following steps give an overview of some of the ways you can edit with the Dynamic Input interface.

1   On the Home tab, click Modify panel > Copy. Select the objects to be copied and press ENTER to complete your selection.

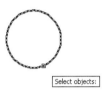

2   The Dynamic Input interface prompts you to Specify a base point. Notice the blue down arrow. Using the arrow keys on your keyboard, you may switch to single copy mode or multiple copy mode . Select a base point on or near the object.

3   The Dynamic Input tooltip provides feedback. Entering **@38.500<180** puts the interface in Relative Coordinate mode and places the values in the correct input fields. Press ENTER to complete the Copy command.

4   Select the circle to activate the grips.

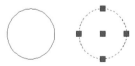

5   Select a quadrant grip to display the Dynamic Input interface. Grip editing displays several
     options. You can resize the circle either by entering a new radius (1), or TAB for one of the
     other options to increase or decrease the radius (2). Enter a value in one of the input fields
     and press ENTER.

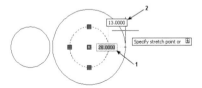

The circle is resized.

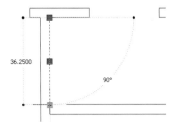

Using the Dynamic Input Interface to Reveal Information

You can see the length or angle of a line or the radius of an arc or circle by using the object grips.
With the command line blank, select the geometry to activate the grips. Hover the cursor over
one of the end grips or circle quadrants without selecting the grip. The Dynamic Input interface
displays size information for the selected geometry.

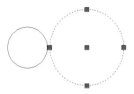

Guidelines for Using Dynamic Input

- When entering length or angle, press TAB to lock the values.
- Before entering the length or angle, you may press TAB to cycle through the available
  input fields. Enter the desired values and press ENTER to complete the command.
- To reveal the length or angle of a line, or the radius of an arc or circle, select the
  geometry (with the command line blank) to activate the grips. Hover the crosshairs
  over one of the grips. The Dynamic Input interface displays size information for the
  selected geometry.

- To Modify an object using Grips, select the object (with the command line blank) and then select a grip. Press TAB to cycle through the available fields. Supply the desired data and press ENTER.
- When Dynamic Input is on, points you enter in response to second or next point prompts default to relative.
- To enter *XY* coordinate values, press # to switch to absolute coordinate entry mode.

Using Direct Distance Entry

Direct distance entry is by far the easiest and quickest way to enter data while using the Draw and Modify commands. You can enter a distance value whenever the software prompts you to select a point. The point coordinates are calculated based on the angle of the cursor from the previous point selected and the distance you enter. It is a good idea to have Polar Tracking on when using this method.

You may use this method of data entry whether the Dynamic Input mode is on or off.

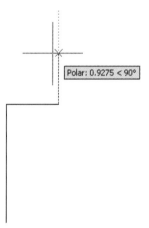

Guidelines for Using Direct Distance Entry

- Turn Polar Tracking on to display the cursor's angle.
- Set the desired incremental polar angles in Polar Tracking settings.
- Enter the desired distance and press ENTER. Be sure that the accurate Polar angle is displayed.
- AutoCAD is accurate 14 places to the right of the decimal point (1.00000000000000). Therefore, it is important to enter the distance and use Polar Snap for absolute precision.
- Although turning Dynamic Input off limits the data fields displayed by your pointer, you may use Direct Distance entry with this feature on or off.

Procedure: Using Direct Distance Entry

The following steps give an overview for using the direct distance entry method.

1   Start a command such as Line and click a point to begin. **Tip**: Toggle off Dynamic Input on the status bar for clearer results.

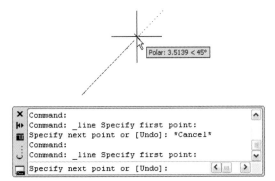

2   When you are prompted to specify the next point, drag your cursor in the direction you want the line to travel, enter a distance on the command line, and then press ENTER.
Tip: Turn polar tracking on to display the current angle of your cursor.

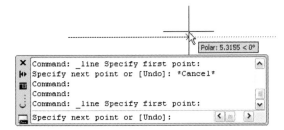

3   Drag the cursor in the direction of the next line segment, enter a distance value, and press ENTER.

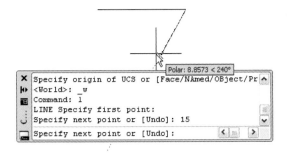

4   Repeat step 2 until the geometry is completed.

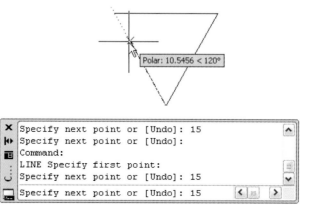

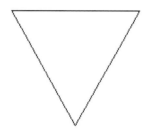

5   Press ENTER to exit the command. Your object is completed.

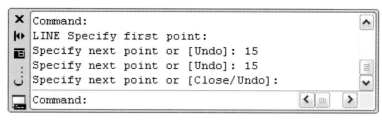

Chapter 2 | Creating Basic Drawings

Exercise | Input Data

In this exercise, you gain familiarity with the various input methods including the command line, the keyboard, and the dynamic interface.

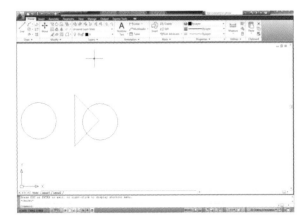

The completed exercise

Completing the Exercise
To complete the exercise, follow the steps in this book or in the onscreen exercise. In the onscreen list of chapters and exercises, click *Chapter 2: Creating Basic Drawings.* Click *Exercise: Input Data.*

1   On the Quick Access toolbar, click New.

2   In the Select Template dialog box, click the arrow next to Open and select Open with no Template - Imperial.

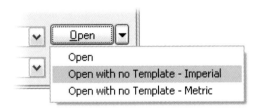

Note: For AutoCAD LT users, select *acadlt.dwt.*

3   On the status bar, make sure dynamic input is off.

4   Use the command line to create a circle:
- Enter **Circle**. Press ENTER.
- Observe the options listed in the brackets.

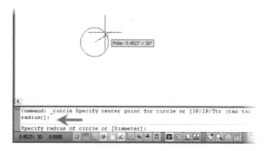

- Click near the center of the graphics window for the center point.
- Enter 1. Press ENTER.
  Zoom to view your drawing, if necessary.

5   To draw a second circle the same size as the first:
- Press ENTER. This repeats the previous command.
- Click to select a point to the left of the first circle.
- Press ENTER to accept the default value for the circle radius.

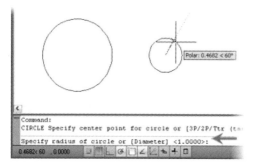

Chapter 2 | Creating Basic Drawings

6   Use the Line command with relative polar coordinates to draw a triangle near the circles:

- To begin the Line command, enter **L** for line. Press ENTER.
- Specify a point in the drawing window for the first point (1).
- Enter the polar coordinate **@2<45** (2). Press ENTER.
- Enter the polar coordinate **@2<135** (3). Press ENTER.

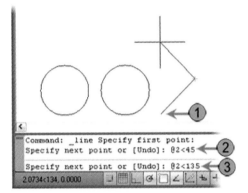

- Enter **c** for the close option. Press ENTER.

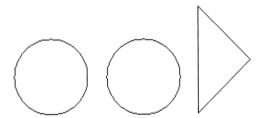

7   Display the command history:

- Press **F2.**
- Review the command history shown. Use the scroll function on the right side of the window or the mouse wheel to display additional history.
- Press **F2** again to turn off the command window.

8   Turn on Dynamic Input. On the status bar, click Dynamic Input.

9   Reveal geometric data using the dynamic interface:

- Click to select the first circle that you created.
- Place your crosshairs over, but do not click the square grip box on the right edge of the circle.
- Verify that the circle radius is 1.
- Press ESC to remove the circle selection.

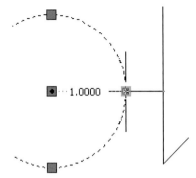

10   Reveal additional geometric data using the Dynamic Input interface:

- Click the two angular lines that you created.
- Place your crosshairs over, but do not click the square grip box at the intersection of the two lines.
- Observe that both the length and angle data are displayed for the selected lines.
- Press ESC to remove the line selection.

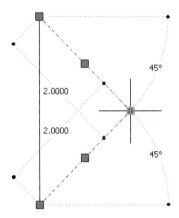

11   Close all files. Do not save.

Lesson 05 | Creating Basic Objects

All drawings consist of basic objects that you create using basic commands. In this lesson, you learn how to create objects such as lines, circles, arcs, rectangles, and polygons. You also learn how to use the Erase command to erase objects.

Learning to create basic geometry is critical to success in the software. As you become proficient with basic geometry creation, you can move on to creating more advanced object types.

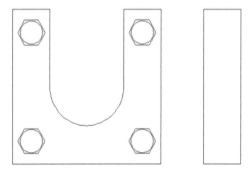

Objectives

After completing this lesson, you will be able to:

- Use the Line command to create lines in the drawing.
- Use the Circle command to create circles in the drawing.
- Use the Arc command to create arcs in the drawing.
- Use the Erase command to erase objects in the drawing.
- Use the Undo and Redo commands to return to previous drawing states.
- Use the Rectangle command to create rectangles in the drawing.
- Use the Polygon command to create equal-sided polygons in the drawing.

Line Command

Use the Line command to create a single line or multiple line segments from a start point to an endpoint.

The following illustration shows a line segment being drawn using the dynamic input interface to specify the length (1) and angle (2) of the segment.

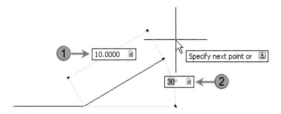

Command Access

Line

Command Line: **Line, L**
Ribbon: **Home tab > Draw panel > Line**

Menu Bar: **Draw > Line**

Command Options

The following Line command options are available from the shortcut menu (right-click) or the command line:

Option	Absolute
First Point	*(default)* Specifies the start point of the line segment.
Next Point	*(default)* Specifies the endpoint of the line segment. Continue to specify next points for additional line segments.
Undo	Removes the previous line segment without exiting the Line command. *Select or enter the capitalized letter only.*
Close	Appears only after you have drawn two line segments. Uses the first point of the line segments as the next point for the current segment to create a closed boundary of line segments. *Select or enter the capitalized letter only.*

Line Command Guidelines

- Use to create a single line or multiple line segments.
- Use the Close option to connect the last segment to the beginning of the first segment.
- Line segments, even though connected, are separate, independent objects.
- If you begin the Line command and press ENTER instead of selecting a start point, the Line will resume at the last point selected, such as the end of the previous line.
- You can Undo a line segment without completely exiting the line command by entering **U** and then pressing ENTER, or selecting Undo.

Practice Exercise | Line Command

In this practice exercise you will practice using the Line command to draw the object below.

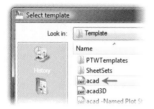

1   Begin a new drawing.

2   In the Select template dialog box, select the *acad* template file (.*dwt*) and click Open.

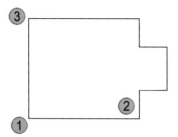

3   Be sure the following status bar settings are on:

- Polar tracking
- Object snap
- Object snap tracking

4   To draw the horizontal line:

- On the ribbon, click Home tab > Draw panel > Line.
- For the start point (1), select a point on the screen.
- Drag the line to the right until you see that the tooltip indicates the polar angle is 0.

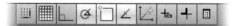

- Enter **4** and press ENTER.

5   Continue with the Line command to draw the remaining line segments from points (2) to (3):

- Drag your mouse up until you see that the tooltip indicates that the Polar angle is 90.

- Enter **1** and press ENTER.
- Drag to < 0, and enter **1** and press ENTER.
- Drag to < 90, and enter **1.5** and press ENTER.
- Drag to < 180, and enter **1** and press ENTER.
- Drag to < 90, and enter **1** and press ENTER.
- Drag to < 180, and enter **4** and press ENTER.

6   Drag the mouse down to Polar < 270 until you see that the object snap indicates you have reached the original endpoint (1), and click the endpoint. Be sure to click inside the Endpoint Object Snap box. Press ENTER to end the Line command.

Circle Command

Use the Circle command to create circles in the drawing. When you start the Circle command, you are prompted to select a center point, then specify the radius. Use the data input methods discussed earlier to input these values.

In the following image, the circle center point is selected and you are prompted to specify a radius.

Command Access

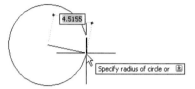

Circle

Command Line: **CIRCLE, C**
Menu Bar: **Draw > Circle >** choose option
Ribbon: **Home tab > Draw panel > Circle**

Circle Command Options

Circle options can be accessed from the drop-down menu next to the Circle button.

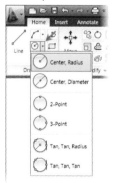

Circle options can be selected from the shortcut menu (right-click) or entered at the command line. Enter the capitalized letter(s) only.

Option	Description
Specify center point	*(default)* Click a point or enter a coordinate for the center of the circle.
D	After you specify a center point, you have the option to specify a Diameter instead of the radius.
3P	Create the circle based on three points you specify to define the circle's diameter.
2P	Create the circle based on two points you specify to define the circle's diameter.
Ttr (tan tan radius)	Create a circle tangent to other objects at a radius you specify.

Tip

The Circle command remembers the radius or diameter of the last circle drawn. If the prompt for the radius or diameter contains a value in brackets, press ENTER to reuse the value for the radius or diameter of the new circle. *Specify radius of circle or [Diameter]* <25.000>: Press ENTER to create a new circle with a 25 unit radius.

Circle Command Guidelines

- The Circle *default* when executed from the command line is Center, Radius. Specify a center point and a radius to define the circle.
- When you specify a Circle option from the drop-down menu, that button remains visible in the toolbar panel.
- After specifying a center point for the Circle, simply press ENTER, if you want the circle to be the same size as the last circle made.
- After specifying a center point, enter **D** and press ENTER if you prefer to enter a diameter for the circle.

Practice Exercise | Circle Command

In this practice exercise, you use the Tan, Tan, Radius, Circle command and the 2-Point Circle. First, you draw two adjacent lines that are 5.25 units each.

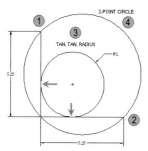

1   Begin a new drawing.

2   In the Select template dialog box, select the *acad.dwt* template file and click Open.

3   Be sure the following status bar settings are on:
    - Polar tracking
    - Object snap
    - Object snap tracking

4   To draw the lines:
    - Start the Line command.
    - For the start point, select the endpoint of the line (1).
    - Drag the mouse down until the Polar angle indicates that it is < 270. Enter **5.25** and press ENTER.
    - Drag the mouse to the right until the Polar angle indicates < 0. Enter **5.25** and press ENTER.
    - Press ENTER to end the Line command.

5   Adjust the display of your drawing using Zoom or Pan Real-time, if necessary.

6   To draw the smaller circle (3):

- On the ribbon, click Home tab > Draw panel > Circle drop-down > Tan, Tan, Radius.
- Move the cursor to the vertical line until you see the Deferred Tangent object snap and then click.
- Now move the cursor to the horizontal line until you see Deferred Tangent again and click.
- Specify the radius of the circle. Enter **2** and press ENTER.

7   To draw the larger circle (4):

- On the Home tab, click Draw panel > Circle drop-down > 2-Point.
- Move the cursor to the end of the vertical line (1) until you see the Endpoint object snap and click.
- Now move the cursor to the end of the horizontal line (2) until you see the Endpoint object snap and click.

Chapter 2 | Creating Basic Drawings

Arc Command

The Arc command creates an arc based on three points. Using the default method for creating an arc, you specify a start point, a second point, and an end point. The arc radius and center point are calculated based on the position of the three consecutive points you specify.

The following illustration represents an arc being created through three points.

Command Access

Arc

Command Line: **ARC, A**
Menu Bar: **Draw > Arc > 3 Points**
Ribbon: **Home tab > Draw panel > Arc**

Command Options

Arc options can be accessed from the drop-down menu next to the Arc button. The most common Arc options are indicated by red arrows in the following illustration.

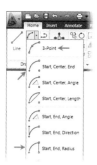

Arc options can be selected from the shortcut menu (right-click) or entered at the command line. Enter the capitalized letter(s) only and follow the command line prompts the capitalized letter(s) only.

Option	Description
C	Specify the center point of the arc. Then you will be prompted to specify the start point of the circle.
Angle	Specify included angle.
Length	Specify the length of the angle chord.

Arc Note

Arcs are drawn in a counterclockwise direction unless using the 3-Point default method.

Practice Exercise | Arc Command

In this practice exercise, you use the Start, Center, End Arc command. First, you draw a rectangle. Remember that arcs are drawn counterclockwise, so it is important that you select your points in the correct order. Draw all of the arcs so that they are outside of the rectangle.

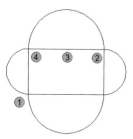

1   Begin a new drawing.

2   In the Select template dialog box, select the *acad.dwt* template file and click Open.

3   Be sure the following status bar settings are on:

- Polar tracking
- Object snap
- Object snap tracking

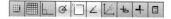

4   To draw the rectangle (any size):

- On the ribbon, click Home tab > Draw panel > Line.
- For the start point, specify the first corner (1).
- Use Polar Tracking to create a rectangle and make sure you snap to the first corner (1) when done.

5   To draw the first arc:

- On the ribbon, click Home tab > Draw panel > Start, Center, End Arc (select the down arrow by the Arc button).
- Specify the start point of the arc. Click the rectangle Endpoint (2).
- Specify the center point of the arc. Enter **MID** and press ENTER.

- Click the midpoint of the rectangle at (3).
- Specify the endpoint of the arc. Click the rectangle endpoint (4).

6   Repeat these steps until you have finished. Remember to draw your arcs in a counter-clockwise direction, using the Start, Center, End Arc command.

Chapter 2 | Creating Basic Drawings

Erase Command

Use the Erase command to remove geometry from the drawing. You can select objects by picking them directly, or using selection options such as a window or crossing window.

Command Access

Erase

Command Line: **ERASE, E**
Menu Bar: **Modify > Erase**
Ribbon: **Home tab > Modify panel > Erase**

OOPS Command

Use the **OOPS** command to retrieve geometry you accidentally erased without undoing any work you did since you last Erased.

Use a Shortcut Menu

Use the shortcut menu to alter your design more quickly. Select the objects you want to erase before entering the command or right-click and select Erase from the shortcut menu.

Practice Exercise | Erase Command

Practice the Erase command. First, draw some lines, circles, and arcs. Then practice removing them from your drawing. Try a few different ways to select the objects.

1   Begin a New drawing.

2   In the Select Template dialog box, select the *acad.dwt* template file and click Open.

3   Draw at least eight objects in the drawing window:

- Start the Line command. Draw some lines.
- Start the Circle command. Draw some circles.
- Start the Arc command. Draw some arcs.

4   To Erase, try these methods:

- On the ribbon, click Home tab > Modify panel > Erase. Select three objects to erase, then press ENTER.
- On the command line, enter **U**. Press ENTER to undo.
- With the command line blank, select three objects. Notice the objects are highlighted and the grips are visible. Right-click and select Erase from the shortcut menu.
- On the command line, enter **U**. Press ENTER to undo.
- Start the Erase command. At the Select objects prompt, enter **L** (for Last) and press ENTER. Notice that the last object you drew is highlighted. Press ENTER to start the Erase command.
- With the command line blank, select an object. Press DELETE.

5   Erase the objects using the Cross window option.

- Enter **E** on the command line and press ENTER. At the select objects prompt, select a spot in the blank area on the right side of the drawing. This will initiate a selection window. Drag your mouse up (or down) and to the left. Notice that the selection window is made of dashed lines.
- Cross the objects in the drawing, but leave some parts of the objects out of the selection window. Select to specify the opposite corner of the selection window.
- Notice that the objects that were completely inside the selection window are highlighted as well as the objects that were crossed by the selection window. Press ENTER to erase the objects.
- Enter **U** at the command line and press ENTER to undo.

6   Erase the objects using the Window option.

- On the command line, enter **E**. Press ENTER. At the select objects prompt, click in a blank area on the left side of the drawing. This will initiate a selection window. Drag your mouse up (or down) and to the right. Notice that the selection window is made of a continuous line.

- Cross the objects in the drawing, so that some are completely within the selection but others are partially out of the window. Click to specify the opposite corner of the selection window.

- Notice that the objects that were completely inside the selection window are highlighted but the objects that were partially out of the selection window are not highlighted. Press ENTER to erase the objects.

- On the command line, enter **U**. Press ENTER to undo.

7   To use the OOPS command on previously erased objects:

- On the command line enter, **E**. Press ENTER. Enter **ALL** at the Select objects prompt and press ENTER.

- Press ENTER again to start the Erase command.

- Now draw some more objects using the Line, Circle, or Arc commands.

- Enter **OOPS** and press ENTER.

- Notice that the objects you erased were returned to the drawing.

8   Close all drawings. Do not save.

Undo and Redo Commands

Use the Undo command to step back through every action you made, including pan and zoom. Use the Redo command to step forward through those actions again. These commands are conveniently located on the Quick Access toolbar. You can Undo at any point in the drawing session, even within some of the draw and modify commands. However you can only Redo immediately after an Undo command.

You may also type the Undo command at the command line. Enter **U** and press ENTER. If you continue to press ENTER, the Undo command will be repeated. If you enter the entire word **UNDO** at the command line and press ENTER, you will see a list of Undo options at the command line prompt.

If you are working in the AutoCAD Classic workspace the Undo and Redo buttons include down arrows that reveal lists which you can choose to undo or redo up to a selected item or step.

Command Access

Undo

Command Line: **U, UNDO**
Menu Bar: **Edit > Undo**
Quick Access Toolbar: **Undo**

Command Access

Redo

Command Line: **REDO**
Menu Bar: **Edit › Redo**
Quick Access Toolbar: **Redo**

Command Options

The following options are available only when you enter the entire word **UNDO** at the command line. Right-click to access the shortcut menu or enter the capitalized letter of the option.

Option	Description
Auto	Groups all actions of a single command, making them reversible with a single U command.
Control	Limits or turns off Undo.
Begin, End	Groups a sequence of actions into a set. After you use the Begin option, all subsequent actions become part of this set until you use the End option.
Mark	Places a mark in the undo information. If you use the Back option, all sequences are undone to the mark.
Back	Undoes all work to the first mark that is encountered. If there are no marks placed in the undo information, the following prompt appears: *This will undo everything. OK? ‹Y›* If you continue, all steps in the drawing are undone to the beginning of the drawing session.

Note

The Mredo command is similar to the expanded Undo command in that it offers other options to redo, such as the last step of all of the prior Undo operations.

Procedure: Using Undo and Redo

The following steps give an overview of how to use the Undo and Redo commands in the drawing.

1   On the Quick Access Toolbar, click Undo (1), or enter **U** in the command line.

2   Each time you click Undo a single operation is undone. If you entered **U** in the command line, you can continue to press ENTER to repeat the Undo command.

3   To Redo an operation, click Redo (2) in the Quick Access toolbar or enter **REDO** immediately following an undo operation.

4   Continue to click Redo until the drawing is returned to the desired state.

5   You can access the Undo or Redo lists on the Standard Toolbar to highlight the steps to undo or redo.

Undo and Redo Guidelines

- Undo information is only saved in the current session of the drawing. If you exit the drawing and reopen it, you cannot undo steps that were done in the previous session.
- The Redo command is only available immediately after an Undo operation.
- You can undo all the way back to the beginning of the drawing.
- Enter **UNDO** on the command line to view advanced Undo options.
- Enter **MREDO** on the command line to view advanced Redo options.
- If you have multiple drawings open at once, each drawing contains separate undo information and, as a result, you can use the Undo command independently within each drawing.

Practice Exercise | Undo and Redo Commands

Most of the time you use Undo and Redo in single steps. In this exercise, you practice using the Undo and Redo commands and some of the Undo options.

1   Begin a new, blank drawing.

2   In the Select Template dialog box, choose the *acad.dwt* template.

3   Draw some circles and then undo them:

- On the command line, enter **C**. Press ENTER. Draw five circles.

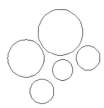

- On the Quick Access toolbar, click Undo until all five circles are gone.

- On the Quick Access toolbar, click Redo repeatedly to bring all five circles back.

4   Draw some lines. Practice using the Undo command within the line command.

- On the command line, enter **L** and press ENTER. Draw several continuous line segments. Press ENTER to complete the Line command.

- On the command line, enter **U**. Press ENTER. Notice that all of the line segments are undone.
- On the command line, enter **L**. Press ENTER. Draw several continuous line segments. Do not exit the line command. Right-click and select Undo from the shortcut menu.

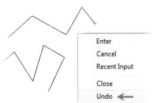

- Notice that the last line segment is undone. Right-click and select Undo again from the shortcut menu. Do not exit the line command. Continue to draw line segments. Press ENTER to complete the Line command.

5   Practice using the Undo options, BEgin and Back.

- On the command line, enter **UNDO**. Press ENTER.
- Enter **BE** (for BEgin). Press ENTER.
- On the command line, enter **L**. Press ENTER. Draw some continuous line segments. Press ENTER to complete the line command.
- Draw some circles, rectangles and arcs.
- With the command line blank, press the up arrow on the keyboard to scroll to the UNDO command. If you pass it, use the down arrow to scroll back. When Undo is in the command line, press ENTER.
- Enter **B** (for Back). Press ENTER.
- This should undo the lines that you created.

Rectangle Command

Use the Rectangle command to create rectangular objects. A single polyline object is created with this command. The simplest method for creating a rectangle is to specify the first corner, then the opposite corner. Other options for creating the rectangle include the Area, Dimension, and Rotation options.

This illustration shows a rectangle with the point used to create it specified.

Command Access

 Rectangle

Command Line: **RECTANGLE, REC**
Menu Bar: **Draw > Rectangle**
Ribbon: **Home tab > Draw panel > Rectangle**

Command Options

These Rectangle options are available after you have selected the first point for the rectangle. Right-click to select from the shortcut menu or enter the capitalized letter at the command line.

Option	Description
Area	Use this option to create a rectangle based on its area and the distance of one side, whether length or width.
Dimensions	Use this option to manually enter the length and width of the rectangle.
Rotation	Use this option to specify a rotation angle for the rectangle.

Tip

When you use the Distance or Area options to specify the rectangle size, the Length prompt refers to the horizontal distance, while the Width prompt refers to the vertical distance. If the rectangle is being rotated, Length refers to the distance along the rotation angle, while Width refers to the distance perpendicular to the rotation angle.

Rectangle Command Guidelines

- The Rectangle command generates polyline objects.
- Because rectangles are polylines, selecting any segment selects the entire rectangle.
- The simplest method for drawing a rectangle is to specify the first corner, then the opposite corner using relative *XY* coordinates. Example: after selecting the fist point, enter **@4,5** to make a rectangle that is 4 x 5.
- Rectangles can be initiated from any corner. After selecting the first point, if you enter **@-4,-5** you will make a rectangle that is located below and to the left of the first point selected.

Note

When using the dimension input option, you need to click to select an orientation. After you enter the length and width values, move your cursor up and down or left and right to view the available orientations. When the orientation you want is displayed, click to create the rectangle.

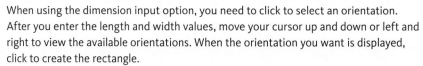

Chapter 2 | Creating Basic Drawings

Practice Exercise | Rectangle Commands

Practice drawing rectangles using coordinate dimensions. Practice other Rectangle options. Adjust your display as you work using the Zoom and Pan Realtime commands.

1   Open a new drawing.

2   Check that the Dynamic Input option on the status bar is not selected.

3   To draw Rectangles using relative coordinates @x,y:

- On the ribbon, click Home tab > Draw panel > Rectangle.
- To specify the first corner, click anywhere in the drawing window.
- At Specify first corner point prompt, enter **@4,5** and press ENTER.
- Notice that a rectangle was drawn up and to the right of the first point selected. If this did not happen, then you forgot to enter **@** before the x,y coordinates. Try again.

4   Continue to draw Rectangles using relative coordinates @x,y:

- On the Home tab, click Draw panel > Rectangle. Click the first corner anywhere in the drawing window.
- Enter the relative coordinates @x,y and press ENTER to make rectangles with the following dimensions:
- 6 x 7 (enter **@6,7**)
- 7 x 6 (enter **@7,6**)
- 9 x 9 (enter **@9,9**)

5   Turn on the Dynamic Input option on the status bar.

6   To draw a rectangle 7 x 10:

- On the Home tab, click Draw panel > Rectangle. Click the first corner anywhere in the drawing window.
- Enter **7,10** (do not enter the @ symbol) and press ENTER.
- A rectangle should have been made up and to the right of the start point. If not, check to be sure that Dynamic Input is on in the Status Bar and try again.
- Press F2.
- Observe that @ symbol was automatically added to the coordinate making it relative to the last point you selected.
- Practice making the following rectangles:
- 2 x 2 (enter **2,2**)
- 4 x 6 (enter **4,6**)

7   To use the Rectangle > Area option:

- On the Home tab, click Draw panel > Rectangle.

- Click a point anywhere in the drawing window for the first corner.
- Enter **A** (for Area) and press ENTER.
- Enter **35** for the area and press ENTER.
- To specify the Length, press ENTER to accept the default if [Length] is already in brackets. Otherwise, enter **L** and press ENTER.
- Enter **7** for the rectangle length and press ENTER.

Polygon Command

Use the Polygon command to create regular polygon geometry by specifying the center point and radius of an imaginary circle, or the start point and endpoint of one of the polygon edges. Regardless of the method you choose to define the polygon, all of its sides are equal in length.

The default method for creating polygons is to specify a center point and radius. When you choose this method, you must choose either the Inscribed or Circumscribed option. Depending on the option you choose, the size of the polygon is calculated as shown in the following image.

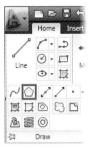

Inscribed   Circumscribed   Edge

Command Access

Polygon

Command Line: **POLYGON, POL**
Menu Bar: **Draw > Polygon**
Ribbon: **Home tab > extended Draw panel > Polygon**

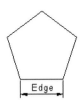

Command Options

The following Polygon command options are available from the shortcut menu (right-click) or the command line. Enter the capitalized letter(s) of the option.

Option	Description
Enter number of sides	Polygons can have between 3 and 1024 sides.
Specify center of polygon	*(default)* Note that while you may pick any point for the center of a polygon, once it is made you will not be able to simply snap to its center.
Inscribe in circle	Draws a polygon within a designated radius.
Circumscribed about circle	Draws a polygon outside of a designated radius.
Edge	Draws a polygon based on the number of sides and the length of a specified edge.

Polygon Command Guidelines

- Polygons can have between 3 and 1024 sides.
- Regardless of the number of sides you choose, all sides are equal in length.
- The Polygon command creates polyline objects.
- Polygon is a good tool for creating balloons and other types of annotation symbols.

Practice Exercise | Polygon Commands

Use the Polygon command to draw a 6-sided polygon that is inscribed about a circle, one that is circumscribed about a circle, and one that has an edge length of 1. First, draw two circles with a radius of 1.5, then draw the polygons.

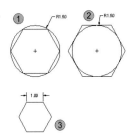

Note: Although you will draw the inscribed and circumscribed polygons inside a circle, it is only to compare the two options. It is not necessary to draw a circle first to make a polygon.

1   Open a new drawing using the *acad.dwt* template.

2   Click the following status bar options so that they are on:

   - Polar tracking
   - Object snap
   - Object snap tracking
     On the status bar, right-click Object Snap and click the Center snap mode so that it is also on.

3   To draw a polygon that is inscribed in a circle, as shown in example 1:

   - On the ribbon, click Home tab > Draw panel > Polygon.
   - Enter **6** for the number of polygon sides.

- Click the center of the circle for the center of the polygon. If object snap is on and center mode is selected, you will see the center snap indicator, as shown below.

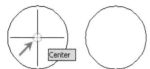

- Enter **I** (for Inscribed). Press ENTER.
- To specify the radius of the polygon circle, enter **1.5**. Press ENTER.

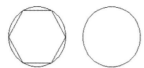

4   To draw a polygon that is circumscribed about a circle, as shown in example 2:
- On the Home tab, click Draw panel > Polygon.
- Enter **6** for the number of polygon sides.
- Click the center of the circle for the center of the polygon. Click when you see the circle's center object snap.
- Enter **C** (for Circumscribed). Press ENTER.
- To specify the radius of the circle, enter **1.5**. Press ENTER.

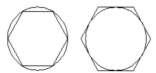

5   To draw a polygon using the Edge option, as shown in example 3:
- On the Home tab, click Draw panel > Polygon.
- Enter **6** for the number of polygon sides.
- Enter **E** (for Edge). Press ENTER.
- Click anywhere in the drawing window to specify the first endpoint of the edge.
- Drag the cursor and notice that with PolarSnap on you can specify the polar angle of the edge. Enter **1**. Press ENTER.

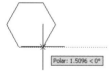

Chapter 2 | Creating Basic Drawings

Exercise | Create Basic Objects

In this exercise, you create a simple mechanical bracket using the basic geometry commands such as Line, Circle, Arc, Rectangle, and Polygon.

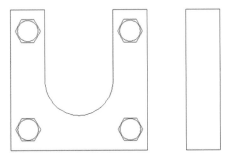

The completed exercise

Completing the Exercise
To complete the exercise, follow the steps in this book or in the onscreen exercise. In the onscreen list of chapters and exercises, click *Chapter 2: Creating Basic Drawings*. Click *Exercise: Create Basic Objects*.

Practice Creating Basic Objects: Part 1

In this part of the exercise, you begin to draw the front view of the bracket, beginning at point (1) and ending at point (2). Then, you resume drawing from point (1) to point (3).

1   Open *M_Create-Basic-Objects.dwg*.

2   On the status bar, make sure the following settings are on:

- Polar tracking
- Object snap
- Object snap tracking
- Dynamic input

3   To begin the line at point (1):

- On the Home tab, click Draw panel > Line.
- Enter **100, 50**. Press ENTER.
- Enter **100**. Press TAB.

- Enter **o**
  The values should appear in the Input interface as shown in the following image.
  Note: The values should appear in the Input interface as shown in the following image.
- Click to create the line.

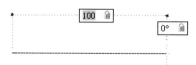

4   To draw a second line perpendicular to the first:
- Drag the cursor upwards and enter **100**. Press TAB.
- Make sure the angle field displays 90 degrees, then click to draw the line.

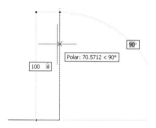

5   To draw another line:
- Drag the cursor to the left making sure that the angle field displays 180 degrees.
- Enter **25**. Press ENTER.
  Note: Using direct distance entry in combination with dynamic input provides you with optimal flexibility in creating your drawings.

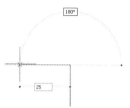

6   To draw another line:
- Drag the cursor downward making sure that the angle field displays 90 degrees.
- Enter **50**. Press ENTER.
- Press ENTER again to finish the line command at point (2).

Chapter 2 | Creating Basic Drawings

7 To undo all the lines that you just drew:

- On the Quick Access toolbar, click Undo.

- Notice that all of the lines that you created in the previous steps are removed.

8 To redo the lines:

- On the Quick Access toolbar, click Redo.

- Notice that all of the lines removed with the Undo command are returned.

9 To draw a line using object snaps:

Note: Object snaps are points on objects which enable you to accurately position other objects. They are covered in detail in another lesson.

- On the Home tab, click Draw panel > Line.
- As you approach the endpoint of the line, the endpoint object snap marker should appear.
- Click to select the endpoint of the line.

10 To draw a line perpendicular to the last:

- Drag the cursor upward making sure that the angle field displays 90 degrees.
- Enter **100**. Press ENTER.

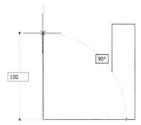

11 To draw a line and correct a mistake using the Undo command:

- Drag the cursor to the right making sure the angle field displays 0 degrees.
- Enter **35**. Press ENTER.

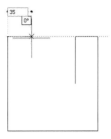

- Right-click near your last point. Click Undo.
- Because you are still in the Line command, only the last line segment that you drew is removed.
- Drag the cursor to the right again, making sure that the angle field displays 0 degrees.
- Enter **25**. Press ENTER.

12 To draw a line perpendicular to the last:

- Drag the cursor downward, making sure that the angle field displays 90 degrees.
- Enter **50**. Press ENTER.

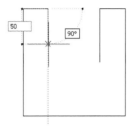

Chapter 2 | Creating Basic Drawings

13 Press ENTER to exit the Line command. Proceed to part two of this exercise.

Practice Creating Basic Objects: Part 2

In this part of the exercise, you draw the arc (1) in the front view of the bracket and add the side view (2). You then place the circles and polygons (3) in the four corners of the front view.

1 Now draw the arc:

- On the Home tab, click Draw panel > Arc.
- Select the endpoint of the previous line.
- Press DOWN ARROW and click End on the shortcut menu.

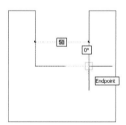

2 Select the endpoint on the right side of the opening.

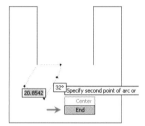

3 To finish the arc:

- Drag the cursor to the left, making sure that the angle field displays 180 degrees.
- Enter **25**. Press ENTER.
- Your drawing should now appear as shown.

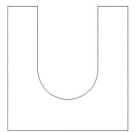

4   Click File menu > Save.

   Tip: You should develop a habit of saving files often.

5   To draw a rectangle:

- On the Home tab, click Draw panel > Rectangle.
- Touch **(DO NOT CLICK)** point (1) as indicated in the following image.
- Drag the cursor to the right. The extension object snap draws a dashed extension line.
- Click near point (2).

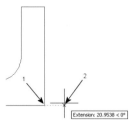

6   To position the rectangle:

- Right-click near your first point and select Dimensions on the shortcut menu.
  Note: This specifies the Dimension option of the Rectangle command.
- For the length, enter **25**. Press ENTER.
- For the width, enter **100**. Press ENTER.
- Click in the upper right of the drawing to position the rectangle.

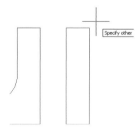

Your drawing should now appear as shown in the following image.

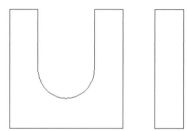

Chapter 2 | Creating Basic Drawings

7 To draw a circle:

- On the Home tab, click Draw panel > Circle.
- Enter **112.50,65**. Press ENTER.
- In the Dynamic Input Radius field, enter **7.5**. Press ENTER.

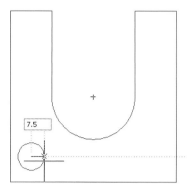

8 To draw a rectangle:

- On the Home tab, click Draw panel > Rectangle.
- Select the center point of the circle (1).
  Note: The object snap marker should appear as you approach the center of the circle.
- Drag the cursor to the upper right (2) and enter **75,70**. Press ENTER.
- Your drawing should appear as shown.

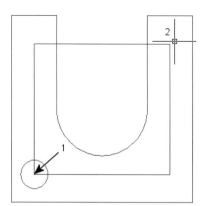

9   To draw three more circles as shown:
- On the Home tab, click Draw panel > Circle.
- Create three circles, each with a 7.5 unit radius, using the corners of the rectangles as center points.
  Tip: The software stores the last radius that you entered. If the command prompt is reading <7.500> you can press ENTER to reuse that value for the radius.

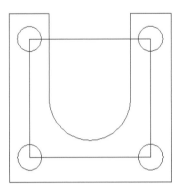

10   On the Home tab, click Modify panel > Erase. Select the rectangle that was used to position the circles. Press ENTER.

11   To draw a polygon circumscribing the top left circle:
- On the Home tab, click Draw panel > Polygon.
- When prompted for the number of sides, enter **6**.
- Select the center of the top left circle.
- In the Dynamic Input menu, select Circumscribed About Circle.
- For the radius, enter **8**. Press ENTER.

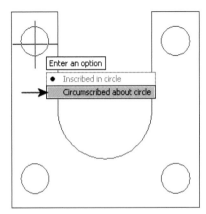

12   To create three similar polygons circumscribing the other circles:

  • Press ENTER to repeat the Polygon command.
  • Create three additional polygons on the remaining circles as shown.

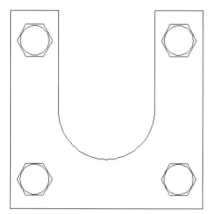

13   Close all files. Do not save.

Lesson 06 | Using Object Snaps

In this lesson, you learn what object snaps are, why they are important, and how to use them effectively in your drawing. You will be able to explain what object snaps are including the difference between running object snaps and object snap overrides. You will also be able to use objects snaps to select snap points in the drawing.

You will use object snaps for all drawing and most editing operations. Using object snaps is the best way to ensure the accuracy of all of your objects.

In the following illustration, the image on the left shows a door placement that used an object snap to place the door. The image on the right shows what the door placement looks like if you do not use an object snap.

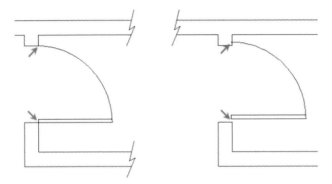

Objectives

After completing this lesson, you will be able to:

- Explain what object snaps are and why they are used.
- State the difference between running object snaps and object snap overrides and identify the different Object Snap modes.
- Use running object snaps and object snap overrides to select snap points in the drawing.

About Object Snap

Every object you create has various selectable points that you can use to position other objects. Every time you create an object you are required to specify a point or location. It is critical that these points be defined accurately if you expect your drawing to be accurate.

Object Snaps Defined

The following image shows three of the most basic types of objects that you can create: a line, a circle, and an arc. In this example, the line has two unique snap types with three possible locations that you can select; the circle has two unique snap types with five possible locations that you can select; the arc has three unique snap types with four possible locations that you can select.

1. Endpoint
2. Midpoint
3. Center point
4. Quadrant

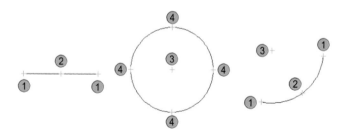

Object snaps exist for each of the previously mentioned points and more. You use them to select those points accurately. Attempting to accurately select these points without using object snaps would be very time-consuming and inaccurate.

Effect of Using Object Snaps

In the following image, the smaller circle needs to be concentric within the larger circle. By using the Center object snap, you can place the smaller circle precisely in the center of the larger circle.

By examining each circle's coordinates, you can verify that they both share the same center point.

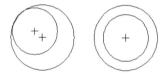

Effect of Not Using Object Snaps

In the following image, the user attempted to create the vertical line at the endpoint of the horizontal line without using objects snaps. Under normal viewing circumstances, the lines appear to be connected correctly; however, after zooming in to the geometry, you can see that the lines are not connected at the endpoints.

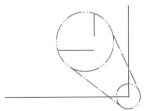

Object Snap Key Points

- Using object snaps to place objects in relation to other objects in the drawing is critical for accuracy.
- Every object you can create contains at least one point that is selectable with an object snap.

Object Snaps

You can access object snaps using several different methods. Running object snaps are generally set and then turned on or off, while object snap overrides represent a one-time use of the selected object snap.

- Running object snaps refer to object snaps that are set and available when the Osnap setting is on.
- Object snap overrides refer to an object snap that you select manually via the toolbar, shortcut menu, or command line. The object snap remains in effect until you specify the next point.

Running Object Snap

If you need to use the same object snap repeatedly, you can set it as a running object snap, which means it stays on until you turn it off. For example, you might set the object snap to center if you need to connect the centers of a series of circles with a line. This feature increases speed and accuracy.

Another feature of running object snap is that multiple object snaps can be on at the same time.

Command Access

Running Object Snap

Command Line: **OSNAP**
Menu Bar: **Tools > Drafting Settings > Object Snap Tab**
Keyboard Shortcut: **F3**
Toolbar: **Object Snap**
Status Bar: **Object Snap**

Object Snap Settings

The quickest way to turn Running Object Snap on or off is from the status bar button (1). If you right-click on this button, you can select Settings (2) to change the object snap options in the Drafting Settings dialog box (shown below). You can also select the snap modes from the shortcut menu. A selected object snap mode will be highlighted (3).

Notice that information in the Object Snap tab of the Drafting Settings dialog box is similar to the shortcut menu shown above.

Next to each available object snap is an icon referred to as the AutoSnap marker. If AutoSnap is turned on, the marker appears whenever you move the cursor over a snap point. Press TAB to cycle through the available snap points. Never turn all the object snap modes on at once. It is better to have several object snaps chosen (such as Endpoint, Midpoint and Intersection) and go back to add others as needed or use the object snap override.

When Are Object Snaps Available

You can specify an object snap whenever the software prompts for a point.

Object Snap Override

Object Snap override means that the snap stays in effect until you specify the next point. You are in snap override mode if you click an object snap from the shortcut menu or the object snap toolbar before selecting the specified point.

Command Access

Running Object Snap

Command Line: **While being prompted to select a point, enter the first 3 letters of the object snap and press ENTER (i.e. MID, INT, NEA)**
Menu Browser: **Tools > Toolbars > ACAD > Object Snap**
Toolbar: **Object Snap** (access from the Menu Browser)
Shortcut Menu: **SHIFT + right-click in the drawing window**

| | Temporary track point |
| --- | Temporary track point |

- Temporary track point
- From
- Mid Between 2 Points
- Point Filters ▸
- Endpoint
- Midpoint
- Intersection
- Apparent Intersect
- Extension
- Center
- Quadrant
- Tangent
- Perpendicular
- Parallel
- Node
- Insert
- Nearest
- None
- Osnap Settings...

Object Snap Modes

Note that an object snap override will cancel:

- If you miss your mark.
- If you select an object snap twice before selecting your point.

In the following examples:

- Point **1** identifies the initial point used to select the object.
- Point **2** identifies the point snapped to, or the second pick point if it is required.
- Point **3** identifies the point snapped to if two pick points were required.

 Endpoint: Snaps to the closest endpoint of an arc, elliptical arc, line, multiline, polyline segment, spline, region, or ray, or to the closest corner of a trace, solid, or 3D face.

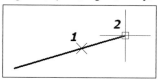

 Midpoint: Snaps to the midpoint of an arc, elliptical arc, line, multiline, polyline segment, region, solid, spline, or xline.

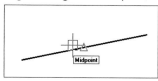

 Center: Snaps to the center points of circles, arcs, or ellipses.

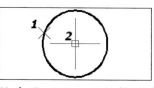

 Node: Snaps to a point object, dimension definition point, or dimension text origin.

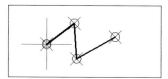

Quadrant: Snaps to quadrant points on a circle, arc, or ellipse.

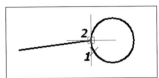

 Intersection: Snaps to the intersection of any two of the following: arc, circle, ellipse, elliptical arc, line, multiline, polyline, ray, region, spline, or xline.

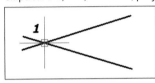

Extended Intersection: Snaps to the imaginary intersection of two objects that would intersect if the objects were extended along their natural paths.

Note: This option is not available as a running object snap. Use the Intersection object snap as an override.

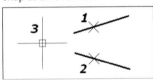

 Extension: Causes a temporary extension line to display when you pass the cursor over the endpoint of objects, so you can draw objects to and from points on the extension line. You can also use the Extension object snap to find the intersection of two objects that would intersect if the objects were extended along their natural paths.

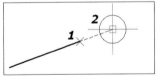

 Insertion: Snaps to the insertion point of an attribute, a block, a shape, or text.

Perpendicular: Snaps to a point perpendicular to an arc, circle, ellipse, elliptical arc, line, multiline, polyline, ray, region, solid, spline, or xline.

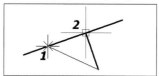

 Tangent: Snaps to a point on a circle or an arc that forms a line tangent to the object. Snaps to the tangent of an arc, circle, ellipse, elliptical arc, polyline arc segment, or spline.

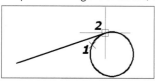

 Nearest: Snaps to the nearest point on an arc, circle, ellipse, elliptical arc, line, multiline, point, polyline, ray, spline, or xline.

 Apparent Intersection: Snaps to the apparent intersection of two objects (arc, circle, ellipse, elliptical arc, line, multiline, polyline, ray, spline, or xline) that do not intersect in 3D space but may appear to intersect in the current view.

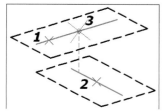

 Parallel: Draws a vector parallel to another object whenever you are prompted for the second point of a vector.

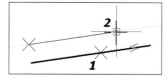

 None: Temporarily turns off all running object snaps for the next selection. Available only as an override, use this object snap when running objects snaps are turned on and you need to temporarily override all object snaps.

Using Object Snap

When you turn on multiple running object snaps, the software uses the object snap most appropriate to the object you select. If two potential snap points fall within the selection area, the software snaps to the eligible point closest to the center of the target box.

You can add to or subtract from your object snap modes without exiting a current command. Right-click OSNAP on the status bar and then click Settings. Add additional modes or remove modes. When you click OK, you return to the drawing area and can continue creating your design.

In the following illustration, the image on the left shows the cursor closer to the midpoint of the line; therefore, the midpoint will be selected. On the right, the cursor is closer to the end of the line; the endpoint will be selected.

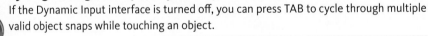

Cycling Through Multiple Object Snaps

If the Dynamic Input interface is turned off, you can press TAB to cycle through multiple valid object snaps while touching an object.

Procedure: Using Running Object Snaps

The following steps are an overview of using running object snaps.

1   On the status bar, right-click Object Snap. Click Settings.

2   In the Drafting Settings dialog box, verify that some of the object snaps are selected and the Object Snap On (F3) option is selected. Click OK.

3   On the Home tab, click Draw panel > Line. Place the cursor near other geometry in the drawing. The AutoSnap marker appears as your cursor approaches a snap point.

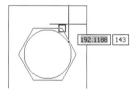

4   Click to select the snap point, then move the cursor to the next point on the screen. As you approach a snap point, the AutoSnap marker appears near the cursor. Click to select the snap point.

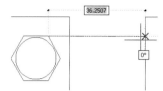

Tip

If you are using a three-button mouse or a wheel mouse, you can set the default behavior for the middle button or wheel to activate the Object Snap shortcut menu. Do this by setting the MBUTTONPAN system variable to o.

- On the command line, enter **MBUTTONPAN**. Press ENTER.
- Enter **o**.
- Press ENTER.

Procedure: Using Object Snap Overrides

The following steps are an overview of how to use the object snap overrides.

1   Begin creating or editing geometry.

2   When the software prompts you to select a point, select an object snap from the shortcut menu. Then position your cursor near the object containing the snap point. The AutoSnap marker should appear (1), indicating the snap point. Click to select the point.

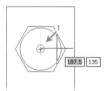

3   SHIFT+right-click and select the object snap from the shortcut menu.

4   Move your cursor to the next object. The AutoSnap marker appears next to the snap point

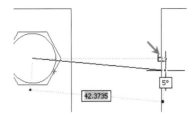

AutoSnap Aperture

You can use the AutoSnap aperture box to inform you when object snaps are active. By default, this option is turned off. The following image shows the AutoSnap aperture box. When any portion of the aperture box touches an object with a valid snap point, the AutoSnap marker appears, indicating a selectable snap point.

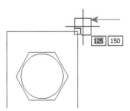

Options Dialog Box: Drafting Settings Tab

Under AutoSnap settings, place a check mark in the box next to the AutoSnap Aperture box.

Under Aperture Size, adjust the aperture size by dragging the slider left or right. You can see a preview of the size to the left of the slider. *Hint: These kinds of adjustments work well just left of center on the sliding adjustment bar.*

Chapter 2 | Creating Basic Drawings

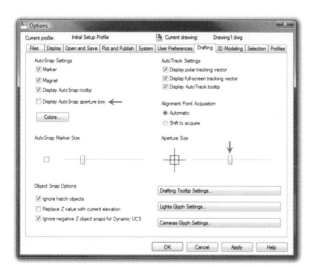

Practice Exercise | Running Object Snap and Object Snap Overrides

In order to practice using running object snap and object snap overrides, you create this drawing two times. The first time, do this drawing with the Running Object Snap option turned on. The second time, turn it off and use the overrides by selecting the object snap each time before you pick your point.

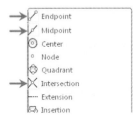

1   Begin a new drawing.

2   Be sure that the object snap is on.

Right-click and check Endpoint, Midpoint, and Intersection.

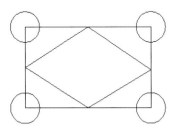

3   Draw a rectangle (any size):
   - On the Home tab, click Draw panel > Rectangle.
   - Click to specify the first corner.
   - Drag your mouse and click to specify the other corner.

4   Draw four circles the same size with the center points at each corner of the rectangle:
   - On the Home tab, click Draw panel > Circle.
   - For the center point of the circle, click the intersection (or endpoint) of the lines at a corner.
   - Make your first circle (any size).

- Press ENTER to repeat the Circle command.
- Click the endpoint of a line at another corner
- Press ENTER to accept the default size [which will be in brackets]
- Repeat for the other two circles.

5   Draw four connecting lines from the midpoint of each line in the rectangle:

- On the Home tab, click Draw panel > Line.
- Move the mouse to the midpoint of a line on the rectangle.
- Click when you see the Midpoint object snap marker.
- Move the mouse to the midpoint of the adjacent line and click when you see that Midpoint marker.
- Repeat for the remaining lines.

6   Erase everything. Begin this drawing again. This time turn object snap off.

7   First, draw the rectangle (any size), then create the same drawing as before using the single object snap overrides. To draw the circles:

- On the Home tab, click Draw panel > Circle.
- Before you specify the center point of the circle, SHIFT+right-click and select Endpoint.
- Click the Endpoint of the line.
- Make the circle any size and repeat these steps for the other three circles.

8   To draw the four connecting lines from the midpoint of each line in the rectangle:

- On the Home tab, click Draw panel > Line.
- SHIFT+right-click and select Midpoint from the shortcut menu.
- Move the mouse to the midpoint and click when you see the Midpoint object snap marker.
- Continue with the Line command. SHIFT+right-click and select Midpoint from the shortcut menu and move the mouse to the midpoint of the adjacent line. Click when you see that marker.
- Repeat these steps for the remaining lines.
  Though it is far easier and quicker to use running object snap, it is also convenient to occasionally use the object snap overrides. In this exercise, you turned object snap off to do the second drawing, however note that it can be left on when the object snap overrides are needed.

9   Close all files. Do no not save.

Exercise | Use Object Snaps

In this exercise, you create geometry using running object snaps and object snap overrides. When you have completed the exercise, you will be able to use object snaps to create and edit geometry. **Note**: The exercise covers most but not all objects snaps.

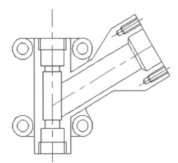

The completed exercise

Completing the Exercise
To complete the exercise, follow the steps in this book or in the onscreen exercise. In the onscreen list of chapters and exercises, click *Chapter 2: Creating Basic Drawings*. Click *Exercise: Use Object Snaps*.

1 Open *M_Object-Snaps.dwg*.

2 On the status bar, make sure the following settings are on:
- Object snap
- Dynamic input

3 To set object snaps:
- On the status bar, right-click Object Snap. Click Settings.
- In the Drafting Settings dialog box, Object Snap tab, set the running object snaps as shown in the following illustration.
- Clear all object snaps in the column on the rightside.
- Click OK.

4   To draw a line:

- On the Home tab, click Draw panel > Line.
- Select the endpoints as shown in the following illustration. Notice the appearance of the object snap.
- Press ENTER to end the Line command.

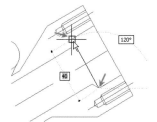

    Tip: You may need to use zoom and pan in order to view and snap to the correct points.

5   Press ENTER to repeat the Line command. Use the Endpoint object snap to create another line right next to the previous one.

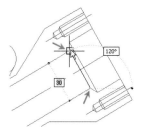

6   To draw a circle:

- On the Home tab, click Draw panel > Circle.
- Touch the outer circle and you should see the Center snap marker. When the marker appears, click to select the center point.

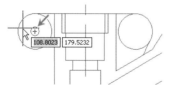

- Enter **6**. Press ENTER.
  Your circle should appear as shown in the following image.

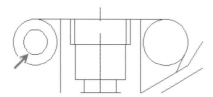

7   Repeat the Circle command for the other three corners of the part.
     Tip: The last radius value that you used is remembered, so when you are prompted for the
     radius, press ENTER. Over the next few steps, you will use the object snap overrides to create
     geometry on the part.

8   To draw a line:

- On the Home tab, click Draw panel > Line.
- SHIFT+right-click and click Quadrant on the shortcut menu.
- Select the lower quadrant of the circle on the bottom left of the part.

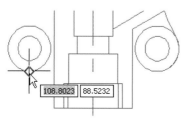

- SHIFT+right-click and click Perpendicular on the shortcut menu.
- Select the vertical line on the part. Press ENTER to end the Line command.

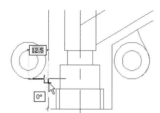

9   Repeat the previous step on the opposite side of the part.

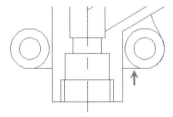

10   Close all files. Do not save.

Lesson 07 | Using Polar Tracking and PolarSnap

In this lesson, you learn how to create geometry at precise distances and angles from other geometry using polar tracking and PolarSnap.

You might not use polar tracking and PolarSnap every day, but knowing how and when to use these tools greatly increases your productivity in certain situations.

In the following illustration, polar tracking and PolarSnap are used to create geometry at precise angles and distances.

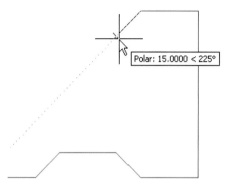

Objectives

After completing this lesson, you will be able to:

- Use the Polar Tracking and PolarSnap modes efficiently and effectively.

Using Polar Tracking and PolarSnap

Because everything that you create requires some degree of precision, it is critical that you learn the different options for creating geometry accurately and yet efficiently. Previously, you learned how to enter coordinate data in the form of absolute and relative coordinates. These methods, though important, are not always the most efficient for creating geometry.

Using polar tracking and PolarSnap, you can create geometry with the same precision as coordinate entry allows you, but more efficiently. To use these features, you need to adjust their options and turn them on using the status bar buttons.

In the following illustration, the same paths are being drawn using polar tracking and PolarSnap. The alignment paths appear as dotted lines extended indefinitely from the point of your cursor. The polar tooltips display the current position of the cursor relative to the last point selected. The path on the left is using polar tracking with an absolute angle measurement, while the path on the right is using the Relative to Last Segment option.

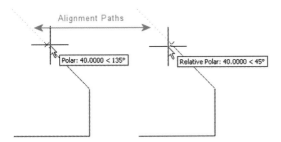

Using polar tracking with PolarSnap, you can accurately draw the previous geometry without having to enter cumbersome coordinates.

Command Access

Polar

Menu Bar: **Tools › Drafting Settings › Polar Tracking tab**
Keyboard Shortcut: **F10**
Status Bar: **Polar Tracking; Right-click › Settings**

Drafting Settings Dialog Box: Polar Tracking Tab

Use the following options to control various aspects of the polar tracking feature.

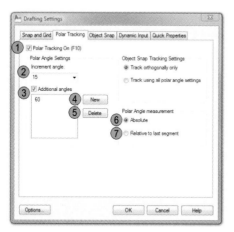

① Select to turn on polar tracking. You can also press F10 to toggle polar tracking on or off.

② Select an angle from the list to increment the polar alignment paths as the cursor approaches the selected angle.

③ Select to snap to the additional angles defined in the list.

④ Click to define an additional PolarSnap angle.

⑤ Click to delete the selected angle in the Additional Angles list.

⑥ Click to display the angle of the alignment path as an absolute angle in the current coordinate system.

⑦ Click to display the angle of the alignment path relative to the last segment drawn.

Drafting Settings Dialog Box: Snap and Grid Tab

Use the Snap and Grid tab of the Drafting Settings dialog box to adjust the snap settings for use with polar tracking. Use the options highlighted in the following illustration to enable precision cursor movement along the polar tracking alignment path.

(1) Click to enable the cursor to snap to predefined distances along the alignment path.

(2) Enter a distance to increment the cursor as it moves along the alignment path. This option is only available when PolarSnap is selected.

Procedure: Using Polar Tracking and PolarSnap

The following steps give an overview of using polar tracking and PolarSnap to create geometry.

1   Right-click Polar Tracking on the status bar and click Settings. In the Drafting Settings dialog box, Polar Tracking tab, you can turn polar tracking on and off and select an increment angle from the list.

2   You can set a PolarSnap increment as shown in the following list or key in values with direct distance entry.

- In the Drafting Settings dialog box, Snap and Grid tab, select the Snap On (F9) option.
- Under Snap Type, click PolarSnap.
- Under Polar Spacing, for Polar Distance, enter a distance.
- Click OK.

3   Begin creating geometry such as lines or polylines. Click a point in the drawing window and drag your cursor to the next point. The polar tracking tooltip displays the polar distance and angle.

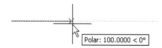

4   Continue selecting points, using the polar tracking tooltips for precise distances and points as shown.

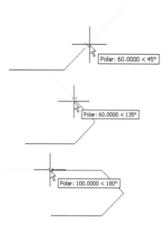

Polar Tracking and PolarSnap Guidelines

- Using polar tracking, you can quickly snap to predefined angle increments while moving the cursor to draw or edit geometry.
- Polar tracking is more flexible than traditional Ortho mode that restricts your cursor movement to horizontal or vertical directions, yet polar tracking offers the same benefit of being able to easily draw lines at common angles. Using PolarSnap, you can select points along the alignment path that would otherwise require the use of cumbersome coordinate entry.
- Unlike Grid snap, which increments all cursor movement, PolarSnap forces the cursor to move in increments only when the angle of the cursor is equal to a polar tracking angle increment. When the cursor angle is not an increment of the polar tracking angle, the cursor can move freely.

Grid and Snap

When you activate the grid, a pattern of dots appears in the background. The area represented by these dots is referred to as the drawing limits.

In the following illustration, the rectangle was drawn with Grid and Snap turned on. Notice how the rectangle is aligned perfectly with the grid pattern.

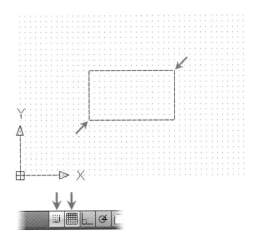

To turn on Grid or Snap, click the appropriate buttons on the status bar.

Note: You can turn these two settings on or off independently of each other.

Ortho Mode

An alternate method to polar tracking is Ortho mode. When Ortho mode is turned on, your cursor can move parallel only to the X or Y axes, so you can quickly draw straight lines or move items easily along the X or Y axes.

In the following illustration, lines were drawn using Ortho mode. The arrow indicates the temporary override symbol that appears when a temporary override key is being used. In this case, the temporary override for Ortho mode is active.

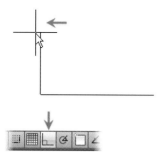

Click ORTHO on the status bar or press F8 to turn Ortho mode on or off.

Note: Press and hold SHIFT while drawing or moving geometry to activate the Ortho mode temporary override. As long as the SHIFT key is pressed, Ortho mode is active.

Exercise | Use Polar Tracking and PolarSnap

In this exercise, you create lines at precise distances and angles using polar tracking and PolarSnap. When you have completed the exercise, you will be able to use the polar tracking and PolarSnap features to create precise geometry.

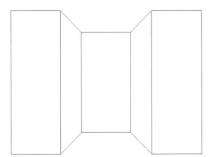

The completed exercise

Completing the Exercise

To complete the exercise, follow the steps in this book or in the onscreen exercise. In the onscreen list of chapters and exercises, click *Chapter 2: Creating Basic Drawings.* Click *Exercise: Use Polar Tracking and PolarSnap.*

1   Open *M_Roller.dwg.*

2   On the status bar, make sure the following settings are on:

   • Snap
   • Polar tracking
   • Object snap
   • Model

   Right-click Polar Tracking and select Settings.

3   In the Drafting Settings dialog box, Polar Tracking tab:

   • Select 15 from the Increment Angle list.
   • Under Polar Angle Measurement, click Absolute.

4   On the Snap and Grid tab:

   • Click PolarSnap.
   • Enter **1** in the Polar Distance field.

5   On the Object Snap tab:

   • Make sure Endpoint and Node are selected.
   • Click OK.

6   To draw the line using polar tracking:

   • Activate the Line tool.
   • Specify the line's start point from the point object, using the Node object snap override.
   • Drag the cursor to the right until the polar tracking tooltip reads 25.00 < 0 degrees. Click the point.

Chapter 2 | Creating Basic Drawings

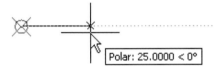

Polar: 25.0000 < 0°

7   Position the cursor so that the polar angle tooltip reads 15.00 < 45. Click the point.

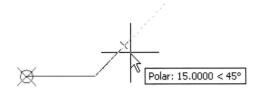

Polar: 15.0000 < 45°

8   Position the cursor so that the polar angle tooltip reads 25.00 < 0. Click the point.

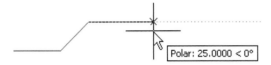

Polar: 25.0000 < 0°

9   Position the cursor so that the polar angle tooltip reads 15.00 < 315. Click the point.

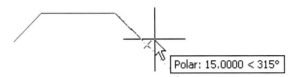

Polar: 15.0000 < 315°

10   Position the cursor so that the polar angle tooltip reads 25.00 < 0. Click the point.

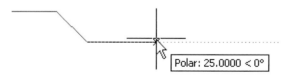

11   Move the cursor upwards until the polar tracking cursor reads 70.00 < 90. Click the point.

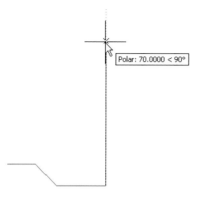

12   Repeat these steps to draw the top half of the object which mirrors the bottom half, changing the Polar angle accordingly. Your final endpoint should be at the original start point.

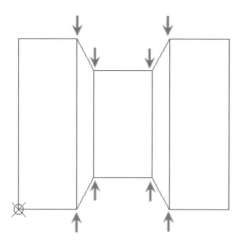

    Chapter 2 | Creating Basic Drawings

13 Press ENTER to repeat the Line command. Select the endpoints indicated in the following image to draw the inner vertical lines. Press ENTER to end the Line command.

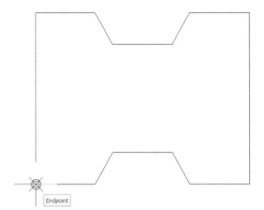

14 Close all files. Do not save.

Lesson 08 | Using Object Snap Tracking

In this lesson, you learn what object snap tracking is and how it can assist you in creating geometry. When you have completed the lesson, you will be able to describe and use object snap tracking to position geometry.

Object snap tracking is the most efficient way to locate a point using your existing objects as reference.

In the following image, object snap tracking is used to quickly locate the center of the rectangle.

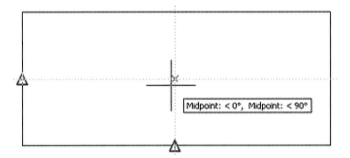

Objectives

After completing this lesson, you will be able to:

- Describe object snap tracking.
- Use object snap tracking to position geometry.

About Object Snap Tracking

You often need to place or create geometry at a location relative to other objects in the drawing. While you could create construction geometry for the purpose of aligning the new geometry, with object snap tracking you can accomplish the same result much faster.

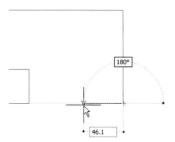

Object Snap Tracking Defined

Object snap tracking works in combination with object snaps to enable you to temporarily acquire and track up to seven points. Once you acquire points, object snap tracking provides horizontal, vertical, or polar alignment paths relative to the points that you have acquired.

In the following image, the table is being moved to the room center using object snap tracking. To center the table in the room, the midpoint of the wall on the left (1) and the midpoint of the wall below (2) have been acquired. Triangular glyphs at the midpoints indicate that the points have been acquired. As the table is positioned near the imaginary intersection, the alignment paths (3) appear indicating the intersection. The Dynamic Input interface displays the current position as 0 degrees from the left midpoint and 90 degrees from the lower midpoint.

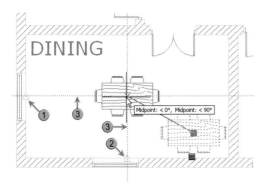

When you need to know the center of a noncircular object such as a rectangle or polygon, use object snap tracking to locate the center point.

Object Snap Tracking Guidelines

- Use object snap tracking to reduce the need to create construction geometry.
- You can use object snap tracking to calculate the center point of noncircular objects.
- When you use object snap tracking in conjunction with dynamic input, the Dynamic Input interface displays position information related to the acquired points.

Using Object Snap Tracking

To use object snap tracking, you acquire points from geometry in the drawing using running object snaps. As you acquire points on the geometry, a small plus (+) sign appears on the point. This indicates that the point is being used for object snap tracking.

In the following image, the midpoint of the left side of the rectangle has been acquired. Notice the plus (+) symbol indicating the acquired point. The midpoint of the bottom of the rectangle is being touched to acquire the point.

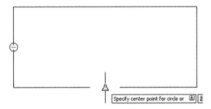

Specify center point for circle or ⊕ 2

Touching to Acquire a Point
To *touch* a point, hover over the point with your cursor, but DO NOT CLICK to select the point. The acquired indicator appears inside the object snap marker when the point has been acquired.

Command Access

Object Snap Tracking
↓

Menu Bar: **Tools › Drafting Settings › Object Snap / Object Snap Tab**
Keyboard Shortcut: **F11**
Status Bar: **Object Snap Tracking › Right-click › Settings**

Drafting Settings Dialog Box

Turn Object Snap Tracking on from the status bar, from the Object Snap tab in the Drafting Settings dialog box, or by pressing F11. Object Snap must be on and modes must be selected for Object Snap Tracking to work.

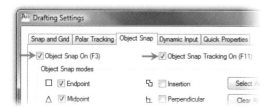

In the Polar Tracking tab, you can choose whether to track Orthogonally Only (simplest method) or to Track using all polar angle settings.

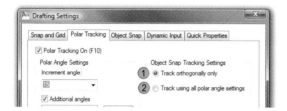

① Alignment paths only appear for horizontal and vertical alignments.

② Alignment paths appear for all polar angles defined.

Tip
Press and hold SHIFT+Q to temporarily turn object snap tracking on or off.

Procedure: Using Object Snap Tracking

The following steps outline how to use object snap tracking to acquire points.

1   On the status bar, make sure the Osnap and Otrack settings are on.

2   Start any command that prompts you to select a point.

3   To specify a point using object snap tracking, touch the point with the cursor. A small plus (+) appears, indicating that the point has been acquired.

4   Touch another point to acquire its location.

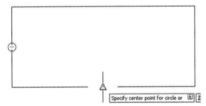

5   If more than two points are required, continue to touch points.

6   Move your cursor to a location that would be considered an intersection of the acquired points, based on orthogonal or polar angle settings. The alignment paths appear as your cursor approaches the calculated intersection.

7   Click to select the calculated point.

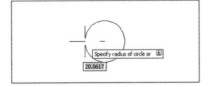

Guidelines for Acquiring Points with Object Snap Tracking

- To acquire a point, touch it with the cursor.
- To release a point, touch an acquired point with the cursor.
- You can acquire up to seven points for object snap tracking.
- If you attempt to acquire more than seven points, previous points are automatically released on a first-acquired, first-released basis.

Object Snap Tracking Settings Key Points

- Object snap tracking uses running object snaps to acquire points.
- To use object snap tracking, object snaps must be turned on with at least one object snap selected.
- Hover over the object snap points, but do not select them.

Practice Exercise | Object Snap Tracking

Practice using object snap tracking *orthogonally*.

1   Begin a new drawing.

2   Be sure that Object Snap and Object Snap Tracking are both selected in the status bar.

Right-click Object Snap and be sure that the Midpoint selection mode is selected.

3   Draw a rectangle any size:
    - On the Home tab, click Draw panel > Rectangle.
    - Click the first corner; click the opposite corner.

4   Draw a circle (any size) in the center of the rectangle:
    - On the Home tab, click Draw panel > Circle.
    - Hold the mouse over the midpoint of one of the lines in the rectangle until you see a small cross.
    - Then hold the mouse over the midpoint of one of the adjacent lines.
    - Then bring your curser to the middle of the rectangle.
    - Click at the intersection of the two dotted lines of the horizontal and polar angles.
    - Specify the circle size by clicking a point in the graphics window, or entering a value on the command line.

5   Close all files. Do not save.

Exercise | Use Object Snap Tracking

In this exercise, you use object snap tracking to create a side view of the part. After completing this lesson, you will be able to use object snap tracking in other drawings.

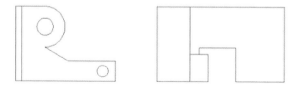

The completed exercise

> **Completing the Exercise**
> To complete the exercise, follow the steps in this book or in the onscreen exercise. In the onscreen list of chapters and exercises, click *Chapter 2: Creating Basic Drawings.* Click *Exercise: Use Object Snap Tracking.*

1 Open *M_Object-Tracking.dwg.*

2 On the status bar, make sure the following settings are turned on:

   - Polar tracking
   - Object snap
   - Object snap tracking
   - Dynamic input

3 Right-click Object Snap Tracking. Click Settings.

4 In the Drafting Settings dialog box, select the running object snaps as shown in the following image. Click OK.

5 To draw a rectangle:

   - On the Home tab, click Draw panel > Rectangle.

- Acquire the lower right corner of the existing shape and move the mouse to the right along the extension path.
- Enter **40** in the Dynamic Input field. Press ENTER.

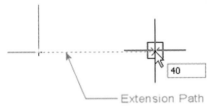

- Move the cursor up and to the right.
- Enter **31.75, 69.85**. Press ENTER.

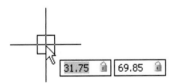

6   To repeat the rectangle command:
- Right-click in the graphics window. Click Repeat RECTANG.
- Select the lower right corner of the previous rectangle as the start point.
- Enter **17.53, 25.4**. Press ENTER.

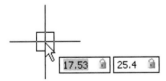

7   To draw a line:
- On the Home tab, click Draw panel > Line.
- Select the top right corner of the first rectangle.
- Move the cursor to the right at 0 degrees. Enter **90.55**. Press ENTER.

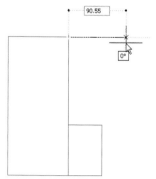

8   Move the cursor to acquire a tracking point from the lower right corner of the second rectangle. Track back to the line until the angle shows 90 degrees. Click to select the point.

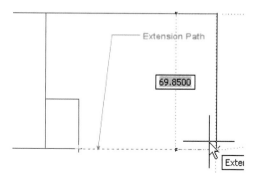

9   Move the cursor to the left. Enter **46.1**. Press ENTER.

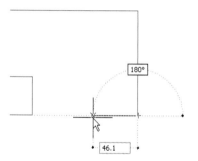

10 Acquire the point where the arc and angled line meet (1). Track back to the point where the current line meets the tracking line (2). Click the intersection of the alignment paths.

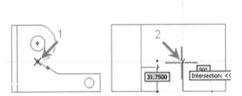

11 Acquire the midpoint of the top line of the second rectangle. Track upwards until you get to the intersection of the two tracking lines. Click that point.

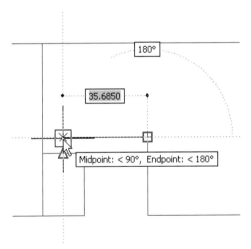

12   Select the midpoint of the top line of the second rectangle. Press ENTER to complete the
      line command.

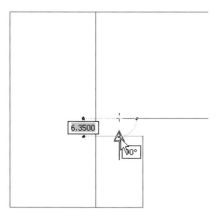

13   Close all files. Do not save.

Lesson 09 | Working with Units

This lesson describes how to set up units in a drawing.

When you create drawings, one of the first things you must do is define the current working units. The units settings determine how you enter distances as well as how the values are returned to you.

The following illustration shows how the software presents the current units through the dynamic input interface.

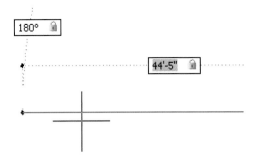

Objectives

After completing this lesson, you will be able to:

- Describe units and how they affect your drawing.
- Use the Units command to set drawing units.

About Units

Units represent the baseline of all the geometry that you create in your drawing. It is up to you to determine what unit of measurement will be used in your drawing.

When you begin a blank drawing, the default units are based in the decimal system. Because the software is not capable of distinguishing inches from millimeters, it assumes that a value of 1 is equal to either 1 inch or 1 mm. Setting the appropriate units determines the format in which the software presents values to you via the command line, status bar, polar tracking, and dynamic input interface.

While the software is not a true units-based system, meaning it doesn't understand the difference between 1 inch and 1 millimeter, there are some assumptions that can affect other settings such as Imperial Architectural units (for example 1'-6"), and alternate dimension display.

Unit Guidelines

The following are some guidelines you should refer to regarding units:

- The software is set by default to decimal units.
- A unit of 1 can be equal to 1 inch or 1 millimeter.
- If you need to input imperial architectural units for distances, you must select the Architectural type drawing units. The software will not understand the architectural units format 1'-6" if the Units are set to Decimal.
- When you are using Architectural Units, enter the foot mark, but it is not necessary to enter inches as the software will assume inches if no symbol is entered. Example 16' -2" can be simply entered: **16'2**.
- When using Architectural units, you may enter **16' -2"** or the equivalent in inches: **194**.
- If you work primarily with metric units, then you should use the default decimal unit setting.
- AutoCAD is accurate 14 decimal places (1.00000000000000). What you see for units precision will be rounded up to the nearest decimal place that you have determined in the Units dialog box.
- Simply picking points in the drawing window will not guarantee that you have specified the precise length or angle unless you use the drawing aids determined in the drafting settings.

Units Example

The following image illustrates the assumptions made regarding units. In this image, a single line was drawn at a length of 18 units. When dimensioned with both a metric and imperial dimension style, the dimensions report different lengths.

This occurs because the default dimension styles have preset conversion factors when you display alternate units. While you could change these conversion factors to represent any conversion imaginable, by default the software assumes a conversion using inches or millimeters as the base unit.

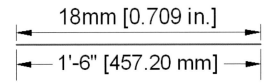

Setting Units

You use the Units command to set up the units for the drawing. You can change the drawing units at any time, but it is recommended that you do so at the beginning of each drawing you create. When you use drawing templates or the New Drawing wizard, the units for the drawing are set accordingly.

In the following image, the drawing units have been set to accept surveyor units for angle input.

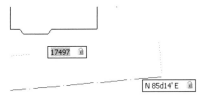

Command Access

Units

Command Line: **UNITS**
Application menu: **Drawing Utilities > Units**

Drawing Units Dialog Box

When you start the Units command, the Drawing Units dialog box is displayed. You set the unit types for length, angle, and insertion scale. You can set the precision for both length and angle units and you can also set the angle direction. The precision options are displayed in the selected unit format.

To set your drawing units, select the appropriate unit in the Length and Angle lists and then set the unit's precision with the Precision lists for length and angle.

Current Unit Setting

The current unit setting affects the manner in which values are presented to you as well as the format in which you can enter distances and angles. Regardless of the unit setting you choose, you can always enter values in decimal format.

Warning!

The Lighting area shown in the Units dialog box is not available in AutoCAD LT.

Procedure: Setting Drawing Units

The following steps give an overview of setting drawing units.

1   On the command line, enter **units** and press ENTER.

2   In the Drawing Units dialog box, select the appropriate length and angle unit types. If necessary, you can also adjust the precision options for both length and angle.

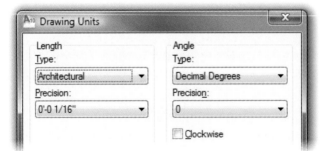

3   Click OK.

4   You can now enter values using the format of the selected unit for length and angle. When the software presents values to you via the interface, they are in the selected unit format.

Guidelines for Setting Units

- While it is possible to set the drawing units at any time, it is recommended that you do this when you start a new drawing.
- Regardless of the current unit setting, you can always enter units in decimal format.
- To input values in a format other than decimal, you must set the appropriate unit type.

Practice Exercise | Setting Units

In this practice exercise, you create a new blank drawing, set the drawing units to Architectural, and draw a rectangle 54' 6" x 34'2". Then you zoom all to see your work.

1   Begin a new drawing. In the Select template dialog box, select the *acad.dwt* drawing template.

2   To set the architectural drawing units:

  • On the command line, enter **units** and press ENTER.
  • In the Drawing Units dialog box, under Length, select Architectural in the Type list.
  • Click OK to exit.

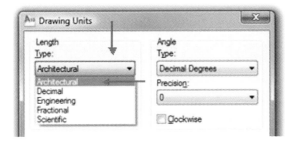

3   To draw the 54'6" x 34'2" rectangle:

  • On the Home tab, click Draw panel > Rectangle.
  • Specify the first corner point.
  • To specify the opposite corner, enter: **@54'6,34'2**
    Note: You do not have to enter inches.

4   To zoom your drawing:

  • Enter **Z** and press ENTER.
  • Enter **A** and press ENTER.

Exercise | Use Architectural Units

In this exercise, you set the drawing to use architectural units. Then, using the dynamic input interface, you sketch the outline of a simple floor plan.

The completed exercise

Completing the Exercise

To complete the exercise, follow the steps in this book or in the onscreen exercise. In the onscreen list of chapters and exercises, click *Chapter 2: Creating Basic Drawings*. Click *Exercise: Use Architectural Units*

1   Open *I_Architectural-Units.dwg.*

2   To set the unit type:
   - Click the Application button > Drawing Utilities > Units.
   - In the Type list under Length, select Architectural.
   - In the Precision list, select 0'-0 1/8".
   - In the Precision list under Angle, select 0.0.
   - Click OK.

3   To draw a line:

- On the Home tab, click Draw panel > Line.
- Enter **10',10'**. Press ENTER.
- Move the cursor to the right.
- Enter **6'-8**. Press TAB.
- Enter **0**. Press TAB.
- Click anywhere in the drawing.

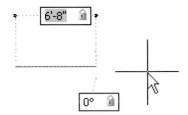

4   For the next point:

- Move the cursor down and to the right.
- Enter **2'4.25**. Press TAB. Enter **45**. Press TAB again.
- Click anywhere in the drawing to accept the point.

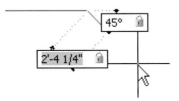

5   For the next point:

- Enter **4'**. Press TAB.
- Enter **0**. Press TAB.
- Move the cursor to the right.
- Click anywhere in the drawing to accept the point.

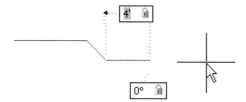

6   For the next point:
- Move the cursor up and to the right.
- Enter **2′4-1/4**. Press TAB.
- Enter **45**. Press TAB.
- Click anywhere in the drawing to accept the point.

7   For the next point:
- Move the cursor to the right.
- Enter **45′-8″**. Press TAB.
- Enter **0**. Press TAB.
- Click anywhere in the drawing.

8   For the next point:
- Move the cursor up.
- Enter **42′-8″**. Press TAB.
- Enter **90**. Press TAB.
- Click anywhere in the drawing.

9   For the next point:
    - Move the cursor to the left.
    - Enter **15'-3"**. Press TAB.
    - Enter **180**. Press TAB.
    - Click anywhere in the drawing.

10 For the next point:
    - Move the cursor down.
    - Enter **6'-2"**. Press TAB.
    - Enter **90**. Press TAB.
    - Click anywhere in the drawing.

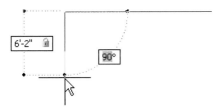

11 For the next point:
    - Move the cursor to the left.
    - Enter **44'-5"**. Press TAB.
    - Enter **180**. Press TAB.
    - Click anywhere in the drawing.

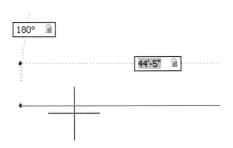

12 Right-click and click Close, or select the endpoint of the line where you started.

13 Close all files. Do not save.

Exercise | Use Surveyor's Units

In this exercise, you set the drawing units to accept Surveyor's Units for angle input, and use the Dynamic Input interface to draw a site boundary.

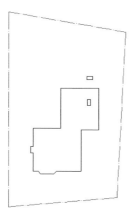

The completed exercise

Completing the Exercise

To complete the exercise, follow the steps in this book or in the onscreen exercise. In the onscreen list of chapters and exercises, click *Chapter 2: Creating Basic Drawings*. Click *Exercise: Use Surveyor's Units*.

1   Open *M_Survey-Units.dwg*.

2   To set the unit type:

   • Click Application Button > Drawing Utilities > Units.
   • In the Angle type list, select Surveyor's Units.
   • In the Angle Precision list, select N odoo'oo" E.
   • Click OK.

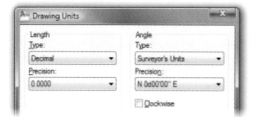

3   To draw a line:
   - On the Home tab, click Draw panel > Line.
   - Enter **4000,4000**. Press ENTER.
   - Enter **17497**. Press TAB.
   - Enter **N85d14' E**. Press TAB.
   - Click anywhere in the drawing.

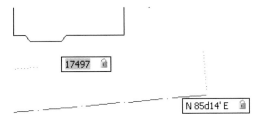

4   For the next point:
   - Move the cursor up and to the right from the previous point.
   - Enter **25498**. Press TAB.
   - Enter **N2d57' E**. Press TAB.
   - Click anywhere in the drawing.

5   For the next point:
   - Move the cursor up and to the left from the previous point.
   - Enter **19000**. Press TAB.
   - Enter **N80d40' W**. Press TAB.
   - Click anywhere in the drawing.
   - Right-click and click Close.
     The site boundary appears as shown.

6   Close all files. Do not save.

Challenge Exercise | Architectural

In this exercise, you use what you have learned in Chapter 2 to draw a basic floor plan.

> **Note**
> You have the option of completing this exercise using either imperial or metric units. Select one version of the exercise to complete the steps.

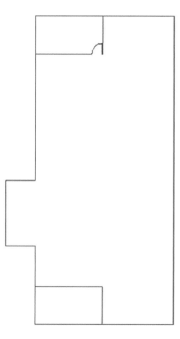

The completed exercise

> **Completing the Exercise**
> To complete the exercise, follow the steps in this book or in the onscreen exercise. In the onscreen list of chapters and exercises, click *Chapter 2: Creating Basic Drawings*. Click *Challenge Exercise: Architectural Metric*.

Metric Units

1 Open *M_ARCH-Challenge-CHP02.dwg.*

2 Draw the floor plan so its lower-right corner matches up with the point in the drawing file as shown in the image.

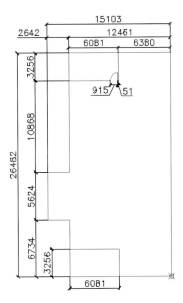

3 Draw the door so it is 51 mm thick.

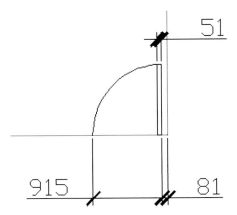

4 Save and close all files.

Imperial Units

1   Open *I_ARCH-Challenge-CHP02.dwg*.

2   Draw the floor plan so its lower-right corner matches up with the point in the drawing file as shown in the image.

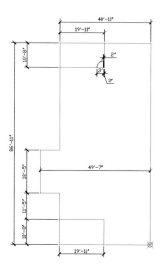

3   Draw the door so it is 2" thick.

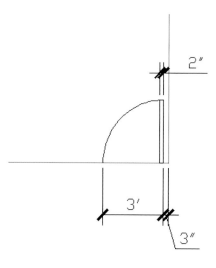

4   Save and close all files.

Challenge Exercise | Mechanical

In this exercise, you use what you have learned in Chapter 2 to create the initial geometry for a small mechanical assembly drawing.

Note: In the following images, the views are closer together than they will appear in your drawing.

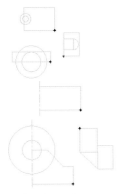

The completed exercise

Completing the Exercise
To complete the exercise, follow the steps in this book or in the onscreen exercise. In the onscreen list of chapters and exercises, click *Chapter 2: Creating Basic Drawings*. Click *Challenge Exercise: Mechanical*.

1 Open *M_MECH-Challenge-CHP02.dwg*.

2 Locate the point in the drawing labeled Start Point 1. Use the basic drawing commands to sketch the following views. You do not need to place dimensions or create centerlines.
Note: Some circles are dimensioned with diameter values, others with radius values. Also, each drawing view contains a point you should use as the start point.

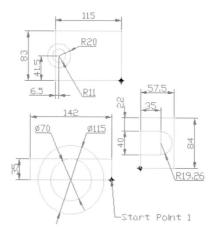

3 Locate the point on the drawing labeled Start Point 2. Use the basic drawing commands to sketch the following views. You do not need to place dimensions or create centerlines.

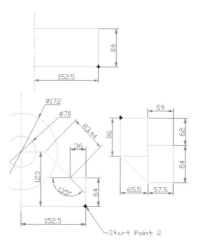

4 Erase the Start Point 1 and Start Point 2 text and leaders.

5 Save and close all files.

Chapter Summary

The concepts and techniques covered in this lesson serve as the building blocks for every drawings that you create. The sooner you master these concepts, the sooner you will be able to move on to more advanced geometry creation and editing.

Having completed this chapter, you can:

- Identify the default coordinate system and use dynamic input, direct distance, and shortcut menus.
- Use the Line, Circle, Arc, Erase, Rectangle, and Polygon commands to create and erase geometry in the drawing.
- Use object snaps to accurately place and create objects in the drawing.
- Activate and use the Polar Tracking and PolarSnap modes to more accurately create geometry at different angles in the drawing.
- Enable and use object snap tracking to position geometry in the drawing.
- Use the Unit command to set up the drawing environment.

Chapter 03

Manipulating Objects

Editing objects is a common part of all design tasks. Whether you make modifications as a result of a design change or in the process of creating more complex objects, editing is something you will be required to do frequently as you draw.

Objectives

After completing this chapter, you will be able to:

- Use different selection methods to select objects in the drawing.

- Move objects in the drawing using object snaps, object tracking, and coordinate entry for precise placement.

- Use the Copy command or grips to create new objects from existing objects in the drawing.

- Change the angle of objects in the drawing by using the Rotate command or with grips.

- Create mirrored images of objects in the drawing using the Mirror command or with grips.

- Use the Array command to create rectangular and circular patterns of objects in the drawing.

- Change the size of objects in the drawing.

- Use grips to edit objects and display geometric information.

Standard Object Snap and Status Bar Settings
Before completing the exercises in this chapter, refer to the "Settings for the Exercises" section in the Introduction.

Lesson 10 | Selecting Objects in the Drawing

This lesson describes how to select objects using several different options and methods.

You need to select objects in your drawing in order to modify and manipulate those objects. As your drawing grows in complexity and contains more objects, you need to use different selection methods to select these objects efficiently.

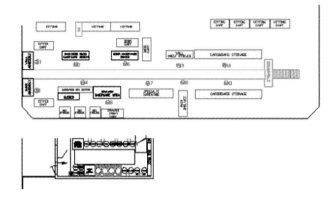

Objectives

After completing this lesson, you will be able to:

- Use implied, manual window, and crossing selection methods to select objects.
- Select objects for grip editing and identify the type of editing that can be done using grips.
- Use several different selection methods to select objects.

Using a Window to Select Objects

An object or group of objects that you select is also called a selection set. There are a variety of methods for selecting, adding, and removing objects within this selection set.

Selection sets are useful when you want to modify a number of objects. You can create a selection set either before or after activating the pertinent command.

If you want to select an individual object, you simply click it. You can continue to select additional objects as needed. As each new object is added to the selection set, the object's appearance changes to dashed lines.

In response to the Select Objects prompt, there are many methods you can use to select several objects at the same time.

Implied Window Selection

An implied window is a method of selecting objects by creating a selection window around those objects. To select objects using an implied window, click in a blank area of the drawing then drag the cursor from left to right and click the opposite corner of the selection window. Objects enclosed completely within the implied window will be selected.

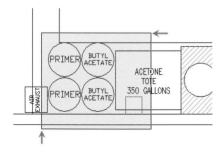

- Only objects that are entirely within the rectangular window are selected.
- If any part of an object is outside the window, that object is not selected.
- Although the drag movement must be from left to right, it can also be up and across, or down and across the drawing area. The drag movement shown here is up and across.
- The window selection area has a solid outline and a differently colored shading to distinguish it from that used in a crossing selection.
- The shaded area indicates the points in space used to define the corners of the rectangular Window.

Manual Window Selection

You can define a selection window by using the Window selection method. In response to any Select Objects prompt, enter **W** and press ENTER. This enables you to create a regular selection window in which you are not restricted as to the direction of the cursor movement when defining the points. When you specify the Window option, you can define the window from left-to-right or right-to-left, and it always results in a regular selection window. Only objects that are completely within the selection window will be included in the selection set.

Implied Crossing Selection

Implied crossing means that you have not manually specified a specific selection method. To make a crossing selection, you specify opposite corners that define a rectangular area. The first corner point must be in your drawing area, but cannot be touching any existing objects. After specifying the first corner point, you drag the cursor from right to left to create a crossing selection that is in the opposite direction of the previous Window selection.

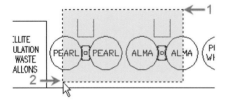

- All objects that are within or touched by the rectangular crossing window are included in the selection set.
- Although the drag movement must be from right to left, it can be up and across or down and across the drawing area.
- The crossing window has a dashed outline and a differently colored shading to distinguish it from that used in a window selection.
- The shaded area indicates the points in space that were used to define the corners of the rectangular window.

Manual Crossing Selection

You can define a non-implied Crossing Window by using the Crossing Window selection method. In response to any Select Objects prompt, enter **C** and press ENTER. This enables you to create a Crossing selection window where the direction of the cursor movement is not restricted when you define the points. When you specify Crossing Window, you can define the window from left to right or right to left, and it always results in a Crossing selection window.

Guidelines

- Implied windowing enables you to automatically create a selection window by clicking two points in a blank part of the drawing area to define the selection window.
- You can create an implied window when the command line is blank (no command is active), or in response to a Select objects prompt.
- Noun-Verb selection is on by default in the software options. This enables you to select objects before starting a command to modify those objects.

Object Selection with Grips

Grips are selectable points on geometry that you use to initiate editing of the selected object. Grips appear when you select an object and no command is currently active.

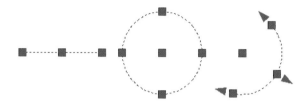

Grips Defined

Grips on selected objects are displayed as colored boxes. If you click a grip, it changes color and becomes a selected, or *hot* grip. If you place your mouse over an unselected grip, the color also changes and it becomes a *hover* grip.

With a hot grip, you can perform editing tasks on the object such as move, mirror, rotate, scale, and stretch. A hover grip can display specific dimension information.

The following illustration shows a common object with grips displayed.

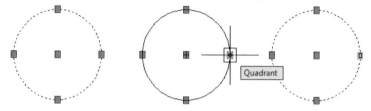

① Unselected grip. This grip is blue by default. Selected grip.

② This grip is red by default.

③ Hover grip. This grip is pink by default.

Using Hover Grips

Place your mouse over a grip without selecting it and the grip becomes a hover grip. These grips are used with Dynamic Input to provide real-time dimensional information such as the current length, angle, and diameter of objects in the drawing. The following illustration on the left demonstrates a hover grip on a rectangle. On the right, a hover grip is shown on a circle object.

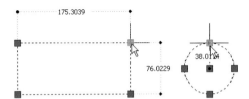

Using Selected Grips

With Dynamic Input turned on, you can select a grip to display fields where you can input new values such as length and radius. On the left, the illustration shows a selected grip where you can change the length of the top line of the rectangle. On the right, the illustration shows the result of changing that value.

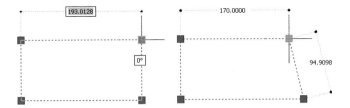

Display Grip Editing Options

Right-click a selected grip to display a menu of grip editing options. The default grip editing option is Stretch. With grip editing, you can perform all of the operations on the menu without having to start a command.

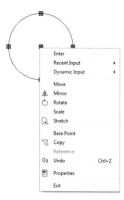

	Enter	
	Recent Input	▶
	Dynamic Input	▶
	Move	
⚠	Mirror	
↺	Rotate	
	Scale	
⌐	Stretch	
	Base Point	
⊶	Copy	
	Reference	
↶	Undo	Ctrl+Z
▦	Properties	
	Exit	

Removing Selection from Grips

To remove a hot grip, press ESC. Press ESC again to remove selection from all grips in the current selection set. To remove a single object from a selection set, press SHIFT + click the object.

Guidelines for Grip Editing

- Grips appear on selected objects only when the command line is blank.
- You can select objects first, so that they are highlighted with grips, then you can choose one of the modify commands for that selection.
- When used in conjunction with Dynamic Input, you can use grips to resize geometry by entering new values for length, angle, radius, and coordinates in the Dynamic Input fields.
- You can combine the grip copy option with your grip editing tasks. Right-click anywhere in the drawing and select Copy. The original object remains unchanged. Multiple copies can be made using the grip editing command options.
- When using the grip copy option, you can make multiple copies at regular intervals based on your first copy by holding down SHIFT when placing your next copy.
- You can perform clipboard edit options of the object selected by right-clicking and choosing: Cut, Copy, Copy with base point or Paste.
- You can change the base point of the object being edited with grips. Right-click anywhere in the drawing and click Base Point to define a new base point for the objects selected.
- You can use the Reference option when rotating or scaling objects during a grip edit. Right-click anywhere in the drawing and click Reference.

Select Objects Options

You can use several keyboard options to select objects on the Select Objects command prompt. These options include Window Polygon, Crossing Polygon, Fence, All, Last, and Previous. Enter the capitalized letter for the option and press ENTER.

The select object options are not so apparent. It is best to memorize those that are most useful. However, if you should enter an incorrect letter at the select object prompt, such as the letter *y* (which is not an option), AutoCAD® will display the entire list of options as shown in the example below.

Selecting with a Window Polygon

To select objects within a non-rectangular window, use the following procedure:

- At the Select Objects prompt, enter **wp** (for Window Polygon).
- Specify points that define an area that entirely encloses the objects that you want in the selection set.
- Press ENTER to close the polygon selection area and complete the selection.

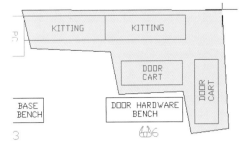

Chapter 3 | Manipulating Objects

Practice Exercise | Windows Polygon Selection

Draw the outer shape shown below and fill it with a random arrangement of rectangles. Then practice using the Windows Polygon selection option to erase the rectangles.

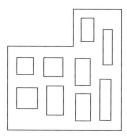

1   Turn Polar Tracking on. Draw the outer shape any size, resembling more or less the shape shown in the illustration:

   • Begin the Line command.
   • Start at the lower left corner (1) and follow the points to draw each line as shown below.
   • If you were able to do this continuously, when you get to point (6), you may enter **C** to close the line segments. Otherwise, you will have to select the Endpoint.

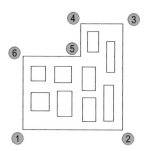

2   To draw the rectangles inside the shape:

   • First check that Object Snap is turned off.
   • Begin the Rectangle command.
   • Pick the first corner, then the opposite corner.
   • Continue until you have filled your object with rectangles.

3   To erase the rectangles using the Windows Polygon selection option:

   • Be sure that Object Snap is turned off.
   • Begin the Erase command.
   • At the Select objects prompt, enter **WP** and press ENTER.
   • Begin the Window Polygon at point (1) and continue until you get back to point (1).

- Press ENTER to complete the Window Polygon and press ENTER again to erase the objects.
  Notice that making the Windows Polygon was like stretching a rubber band around the objects.

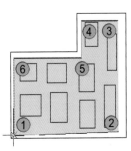

4   Undo. You may Save this drawing in order to practice erasing the objects using the Crossing Polygon option in the next section.

Selecting with a Crossing Polygon

To select objects enclosed or crossed by an irregularly shaped crossing polygon area, use the following procedure:

- At the Select Objects prompt, enter **CP** (for Crossing Polygon).
- Specify points that define an area that encloses or crosses the objects that you want to select.
- Press ENTER to close the polygon selection area and complete the selection.
  Occasionally you will find that it is not possible to completely enclose the objects you want to select. In this situation, you can select objects using a selection fence.

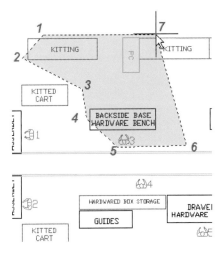

Chapter 3 | Manipulating Objects

Practice Exercise | Crossing Polygon Selection

If you saved the last exercise, you may proceed to step 3. Otherwise, draw the outer shape shown below and fill it with a random arrangement of rectangles. Then practice using the Crossing Polygon selection option to erase the rectangles.

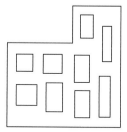

1   Turn Polar Tracking on. Draw the outer shape any size, resembling more or less the shape shown in the illustration:

   • Begin the Line command.
   • Start at the lower left corner (1) and follow the points to draw each line as shown below.
   • If you were able to do this continuously, when you get to point (6), you can enter **C** to close the line segments. Otherwise, you will have to select the Endpoint.

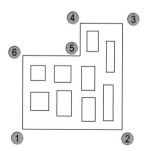

2   To draw the rectangles inside the shape:

   • First check that Object Snap is turned off.
   • Begin the Rectangle command.
   • Pick the first corner, then the opposite corner.
   • Continue until you have filled your object with rectangles.

3   To erase the rectangles using the Crossing Polygon selection option:

- Be sure that Object Snap is turned off.
- Begin the Erase command.
- At the Select objects prompt, enter **CP** and press ENTER.

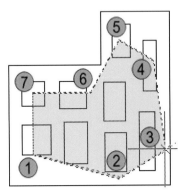

- Begin the Crossing Polygon at point (1) and continue until you get to back to point (1).
- Press ENTER to complete the Crossing Polygon and press ENTER again to erase the objects.
  Note that it was possible to select the complete rectangles because they are *polylines* (connected lines).

4   Undo. You may Save this drawing to in order to practice the Crossing Polygon window in the next section.

Selecting with a Fence

A selection Fence enables you to make a series of line segments across the objects you wish to select. To select objects using the Fence option:

- At the Select Objects prompt, enter **F** (for Fence selection).
- Specify points that define a series of line segments that cross the objects you wish to select.
- Press ENTER to complete the selection fence.

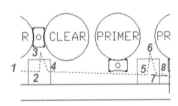

Practice Exercise | Fence Selection

Practice using the Fence selection option. First draw the lines and circles as shown below. Then erase the lines.

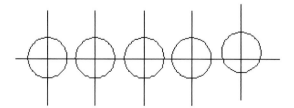

1   Draw the lines and circles (any size):

• Begin the Line command and draw the line segments as shown.
• Next draw the circles near the intersection of the lines.

2   Erase the lines using the Fence selection option:

• Begin the Erase command.
• At the Select objects prompt, enter **F** and press ENTER.
• Click the first fence point at (1)
• Click the second fence point at (2)
• Click the third fence point at (3) and press ENTER.
• Press ENTER to complete the Erase command.

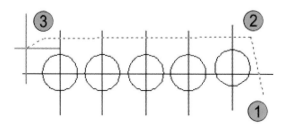

Selecting with the All Option

You can select all of the available objects in a drawing by entering **ALL** at the Select Objects prompt. Be careful using this option as it also affects objects on layers that are turned off, thawed, or unlocked. To use the All option:

- At the Select Objects prompt, enter **ALL**. Press ENTER.
- All displayed objects and all objects that are on layers that are turned off are selected.
- Press ENTER to complete the selection.

Tip
You can use the CTRL+A method to select all objects in the drawing, but you must select the objects first, prior to starting a command. Pressing CTRL+A in response to a Select Objects prompt selects all objects in the drawing, but also cancels the current command.

Selecting with the Last Option

To select the most recently created visible object, enter **L** (Last) at the Select Objects prompt. To use the Last option:

- At the Select Objects prompt, enter **L**. Press ENTER.
- The most recently created object is selected.
- Press ENTER to complete the selection.

Selecting with the Previous Option

Selection sets are stored in memory. You can recall the most recent selection set by entering **P** (Previous) at the Select Objects prompt. To use the Previous option:

- At the Select Objects prompt, enter **P**. Press ENTER.
- All objects in the previous selection set are selected again.
- Press ENTER to complete the selection.

Tip
You can remove objects from the current selection set by holding down SHIFT and selecting the objects again. To remove multiple objects at the same time, you can use both the Implied Window and Implied Crossing methods while holding down SHIFT.

Practice Exercise | Other Selection Options

In this practice exercise, you use selection options that include Last, Previous, All, and Remove. First, you begin by drawing several lines and circles as shown.

1   Draw some lines and circles.

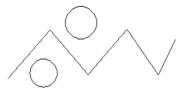

2   Practice using the Last selection option:

- Begin the Erase command.
- At the Select object prompt, enter **L** and press ENTER.
- Notice that the last object drawn is highlighted.
- Press ENTER to execute the command.

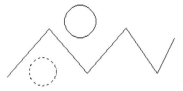

   Note that your last object drawn may be different than the one shown above.

3   Copy one or several objects in your drawing, placing them randomly as shown below.

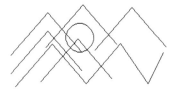

4   Repeat the copy command and try the Previous select object option:

- Begin the Copy command.
- At the Select object prompt, enter **P** and press ENTER.
- Notice the previous selection you made is selected again.
- Press ESC to escape the Copy command.

5 Practice selecting all objects, then remove an object from the selection set:
   - Begin the Erase command.
   - At the Select object prompt, enter **ALL** and press ENTER (only once).
   - Notice all the objects are highlighted.
   - Hold down the SHIFT key and select a single item from the selection set.
   - Notice that it is no longer highlighted.
   - Press ENTER to complete the Erase command.

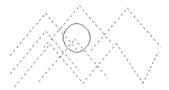

*Note that you can enter **R** and press ENTER to remove the objects from the selection set. Enter **A** to add objects into the selection set.*

Exercise | Select Objects

In this exercise, you use selection methods to erase objects in the drawing. You will be able to use these same methods to create selection sets in other drawings.

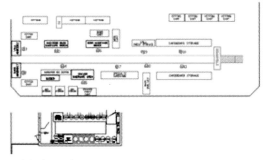

The completed exercise

Completing the Exercise

To complete the exercise, follow the steps in this book or in the onscreen exercise. In the onscreen list of chapters and exercises, click *Chapter 3: Manipulating Objects*. Click *Exercise: Select Objects*.

1 Open *M_Selecting-Objects.dwg*.

2 Zoom into the area shown in the following image.

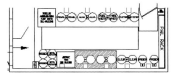

3   Erase using the Implied Window selection option, then remove selected objects from the selection set:

- Begin the Erase command.
- Click near point (1), then near point (2), as indicated in the following image.

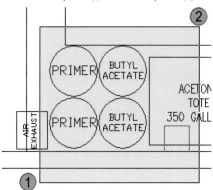

    The selected geometry is highlighted. Only the objects that were completely enclosed by the window should be included in the selection set.

4   To remove objects from the selection set:

- Press SHIFT+select to select the three lines indicated in the following image. This removes them from the selection set.
- Press ENTER to complete the erase command.

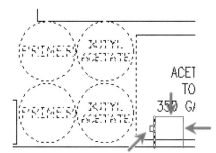

5   To erase using an implied crossing window:

- Start the Erase command.
- Click near point (1), then near point (2) as indicated in the following image. Notice that you are now clicking from right to left. All of the objects that the selection window crosses are highlighted.
- Press ENTER to complete the Erase command.

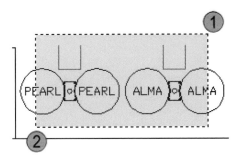

6   In another part of the drawing (zoom in if necessary), erase selected objects using the Crossing Polygon selection option:

- Begin the Erase command.
- At the Select objects prompt, enter **CP**. Press ENTER.
- Click the points for the crossing polygon following the illustration below.
- Begin with (1) and follow the points consecutively until you get to (6) and press ENTER.
- All of the objects that the polygon window has crossed are highlighted.
- Press ENTER to complete the Erase command.

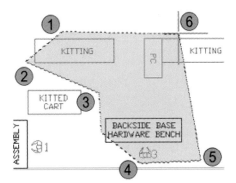

7   This time erase using the Window Polygon selection option:

- Start the Erase command.
- At the Select objects prompt, enter **WP**. Press ENTER.
- Click the points for the window polygon following the illustration below.
- Begin with (1) and follow the points consecutively until you get to (8). Press ENTER.
- Only the objects that are completely within the polygon window are highlighted.
- Press ENTER to complete the Erase command.

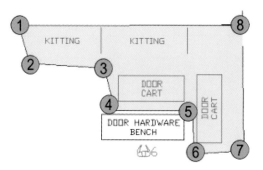

8   Now practice selecting objects with the Fence selection option. Zoom if necessary to the part of the drawing shown below:

- Begin the Erase command
- At the Select objects prompt, enter **F**. Press ENTER.
- Click in the drawing as indicated in the illustration below, beginning with (1).
- When you reach point (7), press ENTER to complete the selection set.
- Press ENTER to execute the Erase command.

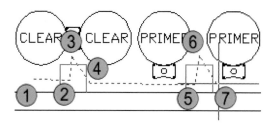

9 Use the Last selection option to erase the last object made in this drawing:

- Zoom to the part of the drawing illustrated below.
- Begin the Erase command.
- At the Select object prompt, enter **L**. Press ENTER.
- Notice that the arrow to the left is highlighted. This was the last object created when this drawing was completed.
- Press ENTER to finish the erase command.

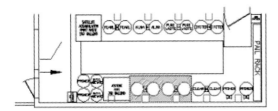

10 View the entire drawing and erase all:

- At the command line, enter **Z** and press ENTER.
- Enter **E** and press ENTER. You should now be viewing the extents of the drawing.
- Start the Erase command.
- At the Select objects prompt, enter **ALL**. Press ENTER.
- Everything visible in the drawing will be highlighted.
- Press ENTER to start the command.
- At the command line, enter **U** . Press ENTER to undo.

11 Close all files. Do not save.

Lesson 11 | Changing an Object's Position

This lesson describes how to use the Move command to reposition objects in the drawing and how to move an object using grips.

Moving objects is a common procedure for changing the position of objects in your drawing. The Move command enables you to move objects to different locations in the drawing using a variety of placement techniques.

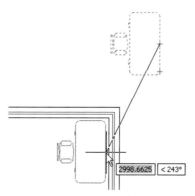

Objectives

After completing this lesson, you will be able to:

- Use grips or the Move command to move objects using object snaps, coordinate entry, and object snap tracking.

Moving Objects

The Move command enables you to reposition an object in the drawing by selecting a base point, where the object is moving from, followed by a point to define where the object is moving to. You can select the two points or use the Displacement option of the command. If you use the Displacement option, the coordinate values you enter specify a relative distance and direction from the base point you selected. Another option is to use grips to reposition an object. You select a grip and then activate the Move command and select a position to move the selected grip and the object to.

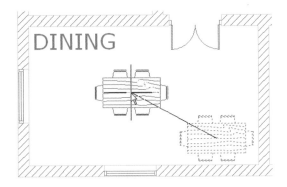

Command Access

 Move

Command Line: **MOVE, M**
Ribbon: **Home tab › Modify Panel › Move**

Menu Bar: **Modify › Move**
Shortcut Menu: **Select objects then right-click anywhere in the drawing window and click move**

Procedure: Moving Objects with the Move Command

The following steps provide an overview for moving objects in the drawing with the Move command.

1   On the ribbon, click Home tab > Modify panel > Move.

2   Select the objects to move and press ENTER to end the object selection.

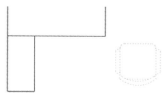

3   Specify a base point (where the objects are moving from).

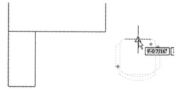

4   Specify a second point (where the objects are moving to).

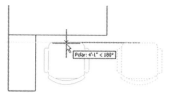

The object is moved to the new point.

Procedure: Moving Objects Using Grips

The following steps provide an overview of using grips to move objects.

1   Select an object to activate its grips.

2   Click a grip to activate grip edit mode. By default, this point will also be used as the base point for the move.

3   Right-click anywhere in the drawing. Click Move.

4   Click to position the object in a new location.

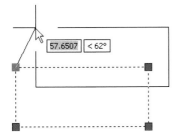

Guidelines

Follow these guidelines when using the Move command:

- When you specify the base point for the move, it should be on or near the object being moved unless you are using other objects to define a reference vector for the move.
- By default, the option for Noun-Verb selection is turned on in the software; this enables you to select the objects to move prior to starting the Move command.

Practice Exercise | Move Objects

In this practice exercise, you draw two rectangles (of any size) then move one of them so that it is one unit to the right of the other rectangle offset from its midpoint. You use two different techniques to move this object.

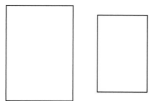

1   Begin a new, blank drawing using the acad.dwt template.

2   To set up the drawing drafting settings:
    • Polar tracking and object snap should be on.
    • Object snap Midpoint mode should be selected.

3   Draw two rectangles any size in the drawing window.

4   To move the rectangle:
    • On the Home tab, click Modify Panel > Move.
    • Select the rectangle on the right and press ENTER.
    • At the prompt to specify the base point, click the midpoint as indicated below.

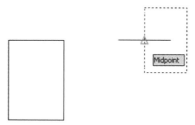

5   Move the rectangle to the midpoint of the other rectangle as indicated in the following illustration:

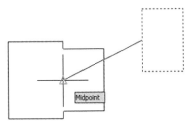

6   Now, move the rectangle again using grips:

- With the command line blank, select the rectangle.
- Select a grip on the rectangle and right-click.
- On the shortcut menu, click Copy.

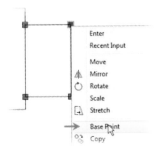

- Select the midpoint on the rectangle as indicated below:

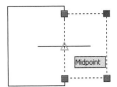

- Select a grip on the rectangle again.
- Right-click and click Move.

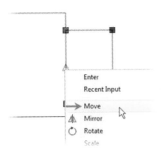

- Drag the rectangle to the right until the polar direction is o degrees.
- Enter **1** and press ENTER.

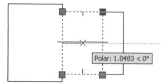

Exercise | Move Objects

In this exercise, you use the Move command to move objects in the drawing. When you've finished, you will be able to move objects in other drawings using object snaps, object tracking, and coordinate entry.

> **Note**
> You have the option of completing this exercise using either imperial or metric units. Select one version of the exercise to complete the steps.

The completed exercise

> **Completing the Exercise**
> To complete the exercise, follow the steps in this book or in the onscreen exercise. In the onscreen list of chapters and exercises, click *Chapter 3: Manipulating Objects*. Click *Exercise: Move Objects Metric*.

Exercise: Move Objects (Metric Units)

In this exercise, you move the furnishings into the designated rooms using the Move command and grips. Polar Tracking, Object Snap, and Object Snap Tracking modes must be on.

1   Open *M_Moving-Objects.dwg*.

2   Zoom into the lower left corner of the drawing, as shown in the following image.

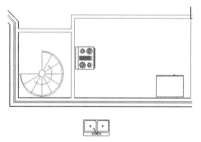

3   Select the sink to move it into the kitchen:

  - With the command line blank, select the sink.
  - Notice that it is a single object with a grip located at the midpoint. You will learn more about these kinds of symbols, or blocks, later in this course.
  - Select the grip on the sink and drag it to the midpoint of the line that represents the wall in the kitchen.
  - Click to relocate the sink to this new position.

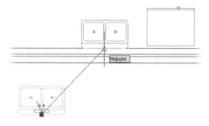

4   Zoom out, then zoom to view the area of the drawing shown in the following image.

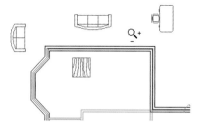

5   To position the love seat as illustrated below:

  - With the command line blank, select the love seat.
  - Select the single grip on it and drag the object towards the wall as indicated. Hover over the midpoint of the wall to acquire a tracking point, then drag the cursor along the alignment path and click to position the object as shown.

Note: An exact distance from the wall is not critical.

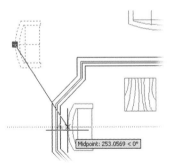

6   Use the Move command to relocate the couch to the interior of the room as indicated:

- Activate the Move command.
- Select the couch object. Press ENTER.
- Select the base point using the midpoint object snap.
- Select the midpoint of the wall to position the couch.

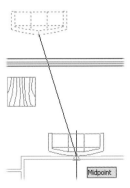

7   Repeat the Move command and select the desk and chair:

- Repeat the Move command.
- Click to create a selection window around the desk and chair as indicated below.
- Press ENTER to end the selection set.

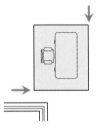

8   To position the desk and chair:
- Select the midpoint of the desk as indicated.
- Hold down SHIFT+D while positioning the cursor. This temporarily turns off all object snaps to prevent the desk from snapping to the wall.
- Drag the cursor to position the desk and chair as shown.

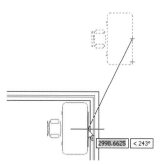

9   Adjust your view to include this area of the drawing.

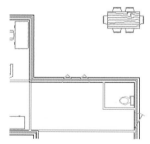

10   Move the dinette set to the interior of the room as shown:
- With the command line blank, select the dinette set.
- Select the grip at the center.
- Drag the dinette set towards the room.
- Hover over the midpoint of the first wall, then the midpoint of the adjacent wall as indicated.
- Drag the dinette set to the middle of the room. Click when you see the tracking lines of the midpoints intersect.

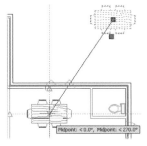

11   To relocate the water closet towards the other wall:
   • With the command line blank, select the water closet.
   • Select the grip and drag it upwards.
   • Enter **650** and press ENTER.

12   Zoom to display your entire drawing.

13   Close all files. Do not save.

Exercise: Move Objects (Imperial Units)

You move the furnishings into the designated rooms using the Move command and grips. Polar Tracking, Object Snap, and Object Snap Tracking modes must be on.

1   Open *I_Moving-Objects.dwg*.

2   Zoom into the lower left corner of the drawing, as shown in the following image.

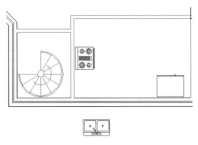

3   Select the sink to move it into the kitchen:
   • With the command line blank, select the sink.
   • Notice that it is a single object with a grip located at the midpoint. You will learn more about these kinds of symbols, or blocks, later in this course.

- Select the grip on the sink and drag it to the midpoint of the line representing the wall in the kitchen.
- Click to relocate the sink to the new position, as shown.

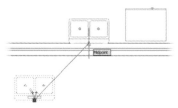

4 Zoom out, then zoom to view the area of the drawing shown in the following image.

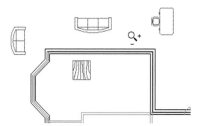

5 To position the love seat as illustrated below:
- With the command line blank, select the love seat.
- Select the single grip on it and drag the object towards the wall as indicated. Hover over the midpoint of the wall to acquire a tracking point, then drag the cursor along the alignment path and click to position the object as shown.
  Note: An exact distance from the wall is not critical.

6 Use the Move command to relocate the couch to the interior of the room as indicated:
- Activate the Move command.
- Select the couch object. Press ENTER.
- Select the base point using the midpoint object snap.
- Select the midpoint of the wall to position the couch.

Chapter 3 | Manipulating Objects

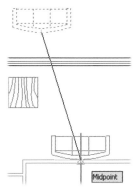

7   Repeat the Move command and select the desk and chair:

   • Repeat the Move command.
   • Click to create a selection window around the desk and chair as indicated below.
   • Press ENTER to end the selection set.

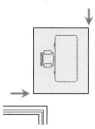

8   To position the desk and chair:

   • Select the midpoint of the desk as indicated.
   • Hold down SHIFT+D while positioning the cursor. This temporarily turns off all object snaps to prevent the desk from snapping to the wall.
   • Drag the cursor to position the desk and chair as shown.

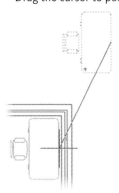

9   Adjust your view to include this area of the drawing.

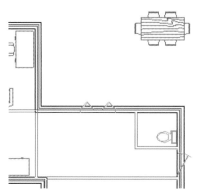

10   Move the dinette set to the interior of the room as shown:

- With the command line blank, select the dinette set.
- Select the grip at the center.
- Drag the dinette set towards the room.
- Hover over the midpoint of the first wall, then the midpoint of the adjacent wall as indicated.
- Drag the dinette set to the middle of the room. Click when you see the tracking lines of the midpoints intersect.

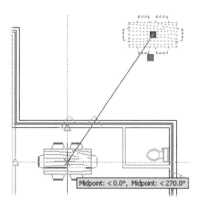

11   To relocate the water closet towards the other wall:

- With the command line blank, select the water closet.
- Select the grip and drag it up. Enter **2'3** and press ENTER.

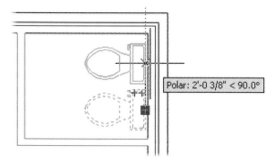

Polar: 2'-0 3/8" < 90.0°

12   Zoom to display your entire drawing.

13   Close all files. Do not save.

Lesson 12 | Creating New Objects from Existing Objects

This lesson describes how to duplicate geometry in the drawing by using the Copy command.

Since the inception of computer aided design, one of the biggest benefits has been the ability to easily copy geometry and use it in other places on the drawing instead of having to manually redraw the geometry when you need it.

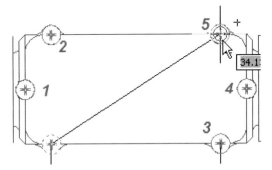

Objectives

After completing this lesson, you will be able to:

- Use grips or the Copy command to copy objects in the drawing.

Copying Objects

In conventional drafting, one of the most time-consuming tasks is to duplicate an object. You use the Copy command to quickly create duplicates of objects at a specified distance from the original.

After starting the Copy command and selecting the object(s) to copy, you then specify the base point (where the object is being copied from) followed by the second point or displacement (where the object is being copied to). To create multiple copies, simply continue specifying second points or displacement values.

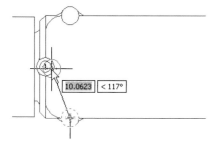

Command Access

Copy

Ribbon: **Draw tab > Modify Panel > Copy**
Command Line: **COPY, CO**
Menu Bar: **Modify > Copy**
Shortcut Menu: **Select objects then right-click anywhere in the drawing window and select Copy.**

Copy Command vs. Clipboard Copy

Do not confuse the Copy command with other similar copy commands found on the shortcut menu. If you select an object and right-click anywhere in the drawing, the Copy and Copy with Base Point options appear on the shortcut menu. These options copy geometry to the clipboard, as in other standard Windows applications, making the geometry available to Paste in other drawings.

Procedure: Copying Objects with the Copy Command

The following steps describe an overview for copying objects in the drawing.

1   On the ribbon, click Home tab > Modify panel > Copy.

2   Select the object(s) to copy and press ENTER.

3   Specify a base point for the copy.

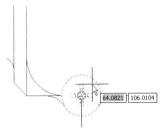

4   Specify a second point or displacement.

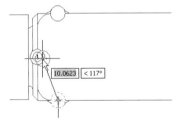

5   Continue to specify second points to create additional copies.

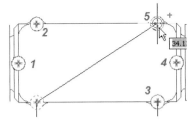

Procedure: Copying Objects Using Grips

The following steps give an overview of using grips to copy objects.

1   Select an object to activate its grips.

2   Click a grip to activate grip edit mode. By default, this point will also be used as the base point for the move.

3   Right-click anywhere in the drawing. Click Move.

4   Right-click anywhere in the drawing. Click Copy.

5   Click to position the copied object in a new location.

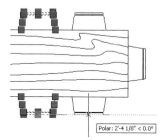

Guidelines

Follow these guidelines when using the Copy command:

- When you specify the base point for the copy, it should be on or near the object being copied unless you are using other objects to define a reference vector for the copy.
- By default, the option for Noun-Verb selection is turned on in the software; this enables you to select the objects to copy prior to starting the Copy command.

Practice Exercise | Copy Objects

In this practice exercise, you use the Copy command and the object grips. First, draw a circle and a line, as shown on the left in the following image.

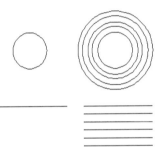

1   To set up the drawing:
   - Draw the circle (any size).
   - Draw the line near the circle (any length).

2   Copy the circle and line to the right:
   - On the Home tab, click Modify panel > Copy.
   - Select the circle and the line and press ENTER.
   - At the prompt, click a base point on or near those objects.
   - Drag the mouse to the right and click. Press ENTER to end the Copy command.

3   Copy the circle using grips:
   - Select the circle on the right.
   - Select one of the quadrant grips to activate it.
   - Right-click the grip, then click Copy.

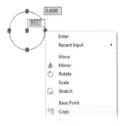

   - Drag the mouse to create a larger copy of the circle and click.
   - Continue to drag and click several times to create multiple copies of the circle.
   - Press ESC to end the grip copy procedure.
   - Press ESC to clear the circle selection.

4   Copy the line using grips:

- With the command line blank, click the line.
- Select a grip at one of the endpoints.
- Right-click the grip and click Move.
- Right-click again and click Copy.
- Continue to click in the drawing window to make multiple copies of the line.
- Press ESC to end the copy procedure.
- Press ESC to clear the line selection.

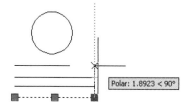

Note the following:

- When using copy with grips, select Copy *after* you have selected an option, such as Move, Mirror, Rotate, Scale, or Stretch.
- Stretch with grips is the default action.
- How the object behaves with grips often depends on which grip you select. For instance, if you had selected the midpoint grip of the line instead of the endpoint, it would have enabled you to move the line as you copied it.

Exercise | Copy Objects

In this exercise, you copy objects in the drawing using the Copy command. When you've finished, you will be able to use the Copy command to duplicate geometry in other drawings.

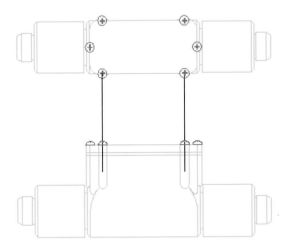

The completed exercise

Completing the Exercise
To complete the exercise, follow the steps in this book or in the onscreen exercise. In the onscreen list of chapters and exercises, click *Chapter 3: Manipulating Objects*. Click *Exercise: Copy Objects*.

1   Open *M_Copy-Objects.dwg*.

2   Zoom into the upper left view of the drawing.

    • On the status bar, right-click Object Snap. Ensure that the Center and Intersection
      options are selected.

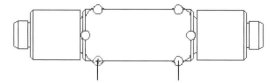

3   To make multiple copies of the red screw head:

    • On the Home tab, click Modify panel > Copy.
    • Select the screw object as shown. Press ENTER.
    • Touch the circle to display the center object snap marker. Click to select the center
      point of the circle as the base point.

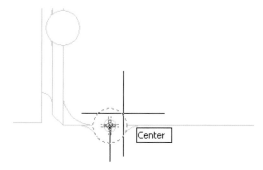

4   Select the center point of the circle as shown in the following image.

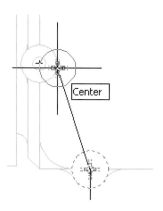

5   Continue selecting the center points of the remaining circles in the top view as shown in the following image. Press ENTER to end the Copy command.

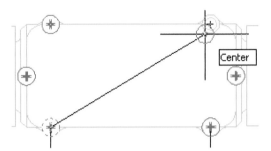

6   To create a copy of the side view of the screw:
    - Press ENTER to repeat the Copy command.
    - Select the edge view of the pan head screw as shown. Press ENTER.
    - Using the center object snap, select the center of the ellipse used to create the pan head screw as the base point.

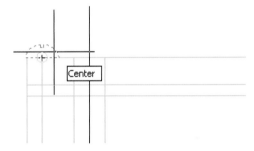

7   To create additional copies:
    - Using the Intersection object snap option, select the intersections as shown in the following image to position the copies.
    - Press ENTER to exit the Copy command.

Chapter 3 | Manipulating Objects

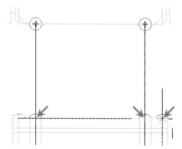

8   Pan or zoom the view to see a side view of the geometry.

9   Next, create a copy of the geometry in the side view for use as a section view:

   • On the command line, enter **co**. Press ENTER.
   • Click two points to define a window selection around the geometry. Press ENTER.

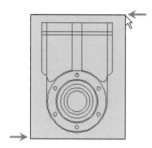

10   To place the copy of the geometry:

   • Select the center of one of the circles in the view as the base point.
   • Verify that Ortho or Polar Tracking mode is turned on.
   • Drag the cursor to the right and enter **50**. Press ENTER.
   • Press ENTER to exit the Copy command.

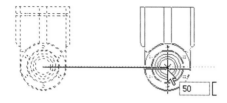

11   Close all files. Do not save.

Lesson 13 | Changing the Angle of an Object's Position

This lesson describes how to use the Rotate command to rotate objects in a drawing. You learn how to use the Rotate command using the default options, and also learn how to use the Reference and Copy options while rotating objects. This lesson also describes how to rotate an object using grips.

After you have created or inserted objects in the drawing, at times you must change the angle of those objects. You can do this easily with the Rotate command, or by using grips to rotate the object.

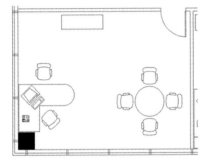

Objectives

After completing this lesson, you will be able to:

- Use grips or the Rotate command to rotate objects in the drawing.

Rotating Objects

You use the Rotate command to rotate objects in the drawing. Command options enable you to rotate the objects simply by entering an angle for the rotation or by defining a reference angle and then entering a new angle for the reference angle. If you need to make a copy of the object while rotating, you can specify the Copy option. When the Copy option is selected, a copy of the object is rotated, leaving the original object in its current position. You can also use grips to rotate the object.

In the following image, two chair objects are being rotated with the Copy option.

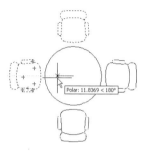

Command Access

Rotate

Command Line: **ROTATE, RO**
Ribbon: **Home tab > Modify Panel > Rotate**

Menu Bar: **Modify > Rotate**
Shortcut Menu: **Select objects then right-click anywhere in the drawing window. Click Rotate.**

Note
Options for the Rotate command are accessible from the shortcut menu. Right-click anywhere in the drawing area while the Rotate command is active. Command-specific options are always in the middle of the shortcut menu.

Procedure: Rotating Objects

The following steps provide an overview of rotating objects using the Rotate command.

1   On the ribbon, click Home tab > Modify Panel > Rotate.

2   Select the object(s) to rotate and press ENTER.

3   Specify a base point for the rotation. The object will rotate around this point.

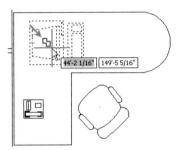

4   Specify a rotation angle by moving the cursor or entering an angle.

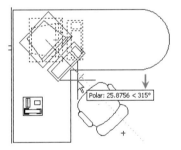

Procedure: Rotating Objects Using Grips

The following steps give an overview of using grips to rotate objects.

1   Select an object to activate its grips.

2   Click a grip to activate grip edit mode. By default, this point will also be used as the center point of rotation.

3   Right-click anywhere in the drawing. Click Rotate.

4   Specify a rotation angle.

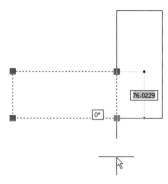

Guidelines

- Rotate the original object or use the Copy option to rotate a copy of the object.
- The base point for the rotation should be on or near the object being rotated. This is critical because the base point represents the point of rotation for the selected object.
- When appropriate, use polar tracking for accuracy and to speed up the process for defining the rotation angle.
- Use the Reference option to refer to the angle of the object that you want to change. You can enter the angle of that object, or specify that angle by selecting two points to determine the angle vector then entering the desired angle.

Practice Exercise | Rotate Objects

In this practice exercise, you draw a rectangle and rotate it using grips, the Rotate command, and the Reference option.

1   Draw a rectangle of any size.

2   To use the grips to rotate the object:
- With the command line blank, select the object.
- Select one of the grips.
- Right-click the active grip. Click Rotate.

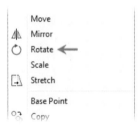

- Drag the mouse around the rotation point, which is the grip that you selected.

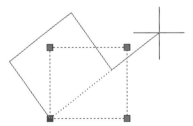

- Click in the drawing window to rotate the rectangle. This is a random rotation angle.
- Press ESC to deactivate the grip selection.

3   Rotate the object again using the Rotate command this time.
- On the Home tab, click Modify Panel > Rotate.

- At the Select object prompt, select the rectangle and press ENTER.
- At the prompt, specify the lower left corner as the base point.
- Enter a rotation angle of **10**. Press ENTER.
- Notice that the object is rotated 10 degrees counterclockwise.

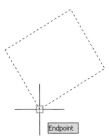

4   Rotate using the Reference option and orient the rectangle back to angle 0:
- On the Home tab, click Modify Panel > Rotate.
- Select the rectangle. Press ENTER.
- Specify the lower left corner as the base point.
- Right-click and click Reference.

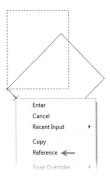

5   Specify the reference angle by selecting the following points on the angle of reference:
- Click the lower left corner endpoint (1).
- Click the endpoint at (2) for the second point (any point along that line will work).
- To specify the new angle, enter **0**, or press ENTER to accept the default ‹0›.

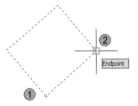

6   The rectangle is now straight.

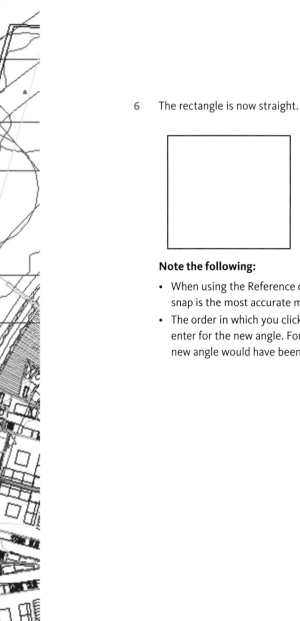

Note the following:

- When using the Reference option, clicking points on the line of reference using object snap is the most accurate method.
- The order in which you click the points on the line of reference determines what you enter for the new angle. For instance, if point (2) was selected before point (1), the new angle would have been 180.

Exercise | Rotate Objects

In this exercise, you use the Rotate command to rotate objects in the drawing. You use the default rotate method for specifying a rotation angle, as well as the Reference and Copy options of the Rotate command. When you have finished, you will be able to use the Rotate command to rotate objects in other drawings.

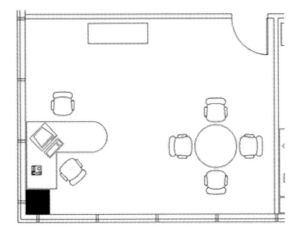

The completed exercise

Completing the Exercise
To complete the exercise, follow the steps in this book or in the onscreen exercise. In the onscreen list of chapters and exercises, click *Chapter 3: Manipulating Objects*. Click *Exercise: Rotate Objects*.

1   Open *C_Rotate-Objects.dwg*.

2   To rotate the computer:
  - Activate the Rotate command.
  - Select the computer object. Press ENTER.
  - Press SHIFT+right-click anywhere in the drawing. Click Insert.
  - Touch the computer block to display the Insert Object Snap marker, then select the point.
    Note: The Insert Object Snap override enables you to select the insertion point of the block.

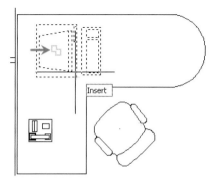

3   To position the computer to face the chair:
  - Verify that the polar setting is selected.
  - Drag clockwise until the PolarSnap display reads 315 degrees. The distance is not critical, just make sure that your cursor is not activating any object snaps.
  - Click to select the point.

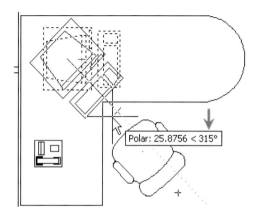

Chapter 3 | Manipulating Objects

4   To select the chair:

- On the Home tab, click Modify Panel > Rotate.
- Click the chair object above the desk. Press ENTER.
- Press SHIFT+right-click anywhere in the drawing. Click Insert.
- Click the chair object to display the Insert Object Snap marker, then click to select the point.

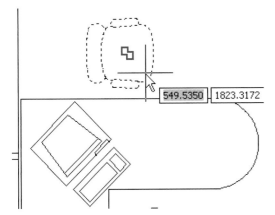

5   To rotate the chair to face the desk:

- Enter **-90.**
- Press ENTER to rotate the chair 90 degrees counterclockwise.
- The chair should be positioned facing the desk.

6   To select the chair and base point:

- Press ENTER to repeat the Rotate command.
- Select the chair object next to the small conference table. Press ENTER.
- Select the center of the conference table as the base point.

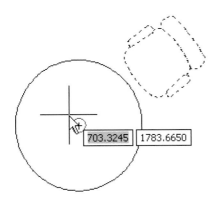

7   To rotate the chair around the round table using the Reference option:

•   Right-click anywhere in the drawing. Click Reference.
•   Define the reference angle by selecting the center of the conference table and the midpoint of the chair back rest.
•   Enter **90**. Press ENTER.
    The chair should be positioned 90 degrees up from the center of the conference table.

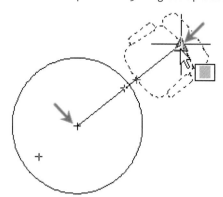

8   To make a copy of the chair while rotating it around the round table:

•   On the command line, enter **RO**. Press ENTER.
•   Select the chair object. Press ENTER.
•   Click the center of the conference table as the base point.
•   Right-click anywhere in the drawing. Click Copy.
•   Position the cursor so that the polar angle displays 90 degrees. Click to select that point.
    A copy of the chair is rotated.

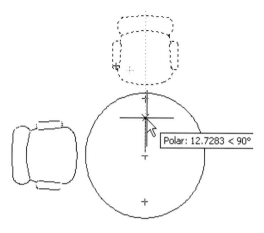

Chapter 3 | Manipulating Objects

9   To rotate both chairs with the Copy option so that four chairs are around your table:

   - Press ENTER to repeat the Rotate command.
   - Select both chair objects. Press ENTER.
   - Click the center of the conference table to specify the base point.
   - Right-click anywhere in the drawing window. Click Copy.
   - Position the cursor so that the polar angle displays 180 degrees. Click to select that point.

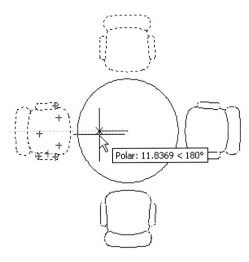

10   Close all files. Do not save.

Lesson 14 | Creating a Mirror Image of Existing Objects

This lesson describes how to create mirrored versions of existing objects in the drawing.

You can use symmetrical copies of objects and spaces to aid you in your designs. Whether they are simple consumer products or whole apartment buildings where adjacent apartments use symmetric floor plans, all make use of symmetry for a variety of reasons.

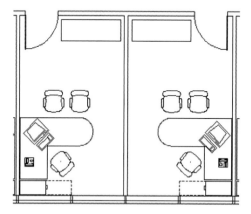

Objectives

After completing this lesson, you will be able to:

- Use grips or the Mirror command to mirror objects in the drawing.

Mirroring Objects

Using the Mirror command, you can create symmetric versions of geometry. When you activate the Mirror command, you are prompted to select the objects to mirror and to define a mirror line. The mirror line defines a vector across which all selected geometry is mirrored. After defining the mirror line, you can decide whether to erase or retain the source geometry. You can also control the Mirror command using grips.

Mirror works for all object types.

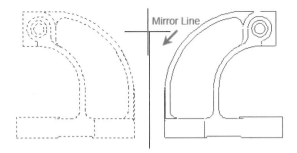

Command Access

Mirror

Command Line: **MIRROR, MI**
Ribbon: **Home tab > Modify Panel > Mirror**

Menu Bar: **Modify > Mirror**

Mirroring Text
You can use the MIRRTEXT system variable to reverse text in a mirror action. By default, the MIRRTEXT system variable is set to 0, which means the text is not reversed when mirrored. If you need the text to be reversed, set MIRRTEXT to 1.

Procedure: Mirroring Objects

The following is an overview of mirroring objects in the drawing with the MIRRTEXT system variable set to 0.

1   Activate the Mirror command.

2   Select the objects to be mirrored. Press ENTER.

3   Select two points to define the mirror line.

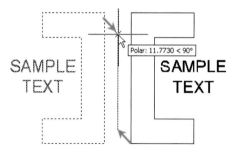

4   Enter **Y** to erase source objects or **N** to keep the source objects. Notice that the orientation of the text remains the same.

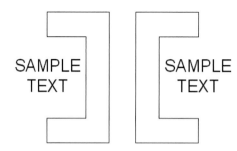

Procedure: Mirroring Text

The following is an overview of mirroring text in the drawing with the MIRRTEXT system variable set to 1.

1   Begin by setting the MIRRTEXT system variable to 1. This turns the mirroring of text on.

- At the command line, enter MIRRTEXT and press ENTER.
- Enter **1** and press ENTER.

2   Activate the Mirror command.

3   Select the objects to be mirrored. Press ENTER.

4   Select two points to define the mirror line.

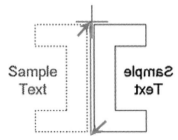

5   Enter **Y** to erase source objects or **N** to keep the source objects.

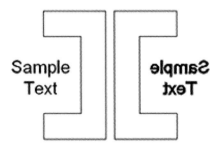

Procedure: Mirroring Objects Using Grips

The following steps give an overview of using grips to mirror objects.

1   Select an object to activate its grips.

2   Click a grip to activate grip edit mode. By default, this point will be used as the first point of the mirror line.

3   Right-click anywhere in the drawing. Click Mirror.

4   Move your cursor to define the mirror line. Click to select the point.

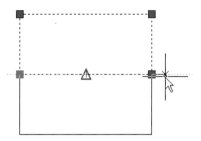

Guidelines for Mirroring Objects

- You can use the Mirror command on all geometry.
- By default, all new drawings have the MIRRTEXT system variable set to 0, so that text is not reversed in a mirror action.
- When MIRRTEXT is set to 0, the text does not mirror; however, the text alignment is mirrored, for example from left alignment to right.
- Drawings that were created in older versions may have the MIRRTEXT system variable set to 1. When you mirror a text object in one of these files, the text is reversed. To avoid reversal of the text, set the MIRRTEXT value to 0.

Practice Exercise | Mirror Objects

In this practice exercise, you mirror an object using the Mirror command and grips. First, you draw an object that you will mirror similar to the one shown.

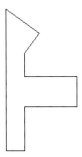

1   Using the Line command, draw an object similar to the one illustrated above. It is best to draw an object that is asymmetric to understand the mirror command.

2   To mirror the object you have just drawn:

- On the Home tab, click Modify panel > Mirror.
- Select the objects. Press ENTER. Click the first point of the mirror line. Click the second point of the mirror line. Note that with polar tracking on, you can mirror the object around a specific angle.

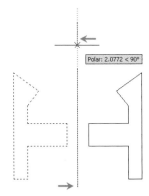

- Press ENTER to accept the default (No <N>), so that you do not erase the source object.

3   Zoom out and mirror the objects using Grips.

- With the command line blank, select the objects.
- Right-click one of the grips (1). Click Mirror (2).
- Right-click again. Click Copy (3).

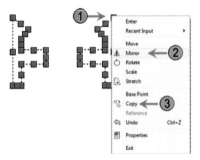

4   Next, change the base point of the objects to mirror:
     • Right-click the selected grip. Click Base point.

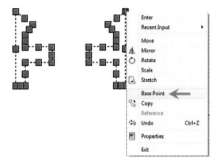

5   Click the first and second points of the mirror line as indicated below. Notice that in this
     example polar tracking is on.

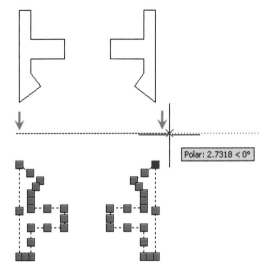

6   Press ENTER to complete the command and ESC to deselect the objects.

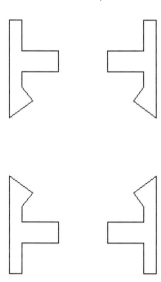

Exercise | Mirror Objects in the Drawing

In this exercise, you use the Mirror command to copy similar geometry from one side of a drawing to another. You also identify and correct a potential problem when mirroring text.

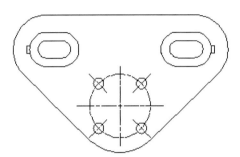

The completed exercise

Completing the Exercise

To complete the exercise, follow the steps in this book or in the onscreen exercise. In the onscreen list of chapters and exercises, click *Chapter 3: Manipulating Objects*. Click *Exercise: Mirror Objects in the Drawing*.

1 Open *M_Mirror-Object.dwg*.

2 To select the objects to mirror:

  • On the Home tab, click Modify panel › Mirror.
  • Enter **WP**. Press ENTER.
  • Create a window polygon around the objects as indicated below. Select points (1) through (4) in the blank area around the objects.
    Hint: To avoid object snaps, zoom in to select the points.

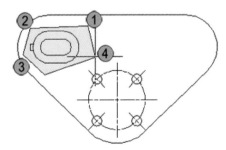

- When you have enclosed the object in the selection window, press ENTER.
- Press ENTER again to complete the object selection.

3   Select the endpoint of the circle centerline as the first point of the mirror line.

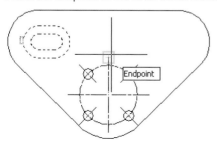

4   Drag the cursor upward. Click anywhere above the first point.

- Verify that polar tracking is on. Make sure that the cursor readout is 90 degrees.
- Right-click and click No to keep the source objects.

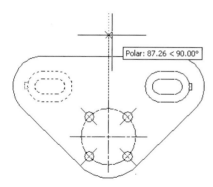

5   Close all files. Do not save.

Lesson 15 | Creating Object Patterns

This lesson describes what an array is and how you can use arrays to create duplicate objects, such as the circular array of chairs around the table in the following floor plan.

Most common patterns contain geometry that is duplicated in a rectangular or circular array. You can use the Array command to duplicate objects in a repeatable pattern.

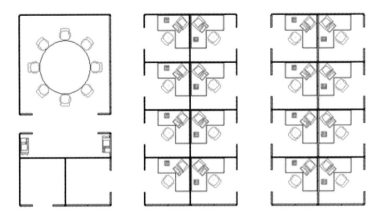

Objectives

After completing this lesson, you will be able to:

- Use the Array command to pattern objects in the drawing.

Creating an Array of Objects

Using the Array command, you can duplicate existing objects in a rectangle or circular (polar) pattern. You can select which type of array to use in the Array dialog box. Click the Rectangular or Polar options to see point, distance, and method requirements for each type.

The following illustration shows a rectangular and polar array.

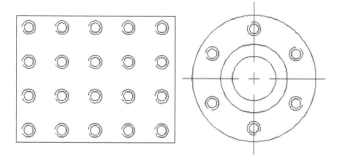

Command Access

Array

Command Line: **ARRAY, AR**
Ribbon: **Home tab > Modify Panel > Array**
Note: Do not confuse this command with the 3D Array command.

Menu Bar: **Modify > Array**

Array Dialog Box: Rectangular Array

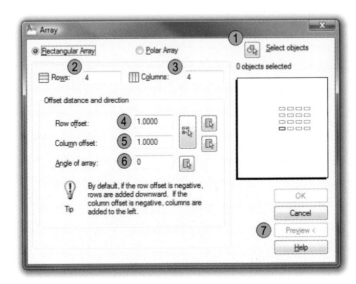

1. Click to select the object(s) to include in the array.

2. Enter the number of rows (horizontal patterns) for the array.

3. Enter the number of columns (vertical patterns) for the array.

4. Enter a distance to offset each row. Use the simulated preview window to see the direction of the pattern.

5. Enter a distance to offset each column.

6. Enter an angle for the pattern.

7. Click Preview to preview the array. Preview is not available until you select an object or objects for the array.

Array Dialog Box: Polar Array

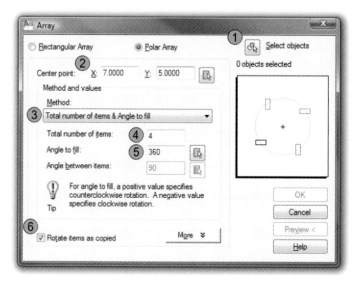

① Click to select the object(s) to include in the array.

② Enter the center point's coordinates in the X and Y fields or click the Select Point icon to select a center point in the drawing window.

③ Select the method for calculating the polar array.

- Total number of items and angle to fill.
- Total number of items and angle between items.
- Angle to fill and angle between items.

④ Enter the total number of items for the array. This includes the original object.

⑤ Enter the total angle for the array. A negative number creates the array in a clockwise direction.

⑥ Select to rotate each object as it is placed in the array.

> ### Zooming while using the Array command
> Although you cannot zoom or pan the drawing using traditional methods while the Array dialog box or Array Preview is active, you can select the Pick Object button, or any of the other pick point buttons to temporarily hide the dialog box, allowing you to zoom and pan. To return to the Array dialog box, press ENTER without selecting any objects or points.

Procedure: Creating a Rectangular Array of Objects

The following steps give an overview of creating rectangular arrays.

1 On the ribbon, click Home tab > Modify Panel > Array.

2 In the Array dialog box, click the Rectangular option. Click Select Objects and select the objects to include in the array.

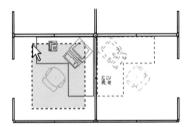

3 Enter row and column values, or click Pick Offset to define the row and column offset values.

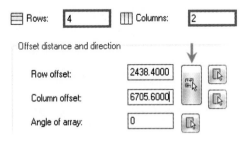

4 If required, enter an angle for the array.

5 Click Preview to preview the array.

6 Right-click to accept and create the array, or press ESC to return to the dialog box.

Procedure: Creating a Polar Array of Objects

The following steps are an overview of creating polar arrays.

1   On the ribbon, click Home tab > Modify Panel > Array.

2   In the Array dialog box, click the Polar option. Click Select Objects and select the objects to include in the array.

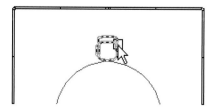

3   In the Center Point fields, enter the X and Y coordinates for the center point of the array, or click Pick Center Point to select the center point in the drawing.

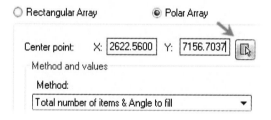

4   In the Method list, select the method to use for the array.

5   Enter values in the appropriate fields according to the method that you chose.

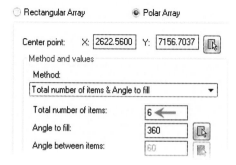

6   Click Preview to preview the array.

7   Right-click to accept and create the array, or press ESC to return to the dialog box.

Guidelines for Rectangular Versus Polar Array

Follow these guidelines when using the Array command:

- To create many regularly spaced objects, the Array command is faster than Copy command.
- For rectangular array, specify the number of rows and columns and the distance between each.

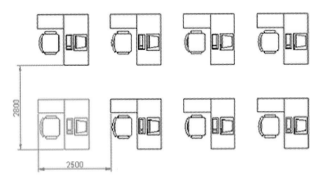

- For Polar Array, specify the number of copies of the object, the angle to fill, and whether the copies are rotated.
- Specify the center point about which the objects will array.
- A Polar Array is drawn counterclockwise or clockwise, depending on whether you enter a positive or a negative value for the angle to fill.

Chapter 3 | Manipulating Objects

Practice Exercise | Creating an Array of Objects

In this practice exercise, you draw a 1 x 1 rectangle and create an array using the Polar and Rectangular array options.

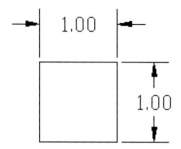

1   Begin by drawing the rectangle:

- Start the Rectangle command.
- Click the first corner in the drawing window.
- For the other corner enter **D** (for Dimensions). Press ENTER.
- Enter a length of **1** and a width of **1**.
- Click to position the rectangle.

2   To create a polar array:

- On the Home tab, click Modify panel > Array.

- In the Array dialog box, click Polar Array (1).
- Click the Select objects button (2) and select the rectangle. Press ENTER to return to the dialog box.
- Click the Center point button (3) and, using object snap tracking, track a center point that is two units down from the midpoint of the rectangle as shown.

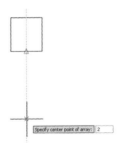

- For Total number of items (4), enter **6**.
- For Angle to fill (5), enter **360**.
- Click OK (6).
- Zoom to display your polar array, which should resemble the following illustration.

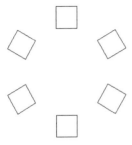

3   To create a rectangular array:

- Create another 1 x 1 rectangle.
- On the Home tab, click Modify panel > Array.

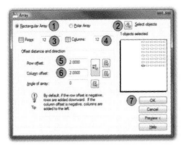

- In the Array dialog box, click Rectangular Array (1).
- Click the Select objects button (2), and click the rectangle. Press ENTER to return to the dialog box.
- Enter **12** for Rows (3) and Columns (4).
- Enter **2** for Row offset (5) and Column offset (6).
- Click OK (7).

Chapter 3 | Manipulating Objects

- Zoom to display your rectangular array, which should resemble the following illustration.

Exercise | Array Objects in the Drawing

In this exercise, you create polar and rectangular arrays of various pieces of office furniture in an office floor plan. When you have completed the exercise, you will be able to use the Array command to create arrays of objects in your drawings.

Note
You have the option of completing this exercise using either imperial or metric units. Select one version of the exercise to complete the steps.

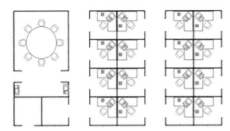

The completed exercise

Completing the Exercise
To complete the exercise, follow the steps in this book or in the onscreen exercise. In the onscreen list of chapters and exercises, click *Chapter 3: Manipulating Objects*. Click *Exercise: Array Objects in the Drawing Metric*.

Exercise: Array Objects in the Drawing (Metric Units)

1   Open *M_Creating-Arrays.dwg*.

2   To create a polar array, zoom into the area shown in the following image.

3   To create an array of the chair around the table:

- On the Home tab, click Modify panel > Array.
- In the Array dialog box, click Polar Array (1).

- Click Select Objects (2). Select the chair.
- Press ENTER to return to the dialog box.

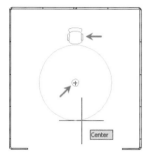

- Click the Center point button (3).
- With Object Snap on, select the center of the table.
- For the total number of items (4), enter **6**.
- For the angle to fill (5), enter **360**.
- Click Preview (6).
- *Do not press* ENTER. Press ESC to return to the dialog box.

4   Change the total number of items:

- In the Array dialog box, enter **8** for the total number of items (4).
- Click OK to complete the polar array.
- Eight chairs are arrayed around the table as in the following illustration.

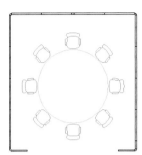

5   Zoom to display the area that is indicated in the following image. Make certain that the walls are visible.

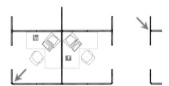

6   Use the Rectangular array option to populate the remaining offices with the objects from the first two:

- On the Home tab, click Modify panel > Array.
- In the Array dialog box, click Rectangular Array.
- Click the Select Objects button.
- Select the objects indicated in the following image. Press ENTER.
  Note: Use two separate crossing windows to select the objects.

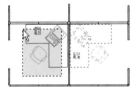

7   Set your desired number of rows and columns:

- In the Array dialog box, for Rows, enter **4**.
- For Columns, enter **2**.
- Under Offset Distance and Direction, click the button indicated below to Pick Both Offsets.

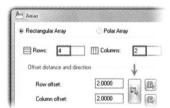

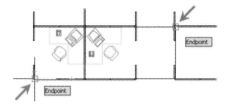

8   Specify the unit cell as indicated:

- Click the endpoint of the line of the lower interior wall.
- For the other corner, click the endpoint of the line of the upper interior wall.

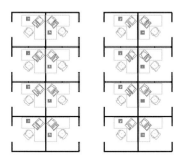

- Click Preview.
- Your rectangular array should appear as illustrated.
- *Do not press* ENTER.
- Use the wheel on the mouse to adjust the display of your drawing.

- If necessary, press ESC to return to the dialog box and reselect the unit cell, or press ENTER to complete the Array command.

9   Close all files. Do not save.

Exercise: Array Objects in the Drawing (Imperial Units)

1   Open *I_Creating-Arrays.dwg*.

2   To create a polar array, zoom into the area shown in the following image.

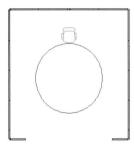

3   To create an array of the chair around the table:

- On the Home tab, click Modify panel > Array.
- In the Array dialog box, click Polar Array (1).

- Click Select Objects (2). Select the chair.
- Press ENTER to return to the dialog box.

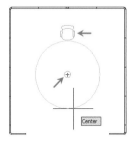

- Click the Center point button (3).
- With Object Snap on, select the center of the table.
- For the total number of items (4), enter **6**.
- For the angle to fill (5), enter **360**.
- Click PREVIEW (6).
- *Do not press* ENTER. Press ESC to return to the dialog box.

4   Change the total number of items:

- In the Array dialog box, enter **8** for the total number of items (4).
- Click OK to complete the polar array.
- Eight chairs are arrayed around the table as in the following illustration.

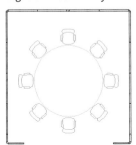

5   Zoom to display the area that is indicated in the following image. Make certain the walls are visible.

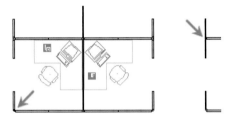

6   Use the Rectangular array option to populate the remaining offices with the objects from the first two:

- On the Home tab, click Modify panel > Array.
- In the Array dialog box, click Rectangular Array.
- Click the Select objects button.
- Select the objects that are indicated in the following image. Press ENTER.
  Note: Use two separate crossing windows to select the objects.

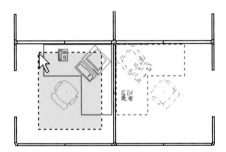

7   Set your desired number of rows and columns:

- In the Array dialog box, for Rows, enter **4**.
- For Columns, enter **2**.
- Under Offset Distance and Direction, click Pick Both Offsets.

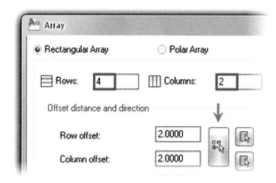

8   Specify the unit cell as indicated:

- Click the endpoint of the line of the lower interior wall.
- For the other corner, click the endpoint of the line of the upper interior wall.

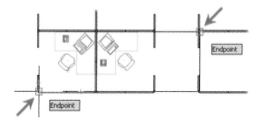

- Click PREVIEW.
- Your rectangular array should appear as illustrated.
- *Do not press* ENTER.
- Use the wheel on the mouse to adjust the display of your drawing.

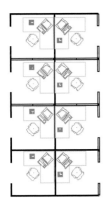 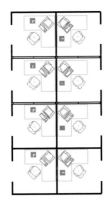

- If necessary, press ESC to return to the dialog box and reselect the unit cell, or press ENTER to complete the Array command.

9   Close all files. Do not save.

Lesson 16 | Changing an Object's Size

This lesson describes how to increase or decrease the size of objects in the drawing using the Scale command.

When you create drawings, it is often quicker to modify existing geometry then to create new geometry from scratch. With the Scale command, you can resize geometry to meet the current design requirements.

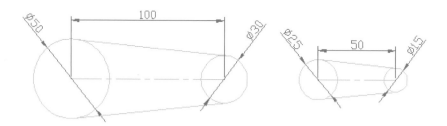

Objectives

After completing this lesson, you will be able to:

• Use the Scale command or grips to scale objects in the drawing.

Scaling Objects

You use the Scale command when you need to change the size of existing geometry in the drawing. The Scale command can scale an entire drawing or just the objects that you select. After you select the geometry to be scaled, you have the option of scaling a copy of the selected geometry. If you choose this option, the original geometry remains unchanged while a copy of the geometry is scaled by the factor you specify. You can also control a scaling operation using grips.

Command Access

Scale

Command Line: **SCALE, SC**
Ribbon: **Home tab > Modify Panel > Scale**
Note: *Do not confuse this command with the 3D Scale command*

Menu Bar: **Modify > Scale**
Shortcut Menu: **Select objects then right-click anywhere in the drawing window. Click Scale.**

Command Options

With the Scale command, you can scale geometry using the following options.

Options	Description
Base Point	Use this option to define the point from which the selected geometry is scaled. If the base point is not coincident with the selected geometry, the distance between the base point and the geometry is scaled.
Copy	Use this option to scale a copy of the selected geometry. The original geometry is not scaled.
Reference	Use this option to specify a reference length, either by entering a value, or selecting two points. After you specify the reference length, enter a new length for the reference length. The scale factor is calculated as Reference Length = New Length.

Procedure: Scaling Objects

The following steps give an overview of scaling objects using the Scale command.

1   On the ribbon, click Home tab > Modify panel > Scale.

2   Select the objects to be scaled. Press ENTER to end the object selection.

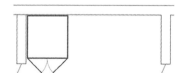

3   Select a base point.

4   Enter a scale factor. Press ENTER.

Procedure: Scaling Objects Using Grips

The following steps give an overview of using grips to scale objects.

1   Select an object to activate its grips.

2   Click a grip to activate grip edit mode. By default, this point will also be used as the base point for the scale.

3   Right-click anywhere in the drawing. Click Scale.

4   Specify a scale factor.

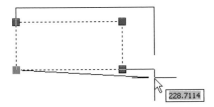

Guidelines for Scaling Objects

- A value less than 1 decreases the size of the geometry. A value greater than 1 increases the size of the geometry. For example, entering a scale factor of .5 halves the size of the selected objects.
- The most recent scale factor used persists for the current editing session.
- To scale using the Reference option, use object snap to click two points on the object to define the reference scale. This is often quicker and more accurate than finding the distance and calculating a scale factor.
- When you use the Reference option, the two points that define the reference distance are independent from the scale base point.

Practice Exercise | Scaling Objects

In this practice exercise, you draw an object and scale it using the Scale command with the Reference option and grips with the Copy option. You draw a rectangle of any size and scale it to a specific size. Then you scale and copy it using grips

1   Draw a rectangle of any size:

  - Start the Rectangle command.
  - Click the first corner.
  - Click the opposite corner.

2   To scale the rectangle using the Reference scale option:

  - On the Home tab, click Modify panel > Scale.
  - Select the rectangle. Press ENTER.
  - Click a base point on or near the rectangle.
  - Right-click and click Reference.

  - To specify the reference length, select the object snap endpoints as indicated below. Notice that the software calculates the exact length of the line based on the two endpoints that you select.

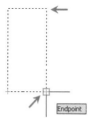

  - To specify a new length, enter **2** and press ENTER.

3   Use grips to scale and copy the rectangle at .5 scale and then at .25 scale of the original size. Select the middle of the rectangle for the base point:

  - With the command line blank, select the rectangle.

- Right-click any grip on the rectangle. Click Scale.

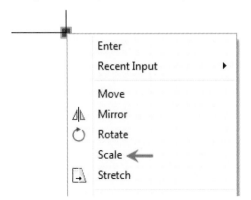

- Using object snap tracking, select the middle of the rectangle for the base point.

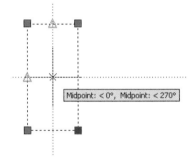

Midpoint: < 0°, Midpoint: < 270°

4   To specify the scale factors:

- Enter **.5**. Press ENTER.
- Enter **.25**. Press ENTER.
- Press ESC to end the scale procedure.
- Press ESC to clear the rectangle selection.
  Your drawing should look similar to the illustration below.

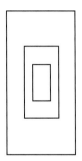

Exercise | Scale Objects Using the Copy Option

In this exercise, you use the Copy option of the Scale command to scale a copy of the link-arm profile geometry and leave the source geometry unchanged. You then rotate the original geometry and dimensions.

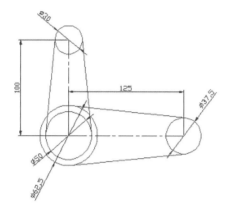

The completed exercise

Completing the Exercise
To complete the exercise, follow the steps in this book or in the onscreen exercise. In the onscreen list of chapters and exercises, click *Chapter 3: Manipulating Objects*. Click *Exercise: Scale Objects Using the Copy Option*.

1   Open *M_Scale-Copy.dwg*.

2   On the Home tab, click Modify panel > Scale. Window select all of the geometry and dimensions in the drawing.

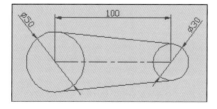

3   Press ENTER to accept the selection.

4   Select the center of the large circle as the base point.

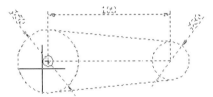

5   Right-click anywhere in the drawing. Click Copy.

6   Enter **1.25** for the scale factor. Press ENTER.

7   To rotate the original objects:

   • Begin the Rotate command.
   • Enter **P**. Press ENTER to select the previous selection set.

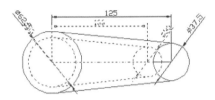

8   Press ENTER to accept the selection set.

9   Select the center point of the larger circle.

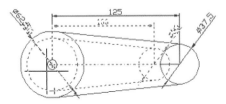

10   Enter **90**. Press ENTER.

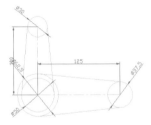

11   Close all files. Do not save.

Challenge Exercise | Grips

In this exercise, you use grips to edit and manipulate objects in a drawing. When you have completed the exercise, you will be able to use grips to effectively manipulate geometry without having to use the standard editing commands.

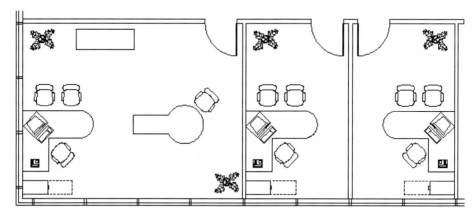

The completed exercise

Completing the Exercise
To complete the exercise, follow the steps in this book or in the onscreen exercise. In the onscreen list of chapters and exercises, click *Chapter 3: Manipulating Objects*. Click *Challenge Exercise: Grip Edit Objects*.

1   Open *M_Grips-Exercise.dwg*.

2   To move a door into position using grips:

  • Select the door.
  • Click the single grip to make it a selected grip.
  • Right-click. Click Move.
  • Drag the door into position. Click the endpoint of the wall. Your object will still be selected.

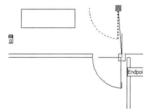

3   To copy the door using grips for the next room:

- Click the grip again to make it a selected grip.
- Right-click. Click Move.
- Right-click. Click Copy.
  Note: With a single object, you do not need to click Move first and can proceed to Copy. With more than one object selected, you always need to click Move before clicking Copy.
- Drag the door one room to the right. Click the endpoint of the wall.
- Press ENTER to complete the copy.
- Press ESC to release your selection.

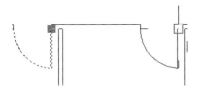

4   To move the plant into position using grips:

- Select the plant.
- Click the grip to make it selected.
- Right-click. Click Move.
- Drag the plant to the upper-left corner as shown below.

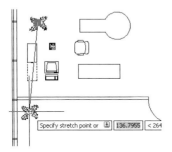

5   To copy the plant using grips:

- Click the plant grip again to make it selected.
- Right-click. Click Move.
- Right-click. Click Copy.
- Drag and place the second plant in the lower-right corner as shown.
- Press ENTER to finish the copy.
- Press ESC to clear your selection.

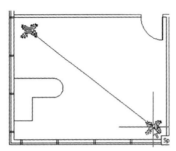

6   To move the credenza and keyhole desk using grips:

   - Using the Move grip mode, drag the credenza into position as shown.
   - Using the Move grip mode, drag the keyhole table into position as shown.

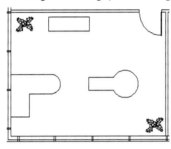

7   To move the file cabinet into position using grips:

   - Select the file cabinet.
   - Click the grip to select it.
   - Right-click. Click Move.
   - Drag the object to the lower-left corner as shown below. Place the object about four units above the lower wall attached to the left side wall.

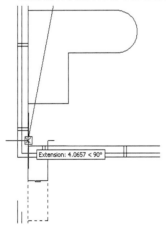

8   To rotate the file cabinet using grips:

- Click the grip again to select it.
- Right-click. Click Rotate.
- Enter **90**. Press ENTER.
- Press ESC to clear your selection set.

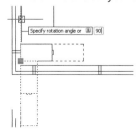

9   Use the Move and Rotate grip modes again to place the computer and phone onto the desk as shown. Refer to the previous step if needed for the step-by-step process.

- The computer object is rotated 45 degrees.
- The phone object is rotated 90 degrees.

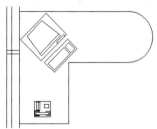

10   Use Move, Rotate, and Copy grip modes to place the chair object in the office as shown:

- The desk chair is rotated -45 degrees and the conference table chair is rotated at 45 degrees. The remaining two chairs are rotated at 90 degrees.
  Your office layout should look like the following image.

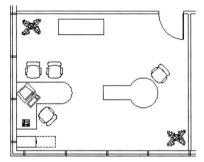

11 Use the Copy and Base Point grip modes to copy many objects at once to populate the next office area to the right:

- Select all of the objects as shown in the following image.
- Pick any one of the available grips to make it hot.
- Right-click. Click Move.
- Right-click. Click Copy.
- Right-click. Click Base Point.
- Pick the inside top-left corner of the room (1) for the base point.
- Pick the top-left inside corner of the next room (2) for the move point.
- Press ENTER to complete the copy.
- Press ESC to release your selection set.

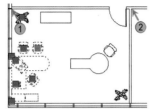

12 Use the Mirror and Copy grip modes to populate the next office area to the right:
- Select all of the objects as shown in the following image.
- Click any one of the available grips to select it.
- Right-click. Click Mirror.
- Right-click. Click Copy.
- Right-click. Click Base Point.
- Pick the midpoint of the outside wall section (1) between the doors for the base point.
- Drag your cursor up at 90 degrees and pick point (2).
- Press ENTER to complete the copy.
- Press ESC to release your selection set.

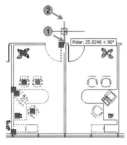

13 Continue to use grips, as time permits, to populate the remaining offices with furniture.

14 Close all files without saving.

Chapter 3 | Manipulating Objects

Challenge Exercise | Architectural

In this exercise, use what you learned about modifying objects to modify the floor plan.

Note
You have the option of completing this exercise using either imperial or metric units. Select one version of the exercise to complete the steps.

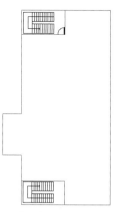

The completed exercise

Completing the Exercise
To complete the exercise, follow the steps in this book or in the onscreen exercise. In the onscreen list of chapters and exercises, click *Chapter 3: Manipulating Objects.* Click *Challenge Exercise: Architectural Metric.*

Metric Units

1   Open the drawing you saved from the previous challenge exercise, or open *M_ARCH-Challenge- CHP03.dwg.*

2   Create geometry to represent the stairs for the building. You will create the stair in an open area of your building and then rotate it and move it into position:
   - Begin with a single line (1).
   - Array the line to create the stairs on the left.
   - Add the vertical lines on the left and the right.
   - Mirror all the lines to create the stairs on the right.
   - Create the remaining lines using Otrack and direct distance entry.

- Do not create the centerline, it is there for dimensional purposes only.

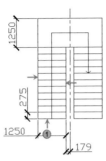

3 Position the stairs in the lower stairwell as shown.

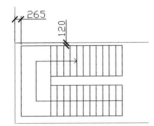

4 Mirror the lower stairs to the top stairwell to complete the drawing.

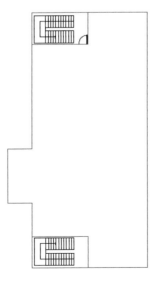

5 Save and close the drawing.

Imperial Units

1   Open the drawing you saved from the previous challenge exercise, or open *I_ARCH-Challenge- CHP03.dwg.*

2   Create geometry to represent the stairs for the building. You will create the stair in an open area of your building and then rotate it and move it into position:

- Begin with a single line (1).
- Array the line to create the stairs on the left.
- Add the vertical lines on the left and the right.
- Mirror all the lines to create the stairs on the right.
- Create the remaining lines using Otrack and direct distance entry.
- Do not create the centerline, it is there for dimensional purposes only.

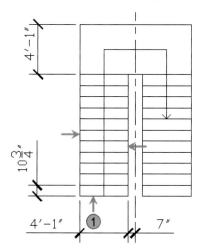

3   Position the stairs in the lower stairwell as shown.

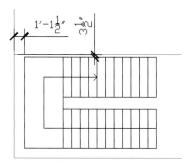

4   Mirror the lower stairs to the top stairwell to complete the drawing.

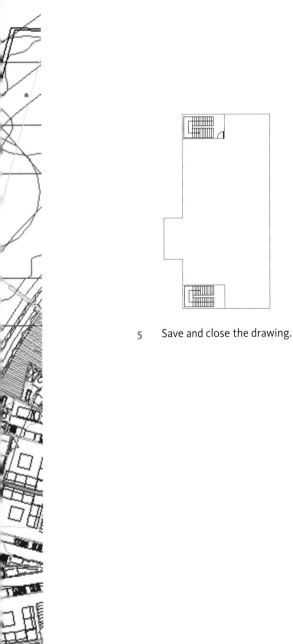

5   Save and close the drawing.

Challenge Exercise | Mechanical

In this exercise, use what you learned about modifying objects to edit geometry.

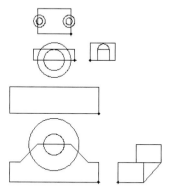

The completed exercise

Completing the Exercise
To complete the exercise, follow the steps in this book or in the onscreen exercise. In the onscreen list of chapters and exercises, click *Chapter 3: Manipulating Objects*. Click *Challenge Exercise: Mechanical.*

1   Open the drawing you saved from the previous challenge exercise, or open *M_MECH-Challenge- CHP03.dwg.*

2   Rotate the right side view 90 degrees as shown.
    Note: The views in the image are closer together than they will appear in your drawing.

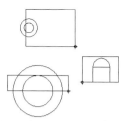

3   Move the top view so that its midpoint aligns with the circles in the main view. Move the side view so that it is correctly aligned with the base view. The views for the Rack Slider Base should appear as shown.
    Note: The views in the image are closer together than they will appear in your drawing.

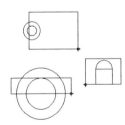

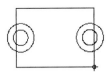

4   Copy or mirror the two circles in the top view to the other side.

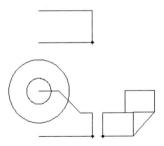

5   Rotate the right side view and move both the top and side view into alignment with the base view.
     Note: The views in the image are closer together than they will appear in your drawing.

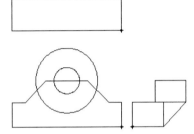

6   Mirror the geometry in the top and main views to complete the sketch as shown.

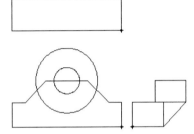

7   Save and close all files.

Chapter 3 | Manipulating Objects

Chapter Summary

Every design you create begins with simple geometry. The procedures you use to edit these basic objects transform them into complex designs.

Having completed this chapter, you can:

- Use different selection methods to select objects in the drawing.
- Move objects in the drawing using object snaps, object tracking, and coordinate entry for precise placement.
- Use the Copy command or use grips to create new objects from existing objects in the drawing.
- Change the angle of objects in the drawing by using the Rotate command or with grips.
- Create mirrored images of objects in the drawing using the Mirror command or with grips.
- Use the Array command to create rectangular and circular patterns of objects in the drawing.
- Change the size of objects in the drawing.
- Use grips to edit objects and display geometric information.

Chapter 04

Drawing Organization and Inquiry Commands

The ability to electronically manipulate, organize, and obtain information in a drawing far surpasses anything that you could accomplish if you were to use manual methods. To achieve this, you must attain proficiency with entering commands and using the other design methods available. This way, you will see how the software is much more useful than pencil and paper.

In this chapter, you learn how to organize objects in a drawing and how to use layers and linetypes to enhance your design practices. You also learn how to take advantage of the electronic design environment and use tools to obtain geometric information from objects in the drawing.

Objectives

After completing this chapter, you will be able to:

- In this lesson, you will use layers to organize objects in your drawing.

- Identify and change the properties of objects.

- In this lesson, you adjust object properties on several different types of objects. You begin by learning about the Quick Properties panel, how to access it and how to control its visibility and behavior. You then use the Quick Properties panel to quickly change object properties.

- Use the Match Properties command to apply the properties from a source object to destination objects.

- Use the Properties palette to change object properties.

- Use linetypes to distinguish objects in the drawing.

- Use the Inquiry commands (Distance, Radius, Angle, Area, List, and ID) to obtain geometric information from the drawing.

Lesson 17 | Using Layers

This lesson describes what layers are and how you can use them to organize objects in your drawing. For example, in the following illustration, objects might be placed on different layers, with dimensions on one layer, hidden lines on another, and the hole features isolated on a third. Each layer may have property settings that determine the color, linetype, and lineweight of the objects on that layer.

In a typical drawing, objects are placed to represent some part of the design. These objects can include geometry, text, dimensions, and borders. To organize your drawing, you need a way to logically group objects based on function, appearance, or other commonalities. There are many industry layering standards and most designers base their own standards on one of these. Most important is that you establish a standard for layering and you follow it.

After completing this lesson, you will be able to use layers to organize objects in your drawing.

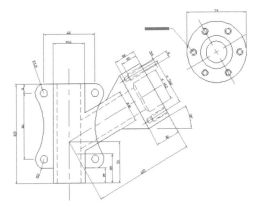

Objectives

After completing this lesson, you will be able to:

- Describe how layers can be used to organize objects in your drawing.
- Describe the purpose of Layer 0.
- Access the Layer Properties Manager and use other commands to manage layers.

Chapter 4 | Drawing Organization and Inquiry Commands

Organizing Objects with Layers

As your drawings increase in complexity, organization of the drawing objects becomes critical to efficiently managing the design data. You can use layers to logically group objects in the drawing.

In the following office layout, you would use layers to separate walls, partition walls, furniture, text, and equipment.

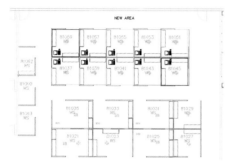

About Layers

Use layers to logically organize the objects in the drawing and to enforce linetype, color, and lineweight standards. When you group objects into layers, you can then control these objects by controlling the single layer. For example, if you put all the dimensions on a single layer, you could chose to hide these dimensions simply by freezing that layer.

The following image illustrates how layers are used to organize objects. The image on the left represents the logical grouping of similar objects, while the image on the right illustrates what you see in the software.

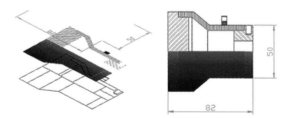

Using layers is similar to using overlays in a manual drafting environment where clear media that contains groups of related design elements are placed throughout the overall design. As a result, you see everything that you create, you have the flexibility to easily remove the overlays, and can focus on any aspect of your design.

A Typical Layer Configuration

A typical drawing could use layers to organize objects in the following way.

Layer Name	Objects
Walls	All geometry representing walls.
Electrical	All geometry representing electrical.
Hidden	Geometry that is represented by hidden lines.
Landscape	Geometry representing landscaping objects.
Construction	Temporary geometry used for sketching or other construction geometry purposes.
Dimensions	Drawing dimensions.
Annotation	Text and notes.
Hatch	Hatch patterns, fills, and gradients.
Titleblock	Borders, Title Block and title block information.

The preceding table is an example of a typical layer configuration. Most companies have layer standards already defined to suit their particular needs. The following example shows a standard architectural layer configuration.

Typical Architectural Layer Configuration

Use the Layer Properties Manager to create and manage the layers in a drawing.

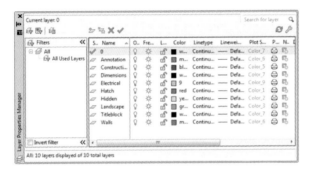

Chapter 4 | Drawing Organization and Inquiry Commands

Layer Key Points

- Use layers to organize objects in your drawing.
- Layers have property settings that determine the color, linetype, and lineweight of the objects on that layer.
- Use the Layer Properties Manager dialog box to create and manage layers.
- Every drawing contains at least the default Layer 0.
- To organize a drawing, consider grouping objects onto layers based on function, appearance, or other commonalities.
- There are many industry standards concerning layering from which you can establish a layering standard for your drawings.
- When your drawing is organized with layers, you can easily control entire groups of objects.

Default Layer

Every drawing that you create has a default layer called 0 (zero). This ensures that every drawing contains at least one layer.

Default Layer Defined

When you create a new drawing, a number of layers may be present depending on the template that you used. Layer 0, however, is persistent regardless of the template used. Every drawing will contain the default layer 0.

Layer 0 cannot be renamed or deleted. AutoCAD® uses that layer to establish predictable behaviors for objects such as blocks, regardless of how other layers are named.

The following illustration shows the Layer Properties Manager dialog box in a drawing created from *acad.dwt*. The only layer present is 0.

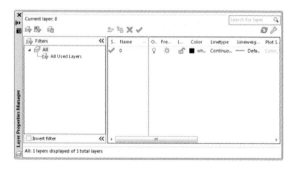

Guidelines for Layer 0

The following are some specific guidelines related to Layer 0.

- You can create layers in addition to Layer 0 in the Layers Properties Manager when you begin a new drawing unless they are already provided in your company's drawing template.
- You can make a layer current first and then draw your objects. This automatically places the geometry on that current layer instead of Layer 0.
- Consider Layer 0 as your working layer when uncertain where to place geometry. Then, move the objects to the appropriate layer.
- You should create simple block geometry on Layer 0 so that when you insert it on another layer it takes on the properties of that layer. For example, a chair block created on Layer 0 and inserted on the Furniture layer will appear with the properties (Color, Linetype, Lineweight) that are assigned to the Furniture layer.
- You should insert blocks with multiple layers on Layer 0 so that the layers and colors assigned to the block appear the way they were created when you insert them into your drawing.

If you do create objects on layer 0, you can assign them to a different layer at any time.

Layer Tools

When you create and manage layers, you use the Layer Properties Manager and the Layer Control list on the ribbon. Together, these commands and tools provide you with the functionality required to effectively create, manage, and assign objects to layers.

Layers Panel

Command Access

Use the Layer Properties Manager to create layers and control the color, linetype, lineweight, and other properties of each layer.

Layers Properties Manager

Command Line: **LAYER, LA**
Ribbon: **Home tab > Layers Panel > Layer Properties**

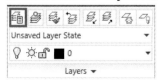

Menu Bar: **Format > Layer...**

To quickly make an object's layer current, use the following command.

Make Objects Layer Current

Command Line: **LAYMCUR**
Ribbon: **Home tab > Layers Panel > Make Objects Layer Current**

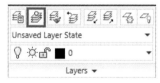

Menu Bar: **Format > Layer Tools > Make Object's Layer Current**

To return to the previous layer settings, use the following command.

Layer Previous

Command Line: **LAYERP**
Ribbon: **Home tab > Layers Panel > Previous**

Menu Bar: **Format > Layer Tools > Layer Previous**

Layer Previous in AutoCAD LT
Layer Previous is not available in AutoCAD LT®.

Layer Properties Manager Dialog Box

Your primary tool for managing layers is the Layer Properties Manager. Use this dialog box to create and manage layers.

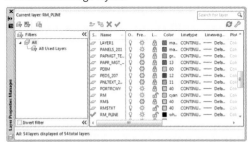

Command Options

The following options are available in the Layer Properties Manager dialog box for essential layer management.

Option	Description
🖙	Click to create a new layer. Enter a name for the layer in the field. Select the layer name twice to rename. Layer names can be listed in the Name column in ascending or descending order.
✕	Click to delete the selected layer. You cannot delete the current layer or layers containing objects. You can Undo by selecting the Undo icon from the Quick Access toolbar.
✓	Click to make the selected layer Current. You can also double-click the layer to make it the current layer.
(color/linetype/lineweight table)	Click the layer row and the appropriate column to assign or change the properties for that layer. Properties include Color (see below), Linetype (see below), Lineweight (see below) and whether the layer will Plot or not.

Option	Description
	Color: Select a color from the AutoCAD Color Index. Note that the Color white will print black and be displayed black on a white drawing background and white on a black background.
	Linetype: A blank drawing will contain the Continuous linetype. Select the Load button to load other linetypes.
	Lineweight: Various lineweights will not be displayed in the drawing window unless the Show Lineweight option is selected in the status bar. Note that the default lineweight is 0.01 inches or 0.25 mm.

New Layer Properties

When you create a new layer, the properties of the currently selected layer are duplicated for the new layer. If your new layer is going to have properties such as color or linetype in common with another layer, select the similar layer before you click New.

Layer Status

The visibility and availability of objects on specific layers are determined by the layer's status. The following table describes the potential status of a layer.

These icons appear in the Layer Properties Manager and the Layer list. Click the icon to change the status of the layer.

Icon	Or	Status
		On: Objects on the layer are visible. **Off**: Objects on the layer are not visible but are still considered when the drawing is regenerated.
		Thawed: Objects on the layer are visible. **Frozen**: Objects on the layer are not visible and are not considered when the drawing is regenerated.
		New VP Freeze: Freezes layer in newly created viewports. **VP Freeze (Layout only)**: The layer is not visible and will not print in the selected or current viewport if frozen.
		Unlocked: You can select and edit objects on the layer. **Locked**: You cannot select or edit objects on the layer.

Layer Control List

The Layer Control list is located on the Layers panel.

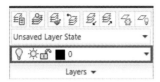

Chapter 4 | Drawing Organization and Inquiry Commands

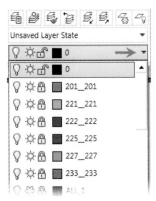

The Layer Control serves a dual purpose.

1   In normal operations, the current layer is displayed. However, when an object is selected with the command line blank, the list displays the layer that the object is on. The following image shows that when the door block is selected, the A-Doors layer is displayed.

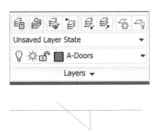

It is helpful to know what layer the object is on. But you may also place the selected object or objects on another layer by choosing the layer from the drop-down list.

2   After you create layers, you can use the Layer Control to select a layer to make it current, to change the layer status to Freeze or Thaw, Lock or Unlock, or turn layers On or Off.

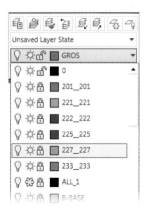

Layer Tools Key Points

- Creating and managing layers requires the use of some key commands, the Layer Properties Manager, and the Layer Control list on the Layers panel.
- Your primary tool for managing layers is the Layer Properties Manager. Use this dialog box to create and manage layers.
- Once a layer is created, you cannot delete it if it is current or if there are objects referenced on that layer.
- Layer o cannot be deleted or renamed.
- Layer properties include color, linetype, lineweight, and whether the layer will plot or not.
- A layer status can be On or Off, Frozen or Thawed, and Locked or Unlocked.
- Layers that are turned off are not visible but are still considered when the drawing is regenerated. Layers that are frozen are not visible and are not considered when the drawing is regenerated.
- With the command line blank, you can select an object and see what layer it is on from the Layers Control list located on the Layers panel.
- You can select an object and move it to another layer using the Layers Control list.
- You can change a layers status from the Layers Control list.
- The Layer Previous command returns you to the previous layer state, to the previous layer setting, and to the previous status of all layers in the drawing.

Performance Tip

For better performance on large drawings, freeze layers instead of turning them off. Objects on layers that are turned off are still considered when the drawing is regenerated, while objects on layers that are frozen are not considered, and thus not calculated when the drawing is regenerated.

Practice Exercise | Layer Tools

In this practice exercise, you create layers in the Properties Manager dialog box and select the layer from the Layer Control list to draw objects on the appropriate layer.

1   To create the layers:
- On the ribbon, click Home tab > Layers panel > Layer Properties.
- In the dialog box, click New. Create the following layers:
    - Layer Name: Circle, Color: Red
    - Layer Name: Line, Color: Blue
    - Layer Name: Rectangle, Color: Green
- **Note**: If you enter the layer name and then a comma, a new layer name field appears. The layers are automatically listed in alphabetical order.

2   Close the Layer Properties Manager dialog box.

3   In the Layer Control list, select the Circle layer to make it current and draw circles on that layer.

4   Repeat the previous step:
- Click the Rectangle layer to make it current and draw rectangles.
- Click the Line layer to make it current and draw lines.

Exercise | Work with Layers

In this exercise, you freeze and thaw layers and lock and unlock them. You create new layers, set the current layer, and create new geometry on the current layer.

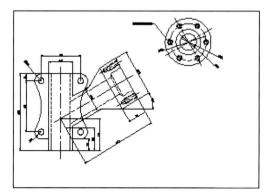

The completed exercise

Completing the Exercise

To complete the exercise, follow the steps in this book or in the onscreen exercise. In the onscreen list of chapters and exercises, click *Chapter 4: Drawing Organization and Inquiry Commands*. Click *Exercise: Work with Layers*.

1 Open *M_Create-Layers.dwg*.

2 Study the drawing, paying particular attention to the color and linetype of the objects. Turn the Dimensions layer off to make it easier to view and make changes to the geometry in the drawing:

   • On the Home tab, click Layers panel > Layer Control list.
   • Click the Sun icon to freeze the Dimensions layer. The icon changes from a sun to a snowflake indicating that the layer is frozen.

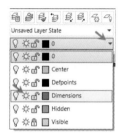

3   To make the hidden layer current:

  • On the Home tab, click Layers panel > Layer Control list.
  • Select Hidden to set it as the current layer.

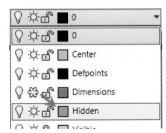

4   Zoom into the area shown and draw lines on the Hidden layer:

  • Using the Line command, create a line from point 1 to point 2 and another from point 3 to point 4 as shown in the following illustration.
  • Make sure you are snapping to the exact endpoint or intersection on the existing objects.

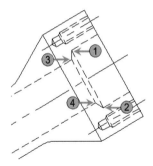

5   Draw a line on the Center layer across the center of the object as indicated below:

  • Zoom out so that the entire drawing is displayed, then zoom into the area shown below.
  • On the Home tab, click Layers panel > Layer Control list. Select the Center layer.
  • Start the Line command.
  • Acquire the 180 degree quadrant point of the large circle and drag your cursor to the left along the extension path.
  • In the dynamic input field, enter **5**. Press ENTER.

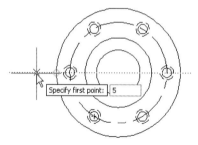

- Drag your cursor outside the large circle to the right along the extension path.
- In the Dynamic Input field, enter **85**. Press ENTER.
- Press ENTER again to end the Line command.

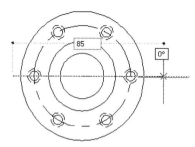

6   To create another line across the center of the object:

- Press ENTER to repeat the Line command.
- Acquire the 270 degree quadrant point of the large circle and drag your cursor downward along the extension path.
- In the Dynamic Input field, enter **5**. Press ENTER.

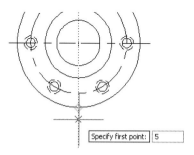

- Drag your cursor outside and above the large circle along the extension path.
- In the Dynamic Input field, enter **85**. Press ENTER.
- Press ENTER again to end the Line command.

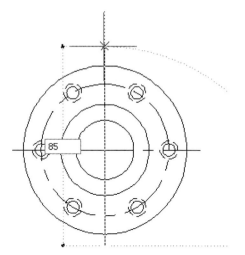

7   Use the Rotate command to rotate both centerlines 30 degrees. Use the center of the large circle as the base point for the rotation.

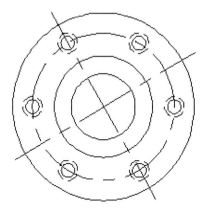

8   Thaw the Dimension Layer:

   • On the Home tab, click Layers panel > Layer Control list.
   • Click the snowflake icon to thaw the Dimensions layer.
   • Zoom out to the extents of your drawing.

9   To observe object properties in the Layer Control list:

- With the command line blank, click any dimension.
- Notice that the Dimensions layer appears in the Layer Control list.

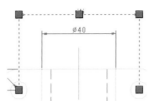

- Press ESC so that the command line is blank.
- Move your cursor over any object on the Visible layer as shown below. Notice the padlock symbol that is displayed. Objects on the visible layer are locked and cannot be modified, however, you may add more geometry to any locked layer.

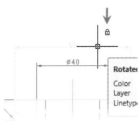

- Select an object on the Visible layer and notice how the layer name displays in the Layer Control list.
- Select any other object, such as a dimension, and notice that now the Layer Control field is blank. Because the list cannot display multiple properties at once, this indicates the objects that you selected are on different layers.
- Press ESC to deselect all objects.

10 Try to move some of the objects including ones which are on a locked layer:
   - Start the Move command.
   - Select all of the objects in the auxiliary view. Press ENTER.
   - Click any point on the drawing. Enter **25**. Press TAB.
   - In the Angle field, enter **30**. Press TAB.
   - Click anywhere in the drawing to complete the Move command. Notice that some of the objects did not move.
   - Undo the Move command.

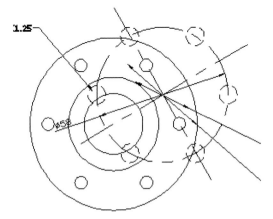

11 This time you will move the objects again, but first you unlock the layer that some of these objects are on:
   - On the Home tab, click Layers panel > Layer Control list. Click the padlock icon on the Visible layer. Note that the padlock changes from a closed lock to an open lock indicating that the layer is unlocked.
   - Repeat the Move command from the previous step. Notice how all of the objects are moved.
   - Relock the visible layer.

12   To create a new layer:

- On the Home tab, click Layers panel > Layer Properties.
- In the Layer Name field, click Visible. The properties of layer Visible are used as the default properties for the new layer.
- In the Layer Properties Manager dialog box, click New Layer (1).
- In the Layer Name field (2), enter **Title Block**.

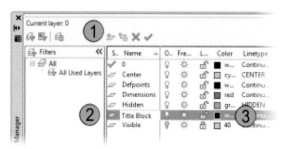

- Click the Color field (3) and select White.

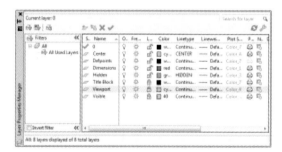

13   To add another layer:

- Click New Layer again.
- In the Layer Name field, enter **Viewport**.
- Click the Color field and select Cyan. Click OK.
- Click in the Plot field. This sets the Viewport layer to nonplotting.
- Click the layer Title Block.
- Right-click. Click Set Current.
- Click the X to close the Layer Properties Manager dialog box.

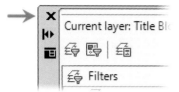

14   Zoom out to the extents of your drawing.

15   To create a rectangular border:

- Start the Rectangle command.
- Enter **0,0**. Press ENTER.
- Right-click. Click Dimensions.
- Enter **400** for the length. Press ENTER.
- Enter **277** for the width. Press ENTER.
- Click anywhere near the Auxiliary view to complete the command.

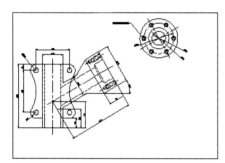

16   Close all files. Do not save.

Lesson 18 | Changing Object Properties

This lesson describes what object properties are and how to change the properties of objects in a drawing. Every object that you create in a drawing has associated properties. For example, a line has an associated color, layer, linetype, and length as shown in the following Quick Properties panel.

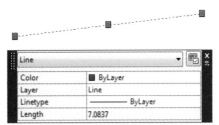

It is very common practice to change the properties of objects as you work on a drawing. One way to access and change some object properties is to select the object and use the Layers and Property panels on the ribbon to change the Layer or override the color, linetype or lineweight. Another method to change object properties is with the Properties palette which provides a number of options depending on the items selected.

The following illustration shows the object properties of a selected circle as displayed in the Properties palette.

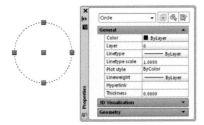

After completing this lesson, you will be able to describe the various properties of objects, identify the current settings, and assign and change object properties for existing objects in the drawing.

Objectives

After completing this lesson, you will be able to:

- Describe what object properties are and explain how they are used.
- Describe the use and effect of the ByLayer property.
- Change object properties.

About Object Properties

The most common object properties include Layer, Color, Linetype, and Lineweight. In most instances, an object's color, linetype, and lineweight are determined by the layer on which it was drawn. When you create new objects, you should make sure that the object properties settings in the layers that you create produce the desired results.

However, you may view, override, or change some object properties from the settings in the Layers and Properties panels. These options are limited to Layer, Color, Linetype, and Lineweight.

In the Properties palette, shown below, you can access a more complete list of object properties that you may view or change. The list of properties that is displayed depends on the type of object or variety of objects that you select.

Object Properties - Line

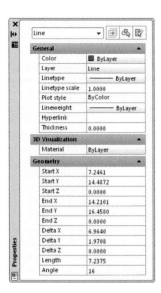

Warning!
The 3D Visualization group show in the previous image is not available in AutoCAD LT.

Definition of Object Properties

Object properties control how an object looks, both on screen and in print. The following image shows objects with specific Linetype, Lineweight, and Color properties.

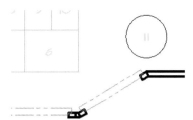

Example of Object Properties

It is common practice in 2D drafting to represent a feature or surface that is obscured by another with a hidden linetype. The hidden line indicates that the feature exists behind the current visible surface. Another common practice is to use colors to distinguish between objects in complex drawings and assigning different colors to different object types.

In the following image, the object lines are shown with the Continuous linetype and a unique color. The section line is shown with the Phantom linetype and unique color. The hole centerlines are shown with the Centerline linetype and a unique color. The hidden edge lines are shown with the Hidden linetype and a unique color. More than likely, the information in this drawing is organized into layers which determine the color and linetype of these objects. However, at a glance, it would be impossible to know precisely how the object properties have been assigned without further investigation.

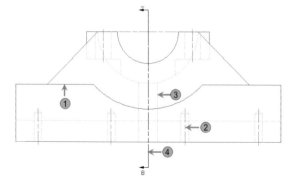

1. Object lines shown as Continuous linetype.

2. Hole centerlines shown as Center linetype.

3. Hidden edge lines shown as Hidden linetype.

4. Section line shown as Phantom linetype.

ByLayer Property

The Properties panel in the Home tab of the ribbon displays the current property settings for objects that you create in a drawing. The default settings are ByLayer which means that the object properties are determined by the layer. By default, all objects use the ByLayer setting for color, linetype, and lineweight.

The following image shows the default ByLayer settings on the object Properties panel.

Definition of the ByLayer Property Setting

The ByLayer property setting is assigned to objects and specifies its color, linetype, lineweight, and plot style. This special property setting is the equivalent to using a specific color such as red or a specific linetype such as Hidden. When property types are set to ByLayer, the object assumes the property setting that is defined in the object's layer. If you change the property in the layer, all objects with the ByLayer setting update accordingly.

The ByLayer setting not only enables consistency across objects on the same layer, it also ensures that all objects update accordingly if you change the layer's color, linetype, or lineweight properties.

> **Tip**
> You should only override an object's color, linetype, or lineweight property to something other than ByLayer when absolutely necessary. When you look at a drawing that contains objects of the same colors and linetypes, the natural inclination is to assume those objects are on the same layers.

Example of Changing Object Properties from the ByLayer Default

It is common drafting practice to place certain object types on their own layers. For example, all centerlines would be on the same layer, all object lines on their own layer, and so forth. By following this structure, you can readily control the display of all your objects both on screen and in print.

In the following image, the object lines, centerlines, and hidden lines all have their properties set to ByLayer.

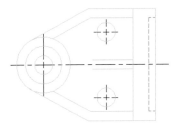

If you change the lineweight of the layer of the object lines, all of the objects on that layer change to reflect the layer setting. This change is shown in the following image.

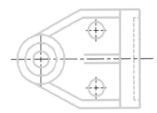

Changing Object Properties

One way to change the properties of objects is to use the controls in the Layers and Properties on the ribbon. By selecting the object or objects, you can view properties and make changes simply by selecting the desired options from the lists.

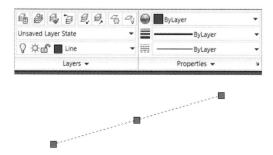

To turn the Layers or Properties panels on, right-click on the Home tab and click Panels. Then select Layers and Properties from the list.

Layers Panel - Layer Control List

The following image shows the Layers panel. With an object selected, you can view and modify the layer associated with that object.

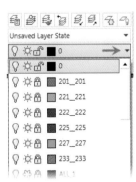

Properties Panel - Select a Linetype

The following image shows the Properties panel with the linetype list selected. Using this panel, you can view and modify an object's color, linetype, and lineweight.

Show/Hide Lineweight

The Show/Hide Lineweight option on the status bar controls the visibility of lineweights in the drawing.

Click to turn this feature on or off. Right-click and select Settings to adjust the display scale.

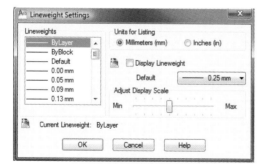

Procedure: Changing an Object's Layer Property

The following steps give an overview of how to change an object's layer property using the Layer Control list in the Layers panel.

1   Select one or more objects in your drawing that need to be moved to a different layer.

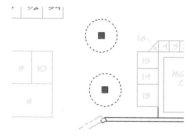

2   On the Home tab, click Layers panel > Layer Control list. Select the layer where you want to move the objects.

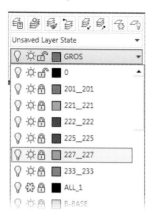

3   Press ESC to clear your selection.

Procedure: Changing an Object's Color Property

The following steps describe how to change an object's color by selecting a color from the list on the Properties panel.

1   Select one or more objects in your drawing that need to have their color changed.

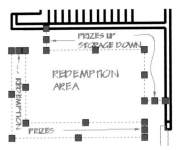

2   On the ribbon, click Home tab > Properties panel > Object Color. Select the desired color from the list.

3   Press ESC to deselect the objects.

Procedure: Changing an Object's Linetype Property

The following steps describe how to change an object's linetype by selecting the list of linetypes from the Properties panel. You can load desired linetypes that are not in the list by selecting Other.

1   Select one or more objects in your drawing that need to have their linetype changed.

2   On the ribbon, click Home tab > Properties panel > Linetype. Select the desired linetype from the list.

3   Press ESC to deselect the object.

Procedure: Changing an Object's Lineweight Property

The following steps describe how to change an object's lineweight by using the lineweight list on the Properties panel.

1   Select one or more objects in your drawing that need to have their lineweight changed.

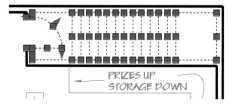

2   On the ribbon, click Home tab > Properties panel > Lineweight. Select the desired lineweight from the list.

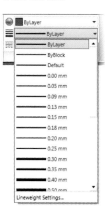

3   Press ESC to deselect the object.

Change Properties Guidelines

- Make sure that you display the Layers and Properties panels. If they are not visible, right-click in the Home tab of the ribbon to turn them on.
- Be sure the command line is blank, then use the window or crossing selection to quickly select one or more objects to view or change their properties.
- If you select the wrong object, just press SHIFT and select it again to remove it from the selection set.
- When you select more than one object with different properties, the field in the property option will be blank. This is because only one property can be listed at a time.
- You can select more than one object and choose a property that you want to assign to all of the objects selected.
- Object properties should be determined by the layer (ByLayer) whenever possible.
- Linetypes not shown in the list can be loaded into the drawing.
- Be sure the Lineweight display option is on in the status bar and adjust the lineweight display in the Settings dialog box.

Object Selection

Remember to press ESC after you complete each change and before you select more objects. This prevents accidental changes to the properties of previously selected objects.

Practice Exercise | Changing Object Properties

In this practice exercise, you draw simple objects on the default layer 0. Then you create additional layers with object properties as specified. Finally, you select the objects and change the properties using the lists from the Layers and Properties panels.

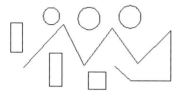

1   Begin a new drawing from the *acad.dwg* template and draw some lines, circles, and rectangles on the default layer 0.

2   On the Home tab, click Layers panel > Layer Properties. In the Layer Properties Manager, create several layers with the following names and colors:

   - Circles - red
   - Lines - blue
   - Rectangles - cyan

3   To assign a hidden linetype to the Lines layer

   - In the Layer Properties Manager, on the Lines layer, click Continuous.

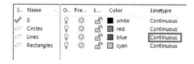

   - In the Select Linetype dialog box, click Load.

   - In the Load or Reload Linetypes dialog box, scroll to and click HIDDEN.

- Click OK to exit the dialog boxes.

4   To assign a Lineweight of 0.35 to the layer named Rectangles:

- In the Layer Properties Manager dialog box, click the Default lineweight of the Rectangles layer.
- In the Lineweight dialog box, click 0.35 mm lineweight.

- Click ok to exit the dialog box.
- Close the Layer Properties Manager.

5   To change the object properties:

- With the command line blank, select all of the circles. On the Home tab, click Layers panel > Layer. Select the Circle layer. Press ESC to deselect the objects.
- Repeat this step for the lines and rectangles and place them on their designated layers.
- Press ESC to deselect all objects.
- Your drawing should look similar to what is shown in the following illustration.

6   On the status bar, be sure the Show Lineweight setting is on.

7   To change the object properties again:
- With the command line blank, select the object you have drawn.
- On the Home tab, click Properties panel > Linetype (1) > Hidden.
- In the Lineweight list (2), click 0.40.
- From the Color list (3), select White.

- Now all of the objects in your drawing should have the same color, linetype, and lineweight as in the following image.

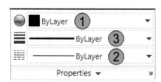

    It is difficult to tell at a glance which objects are on the layers.

8   Change the object properties back to ByLayer:
- With the command line blank, select all of the objects that you have drawn.
- On the Home tab, click Properties panel > ByLayer for (1) Color, (2) Linetype, and (3) Lineweight.

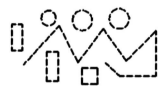

- Press ESC to deselect all of the objects.
- Your objects should display the properties that you assigned to each object in step 5.

Exercise | Change Object Properties

In this exercise, you use the Layers and Properties toolbars to change the layer, linetype, and lineweight of selected objects.

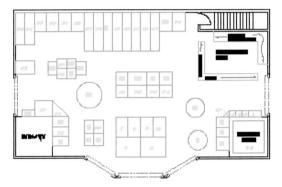

The completed exercise

Completing the Exercise

To complete the exercise, follow the steps in this book or in the onscreen exercise. In the onscreen list of chapters and exercises, click *Chapter 4: Drawing Organization and Inquiry Commands*. Click *Exercise: Change Object Properties*.

1   Open *I_Change-Properties.dwg*.

2   To change the linetype of the overhead doors to ByLayer:

   • Select the overhead doors indicated by the arrows.
   • On the Home tab, click Properties panel > Linetype.
   • Select ByLayer. Press ESC to clear your selection set.

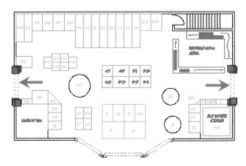

3   To move some of the machine labels to another layer:

- With the command line blank, select the text for machine numbers 47 through 54.
- On the Home tab, click Layers panel > Layer.
- Select the machine labels layer to move the numbers to this layer.
- Press ESC to clear your selection set.

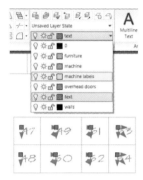

4   To move some tables to another layer:

- Select the three round tables as shown.
- On the Home tab, click Layers panel > Layer.
- Click the furniture layer to move the tables to this layer.
- Press ESC to clear your selection set.

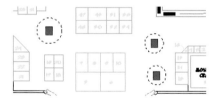

5   To change the lineweight of objects:

- On the status bar, click Show/Hide Lineweight to turn on the lineweight visibility.

- Zoom into the stairwell area on the drawing.
- Select the inside walls of the stairwell, all stair treads, and the door lines.
- On the Home tab, click Properties panel > Lineweight.
- Click ByLayer. Press ESC to clear your selection set.

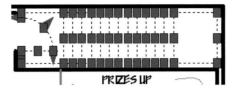

6   To change the color of objects:
   - Zoom into the upper right part of your drawing.
   - Select the lines of the counter space as indicated.
   - On the Home tab, click Properties panel > Color.
   - Select the ByLayer property to change each object's color to that of its layer.
   - Press ESC to clear your selection set.

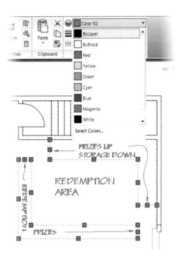

7   To move some machines to another layer:
   - Select the machines labeled 5 through 10 without selecting the numerical label.
   - On the Home tab, click Layers panel > Layer.
   - Click the machine layer to move these machines to that layer.
   - Press ESC to clear your selection set.

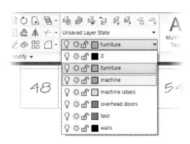

8   Close all files. Do not save.

Lesson 19 | Quick Properties

In this lesson, you adjust object properties on several different types of objects. You begin to learn about the Quick Properties panel, how to access it, and how to control its visibility and behavior. You then use the Quick Properties panel to quickly change object properties.

Object properties are adjusted frequently in each drawing editing session. The Quick Properties panel enables you to streamline and simplify the process because you only see the properties that you need. This enables you to make object property changes much faster.

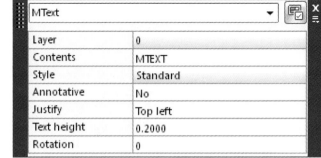

Objectives

After completing this lesson, you will be able to:

- Describe the Quick Properties panel and settings.
- View object properties using the Quick Properties panel.

About Quick Properties

The Quick Properties panel is a convenient way to view and modify object properties without losing space to the larger Properties palette. Quick Properties are automatically displayed when you select an object, and they disappear when the object is deselected. You can view and modify the properties of the object that are displayed in the Quick Properties panel. While beyond the scope of this lesson, you can use the CUI dialog box to change the properties that are displayed on the Quick Properties panel to show the properties that you use the most.

Quick Properties Panel

The following options are available in the Quick Properties panel.

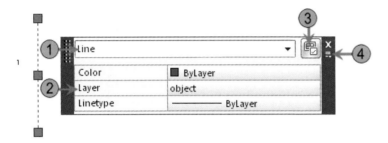

① **Object Type**: Displays the type of object selected.

② **Object Properties**: Lists object properties.

③ **Customize**: Displays the Customize User Interface (CUI) dialog box where you can specify the object types and the properties that display for them in the Quick Properties panel.

④ **Options**: Displays the options menu where you can close, customize, and change Quick Properties settings. You can also set the location mode to cursor or float and specify whether the Quick Properties panel automatically collapses.

> **Note**
> When multiple objects are selected, the Quick Properties panel only displays properties that are common to all selected objects. You can select a specific type of object from a drop-down list to display all of the Quick Properties for that object type.

Quick Properties Settings

You can specify how and where the Quick Properties panel is displayed in the Drafting Settings dialog box, Quick Properties tab. The following settings are available:

(1) **Enable Quick Properties Palette**: Displays the type of object selected. When multiple objects are selected, a drop-down list enables you to select a specific type of object.

(2) **Palette Display**: Sets the Quick Properties panel to display all objects or only the objects that have defined Quick Properties in the Customize User Interface (CUI).

(3) **Palette Location**: Sets the location mode of the Quick Properties panel to Cursor or Static.

(4) **Palette Behavior**: Enables the Quick Properties panel to display only the number of properties specified for Default Height. You must scroll or expand the Quick Properties panel to view properties if more than the default number are available.

Location Modes

The Quick Properties panel can be displayed in three different modes:

- **Cursor mode** – Use this option to display the panel alongside the cursor when an object is selected.
- **Static mode** – Use this option to display the panel in the same place on the screen unless you manually reposition it.

Using Quick Properties

When Quick Properties are turned on, the Quick Properties panel displays when you select an object. The Quick Properties panel no longer displays when you deselect that object. If you do not want the Quick Properties panel to display each time you select an object, use the toggle functionality on the status bar or in the Drafting Settings dialog box to turn Quick Properties off.

Command Access

Quick Properties

Keyboard Shortcut: **CTRL+SHIFT+P**
Object Shortcut Menu: **Quick Properties**
Status Bar: **Quick Properties**

Procedure: Using Quick Properties

The following steps give an overview of using Quick Properties.

1   On the status bar, verify Quick Properties is turned on.

2   Select an object.

3   In the Quick Properties panel, view or change the desired object property.

4   Press ESC to exit the Quick Properties panel.

Exercise | Use Quick Properties

In this exercise, you use the Quick Properties palette to view various object properties. You also customize the Quick Properties palette to control the circumstances in which the palette appears and the options it displays.

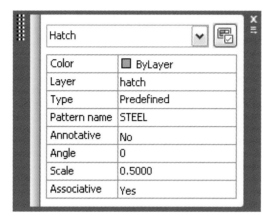

The completed exercise

Completing the Exercise

To complete the exercise, follow the steps in this book or in the onscreen exercise. In the onscreen list of chapters and exercises, click *Chapter 4: Drawing Organization and Inquiry Commands.* Click *Exercise: Use Quick Properties.*

1   Open *c_quick properties.dwg.*

2   On the status bar, right-click Quick Properties. Click Settings.

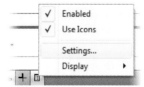

3   In the Drafting Settings dialog box, Quick Properties tab:
  - Place a check mark in the box next to the Enable Quick Properties Palette option.
  - For the Palette Display, click All Objects.

□ Enable Quick Properties Palette(CTRL+SHIFT+P)

Palette Display
    ◉ All objects
    ○ Only objects with specified properties

4   Under Palette Location:

- Click Cursor-dependent.
- For Quadrant, select Bottom-Right.
- For Distance in Pixels, enter **20.**

Palette Location
    ◉ Cursor-dependent
        Quadrant   Bottom-Right ▼
        Distance in pixels 20
    ○ Static

5   Under Palette Behavior:

- Verify that Collapse Palette Automatically is selected.
- For the minimum number of rows, enter **2.**

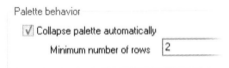

Palette behavior
    ☑ Collapse palette automatically
        Minimum number of rows 2

6   Click OK.

7   Select a line object in the drawing. The Quick Properties panel automatically appears to the bottom right of the cursor.

8   Move your cursor over the Quick Properties panel. The panel expands to display
    more properties.

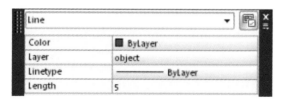

9   Press ESC to clear the selected line.

10 Select a dimension in the drawing. The Quick Properties panel automatically displays two
    property rows.

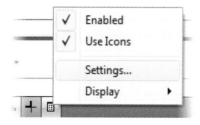

11 On the status bar, right-click Quick Properties. Click Settings.

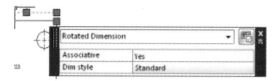

12 In the Drafting Settings dialog box, Quick Properties tab, under Palette Behavior, clear the
    check mark for the Collapse Palette Automatically option. Click OK.

13 Select a dimension in the drawing. The Quick Properties panel automatically expands.

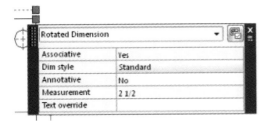

Rotated Dimension	
Associative	Yes
Dim style	Standard
Annotative	No
Measurement	2 1/2
Text override	

14 Press ESC to clear the selected dimension.

15 Close all files. Do not save.

Lesson 20 | Matching Object Properties

This lesson describes how to change the properties of objects in a drawing to match the properties of other objects in the drawing or in another drawing.

A typical drawing will contain objects with properties that are unique to the individual object and properties that are shared by other objects in the drawing.

After completing this lesson, you will be able to use the Match Properties command to apply the properties from a source object to destination objects.

The following illustration shows how several objects in the drawing can have common properties.

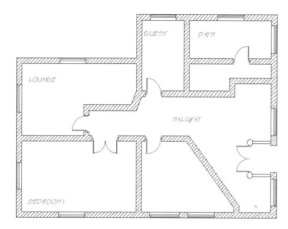

Objectives

After completing this lesson, you will be able to:

- Use the Match Properties command to apply the properties from a source object to destination objects.

Matching an Object's Properties

You use the Match properties command to assign properties of one object to another by selecting a source object and a destination object.

In the following illustration, the properties from a source hatch object (1) are applied to the destination hatch (2).

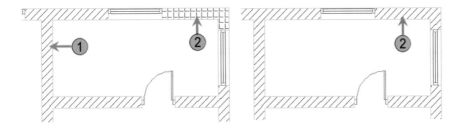

Command Access

 Match Properties

Command Line: **MATCHPROP**
Ribbon: **Home tab >Clipboard panel > Match Properties**

Menu: **Modify > Match Properties**

Property Settings Dialog Box

The properties that you select in the Property Settings dialog box determine which properties from the source object are copied to the destination objects. To adjust the Match Properties settings, after you activate the Match Properties command and select the source object, right-click anywhere in the drawing and select Settings.

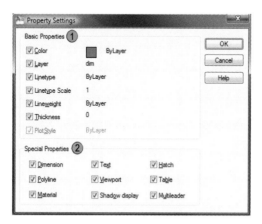

The Property Settings dialog box is divided into two areas, Basic Properties and Special Properties.

(1) Basic Properties are properties that are common to most objects.

(2) Special Properties are properties that are specific to a certain type of object. For example, if you select the Text option, the text style of the source object is assigned to the destination text object. In some situations, you may not want to copy the text style to the destination text, so you would clear the Text option. Only the basic properties that are selected are copied to the destination text.

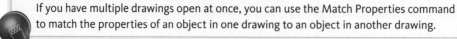

Match Properties Across Multiple Drawings

If you have multiple drawings open at once, you can use the Match Properties command to match the properties of an object in one drawing to an object in another drawing.

Procedure: Matching Object Properties

The following steps give an overview of using the Match Properties command to apply properties from a source object to a destination object.

1   On the ribbon, click Home tab > Clipboard Panel > Match Properties.

2   Select a source object.

3   To control which properties are assigned to the destination object, right-click anywhere in the drawing and click Settings. Select the properties in the Properties Settings dialog box.

4   Select the destination objects.

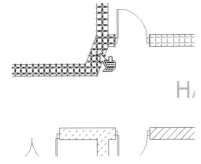

Guidelines for Matching Properties

- When you use the Match Properties command, you can select only one source object.
- You must select the source object directly. Implied windowing or other window selection methods are not available.
- You can match the properties from the source object to an unlimited number of objects. When selecting the destination objects, you can use any selection method.
- You can match properties from objects in one drawing to objects in another drawing that is opened.
- To adjust the matching properties settings, begin Match Properties, select the source object and right-click to access the Settings dialog box.

Practice Exercise | Match an Object's Properties

In this practice exercise, you create several rectangles on Layer 0. You create a new layer with specified properties and draw some rectangles on that layer. Then you use the Match Properties command on selected rectangles.

1   Begin a new, blank drawing.

2   Draw several rectangles on the default Layer 0.

3   Create a new layer:
   - In the Layer Properties dialog box, create a new layer with the following object properties:
     - Name: Test.
     - Color: blue.
     - Linetype: Hidden (first Load the hidden linetype into the drawing).
     - Lineweight: 0.35 (select Show Lineweight in the status bar).
   - Set this layer current.
   - Exit the dialog box.

4   Draw several more rectangles. The second set of rectangles should have the object properties designated in the new layer settings, and the first set of rectangles should have the default object properties.

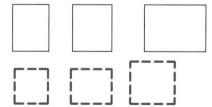

Note: *Select Show Lineweight on the status bar to view the new layer properties.*

5   To match the properties:
   - On the Home tab, click Clipboard Panel > Match Properties.
   - On the new layer, select one of the rectangles (1) that you have drawn.
   - Create a crossing window as indicated below to select the rectangles that are on layer 0.
   - Press ENTER to exit the Match Properties command.

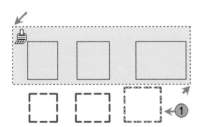

6   The object properties of the rectangles should now match.

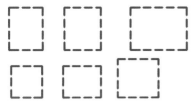

Exercise | Match Object Properties

In this exercise, you use the Match Properties command to apply one object's properties to other objects. When you have completed the exercise, you will be able to use the Match Properties command to aid in more efficient drawing creation.

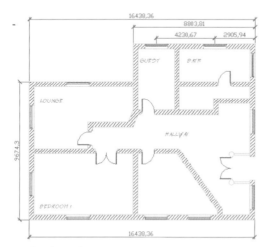

The completed exercise

Completing the Exercise
To complete the exercise, follow the steps in this book or in the onscreen exercise. In the onscreen list of chapters and exercises, click *Chapter 4: Drawing Organization and Inquiry Commands*. Click *Exercise: Match Object Properties*.

1   Open *C_Match-Properties1.dwg*.

2   To match the properties of one window block to others:
   • On the Home tab, click Clipboard Panel > Match Properties.
   • Select the window block (1) as the source object.
   • For the destination objects, select the window blocks located at (2), (3), and (4).
   • Press ENTER to exit the command.

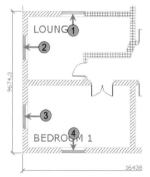

3   To match some of the properties from the single door to the double doors:

   • On the Home tab, click Clipboard Panel > Match Properties.
   • Select the single door swing arc (1).

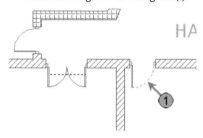

   • Right-click in the drawing window. Click Settings.
   • In the Property Settings dialog box, under Basic Properties, make sure the Color (2)
      option is cleared.
   • Click OK to return to the drawing window.

   • Make a crossing window at (3) and (4) to select the double doors as indicated below.

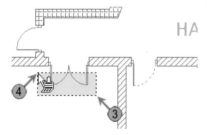

- Press ENTER to exit the Match Properties command.
  Note: Since the color of the double door was not set to ByLayer, it did not change. If you click any object on the double door, you notice that the Doors layer is displayed in the Layer Control list on the Layers panel.

4   To match some of the properties from one wall hatch to another:

- On the Home tab, click Clipboard Panel > Match Properties.
- Select the wall hatch (1) between the two doors as shown in the image below.

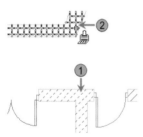

- Right-click in the drawing area. Click Settings.
- In the Property Settings dialog box, make sure the Hatch option is cleared and the Color option is selected.

- Click OK to exit the dialog box and return to the drawing window.
- Select the wall hatch (2) immediately above the source hatch.

Only the basic properties of the hatch change. Since the hatch style is not part of the basic properties, the hatch's pattern stays the same.

5   To match hatch styles between wall hatches:

- With the Match Properties command started, right-click and click Settings to open the Property Settings dialog box.
- Select the Hatch option. Click OK.
- In the drawing window, select the same hatch as in the previous step. This time, the hatch style changes along with the basic properties.
- Continue to select the rest of the mismatched wall hatches.
- Press ENTER to end the command.

6   To match properties across dimensions:

- On the Home tab, click Clipboard Panel > Match Properties.
- Select the overall dimension across the bottom of the drawing as the source object.

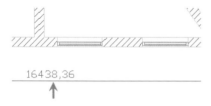

- Select all of the dimensions across the top of the drawing.
- Press ENTER to exit the Match Properties command.

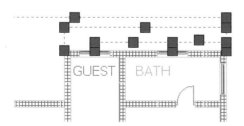

7   Open another drawing and match properties from objects in one drawing to another:

- Open the *C_Match-Properties2.dwg drawing*.
- On the View tab, click Window panel > Tile Vertically to view each drawing side by side.
- Select one drawing to activate the window and Zoom Extents.
- Select the other drawing window and repeat the Zoom Extents command.
- In the drawing that you just opened, zoom to the lower right corner where it reads CONFERENCE ROOM.

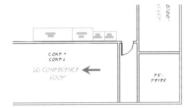

8   To match properties from one drawing to the next:

- On the Home tab, click Clipboard Panel > Match Properties.
- Select the LG. CONFERENCE text in the drawing as indicated above.
- Select the other drawing *C_Match- Properties1.dwg* to activate the drawing window.
- Select the text objects in the drawing.

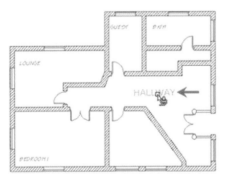

- Continue to select all of the text objects.
- Press ENTER to exit the command.

9   When object properties are matched from one drawing to another, all referenced object properties (i.e. layer, text style, linetype) are brought into the matched drawing.

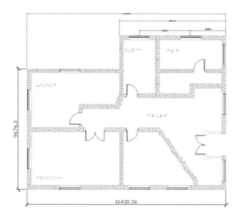

10   Close all files. Do not save.

Lesson 21 | Using the Properties Palette

This lesson describes the Properties palette and how to use it to modify object properties.

Each object you create has a set of properties that defines how the object appears in the drawing. In fact, as you create the objects, you are assigning properties as part of the geometry creation process. You can view and modify these properties with the Properties palette.

After completing this lesson, you will be able to use the Properties palette to adjust object properties.

The following illustration shows a typical drawing containing objects of different types. You can use the Properties palette to modify the common property types of dissimilar objects at the same time.

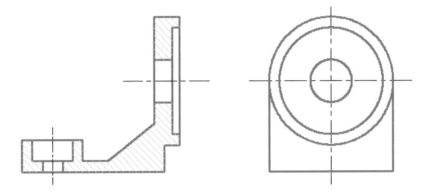

Objectives

After completing this lesson, you will be able to:

- Use the Properties palette to adjust object properties.

Using the Properties Palette

You can use the Properties palette to change the characteristics of an object such as its color, linetype, lineweight, or layer. The Properties palette is context sensitive, so it only displays the properties that are relevant to the type of object that you select.

Object Properties

Properties are organized into separate groups, such as General, Geometry, and Misc. Click the arrows on the title area for each group to collapse or expand the group.

Read-only properties are indicated by a gray background in the values column, and cannot be selected.

You can select read-write properties. Options for changing these properties vary with the property. Some are lists, some are simple text boxes, and others require you to click an icon in the field to redefine a point.

Command Access

Properties Palette

Command Line: **PROPERTIES**

Ribbon: **Home tab > Properties Panel > Dialog Box Launcher**

Menu: **Modify > Properties; Tools > Palettes > Properties; right-click an object > Properties**

Keyboard Shortcut: **CTRL+1**

Tip

You can also double-click on some objects to access the Properties palette.

Selecting Objects Using the Object Types List

When you have multiple object types selected, the Object Types list shows all of the objects. When you select different types of objects, the Properties palette displays only those property types that are common to all object types that are selected. For each object type that you select, the object type name appears in the list. You can select an object type in the list to adjust properties for the selected objects of that type.

For example, in the following illustration, the Object Type list is shown with two objects that are selected, a polyline and a text object.

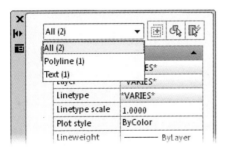

Procedure: Using the Properties Palette to Change Object Properties

The following steps give an overview of using the Properties palette to change object properties.

1   On the ribbon, click Home tab > Properties panel > Dialog Box Launcher > Properties or press CTRL+1.

2   Select the objects to adjust properties for.

3   You can change any value in a read-write field and all changes occur in real time.

4   Press ESC to cancel the object selection. The Properties palette remains open.

Key Points for Using the Properties Palette

- The Properties palette differs from a traditional dialog box interface in that it can remain open while you are using other commands.
- Other methods are available for editing an object's properties, but the Properties palette provides a common interface for changes to different object types and to the properties of multiple objects simultaneously.
- Click the Auto-hide icon on the Properties palette (shown in the following illustration) to make the palette collapse when the cursor moves away from it.

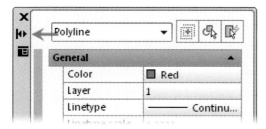

Exercise | Manipulate Object Properties

In this exercise, you learn how the Properties palette functions. When you have completed the exercise, you will be able to effectively manipulate objects and their properties using the Properties palette.

The completed exercise

Completing the Exercise

To complete the exercise, follow the steps in this book or in the onscreen exercise. In the onscreen list of chapters and exercises, click *Chapter 4: Drawing Organization and Inquiry Commands*. Click *Exercise: Manipulate Object Properties*.

---

1   Open *C_Properties-Palette.dwg*.

2   To open the Properties palette, press CTRL+1.
    Note: If the Properties palette is already open, CTRL+1 will close it. You can also access the Properties palette by double-clicking an object in the drawing. This either opens the Properties palette if it is not currently open, expands the palette if Auto-hide is set, sets the focus to the palette if it was already open, or launches the PEDIT command if you double-click a polyline.

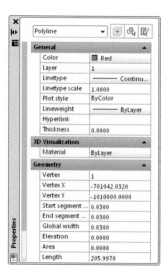

3   Click the Auto-hide button in the upper left corner of the Properties palette as shown in the image.

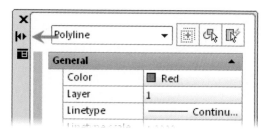

This causes the Properties palette to expand when you move the mouse over it and contract when the mouse moves away. You can also dock the palette by dragging it to the edge of the application window.

4   Change object properties using the palette:

- Select all of the objects in the drawing.
- On the Properties palette, change the color and linetype to ByLayer.
- Press ESC to clear the selection and notice the change in color.

5   Zoom in to the area shown.

-701263.4518

6   To change the color of selected polylines:

- Select all of the geometry in the window.
- On the Properties palette, select Polyline from the Object Type list.
- Select the Color property and set it to Blue.
- Press ESC and notice that all polylines in the selection are now blue.

Kosmonosy

7   To change the display of the drawing:

- Zoom to the extents of the drawing.
- Zoom to the area shown in the image.

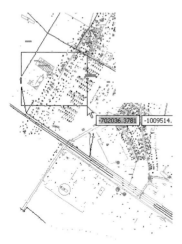

8   To select objects to change:

- On the Home tab, click Layers panel > Layer. Turn off Layer 1 in the Layer list.
- Select the large circle in the view.

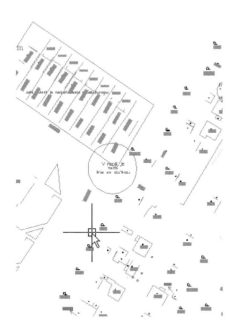

9   To change the diameter of the circle using the palette:

- On the Properties palette, change the Diameter to **64.**
- Press ENTER.
  The diameter changes.

Center Z	0.0000
Radius	32.0000
Diameter	64.0000
Circumference	201.0619
Area	3216.9909
Normal X	0.0000
Normal Y	0.0000
Normal Z	1.0000

10   Use a crossing window selection to select more objects in the view.

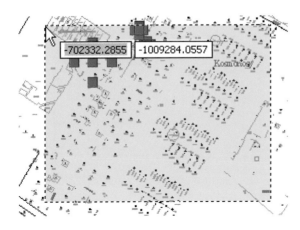

11   To change object properties by filtering:

- Use the Object List at the top of the Properties palette to filter just the circle objects.
  The properties common to all circles appear in the Properties palette.
- Change the diameter to **32** units.
- Press ENTER.
- The diameters of all circles in the selected view change to 32.

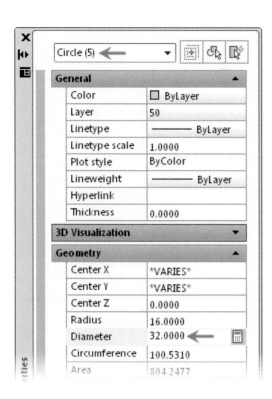

12 Close all files. Do not save.

Lesson 22 | Using Linetypes

This lesson describes how to use linetypes in your drawings. After completing this lesson, you will be able to describe linetypes and how they are used in a drawing and use the Linetype Manager to add linetypes to your drawing.

Linetypes are used to distinguish objects in the drawing from one another. You can use them to represent hidden geometry in a specific view, to show centerlines for dimensioning, or perhaps just to add clarity to the drawing.

For example, the following illustration shows a solid linetype used for geometry and a centerline linetype used for centerlines for dimensioning. The dashed linetype indicates hidden geometry.

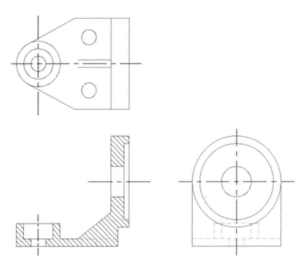

Objectives

After completing this lesson, you will be able to:

- Describe linetypes and how they are used in a drawing.
- Use the Linetype Manager to add linetypes to your drawing.

About Linetypes

In a typical drawing, you find linetypes associated with many objects. While the specific linetypes used may vary from one discipline to another, the concept of using linetypes remains consistent. They are always used to distinguish objects from one another and to make the drawing easier to read and understand.

The following illustration contains continuous, hidden, and center linetypes. Each of these linetypes have meaning within the discipline in which they are used.

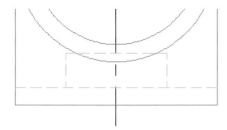

Linetypes Defined

Linetypes are an attribute of an object that determines how it looks. The linetype helps to distinguish one object from another in a design. For example, a hot water line could be represented by the HW linetype and a gas line in a building could be represented by the GAS linetype.

This image shows common linetypes used in drafting and design.

——————————   —— ——————————

—— —— —— —— —— —— —— —— ——

——— GAS ——— GAS ——— GAS ———

——— HW ——— HW ——— HW ———

Linetype Examples

In the following image, you see two pieces of steel overlapping one another. It is impossible to tell which object lies on top of the other.

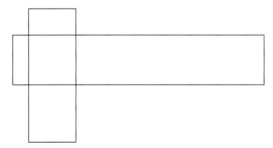

This second image uses hidden lines on the vertical steel object to show you that it lies beneath the horizontal piece of steel.

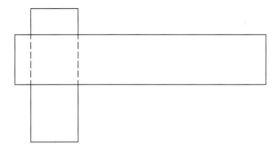

Linetype Key Points

- Linetypes are used to distinguish objects from one another.
- Linetypes add visual clarity to the drawing.

Adding Linetypes to Your Drawing

To add linetypes to your drawing, you generally assign the linetype to layers and then create objects on the appropriate layers. The object's linetype can be set to ByLayer, which means the object assumes the linetype of the layer.

By default, the only linetype available in the drawing is Continuous. To use additional linetypes, you must load them into the drawing. The primary method for adding linetypes to the drawing is with the Linetype Manager.

Command Access

Linetype Manager
Command Line: **LINETYPE**
Ribbon: **Home tab > Properties Panel > Linetype list > Other**

Menu Bar: **Format > Linetype**

About the Linetype Manager

The Linetype Manager dialog box displays all of the linetypes that are currently loaded in the drawing. To load additional linetypes, click Load. To delete linetypes, select the linetype and click Delete. You cannot delete a linetype if it is currently being referenced by other objects in the drawing.

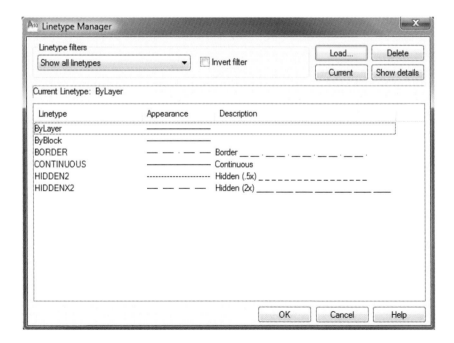

Loading Linetypes

When you select Load from the Linetype Manager dialog box a list of linetypes provided by AutoCAD appears that lets you add additional linetypes to the drawing. You can scroll through the list and select the desired linetypes.

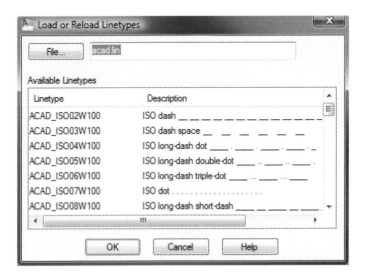

Loading Linetypes from the Layer Property Manager

You can also add linetypes to a drawing from the Layer Properties Manager. Click to assign the linetype to a layer. If the linetype is not available in the Select Linetype dialog box, click Load to load the linetype using the Load or Reload Linetypes dialog box.

Controlling Linetype Scale

Depending on the size of the objects in your drawing, you may have to adjust the linetype scale in order for the lines to appear correctly. For example, to see the gaps in a centerline that is 12 units long, you would set your linetype scale to 1.0, but to see the gaps correctly in a centerline that is 240 units long, you would set your linetype scale to 10.0.

In the following illustration, both lines are center linetypes, but the lower line appears with a more dense pattern as a result of a smaller linetype scale.

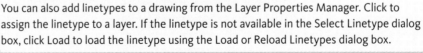

You can control linetype scale in the drawing using two different methods.

- **LTSCALE**: This is a global linetype scale factor that affects all of the objects that use linetypes in the drawing. To change the global linetype scale, on the command line, enter **LTSCALE** and then enter a positive number. The default scale factor is set to 1.
- **Linetype Scale property**: You can set the linetype scale factor for selected objects. Double-click the object to access the Properties palette (or right-click and select Properties from the shortcut menu). Enter a new value in the Linetype Scale property field. The Linetype Scale property works in combination with the global linetype scale factor for the drawing. For example, if the global linetype scale factor is set to 2 and the linetype scale property is set to 0.5, the net result is a linetype scale factor of 1 for the selected object.

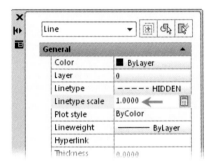

Properties Palette

Procedure: Adding Linetypes to a Drawings

The following steps give an overview of adding linetypes to a drawing.

1   On the ribbon, click Home tab > Properties panel > Linetype list > Other.

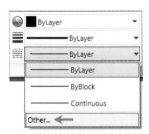

2   In the Linetype Manager, click Load.

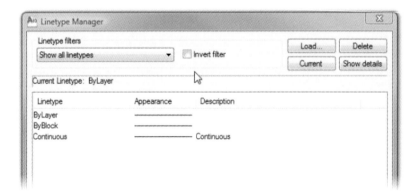

3   In the Load or Reload Linetypes dialog box, select the linetypes. Click OK.

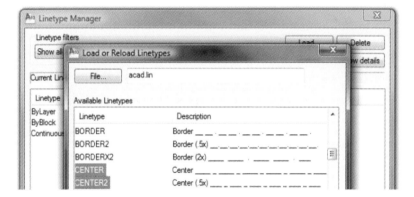

Press SHIFT or CTRL to select more than one linetype.

4   The selected linetypes appear in the Linetype Manager. Click OK.

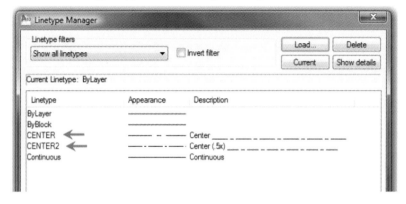

5   The linetypes are now available to apply to layers or individual objects.

Linetype Management Guidelines

- By default, a blank drawing will contain only one linetype, the continuous linetype.
- Add only the linetypes that you need for your drawing.
- Delete linetypes that are not being referenced or used from the Linetype Manager dialog box or with the PURGE command.
- A linetype that is being referenced or used cannot be deleted.
- To use other linetypes, you must load them into the drawing first and then apply them to the object or layer.
- Control linetype scale with the LTSCALE command. For example, an LT scale of 24 will multiply the size of all of the linetypes in a drawing by 24.
- Set the linetype scale of individual objects only when necessary using the Properties palette. Linetype scale settings made to individual objects are multiplied by the overall LTSCALE factor.
- Certain linetypes are available at 2 times the normal size. Example: HIDDEN, HIDDEN2 (.5x) and HIDDENX2 (2x).
- By default, all object properties are drawn in the ByLayer mode, so objects will take on the property settings of the current layer. You can override the default mode by selecting a specific linetype from the Linetype list on the Properties panel.

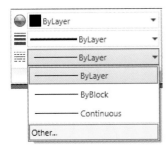

Practice Exercise | Add Linetypes to Your Drawing

In this practice exercise, you draw a simple object. You add the HIDDEN linetype to the drawing, apply it to the object that you create, and then change the LTSCALE.

1   Begin a new drawing and make a rectangle.

2   To access the Linetype Manager:

- On the Home tab, click Properties panel > Linetype list > Other.

3   To load the linetype:

- In the Linetype Manager dialog box, click Load.
- In the Load or Reload Linetypes dialog box, scroll to find the HIDDEN linetype.

- Click the HIDDEN linetype.
- Click OK to load and exit the dialog boxes.

4   To apply the hidden linetype to the object:

- With the command line blank, click the rectangle.
- On the Home tab, click Properties panel > Linetype list.
- Select HIDDEN.

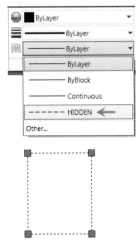

- Press ESC to deselect the rectangle and view the results.

5   To change the linetype scale:

- On the command line, enter **LTSCALE**. Press ENTER.
- Enter a new scale factor of **2**. Press ENTER. View the results.

Exercise | Use Linetypes

In this exercise, you load linetypes into the drawing and assign them to layers. You then create new geometry using the new linetypes.

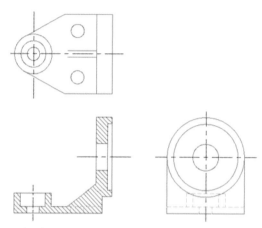

The completed exercise

Completing the Exercise

To complete the exercise, follow the steps in this book or in the onscreen exercise. In the onscreen list of chapters and exercises, click *Chapter 4: Drawing Organization and Inquiry Commands*. Click *Exercise: Use Linetypes*.

1   Open *M_Using-Linetypes.dwg*.

2   To load linetypes:

   • On the Home tab, click Properties panel > Linetype list > Other.

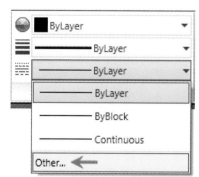

- In the Linetype Manager dialog box, click Load.
- In the Load or Reload Linetypes dialog box, locate and click the CENTER linetype.
- Locate the HIDDEN linetype and press CTRL+click the linetype (this enables you to select more than one option from the list, but not the options in between).

- Click OK to load the lines and to exit the dialog boxes.

3   To apply the loaded linetypes to the selected layers:

- On the Home tab, click Layers panel > Layer Properties.

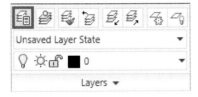

- In the Layer Properties Manager dialog box, find the CENTER layer and click the linetype field for that layer (currently Continuous).
- In the Select Linetype dialog box, click the CENTER linetype. Click OK.
- This applies the CENTER linetype to the CENTER layer.

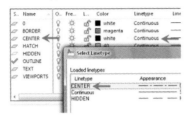

- Repeat the steps to apply the HIDDEN linetype to the HIDDEN layer.
  Note: Linetypes may also be loaded from this dialog box.
- Click OK to exit the dialog box and close the Layer Properties Manager.

4   Notice that the centerlines now appear in the drawing. To change the linetype scale:

- On the command line, enter **LTSCALE**. Press ENTER.
- For the scale factor, enter **.75**. Press ENTER.
  Notice the effect that the new linetype scale has on the centerlines.

5   To create another centerline, first make the Center layer current:

- On the Home tab, click Layers panel › Make Object's Layer Current.

- Select any centerline on the drawing. The current layer should now be the Center layer.

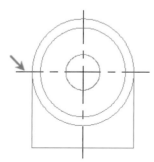

- Start the Line command.
- Use object snap tracking to track a line from the center object snap above and below the object as indicated below.

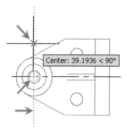

6   Before drawing the hidden lines, make the HIDDEN layer current. Freeze the HATCH layer and select the appropriate object snap settings:

- On the Home tab, click Layers panel > Layer list. Select HIDDEN to make it current.

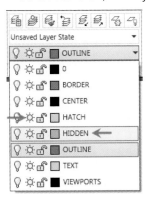

- Select the Layer List again and Freeze the HATCH layer.
- On the status bar, be sure that polar tracking, object snap, and object snap tracking are all selected.
- On the status bar, right-click Object Snap. Click Settings.

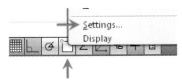

- Select the Endpoint, Quadrant, Intersection, and Perpendicular object snap modes.

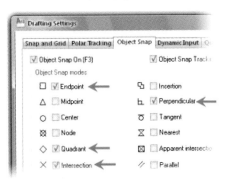

- Use the Line command to draw two line segments in the front view that track the right and left quadrants of the small circles in the top view. Draw the line segments so that they intersect the slanted line and are perpendicular to the bottom line as indicated below.

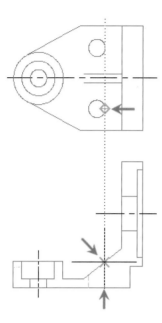

7 Use the same technique to draw the hidden lines in the side view:

- Using the line command, track the endpoint of the corner in the front view as indicated *(do not select this endpoint!)*.
- Drag the cursor to the side view until it intersects with the left vertical line of the object and click.
- Drag the cursor to the right side of the object to draw the line perpendicular to the right vertical line and click.
- Press ENTER to complete the line command.
- Repeat to create the other horizontal line using the adjacent corner in the front view.

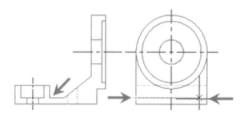

8 To refine the hidden hole detail in the front view:

- Zoom to this area.
- Trace the endpoint of the inside corner *(DO NOT click the endpoint)*.
- Drag the cursor until it intersects with the vertical hidden line and click.

Chapter 4 | Drawing Organization and Inquiry Commands

- Drag the line until it is perpendicular with the vertical hidden line to the right and click.

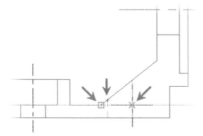

- Zoom in closer to view the hidden line segments.
- With the command line blank, select the vertical lines.
- Drag the upper endpoints down to the endpoints or perpendicular to the horizontal line.

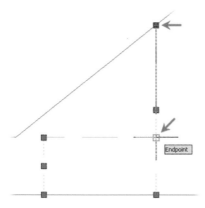

9   To refine the hidden hole detail in the side view, you copy lines from the front view and modify them:

- Start the Copy command.
- Window select from left to right to select the hole detail in the side view.

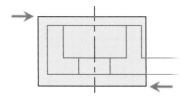

- Press ENTER to complete the selection.

- Click the intersection of the centerline and the bottom line in the front view as the base point.

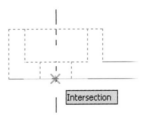

Intersection

- Drag the copied objects to the right. Click the intersection point of the centerline and bottom line in that view.

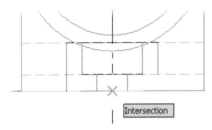

Intersection

- Press ENTER to complete the Copy command.

10   To change the linetypes and modify the copied lines:

- With the command line blank, select the lines that you just copied.
- Click the lower grip in the line segment on the left. Drag it perpendicular to the horizontal line as indicated.

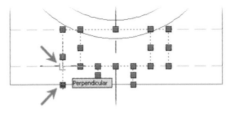

Perpendicular

- With the objects still selected, on the Home tab, click Layer Control list > Hidden.

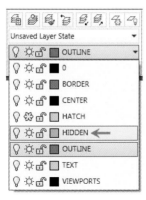

- Press ESC to deselect all lines.
  The previously selected lines should all be on the HIDDEN layer.
- With the command line blank, select the upper hidden horizontal line.
- Select the endpoint on the right and drag it to the endpoint object snap of the vertical hidden line as indicated below. Use the intersection or perpendicular object snap mode.

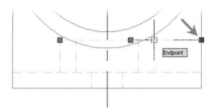

- Repeat this for the opposite endpoint.

11 To change the linetype scale of the selected line segments:

- With the command line blank, select the two short hidden line segments as indicated below.
- Right-click and select Properties.

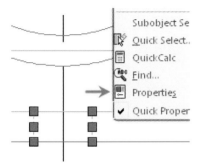

- In the Linetype scale field, enter **.5**.
- Press ENTER to apply this change to the selected lines.
- Click the X in the upper left corner of the Properties dialog box to close it.
- Press ESC to deselect the line segments.

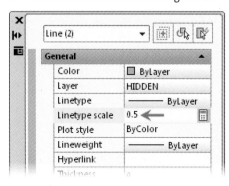

- Observe that the linetype scale changes to the scale of the previously selected lines.

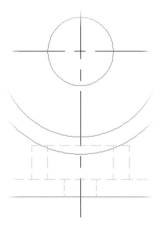

12   To convert other lines to the HIDDEN layer:

- With the command line blank, select the hole details as indicated below.

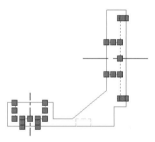

- In the Layer Control list, select the HIDDEN layer.
- Press ESC to deselect the lines and observe the change.

13 To complete this side view, it will no longer be a section view. Modify the lines accordingly:

- With the command line blank, select the vertical line as indicated below.
- Click the lower grip and use object tracking to track the inside corner as indicated.
- Press ESC to deselect the line and grips.

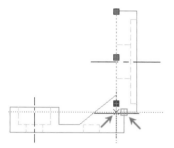

14 To adjust the horizontal lines:

- With the command line blank, select the line that is indicated below.
- Select the left grip and drag it to the newly located endpoint of the vertical line.

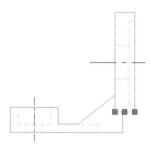

- Press ESC to deselect the line, then click the other horizontal line that is indicated below. Select the right endpoint grip and drag it so that the line is perpendicular to the vertical line to its right.

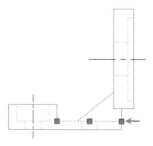

15 To delete the underlying line segment:

- With the command line blank, use a window to select the short line segment, clicking from left to right.

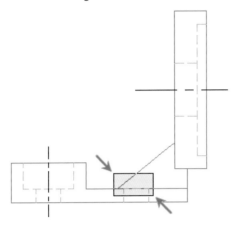

- Use the Erase command or press DELETE.

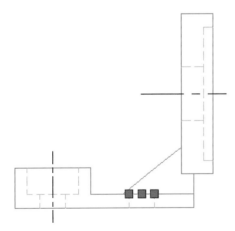

Note: It is important to pay attention to the lines that are on top of other lines and delete those that are not necessary.

16 To erase the hatch pattern that is no longer necessary:

- In the Layer Control list, thaw the HATCH layer.
- With the command line blank, select the hatch pattern.
- When it is highlighted, enter **E**. Press ENTER.
- Zoom out to observe the changes.

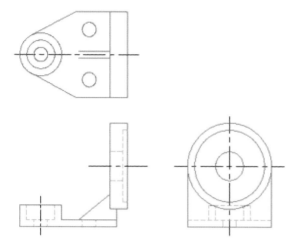

17 Close all files. Do not save.

Lesson 23 | Using Inquiry Commands

This lesson describes how to use the Measuregeom command and other inquiry commands to obtain geometric information on objects in the drawing.

As you create objects, the defining points and object types are stored in the drawing database. You can use the commands on the Inquiry toolbar to retrieve this information or to obtain distances, angles, areas, object types, and other important data for objects.

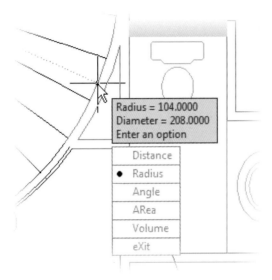

Objectives

After completing this lesson, you will be able to:

- Describe measuring and explain why the data is useful.
- Describe how to use measure tools including distance, radius, angle, area, and volume.
- Obtain information about objects, such as type, location, dimensions and properties.

About Measuring

You can calculate the distance, radius, angle, area, and volume of selected objects or a sequence of points by measuring.

Measuring is especially useful when collecting data for building and manufacturing. In the following illustration, Radius is used to obtain the brick arch radius and is mandatory for accurate construction.

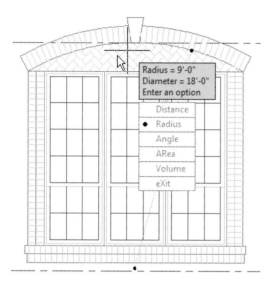

Definition of Measuring

Measuring is used to ascertain the extent, dimensions, and capacity of certain objects. Measuring enables you to obtain geometric information from such things as arches, room areas, polylines, and 3D solids.

Example of Area Measurement

The following illustration shows the results of using the Area tool to obtain the total square footage of a floor plan.
Note: The Area tool also provides perimeter data.

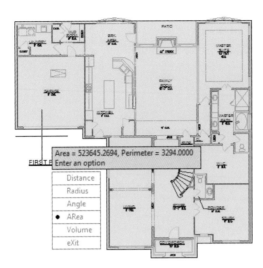

Using Measure Tools

Measure tools are used to pull specific data from objects. They provide a quick and effective way to collect useful information such as the total amount of concrete needed for a foundation or the precise volume of an excavation area. This information is frequently necessary to communicate pertinent measurements to outside sources or to ensure that a design meets criteria. The process for obtaining such information is combined into a single command in which different measurement options are chosen.

The following illustration shows the Volume option that is used to acquire data from a 3D object.

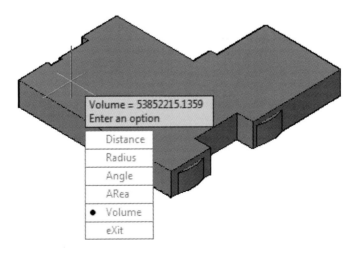

Command Access

Measuregeom

Command entry: **measuregeom**

Ribbon: **Home tab > Utilities panel > Measure drop-down > Distance/Radius/Angle/Area/Volume**

Menu: **Tools > Inquiry > Distance/Radius/Angle/Area/Volume**

Measure Command Options

The following illustrates the different measuring tools and what they are used for.

Option	Description
Distance	Measures the distance between two specified points or totals the distance between multiple points.
Radius	Measures the radius and diameter of a specified arc or circle.
Angle	Measures the angle of a specified arc, circle, line, or vertex.
Area	Measures the area and perimeter of an object or defined area. There are also options to keep a running total as you define areas or to subtract specified regions from total calculated area.
Volume	Measures the volume of an object or a defined area. There are also options to keep a running total as you define volume or to subtract specified regions from total calculated volume.

> **Selection Accuracy is Key**
>
> For the same reason you use object snaps to create geometry, using object snaps to select points for Inquiry commands is critical. If you estimate the point selection, the value returned will not be accurate.

Measure Distance

The Distance option of the Measuregeom command prompts you to select two points on the drawing and then returns information about the distance between them, their angles in and from the XY plane, and their delta values (distance traveled along each axis) in both 2D and 3D planes. The information is presented to you on the command line in the format shown below. You can also see it in the Text Window by pressing F2.

Distance = 157.1924, Angle in XY Plane = 34, Angle from XY Plane = 0Delta X = 130.3938, Delta Y = 87.7889, Delta Z = 0.0000

The following image illustrates the values returned with the Distance command.

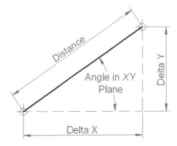

Process: Measuring Distance

The following steps give an overview for acquiring the distance between two points using the Distance option of the Measuregeom command.

1. On the ribbon, click Home tab > Utilities panel > Measure drop-down > Distance.

2. Select first point.

Chapter 4 | Drawing Organization and Inquiry Commands

3   Enter **M** for Multiple Points and select second point.

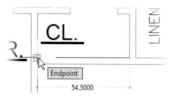

4   Continue to select points until you arrive at starting point.

5   Right-click and select Enter to close command.

6   Note running total of the distance acquired.

Process: Measuring Radius

The following steps give an overview for acquiring the radius using the Radius option of the Measuregeom command.

1   On the ribbon, click Home tab > Utilities panel > Measure drop-down > Radius.

2   Select arc.

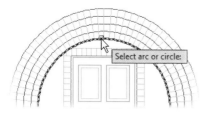

3   Note radius and diameter of arc.

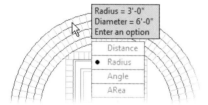

Procedure: Measuring an Angle

The following steps give an overview for acquiring the angle of two lines using the Angle option of the Measuregeom command.

1   On the ribbon, click Home tab > Utilities panel > Measure drop-down > Angle.

2   Select first line.

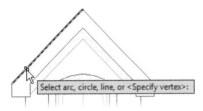

3   Select second line.

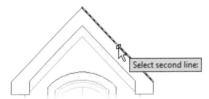

4   Observe resulting angle.

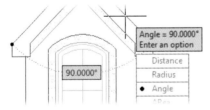

Process: Measuring Area

The following steps give an overview for acquiring the area of a space using the Area option of the Measuregeom command.

1   On the ribbon, click Home tab > Utilities panel > Measure drop-down > Area.

2   Enter **Add** at the command prompt and select the first point.

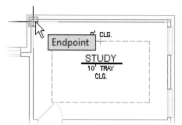

3   Continue selecting points in a sequence that defines the perimeter of the area. Press Enter.

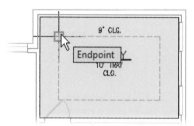

4   Enter **Subtract** at the command prompt and select the first point of the area to subtract.

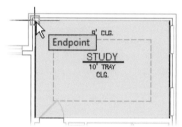

5   Continue selecting points until you arrive back at the starting point. Press ENTER and note the new total area.

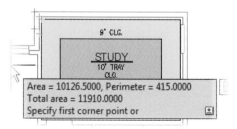

ID Point

With the ID Point command, you can retrieve the precise location of any point in the drawing. When you start the ID Point command, you are prompted to specify a point. This can be a point in the drawing or a point on an object. The ID Point command returns the coordinate of the point you select, as shown below.

X = 624.3266 Y = 208.1684 Z = 0.0000

As with all other Inquiry commands, the values are returned in the current units of the drawing.

Command Access

 ID Point

Command Line: **ID**
Ribbon: **Home tab > Utilities panel > ID Point**

Menu bar: **Tools > Inquiry > ID Point**

Selection Accuracy is Key

For the same reason you use object snaps to create geometry, using object snaps to select points for Inquiry commands is critical. If you estimate the point selection, the value returned will not be accurate.

Procedure: Identifying a Precise Location

The following steps give an overview of identifying a precise location in the drawing.

1   Start the ID command.

2   Use an object snap to accurately select a point in the drawing. The coordinate is displayed on the command line.
Note: F2 will display the entire AutoCAD Text Window.

Guidelines

Consider the following guidelines when using the Measure tools:

- When you measure an object, the position at which you select the object determines the measurement of the object.
- If you use multiple points, a running total of the distance based on existing line segments and the current rubber band line is calculated.
- The Measuregeom command cannot calculate the area of a self-intersecting object.
- With the Area tool you may turn on the Add or Subtract mode and either keep a running total of area as you define areas or subtract a specified area from the total area.
- With the Volume tool you may turn on the Add or Subtract mode and either keep a running total of volume as you define regions or subtract a specified region from the total volume.
- When using the Volume tool, you may select 3D solids or 2D objects. However, if you select a 2D object you must specify a height for that object.
- You can select polylines when using the Distance, Area, and Volume options.

Practice Exercise | Acquiring Distance and Coordinates

In this practice exercise you make a simple drawing, then you inquire about the distance between two points and coordinate the information.

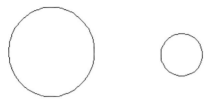

1   Draw two circles (any size).

2   To acquire the distance between two points:

- Begin the Distance command.
- With Object Snap on, specify the Center of one circle as the first distance.

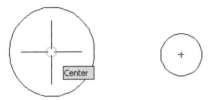

- Specify the Center of the other circle.
- View the distance in the command line or in the AutoCAD Text Window (F2)

3   To view the X and Y coordinates of a specific point:

- Begin the ID command.
- With Object Snap on, specify the Center of one of the circles you have drawn.
- View the coordinate in the command line or in the AutoCAD Text Window (F2).
  Note that the type and precision of the coordinate and distance information is determined by the settings in the Drawing Units.

Obtaining Object Information

List Command

The List command returns information on objects you select in the drawing. The information is displayed in the text window. The type of information retrieved is dependent on the type of object you select. You can select one or more objects to obtain information such as:

- Object type.
- Space (model or paper).
- Layer.
- Handle (unique identifier in the drawing database).
- Geometric data (location, size, etc.).

The following image represents an object created with the Polygon command. The information following the image represents the information provided by the List command when this type of object is selected.

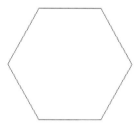

```
           LWPOLYLINE  Layer: "0"
                    Space: Model space
            Handle = 189
       Closed
Constant width     0.0000
         area     18.0708
    perimeter     15.8239

    at point   X=  14.6546  Y=  10.4486  Z=   0.0000
    at point   X=  13.3359  Y=  12.7325  Z=   0.0000
    at point   X=  10.6986  Y=  12.7325  Z=   0.0000
    at point   X=   9.3799  Y=  10.4486  Z=   0.0000
    at point   X=  10.6986  Y=   8.1646  Z=   0.0000
    at point   X=  13.3359  Y=   8.1646  Z=   0.0000
```

Command Access

List

Command Line: **LIST, LI**
Ribbon: **Home tab > Properties panel > List**

Menu bar: **Tools > Inquiry > List**

Listing Multiple Objects
If you select multiple objects, the properties for each object will be listed sequentially in the text window.

Procedure: Obtaining Information About Objects

The following steps give an overview of using the List command to information about objects.

1   Start the List command.

2   Select one or more objects. Press ENTER.
    Information about the selected objects is listed in the text window.

Practice Exercise | Obtaining Object Information

In this practice exercise, you draw each type of object that you have learned: circle, arc, line, and rectangle. You also practice the List command and observe what information is displayed for each unique object.

1   Draw the following objects (any size):
    - Circle
    - Line
    - Arc
    - Rectangle
2   To List each object separately:
    - Begin the List command.
    - Select the circle and press ENTER.
    - Observe the information listed in the AutoCAD Text Window.
    - Press F2 to close the text window.
3   Repeat the previous steps for each object drawn.

Exercise | Obtain Geometric Information

In this exercise, you use the Inquiry commands to obtain geometric information about objects and points in a drawing.

You obtain information about the numbered objects and points in the following illustration.

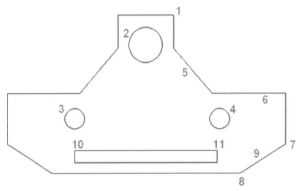

The completed exercise

Completing the Exercise
To complete the exercise, follow the steps in this book or in the onscreen exercise. In the onscreen list of chapters and exercises, click *Chapter 4: Drawing Organization and Inquiry Commands*. Click *Exercise: Obtain Geometric Information*.

1   Open *M_Inquiry.dwg*.

2   On the ribbon, click Home tab > Utilities panel. If the Utilities panel is not visible, right-click anywhere on the ribbon and then click Panels > Utilities panel.

3   On the Utilities panel click Measure and then click Distance. Use the Endpoint object snap and select points (7) and (8).

  • What is the distance? _____
  • What is the angle? _____

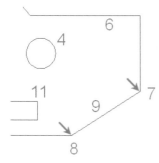

4   On the Utilities panel click Measure and then click Radius. Select circle (2) and press ENTER. Repeat this procedure for circle (3) and circle (4).

   - What is the radius for circle (2)? _____
   - What is the radius for circle (3)? _____
   - What is the radius for circle (4)? _____
     Note: The List command also displays the radius of circles.

5   Enter **List** on the command line and select the rectangle between points (10) and (11). Press ENTER.

   - What type of object is it? _____
   - What Layer is the rectangle on? _____
   - What is the area of the rectangle? _____
   - What is the perimeter of the rectangle? _____

6   Close the Text Window.

7   On the Utilities panel, click Measure and select Distance. Then select Distance and select the center points of circles (2 and 3).

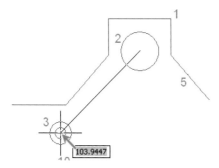

8   Repeat the Distance command and select the center points of circles (2 and 4).

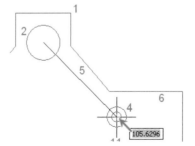

9   Press F2 to open the Text Window.

- What is the Distance between circle (2) and circle (3)? _____
- What is the Distance between circle (2) and circle (4)? _____

10 Close the Text Window.

11 Repeat the List command and select line (5). Press ENTER.

- What is the angle of the line? _____
- What is the Delta X value? _____
- What is the Delta Y value? _____

12 Close the Text Window.

13 On the Utilities panel, click ID Point and use the Endpoint object snap to select point (1).

- What are the coordinate values?
- X:_____
- Y:_____
- Z:_____

14 On the Utilities panel, click Measure and then select Area. Click Area.

- Right-click anywhere in the drawing. Click Add.
- Beginning at point (1), use objects snaps to select the endpoints around the outer profile.
- After you select all points, press ENTER.
- Right-click anywhere in the drawing. Click Subtract.
- Right-click anywhere in the drawing. Click Object.
- Select each of the three circles.
- Select the rectangle.
- Press ENTER.
- What is the net area of the profile after subtracting the circles? _____

15 Exit the Area command.

16 Close all files without saving.

Answers to Exercise Questions

Step	Answer

3. Distance = 55 mm.
Angle = 212 degrees.

4. Radius for circle 2 = 17.25 mm
Radius for circle 3 = 10.00 mm
Radius for circle 4 = 10.00 mm

5. Object type = LWPOLYLINE
Layer = Visible
Area = 1764.00 mm
Perimeter = 318.00 mm

9. Distance between circles 2 and 3 = 103.9447 mm
Distance between circles 2 and 4 = 105.6296 mm

11. Angle = 131 degrees
Delta X = -39.6953 mm
Delta Y = 44.9275 mm

13. X = 253.1353
Y = 0.0000
Z = 0.0000

14. Net area = 24255.3940 mm

Exercise | Measure Objects

In this exercise, you use distance, radius, angle, area, and volume to extract specific data from the floor plan.

The completed exercise

Completing the Exercise

To complete the exercise, follow the steps in this book or in the onscreen exercise. In the onscreen list of chapters and exercises, click *Chapter 4: Additional Enhancements*. Click *Exercise: Measure Objects*.

1   Open *I_Measure.dwg*.

2   Zoom into the powder room at the right side of drawing.

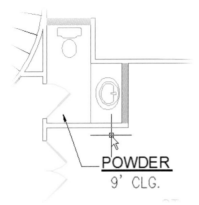

3   On the Home tab, click Utilities panel > Measure drop-down > Distance.

4   Acquire the total lengths of the walls in the powder room.

- Select the first point in the powder room
- At the command line prompt, enter **M** and press ENTER to use the Multiple points option.

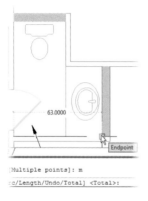

- Continue clicking each inside corner until you arrive back at the original starting point.
- Notice the total length of all walls in the powder room.

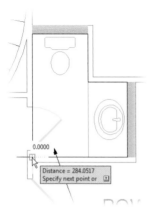

5   Acquire the radius of the stairway wall.

   • On the Home tab, click Utilities panel > Measure drop-down > Radius.
   • Select the outside edge of the curved stairway wall to the left of the powder room.

   • Click the wall to acquire the wall's radius.

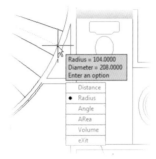

6   Use the angle option to ensure the walls are at a 90 degree angle.

   • On the Home tab, click Utilities panel > Measure drop-down > Angle.
   • Select the bottom wall of the powder room.

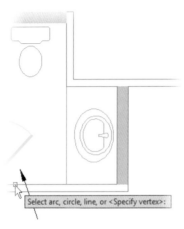

- Select the wall behind the sink.

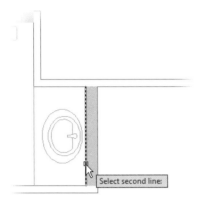

- Verify that the two walls are at a 90 degree angle.

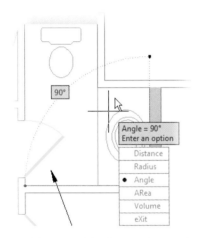

7   Find the area of the floor in the powder room.

- On the Home tab, click Utilities panel > Measure drop-down > Area.
- Click each of the interior corners of the powder room consecutively.

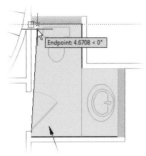

- Finish clicking points at your starting point.
- Press ENTER to view the area of the powder room floor.

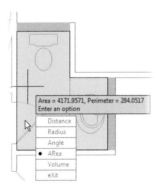

8   Find the volume of the powder room.

- On the Home tab, click Utilities panel > Measure drop-down > Volume.
- Click each of the interior corners of the powder room consecutively.
- Press ENTER. You are prompted to enter a height.
- For height, enter **108** (note the 9' ceiling height). Press ENTER.
- Notice the volume of the room.

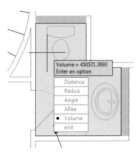

9   Close all files. Do not save the drawings.

Challenge Exercise | Architectural

In this exercise, you use what you learned about drawing organization and inquiry commands to create layers, manipulate objects and their layers, and create additional geometry on the correct layer.

> **Note**
> You have the option of completing this exercise using either imperial or metric units. Select one version of the exercise to complete the steps.

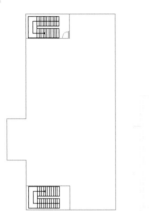

The completed exercise

> **Completing the Exercise**
> To complete the exercise, follow the steps in this book or in the onscreen exercise. In the onscreen list of chapters and exercises, click *Chapter 4: Drawing Organization and Inquiry Commands*. Click *Challenge Exercise: Architectural Metric*.

Metric Units

1 Open the drawing you saved from the previous challenge exercise, or open *M_ARCH-Challenge- CHP04.dwg.*

2 Create nine layers with the following names and color properties:

- Annotation = white
- Dimension = red
- Doors = 30
- Plumbing Fixtures = magenta

- Stairs = white
- Titleblock = red
- Wall-Interior = cyan
- Windows = blue
- Viewports = 9

3   Put the stair geometry on the Stairs layer and the door geometry on the Doors layer.

4   Thaw the Existing Building - Apparatus Bay layer.

5   Save and close the drawing.

Completing the Exercise

To complete the exercise, follow the steps in this book or in the onscreen exercise. In the onscreen list of chapters and exercises, click *Chapter 4: Drawing Organization and Inquiry Commands*. Click *Challenge Exercise: Architectural Imperial*.

Imperial Units

1   Open the drawing you saved from the previous challenge exercise, or open *I_ARCH-Challenge- CHP04.dwg*.

2   Create nine layers with the following names and color properties:

- Annotation = white
- Dimension = red
- Doors = 30
- Plumbing Fixtures = magenta
- Stairs = white
- Titleblock = red
- Wall-Interior = cyan
- Windows = blue
- Viewports = 9

3   Put the stair geometry on the Stairs layer and the door geometry on the Doors layer.

4   Thaw the Existing Building - Apparatus Bay layer.

5   Save and close the drawing.

Challenge Exercise | Mechanical

In this exercise, you use what you learned about drawing organization and inquiry commands to add layers and hidden geometry to the drawing views.

Note: The following image depicts only some of the views requiring hidden line geometry.

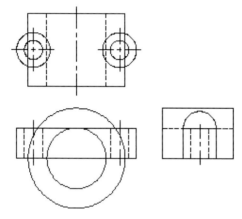

The completed exercise

Completing the Exercise

To complete the exercise, follow the steps in this book or in the onscreen exercise. In the onscreen list of chapters and exercises, click *Chapter 4: Drawing Organization and Inquiry Commands*. Click *Challenge Exercise: Mechanical*.

1   Open the drawing you saved from the previous challenge exercise, or open *M_MECH-Challenge- CHP04.dwg*.

2   Open the Layer Properties Manager:

- Create a new layer named **Hidden** and make it the current layer.
  - Color = 151
  - Linetype = Hidden
- Create a new layer named **Centerline**.
  - Color = Magenta
  - Linetype = Center
- Create a new layer named **Annotation**.
  - Color = Magenta
  - Linetype = Continuous
- Freeze and lock the Start Points layer.

3   Set the LTSCALE system variable to **0.75**.

4   With the Hidden layer current, create the hidden geometry in these views using points in each view as references. Then create the centerline objects and place them on the Centerline layer. **Note**: In the following image, the views are closer together than they are in the drawing.

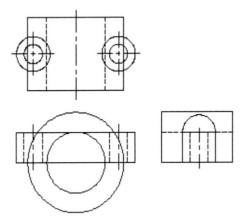

5   Save and close all files.

Chapter Summary

There is more to creating drawings than drawing lines, circle, and arcs. Part of the drawing process involves the use of layer and linetype standards as well as retrieving geometric information from objects in the drawing.

Having completed this chapter, you can:

- Use layers to organize objects in your drawing.
- Identify and change the properties of objects.
- Use the Quick Properties palette to quickly change object properties.
- Use the Match Properties command to apply the properties from a source object to destination objects.
- Use the Properties palette to change object properties.
- Use linetypes to distinguish objects in the drawing.
- Use the Inquiry commands (Distance, Radius, Angle, Area, List, and ID) to obtain geometric information from the drawing.

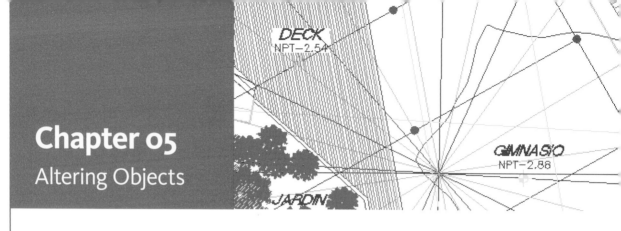

Chapter 05
Altering Objects

Of all CAD design tasks, editing objects is most common. Editing is something you will be required to do nearly every time you draw whether as the result of design changes or just the standard practice of creating more complex objects from simple ones.

Objectives

After completing this chapter, you will be able to:

- Change the length of objects using the Trim and Extend commands.

- Create parallel and offset geometry in your drawing by using the Offset command.

- Use the Join command to combine multiple objects into a single object.

- Break objects into two or more independent objects.

- Apply a radius corner to two objects in the drawing.

- Apply an angled corner to two objects in the drawing.

- Use the Stretch command to alter the shape of objects in the drawing.

Standard Object Snap and Status Bar Settings
Before completing the exercises in this chapter, refer to the "Settings for the Exercises" section in the Introduction .

Lesson 24 | Trimming and Extending Objects to Defined Boundaries

This lesson describes how to trim and extend objects in the drawing.

A typical design process involves shortening or lengthening the construction lines or other geometry at various times to represent the design's features.

After completing this lesson, you will be able to describe the uses of the Trim and Extend commands to modify objects, cut edges, and extend boundaries in your drawing.

The following image illustrates lines that need to be trimmed.

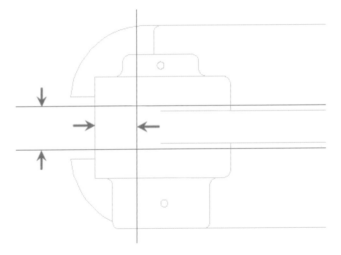

Objectives

After completing this lesson, you will be able to:

- Use the Trim and Extend commands to modify geometry in your drawing.

Using the Trim and Extend Commands

You can use the Trim command to shorten and the Extend command to lengthen existing geometry to meet the edges of other objects. This means that you can create an object such as a line and later adjust it to fit precisely between other objects.

When you use the Trim command, you select objects to use as cutting edges and trim geometry back to those objects. You select the portion of the object to trim, not the portion to keep.

In the following image, the arrows indicate where you would click to trim the lines.

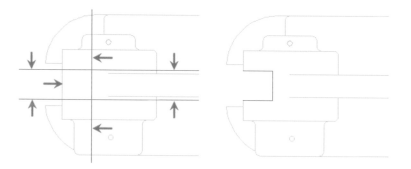

When you use the Extend command, you select objects to use as boundary edges and extend geometry to those objects.

In the following illustration, the boundary edge (2) is indicated with an arrow. Selecting the lines (1) at the location of the arrows extends each line to the first boundary edge it encounters. The completed command is illustrated in the image on the right.

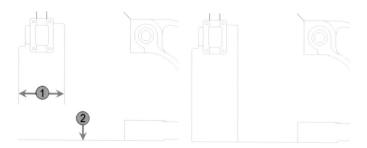

Before extend and after extend

Command Access

Trim

Command Line: **TRIM, TR**
Ribbon: **Home tab > Modify panel > Trim**

Menu Bar: **Modify > Trim**

Command Access

Extend

Command Line: **EXTEND, EX**
Ribbon: **Home tab > Modify panel > Extend**

Menu Bar: **Modify > Extend**

Procedure: Trimming Objects

The following steps give an overview of using the Trim command to shorten objects to cutting edges.

1. On the ribbon, click Home tab > Modify panel > Trim.

2. Either select the objects to serve as cutting edges (1) and then press ENTER, or press ENTER without selecting any objects. Pressing ENTER without selecting activates implied selection, where all suitable objects in the drawing are treated as potential cutting edges.

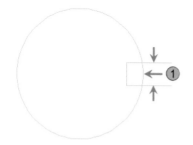

3. Select the objects to trim (2).

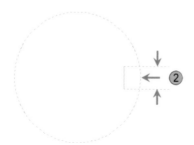

4. Press ENTER to end the command and view your completed operation.

Procedure: Extending Objects

The following steps give an overview of using the Extend command to lengthen objects to boundary edges.

1   On the ribbon, click Home tab > Modify panel > Extend.

2   Either select the objects to serve as boundary edges (1) and then press ENTER, or press ENTER without selecting any objects. Pressing ENTER without selecting, activates implied selection, where all suitable objects in the drawing are treated as potential boundary edges.

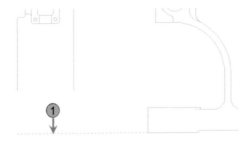

3   Select the objects to extend (2).

4   Press ENTER to end the command and view your completed operation.

Guidelines for Trim and Extend

Consider the following guidelines when using the Trim and Extend commands:

- Cutting or boundary edges may be lines, arcs, circles, polylines, ellipses, splines, xlines, regions, blocks, text, and rays.
- If you do not specify a cutting or boundary edge and press ENTER instead at the Select Objects prompt, all objects become potential cutting edges or boundaries. This is called implied selection.
- If you hold down SHIFT, you can SHIFT + select to switch between Trim and Extend. For example, if you are in the Trim command, you can hold down SHIFT and select objects to be extended to the boundary edge. Similarly, you can be in the Extend command and use SHIFT + select to trim objects to a cutting edge.
- Cutting and boundary edges do not have to intersect the object being trimmed or extended if you use the Edge option set in the Extend mode. With this setting, you can trim or extend an object to where it would intersect if the cutting or boundary edges were extended. For example, in the following illustration, the lower line (2) in the left illustration can be extended as if line (1) really was extended to point (3) as shown in the illustration on the right.

Extended Edge Mode

Guidelines for Trim and Extend Options

- The default edge mode for Trim and Extend is No Extend. Most of the time, you will want to use these commands with this default setting.
- The Trim or Extend Project option is for 3D.
- The Trim or Extend eRase option enables you to erase line segments within either of these commands.
- The Trim or Extend Undo option enables you to reverse an action you have made to trim or extend without exiting either of these commands.
  Note: You can right-click to select these options from the shortcut menu or you can type the capitalized letter of the option at the command line and press Enter.

Practice Exercise | Trim and Extend

In this practice exercise, you use the Trim and Extend commands. First, draw two rectangles. Across one rectangle, draw a series of lines that intersect the rectangle. Inside the other rectangle, create lines that do not touch the sides of the rectangle as shown below. You also practice the Trim and Extend commands using the Fence selection option.

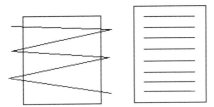

1   To set up this practice exercise:
   • Draw two rectangles of any size.
   • Across one rectangle, draw a series of lines that intersect the rectangle.
   • Inside the other rectangle draw a line that is completely inside and copy it several times.

2   To use the Trim command, select the cutting edges first:
   • On the Home tab, click Modify panel > Trim.
   • Select the rectangle for the cutting edge.
   • Press ENTER.

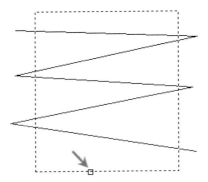

3   To trim the lines:
   • Click the portion of the line segment that you want to remove.
   • Trim all of the line segments to the left of the rectangle as indicated below.

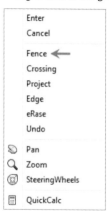

4   Continue to trim, this time using the Fence option:

  - Right-click in the graphics window. Click Fence.

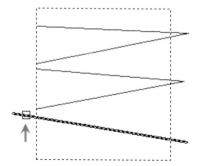

  - Click the first fence point just above the series of line segments to the right of the rectangle (1).
  - Click the next fence point just below the bottom line segment to the right of the rectangle (2).

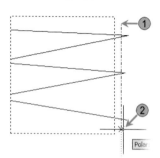

5   To complete the Trim command:
    - Press ENTER to complete the Fence selection option.
    - Press ENTER to exit the Trim command.

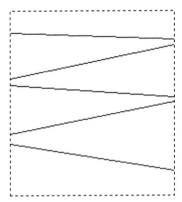

6   To use the Extend command, select the boundary edges first:
    - On the Home tab, click Modify panel > Extend.
    - Select the rectangle for the boundary edge.
    - Press ENTER.

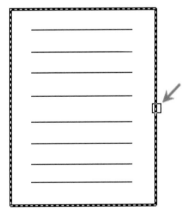

7   To extend the lines, select the line near the end that you want to extend:
    - Click each line towards the left of the rectangle (1).

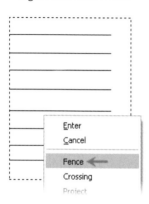

- Right-click. Click Fence.

- Click just above the line towards the right side of the rectangle (1).
- Click just below the bottom line (2) as indicated below.

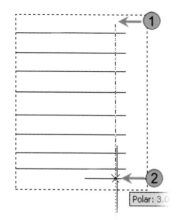

8   To complete the Extend command:

- Press ENTER to complete the Fence selection line option.
- Press ENTER to exit the Extend command.
- View your results.

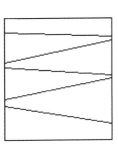 

Exercise | Trim and Extend Objects

In this exercise, you use the Trim and Extend commands to trim and extend edges on the drawing. When you have completed the exercise, you will be able to trim and extend geometry using standard trim and extend methods. You will also be able to use the Edge option to extend or trim geometry to implied intersections and the SHIFT+select feature to switch between trimming and extending.

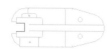

The completed exercise

Completing the Exercise
To complete the exercise, follow the steps in this book or in the onscreen exercise. In the onscreen list of chapters and exercises, click *Chapter 5: Altering Objects*. Click *Exercise: Trim and Extend Objects*.

1   Open *M_Trim-Extend.dwg*.

2   Zoom to display the view as shown in the following image.

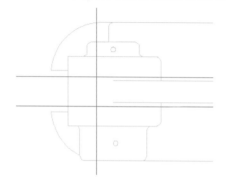

3   Use the Trim command to complete the slot geometry:

- On the Home tab, click Modify panel > Trim.
- Select the lines highlighted in the following image as the cutting edges.
- Press ENTER.

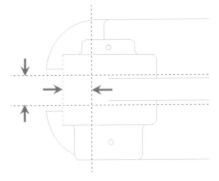

4   Select the lines to trim at the points indicated in the following image. Press ENTER.

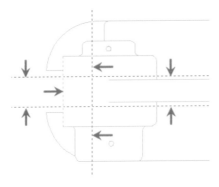

Your drawing should appear as shown in the following image.

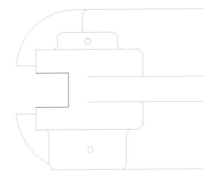

5   Zoom out to display the entire drawing.

6   To use the Extend command:

- On the Home tab, click Modify panel > Trim drop-down > Extend.
- Select the geometry highlighted in the following image as your boundary edges.
- Press ENTER.

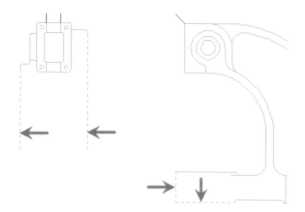

7   To complete the view on the left:

- Right-click anywhere in the drawing window. Click Edge.
- Right-click anywhere in the drawing window. Click Extend.
- Select the geometry indicated in the following image as the objects to extend.
  Note: You need to select the two horizontal lines twice because they are initially extended to the first boundary. The second selection extends them to the next boundary that the edge intersects.

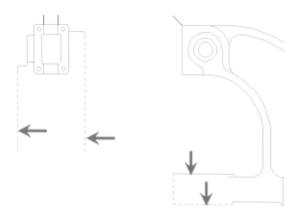

Your drawing should appear as shown in the following image.

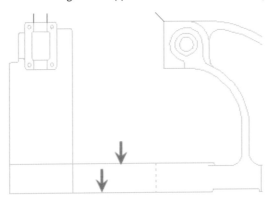

8   SHIFT+select the lines indicated in the previous image to trim them.

9   Press ENTER to end the Extend command.

10 To remove the construction lines:

   - Start the Erase command.
   - Select the lines indicated in the following image. Press ENTER.

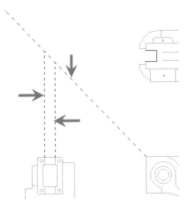

11 Your completed drawing.

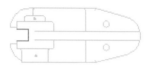

12   Close all files. Do not save.

Lesson 25 | Creating Parallel and Offset Geometry

This lesson describes how to use the Offset command to create geometry that is offset from or parallel to other geometry in the drawing.

In a typical drawing, you are likely to find several objects that are parallel to or offset from each other. You can use the Offset command to create this effect on geometry in the drawing and increase efficiency by reusing existing geometry.

The following illustration shows several parallel lines and concentric circles. The Offset command can be used to create these types of objects..

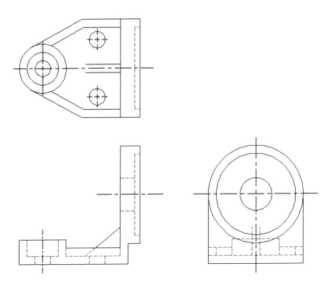

Objectives

After completing this lesson, you will be able to:

- Use the Offset command to create parallel and offset geometry.

Offsetting Objects

The Offset command creates a new object whose shape parallels the shape of a selected object.

For example, in the following image, the inside shape has been offset twice using the Offset command with the Multiple option.

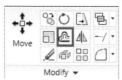

Command Access

Offset

Command Line: **OFFSET, O**
Ribbon: **Home tab > Modify panel > Offset**

Menu Bar: **Modify > Offset**

Command Options

The Offset command has the following options. From the shortcut menu, either right-click to select the option or enter the capitalized letter and press ENTER.

Option	Description
Through	Offsets a selected object the distance of a point picked in the drawing window.
Erase	Erases the source object after it has been offset.
Layer	Offsets the object to the original source layer or the current layer.
Multiple	Makes multiple offsets of the object in increments specified by the offset distance.

Procedure: Offsetting Geometry a Specific Distance

The following steps give an overview of offsetting geometry a specified distance.

1 On the ribbon, click Home tab > Modify panel > Offset.

2 Specify the offset distance by selecting two points.
   Note: You can enter a value instead of selecting points.

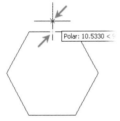

3 Select the object to offset.

4   Select a point on the side where you want to place the new objects.

5   Select another object to offset or exit the command.

Procedure: Offsetting Geometry Through a Point

The following steps give an overview of using the Offset command with the Through option to offset a line through a point on a circle.

1   On the Home tab, click Modify panel > Offset.

2   Right-click anywhere in the drawing. Click Through. You can also enter **t** on the command line.

3   Select the object to offset.

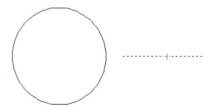

4   Specify the point through which to offset the object.
     Note: The top horizontal line represents the position of the object after the offset. If it were extended, it would pass through the point indicated by the cursor.

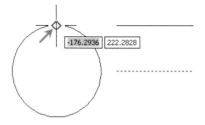

5   Select another object to offset or exit the command.

Procedure: Offsetting Multiple Objects

The following steps give an overview of serially offsetting geometry a specified distance using the Multiple option.

1   On the Home tab, click Modify panel > Offset.

2   Specify the offset distance by entering a value or selecting two points.

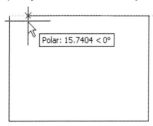

3   Select the object to offset.

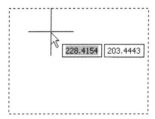

4   Right-click anywhere in the drawing. Click Multiple.

5   Select a point on the side where you want to place the new objects.

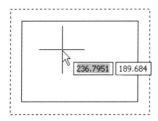

6   Select another point to offset the last object by the same amount.

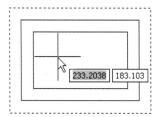

7   Continue selecting points to repeat the offset on the last object created.

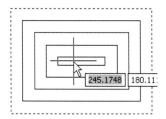

Guidelines for Using the Offset Command

- Setting the offset distance is the default and most common method for using offset. Enter the distance and press ENTER.
- The offset distance may also be set by picking two points in the drawing window. When using this method, it is best to use object snap and reference objects in the drawing to accurately set a distance.
- When you begin the Offset command, the last offset distance used is displayed in the command line. Press ENTER to accept this distance, or enter a new offset distance then press ENTER.
- Use the Multiple option to create a series of offsets once you have selected the original object to offset. Then simply click the side to offset as many times as needed.
- An offset object will automatically retain the color, layer, and linetype of the source object unless you change the offset Layer option to Current. The most common method is to keep the offset objects on the source layer.
- When you offset a circle, arc or polyline, at some point it may not be possible to create the offset to the inside or outside of the object because of geometry restrictions. For example, if the offset distance is greater than the radius of a circle, it would be impossible to offset to the inside of that circle.
- You remain in the Offset command until you press ENTER, unless you have initiated the Through option. Then only one offset is created through the object selected.

Practice Exercise | Offsetting Objects

In this practice exercise, you practice using the Offset command with three different methods. First, draw a circle, a line, and a rectangle, and then offset the rectangle a specific distance. Offset the circle through a selected point. Make multiple offsets of the line.

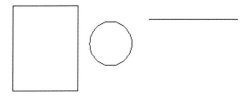

1   To offset a distance:

- On the Home tab, click Modify panel > Offset.
- Enter an offset distance of **.05**. Press ENTER.
- Select the rectangle (1).
- Click inside the rectangle.
- Select the new rectangle (2).
- Click inside the rectangles.

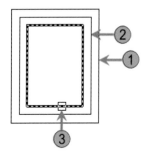

- Select the next rectangle (3) and click inside the rectangles.
- Press **ENTER** to complete the Offset command.

2   To offset through a point:

- On the Home tab, click Modify panel > Offset.
- Right-click in the drawing window. Click Through.
- Select the object to offset. Select the Circle.

- Specify a point through another object. Select anywhere on the adjacent rectangle.

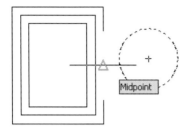

- Press ENTER to exit the Offset command.

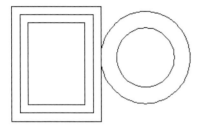

3   To make multiple offsets:
- On the Home tab, click Modify panel > Offset.
- Enter an offset distance of **.1**. Press ENTER. Select the line to offset.
- Right-click the selected object. Click Multiple.
- Specify a point on the side of the line to offset.
- Continue to make offsets of the line. Press ENTER to end the Offset command.

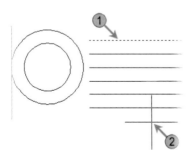

Exercise | Create Parallel and Offset Geometry

In this exercise, you use the Offset command to create geometry that is offset from existing geometry in the drawing. You also use the Trim command to clean up the geometry after it has been offset. When you have completed the exercise, you will be able to use the Offset command in other drawings.

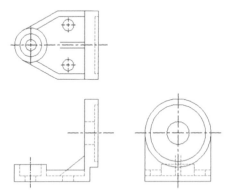

The completed exercise

> **Completing the Exercise**
> To complete the exercise, follow the steps in this book or in the onscreen exercise. In the onscreen list of chapters and exercises, click *Chapter 5: Altering Objects*. Click *Exercise: Create Parallel and Offset Geometry*.

1   Open *M_Offset-Objects.dwg*.

2   Zoom to display the upper-left view as shown.

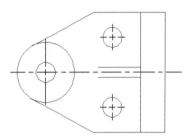

3   To offset a circle:

- On the Home tab, click Modify panel > Offset.
- On the command line, verify that the current settings for the offset are as follows:
  - *Current settings: Erase source=No*
  - *Layer=Source*
  - *OFFSETGAPTYPE=0*
- If the settings are different from the above, do the following, otherwise continue at the next primary bullet:
  - Right-click anywhere in the drawing window. Click Erase. Click No.
  - Right-click anywhere in the drawing window. Click Layer. Click Source.
- Enter **7.5**. Press ENTER.
- Select the small circle, then select a point outside the circle.

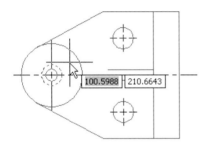

4   Select the top outside edge of the part and select a point below the profile as shown.

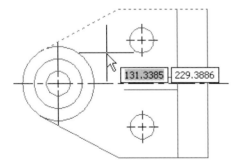

5   To complete the offset:

- Select the bottom outside edge of the part and select a point above the profile as shown.
- Press ENTER to exit the Offset command.

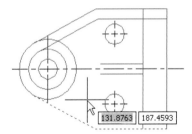

6   To trim the objects created in the previous step:

- On the Home tab, click Modify panel > Trim.
- Use the large circle and vertical line as the cutting edges.
- Select the objects created with the Offset command near the points indicated with arrows.

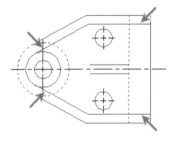

7   To offset the vertical line and place it on the current layer:

- On the Home tab, click Modify panel > Offset.
- Right-click anywhere in the drawing. Click Layer. Click Current.
- Enter **5.25**. Press ENTER.
- Select the vertical line indicated in the following image and then select a point to the left of the line.
- Press ENTER to end the Offset command.

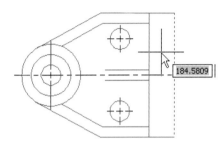

8 Zoom to display the entire drawing.

9 To offset the centerlines using existing views to set a distance:

- On the Home tab, click Modify panel > Offset.
- Select the two points indicated in the following image to specify the offset distance.

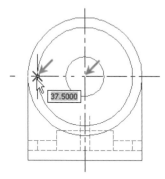

10 To complete the offset:

- Select the centerline in the upper left view and select a point above the centerline.
- Select the centerline again and select a point below the centerline.
- Press ENTER to exit the Offset command.

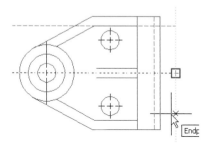

11 Using the Trim command, clean up the hidden lines as shown in the following image.

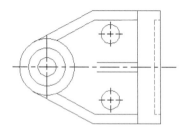

12   To create a hidden pocket in the front view:

- On the Home tab, click Modify panel > Offset.
- Right-click anywhere in the drawing window. Click Through.
- When prompted for the object to offset, select the centerline in the left view (1).
- When prompted for the through point, select the point indicated in the following image (2).

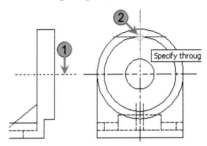

13   To offset another line:

- When prompted for the object to offset, select the centerline again (1).
- When prompted for the through point, select the point indicated in the following image (2).

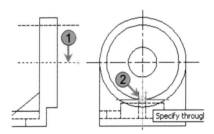

14   To complete the pocket:

- When prompted for the object to offset, select the vertical line in the lower left view (1).
- When prompted for the through point, select the point on the top-left view (2).
- Press ENTER to exit the Offset command.

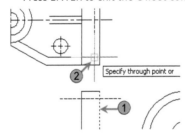

15 Use the Offset command with the Through option to offset the centerline through the quadrants of the smaller circle, then use the Trim command to clean up the lines as indicated in the following image.

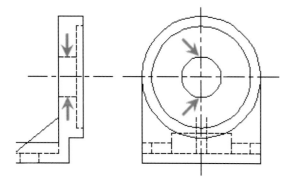

16 Close all files. Do not save.

Lesson 26 | Joining Objects

When you edit drawings, extra objects that are produced increase the overall size of the drawing and may complicate your drawing process.

Several situations can lead to incomplete or incorrect geometry such as broken line segments, arcs, or open polylines. Importing geometry from other programs or 2D geometry that originated in a 3D model could result in geometry that appears to be correct but, on closer examination, contains unwanted breaks. Use the Join command to fix these broken objects and combine them into single objects.

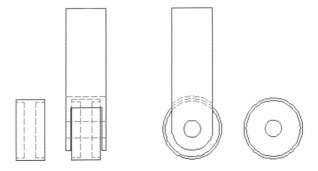

Objectives

After completing this lesson, you will be able to:

- Use the Join command to join similar objects.

Chapter 5 | Altering Objects

Joining Objects

Use the Join command to combine individual segments of like objects into a single object, to reduce file size, and to improve drawing quality. The Join command can be used on polylines, lines, arcs, elliptical arcs, and splines.

Command Access

Join

Command Line: **JOIN, J**
Ribbon: **Home tab › extended Modify panel › Join**

Menu Bar: **Modify › Join**

Command Options

With the Join command, you can combine similar objects into one object.

Option	Description
Select source object	Offsets a selected object the distance of a point picked in the drawing window.
Select objects to join to source	Use this option to select objects that you join to the source object.
Select arcs to join to source or [cLose]	This option appears if the source object is an arc. The close option closes the arc and converts it to a circle.
Select elliptical arcs to join to source or [cLose]	This option appears if the source object is an elliptical arc. The close option closes the elliptical arc.

Join Command Example

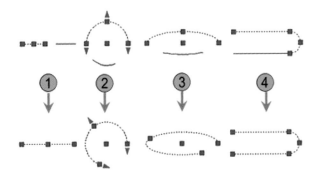

1. Two lines with a gap are joined into a single line.

2. Two concentric arcs are joined into a single arc.

3. Two concentric ellipse objects are joined into a single ellipse.

4. A line is joined to an open polyline.

Procedure: Joining Lines with the Join Command

The following steps provide an overview of joining lines using Join.

1. On the Modify panel, click Join.

2. Select the source line.

3. Select the other lines to join to the source line and press ENTER.

The selected line segments are joined together.

Procedure: Converting an Arc to a Circle with the Join Command

The following steps provide an overview of converting an arc to a circle using the Join command.

1 On the Modify Draw panel, click Join.

2 Select an arc.

3 Right-click and click Close on the shortcut menu. The arc is converted to a circle.

Guidelines

When you use the Join command to join objects, the following rules apply.

- **Lines**:
  - Segments must be collinear.
  - Segments can overlap.
  - Segments can have a gap between them.
- **Polylines and splines**:
  - Must be coplanar.
  - Must share a common endpoint.
  - Segments cannot overlap.
  - Lines and arcs can be joined to polylines if a polyline is selected as the source object.
- **Arcs**:
  - Must share the same circular path.
  - Segments can overlap.
  - Segments can have a gap between them.
- **Elliptical Arcs**:
  - Must share the same elliptical path.

Joining Arcs or Elliptical Arcs

When you join arcs or elliptical arcs together, the source object is always extended to the other objects in a counterclockwise direction. In the following image, the source arc is selected at point (1) while the other arc is selected at point (2). The source arc is extended counterclockwise to meet the other arc.

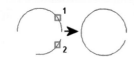

Practice Exercise | Joining Objects

Quite often when you edit your drawing, changes occur that require you to join or rejoin segments. In this practice exercise, you draw a circle and a line with a rectangle that overlaps both objects. First trim these objects, then erase the rectangle. Use the Join command to reconnect the circle and line segments.

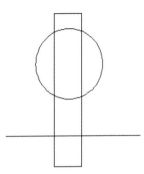

1   Draw the circle, line and rectangle as illustrated above.

2   To Trim the circle and the line:
- Begin the Trim command.
- Select the rectangle for the cutting edge and press ENTER.
- Select the portion of the line and circle inside the rectangle to trim.

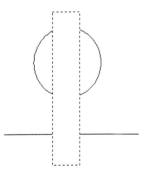

3   Erase the rectangle.

4   To join the line segments:
- Begin the Join command.
- Select the Source object (1).
- Select the object to join (2).

- Press ENTER to complete the command.

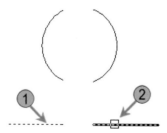

5   To Join the arc segments and close them. Method 1:
- Begin the Join command.
- Select one arc (1) then select the other (2). Press ENTER to join the two arcs.

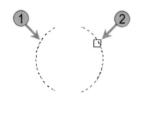

Notice how the arcs work in a counterclockwise direction. The order in which you select the arcs determines how they are joined. For instance, if you had selected arc (2) first then arc (1), the segments would have been joined at the top.
- Repeat the Join command
- Select the arc.
- Right-click on the selected object. Click Close.

Note: If you were to enter this option at the command line, you would enter **L** and press ENTER, indicated by the capitalized letter L.

- The arc is now closed, making it a circle again.

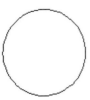

6   To Join the arc segments and close them. Method 2:

- Begin the Join command.
- Select one arc segment.
- Right-click the selected object. Click Close.

The arc is now closed to form a circle, but the remaining arc segment should be erased.

- Begin the Erase command.
- Hold down SHIFT+SPACEBAR and select the circle in the area of the remaining arc segment. Click until you see that the arc segment is selected.
- Press ENTER to erase the arc.

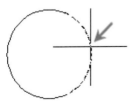

Exercise | Join Objects

In this exercise, you use Join to join lines and arcs.

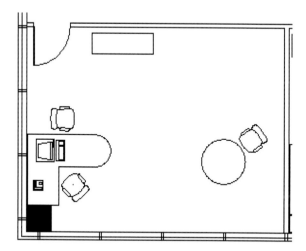

The completed exercise

> **Completing the Exercise**
> To complete the exercise, follow the steps in this book or in the onscreen exercise. In the onscreen list of chapters and exercises, click *Chapter 5: Altering Objects*. Click *Exercise: Join Objects*.

1   Open *M_Join-Objects.dwg*.

2   Mirror a door from the right side of the room to the left side. Use the Mid Between 2 Points object snap to obtain the midpoint of the room and erase the source object.

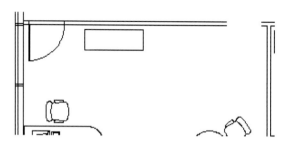

3   To join the wall lines to the shorter segments left from removing the door:

  - On the Modify panel, click Join.
  - When prompted for the source object, select the inside wall line (1).
  - When prompted for the line to join, select the inside short line (2).
  - Press ENTER.

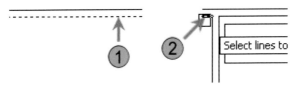

4   Join the two outer wall lines following the same method used in the previous step. Your drawing should now look like the following image.

5   Use Trim to remove the wall sections at the new door location. Your drawing should now look like the following image.

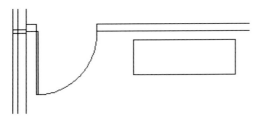

6   To modify the conference desk in this office by removing the rectangular wing:

- Zoom in to the table.
- Delete the three lines as shown.

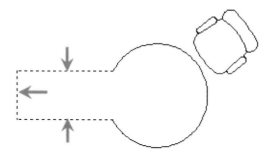

7   Use Join to close the circle that represents the table:

- Start the Join command.
- When prompted for the source object, select the open circle.
- Right-click the selected object. Click close.

8   Close all files without saving.

Lesson 27 | Breaking an Object into Two Objects

This lesson describes how to break objects into two separate objects using the Break command. The two new objects have the same properties as the original, but you can modify them independently.

There may be instances when you need to break an object into two or more separate pieces. While the Trim command can accomplish this, the Break command can break objects without the need for cutting geometry and the resulting pieces can have coincident endpoints.

After completing this lesson, you will be able to identify the command options for Break and use the command to break objects.

In the following illustration, the Break command was used to break an existing line (1) so that the properties of the resulting new object could be changed independently (2).

Objectives

After completing this lesson, you will be able to:

- Use the Break command to break objects.

Breaking Objects

Using the Break command, you can break a single object into two independent objects. You accomplish this by first selecting the object to break and then specifying the break points.

The Modify panel contains two versions of the Break command. While each version executes the core Break command, one breaks the object leaving a gap between the two remaining pieces and the other breaks the object at one point, leaving the ends coincident (touching). In this lesson, you learn both Break methods.

In the following image, the Break command was used to break the line indicated by the middle arrow, at the points indicated by the arrows pointing to the intersections.

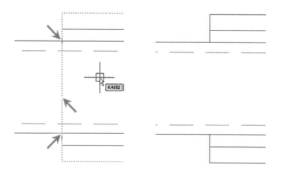

Command Access

Break

Command Line: **BREAK, BR**
Ribbon: **Home tab > Modify panel > Break**

Menu Bar: **Modify > Break**

Command Access

Break at Point

Command Line: **BREAK, BR**
Ribbon: **Home tab > Modify panel > Break at Point**

Menu Bar: **Modify > Break**

Command Options

The Break command provides the following options. Select the Break at Point option on the 2D Draw panel if you want both first and second break points to be the same.

Option	Description
First Point	Specifies the first point of the break. If this option is not specified, the point where you select the object is used as the first point.
Second Point	Specifies the second point of the break. Select any point on the object or enter @ and press ENTER to use the first point as the second point (results in the object broken so that endpoints are coincident).

Procedure: Breaking Objects Using the Break Command

The following steps give an overview of breaking objects using the Break command.

1   On the Modify panel, click Break.

2   Select the object to break. If you do not manually specify the first point of the break, then the point at which you select the object is used as the first point of the break.

Chapter 5 | Altering Objects

3   Right-click anywhere in the drawing. Click First Point.

4   Select the first point of the break.

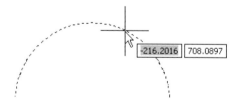

5   Select the second point of the break.

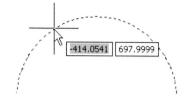

The selected object is broken at the points specified.

Procedure: Breaking Objects Using the Break at Point Command

The following steps give an overview of breaking objects using the Break at Point command.

1   On the Modify panel, click Break at Point.

2   Select the object to be broken.

3   Select the first break point.

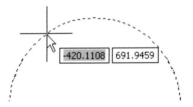

4   The first break point is automatically used for the second break point, resulting in two objects with coincident endpoints.
     Note that when the object is selected the grips display the broken segment.

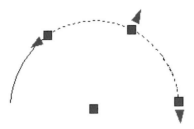

Guidelines for Breaking Objects

- You can use the Break command on lines, circles, arcs, polylines, and splines.
- If you do not manually specify the first point, the point at which the object was selected is used as the first point.
- When breaking an object at the intersection of another object, be sure to specify which object you want to break first.
- Circles break in a counterclockwise direction. The portion that gets removed depends on the order in which you select the breakpoints.
- You can enter @ and press ENTER to use the first point as the second point, which results in the object being broken in such a way that the resulting endpoints are coincident.

When to use Break
Use the Break command only when there are no cutting edges that would allow you to use the Trim command or to break an object at a specific point without a gap.

Practice Exercise | Breaking Objects

In this practice exercise, you practice the Break command by drawing a vertical line with a series of offset lines that intersect as shown below on the left, and practice the *Break at a Point* command by drawing two intersecting lines as shown below on the right.

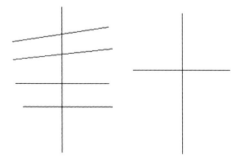

1   Draw the lines as shown above.

2   To break the lines leaving a gap:

- Turn Object Snap off to avoid selecting the intersections.

- Begin the Break command.
- Select a line at point (1).
- Click the second break point (2).

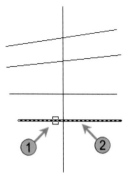

- Repeat the Break command.
- Continue to select the break points of each line on one side of the vertical line, then the other as shown below.

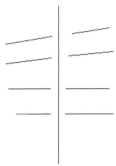

3   To Break an object at a select point:

     •   Turn Object Snap on.

     •   Begin the *Break at a Point* command.

     •   Select the line segment as indicated below.

     •   Select the intersection of the two lines.

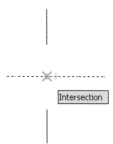

Intersection

- The line segment is now broken at the intersection.

Exercise | Break Objects

In this exercise, you use the Break and Break at Point commands and change the layer in order to show the hidden parts of the object in two different ways. When you have completed the exercise, you will know the difference between breaking at single points and breaking an object at two points.

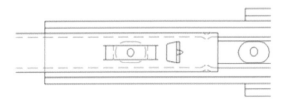

The completed exercise

Completing the Exercise
To complete the exercise, follow the steps in this book or in the onscreen exercise. In the onscreen list of chapters and exercises, click *Chapter 5: Altering Objects*. Click *Exercise: Break Objects*.

1   Open *C_Break-Object.dwg*.

2   Zoom in on the part of the drawing shown.

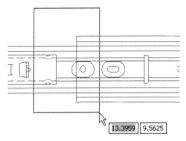

3   To remove a portion of a line:

• Start the Break command.

• Select the outside object as shown.

• Right-click and click First Point.
  Note: The benefit of using this option is that you can select the object and then precisely select the two break points.

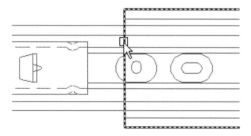

4   Select the first break point (1). Then select the second point (2).

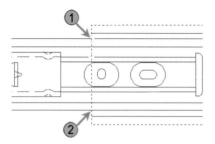

5   Zoom out to display your entire drawing. Zoom in to the area shown.

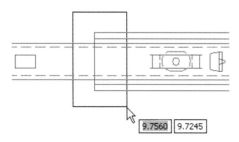

6   To break the line at a point without removing any of it:
    • Start the Break at Point command.
    • Select the outer object as shown.

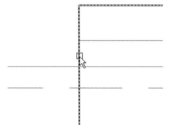

7   Select point (1) to specify the break point.

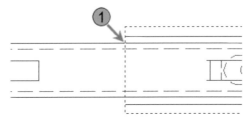

8   Break the line again without removing any of it:
    • Start the Break at Point command.
    • Select the outer object again (1).

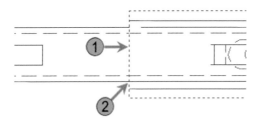

    • Select the Intersection at point (2) to specify the break point.
9   Select the line between the two break points to highlight it.

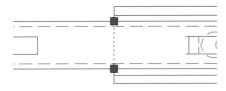

10 To move this object to the Hidden2 layer:
    • On the Layers panel, click the Layers list.
    • Click the Hidden2 layer to move the selected object to this layer.

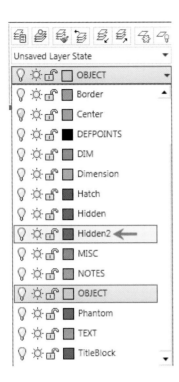

11   Press ESC. Your drawing should look like the following image.

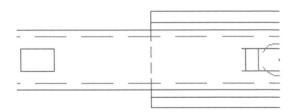

12   Close all files without saving.

Lesson 28 | Applying a Radius Corner to Two Objects

This lesson describes how to fillet objects using the Fillet command.

Fillets and rounds are common in mechanical drawings, but you can use the Fillet feature across all design disciplines to create radius geometry connecting two objects.

After completing this lesson, you will be able to identify options of the Fillet command and use the command to create radius geometry between two objects.

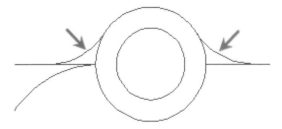

Objectives

After completing this lesson, you will be able to:

- Use the Fillet command to create radius geometry connecting two objects.

Chapter 5 | Altering Objects

Creating Fillets

You can use the Fillet command to connect two objects quickly with a smoothly fitted arc of a specified radius. You usually use it to represent a rounded edge on a corner; an inside corner is called a fillet and an outside corner is called a round. You can fillet lines, arcs, circles, ellipses, polylines, xlines, splines, and rays.

You can also create a sharp corner with the Fillet command by specifying a radius value of 0.

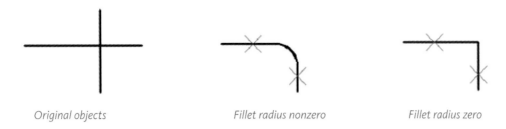

Original objects	Fillet radius nonzero	Fillet radius zero

Command Access

Fillet

Command Line: **FILLET, F**
Ribbon: **Home tab > Modify panel > Fillet**

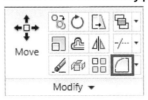

Menu Bar: **Modify > Fillet**

Command Options

The following options are available for the Fillet command.

Option	Description
Undo	Reverses the previous action of the Fillet command.
Polyline	Fillets all vertices of a polyline using the current radius value.
Radius	Sets the radius for the fillet arc.
Polyline	When Trim mode is selected, the lines are trimmed to be tangent with the fillet. If Trim mode is set to No Trim, the fillet radius is drawn but the lines are not trimmed.
Multiply	When the Multiple option is selected, you can create multiple fillets without restarting the command.

Procedure: Applying a Radius Corner with the Fillet Command

The following steps give an overview of how to apply a radius corner with the Fillet command.

1   Start the Fillet command.

2   On the command line, verify the current fillet settings. If required, set the options appropriately.
    Command: FILLETCurrent settings: Mode = TRIM, Radius = 1.0000Select first object or [Undo/ Polyline/ Radius/Trim/Multiple]:

3   Select the first object to fillet.

4   Select the second object to fillet. The fillet is created.
    Note: If you choose the Polyline option, the last step is not required, since all vertices of the polyline are filleted at once.

> **SHIFT+Select for Zero-Radius Fillet**
> Regardless of the current Fillet Radius setting, if you SHIFT+select the two objects, a zero-radius fillet is applied.

Chapter 5 | Altering Objects

Guidelines

- Depending on the locations you specify, more than one possible fillet can exist between the selected objects. Always select the part of the objects that you want to keep.

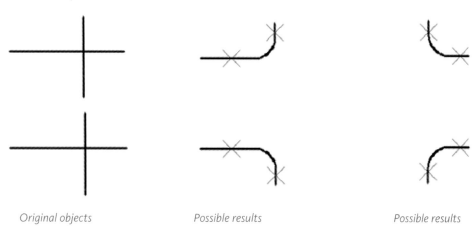

Original objects   *Possible results*   *Possible results*

- You can fillet parallel lines, xlines, and rays. The current fillet radius is ignored and an arc is created that is tangent to both parallel objects and located in the plane common to both objects.

- You can also fillet a polygon, or an entire polyline, or remove fillets from an entire polyline.

- If you set a nonzero fillet radius, fillet arcs are inserted at the vertex of each polyline segment that is long enough to accommodate the fillet radius.

Key Points

- The fillet radius is the radius of the arc that connects the objects.
- If both objects being filleted are on the same layer, the fillet arc is created on that layer. Otherwise, the fillet arc is created on the current layer.
- Entering a radius value of **o** creates a sharp corner.
- Holding down the SHIFT key while selecting the object to fillet will override the current radius value and create a radius of o.
- An object that is filleted to a polyline becomes part of that polyline.
- A polyline cannot be filleted to an arc. Explode the polyline, then fillet the objects and join them again using the Polyedit command.

Practice Exercise | Creating Fillets

In this practice exercise, you use the Fillet command on a simple rectangle.

1   Draw a rectangle.

2   To Fillet a single corner:
   - Begin the Fillet command.
   - Enter **R** and press ENTER.
   - Specify a fillet radius of **.25** and press ENTER.
   - Click the lines near one corner of the rectangle as indicated below.

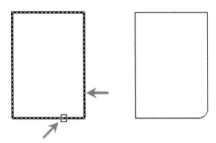

3   Now change the radius and use the Fillet polyline option:
   - Begin the Fillet command.
   - Enter **R** and press ENTER.
   - Enter a fillet radius of **.5** and press ENTER.
   - Enter **P** and press ENTER.
   - Select the rectangle.

Note: If this rectangle was made of separate line segments instead of a polyline, the previous radius would have remained and you could not have used the Polyline option to fillet all of the corners at once.

4   Now change the fillet radius to 0 to make sharp corners on the rectangle:

- Begin the Fillet command.
- Enter **R** and press ENTER.
- Enter a fillet radius of **0** and press ENTER.
- Enter **P** and press ENTER.
- Select the rectangle.

Exercise | Create a Filleted Corner

In this exercise, you create fillets on the objects in the drawing. You use different options of the Fillet command to create the desired results. When you have finished, you will be able to use the Fillet command in other drawings.

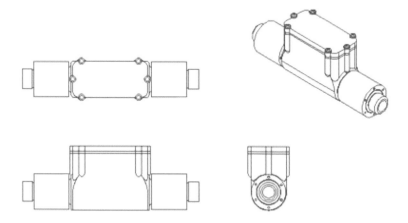

The completed exercise

Completing the Exercise
To complete the exercise, follow the steps in this book or in the onscreen exercise. In the onscreen list of chapters and exercises, click *Chapter 5: Altering Objects*. Click *Exercise: Create a Filleted Corner*.

1   Open *M_Create-Fillets.dwg*.

2   Zoom in to the lower-left area of the drawing.

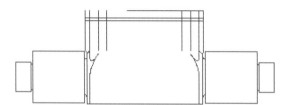

3   To use the Fillet command to create an end cap on parallel lines:

- Start the Fillet command.
- Right-click anywhere in the drawing area. Click Multiple.
- Select the lines as shown.

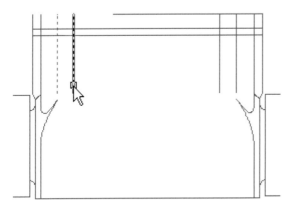

4   To complete the fillet:

- Select the lines on the opposite side of the view.
- Press ENTER to end the Fillet command.

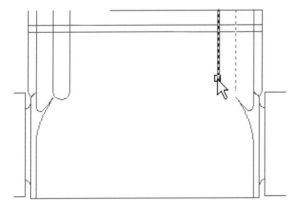

5   Pan or zoom to the top-left of the drawing.

6   To create a blend between the part profile and the screw bosses:

- Start the Fillet command.
- Right-click anywhere in the drawing area. Click Multiple.
- Right-click anywhere in the drawing area. Click Trim. Click No Trim.
- Right-click anywhere in the drawing area. Click Radius.
- Enter **2**. Press ENTER.
- Select the horizontal line, and then select the larger circle.

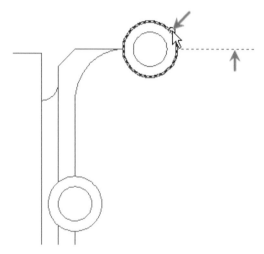

7   Repeat the selection on the opposite side of the circle. The fillet should appear as shown.

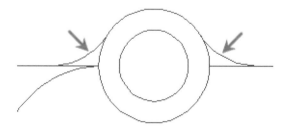

8   To complete the boss creation:

• Repeat the selection process on the other bossed areas in the drawing, as indicated in the following image.

• Press ENTER to end the Fillet command.

9   Zoom to display the entire drawing.

10   To ignore the radius setting and create a sharp corner while using the fillet command:

• Start the Fillet command.

• On the command line, confirm the radius is still set to 2.0000.

• Select the horizontal line.

• Press SHIFT+select the vertical line to create a zero-radius fillet.

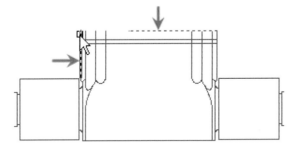

11   To complete the right view:

- Press ENTER to repeat the Fillet command.
- On the right-side view, select the top horizontal line.
- Press SHIFT+select the right-side vertical line to create a zero-radius fillet.

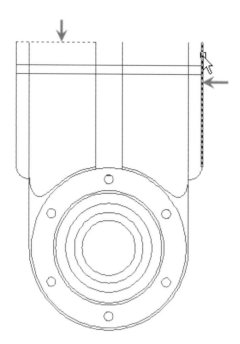

12   Close all files without saving.

Lesson 29 | Creating an Angled Corner Between Two Objects

This lesson describes how to use the Chamfer command to create chamfer features on objects in the drawing.

There are many situations that call for a chamfer. Any time you need to create an angled intersection on objects in the drawing, the Chamfer command should be your first choice.

After completing this lesson, you will be able to identify options of the Chamfer command and use the command to create chamfered features.

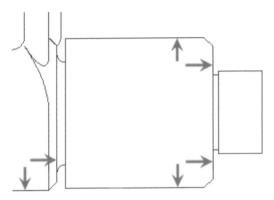

Objectives

After completing this lesson, you will be able to:

- Use the Chamfer command to create chamfer features.

Creating Chamfers

You use the Chamfer command to quickly create a line between two nonparallel lines. It is usually used to represent a beveled edge on a corner. You can chamfer lines, polylines, xlines, and rays.

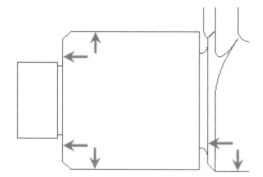

Command Access

Chamfer

Command Line: **CHAMFER, CHA**
Ribbon: **Home tab > Modify panel > Chamfer**

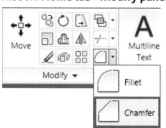

Note: *Select the Chamfer command from the drop-down menu.*
Menu Bar: **Modify > Chamfer**

Command Options

The following options are available when using the Chamfer command.

Option	Description
Undo	Use this option to undo the previous action of the Chamfer command.
Polyline	Use this option to chamfer a 2D polyline. All polyline vertices are chamfered at the current distance or angle settings.
Distance	Use this option to specify distance values for the chamfer.
Angle	Use this option to create the chamfers based on one distance and an angle.
Trim	Use this option to set the Trim and No Trim modes. When Trim mode is active, the objects being chamfered are trimmed to the start of the chamfer lines. When No Trim mode is set, the objects selected for the chamfer are not trimmed.
Method	Use this option to switch between the Distance or Angle methods for creating the chamfer.
Multiple	Use this option to create multiple chamfers without having to restart the command.

Using Chamfer Options

- With the Distance method, you specify the amount that each line should be trimmed or extended.

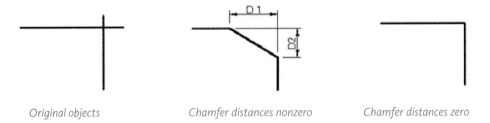

Original objects   *Chamfer distances nonzero*   *Chamfer distances zero*

- With the Angle method, you can also specify the length of the chamfer and the angle it forms with the first line.

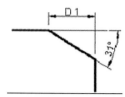

- Using the Trim and No Trim modes, you can trim or extend chamfered objects to the chamfer line or retain the chamfered objects as they were before the chamfer, as shown next.

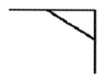

- You can chamfer all corners of a polyline using the Polyline option.
- The Multiple option allows you to chamfer more than one set of objects without leaving the command. For example, you could chamfer the four corners of the square shown next with one Chamfer command.

Procedure: Creating Chamfers

The following steps give an overview of creating chamfers with the Chamfer command.

1   Start the Chamfer command.

2   Confirm the settings on the command line. If necessary, adjust the options as required for the design intent.
     Command: _chamfer(NOTRIM mode) Current chamfer Dist1 = 1.0000, Dist2 = 1.5000Select first line or [Undo/Polyline/Distance/Angle/Trim/mEthod/Multiple]:

3   Select the first object to be chamfered.

4   Select the second object to be chamfered. The chamfer feature is created.
     Note: If you choose the Polyline option, step 4 is not required, as all vertices of the polyline will be filleted at once.

Chamfer Guidelines

- If both objects being chamfered are on the same layer, the chamfer line is created on that layer. Otherwise, the chamfer line is created on the current layer.
- Entering chamfer distances of 0 creates a sharp corner.
- Setting equal chamfer distances is the same as setting the angle at 45 degrees.
- When setting chamfer distances the first distance is always applied to the first line you pick.
- Chamfering a line to a polyline will automatically join it to the polyline.
- A closed polyline will chamfer in a counter-clockwise direction.
- Hold down SHIFT while selecting the object to override the chamfer distance values and create a sharp corner.

Practice Exercise | Creating Chamfers

In this practice exercise, you draw an 8 x 6 rectangle and create chamfers using the Chamfer command.

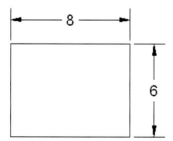

1   To draw the rectangle:
   - Begin the Rectangle command.
   - Click in the drawing window to specify the first corner.
   - For the other corner, enter **@8,6** and press ENTER.

2   To make a 45 degree corner using the chamfer command:
   - Begin the Chamfer command.
   - Right-click anywhere in the drawing. Click Angle.

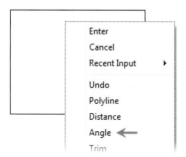

   - Enter **1** and press ENTER for the chamfer length on the first line.
   - Enter **45** and press ENTER to specify the chamfer angle from the first line.
   - Select the first corner then the adjacent corner as indicated below.

- Repeat until all 4 corners are chamfered.
- Press ENTER to exit the chamfer command.
  Note: You could have used the Distance option and entered both distance lengths at 1 for the same results.

3   To chamfer using the polyline option:
- Draw another 8 x 6 rectangle (see #1).
- Begin the Chamfer command.
- See that the current chamfer length is 1 and the angle is 45 degrees.
- Right-click anywhere in the drawing. Click Polyline.

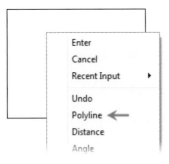

- Select the rectangle.
- All corners are chamfered.

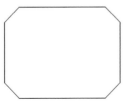

4   To chamfer using the Distance option where the distances are not equal:
- Draw another 8 x 4 rectangle.
- Begin the Chamfer command.
- Right-click anywhere in the drawing. Click Distance.

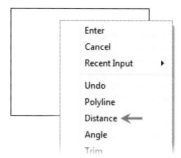

- Enter **1** for the first chamfer distance and press ENTER.
- Enter **.5** for the second chamfer distance and press ENTER.
- Select the first line (1) and select the second line (2).
- Repeat the Chamfer command.
- Select the line at (3) and then select the line at (4).
  Remember that the first distance is always applied to the first line you select and the second distance is applied to the second line selected.

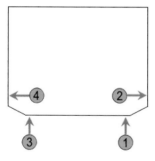

- Repeat the Chamfer command and add chamfers to all four corners as shown below.

5   To chamfer using the Distance option combined with the Polyline option when the distances are not equal:

- Draw an 8 x 6 rectangle.

- Begin the Chamfer command.
- Note that the current chamfer distance 1 is 1 and distance 2 is .5.
- Right-click anywhere in the drawing. Click Polyline.

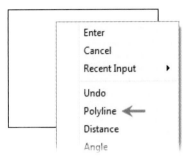

- Select the rectangle.

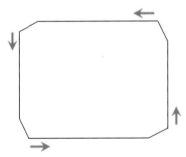

Chamfer works in a counterclockwise direction. Therefore, chamfering a polyline with non-equal distances gives you this kind of result.

Exercise | Create a Chamfered Corner

In this exercise, you create chamfer features using the Multiple, Distance, and Angle options of the Chamfer command. When you have completed the exercise, you will be able to use the Chamfer command to add chamfer features to geometry in other drawings.

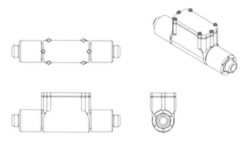

The completed exercise

> **Completing the Exercise**
> To complete the exercise, follow the steps in this book or in the onscreen exercise. In the onscreen list of chapters and exercises, click *Chapter 5: Altering Objects*. Click *Exercise: Create a Chamfered Corner*.

1   Open *M_Create-Chamfers.dwg*.

2   Zoom in on the lower left view of the drawing.

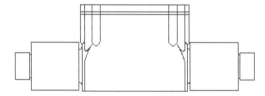

3   To create a 1-unit chamfer:
   - Start the Chamfer command.
   - Right-click anywhere in the drawing window. Click Distance.
   - When prompted for the first chamfer distance, enter **1**. Press ENTER.
   - Press ENTER for the second chamfer distance, as it defaults to the value of the first chamfer distance.
   - Right-click anywhere in the drawing window.
   - Click Multiple. This enables you to create multiple chamfers without restarting the Chamfer command.

4   To complete the chamfer:

- Select the lines indicated in the following image near their intersections.
  Note: The chamfers have already been applied in this image. You may need to turn on the Trim option if it is off.
- DO NOT exit the chamfer command. Proceed to the next step.

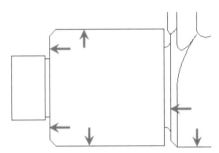

5   Select the lines near their intersections as shown in the following image. Press ENTER to end the Chamfer command.

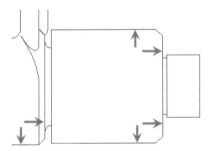

6   Use Zoom and Pan to display the top-left view in the drawing.

7   To create more 1-unit chamfers in this view:

- Start the Chamfer command.
- Right-click anywhere in the drawing window. Click Multiple.
- Select the lines indicated in the following image.
  Note: The lines have already been chamfered in this image.

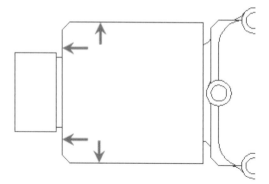

8   Repeat the chamfers on the right side of the view. Press ENTER to end the Chamfer command.

9   To create additional chamfers using the Angle and Multiple options:
    • Press ENTER to repeat the Chamfer command.
    • Right-click anywhere in the drawing window.
    • Click Angle.
    • Enter **1** for the chamfer length on the first line.
    • Enter **60** for the chamfer angle from the first line.
    • Right-click anywhere in the drawing window.
    • Click Multiple.
    • Select the edges in the order indicated in the following image.
       Note: The chamfers have already been applied in this image.

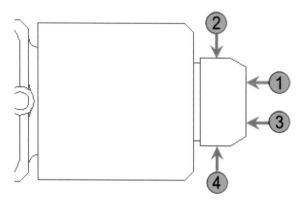

10 Select the edges on the opposite side of the view.

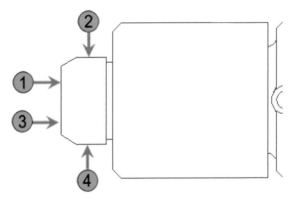

11 Use Zoom and Pan to display the lower-left view as shown.

- Apply the chamfers to the edges of the part on both sides of the view.
- Press ENTER to end the Chamfer command.

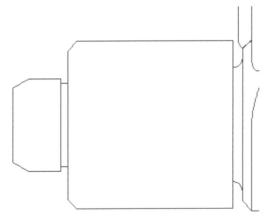

12 Using the Line command, draw line segments at each location in which a chamfer was created.

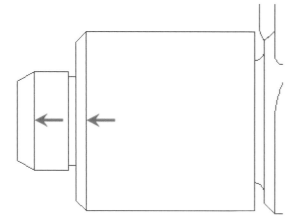

13 Zoom to display your entire drawing.

14 Close all files without saving.

Lesson 30 | Changing Part of an Object's Shape

This lesson describes how to use the Stretch command to change part of an object's shape.

Reusing objects and ease of editing are key benefits of using the Stretch command. As your design evolves, changes to features naturally occur as part of the process, or perhaps you are attempting to reuse geometry from another drawing and some features require a change in length or shape. The Stretch command can help in these situations by enabling you to modify the shape of existing objects easily.

After completing this lesson, you will be able to describe key aspects of the Stretch command and use the command to stretch objects.

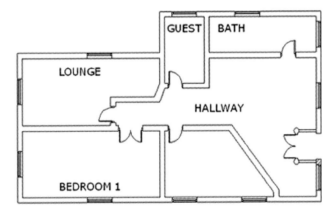

Objectives

After completing this lesson, you will be able to:

- Use the Stretch command to stretch objects.

Stretching Objects

You use the Stretch command to change the shape of objects in the drawing, defining the area to be stretched with a crossing window or crossing polygon selection tool. After you define the stretch window, you then specify a base point and a second point for the stretch.

Defining the stretch operation with a crossing window or crossing polygon is critical, because the area that is crossed by the selection method determines how the objects are stretched.

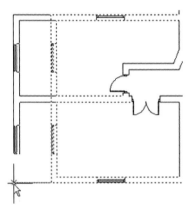

Command Access

Stretch

Command Line: **STRETCH, S**
Ribbon: **Home tab > Modify panel > Stretch**

Menu Bar: **Modify > Stretch**

Procedure: Stretching Objects Using Grips

The following steps give an overview of using grips to stretch objects.

1   Select an object to activate its grips.

2   Select any grip (use SHIFT+select to select multiple grips).

3   Click and drag the grips to a new location.

Procedure: Stretching Objects

The following steps give an overview of stretching objects in a drawing.

1   Start the Stretch command.

2   Select the objects to be stretched by defining a crossing window or crossing polygon selection.

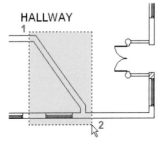

3   Select the base point for the stretch.

4   Select the second point or enter a value for the stretch distance.

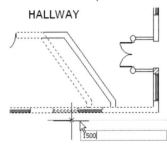

Stretch Guidelines

- When you stretch objects, you must define the stretch window using a crossing window (CW) or crossing polygon (CP). If you use implied windowing, you must create the selection from right to left.
- Objects that are crossed by the selection window are stretched, while objects that are completely enclosed by the window are moved.
- To stretch an object in a straight line, be sure that Polar Tracking or Ortho Mode is on.
- After you have selected your object(s) to Stretch, pick a base point near the object but far enough away from any other objects you might snap to accidentally.

Practice Exercise | Stretching Objects

In this practice exercise, you draw some rectangles and then practice using the Stretch command to stretch using grips.

Keep in mind that object endpoints included in the crossing selection window are moved or stretched to a new location. Endpoints left out of the crossing selection window remain anchored to their position.

1   To Stretch the large rectangle:

*   Draw a rectangle with another one inside, as shown above.
*   Begin the Stretch command.
*   Begin an implied crossing window by clicking the right corner (1) of the selection window then click the opposite corner to the left (2), as indicated below.

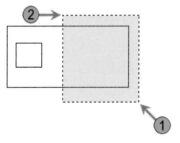

*   Press ENTER to complete your selection.
*   Click a base point near the object (1). DO NOT SELECT the next point. Drag the cursor to the left (2) as shown below, enter **2**, and press ENTER.

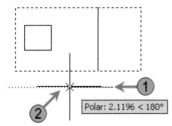

Notice that Polar Tracking or Ortho Mode must be on to ensure that you drag the objects in a straight line.

2   To stretch both rectangles:

- Begin the Stretch command.
- Begin an implied crossing window picking corners first at (1) and then at (2) as shown below.

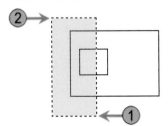

- Press ENTER to complete the selection.
- Click a base point near the object as shown below and drag to the left.

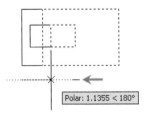

- Enter **2** and press ENTER.

Notice that Polar Tracking or Ortho Mode must be on to ensure that you drag the objects in a straight line.

3   To stretch the large rectangle and move the small rectangle using the Stretch command:

- Begin the Stretch command.
- Begin an implied crossing window first at point (1) then at point (2). Be sure the smaller rectangle is completely inside the selection window.

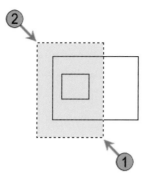

- Press ENTER to complete the selection.
- Click a base point near the object as indicated below.
- Drag the cursor to the left.

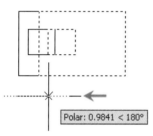

Polar: 0.9841 < 180°

- Enter **2** and press ENTER.

Notice that the small rectangle was completely within the selection window so all endpoints or vertex points were moved.

4   To stretch an object using grips:

- With the command line blank, select a rectangle.
- Hold down SHIFT and click two endpoints as indicated below.

- Release SHIFT and click one of those points again.

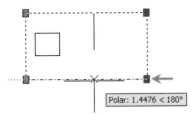

Polar: 1.4476 < 180°

- Drag the cursor to the left and click on the Midpoint of that line.

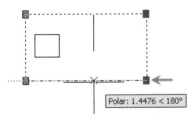

Polar: 1.4476 < 180°

5   To stretch a single vertex or endpoint of an object:
- With the command line blank, select the rectangle.
- Click a corner endpoint.
- Drag to the right and click.
- Press ESC to deselect the object.

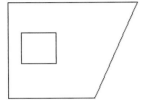

Notice that the single endpoint or vertex was moved and the other endpoints remained anchored. The lines in between were stretched.

Exercise | Stretch Objects

In this exercise, you use the Stretch command to increase the area of the rooms in the floor plan. When you have finished, you will be able to use the Stretch command to stretch geometry in other drawings.

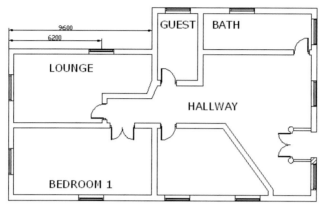

The completed exercise

Completing the Exercise

To complete the exercise, follow the steps in this book or in the onscreen exercise. In the onscreen list of chapters and exercises, click *Chapter 5: Altering Objects*. Click *Exercise: Stretch Objects*.

1   Open *M_Stretch-Objects.dwg*.

2   On the status bar, turn Osnap off.

3   To add 2000 units to the left side of the structure:

- On the Modify panel, click Stretch.
- Click point (1) then point (2) to define the stretch crossing window.
- Press ENTER.

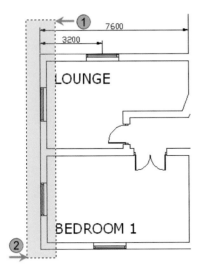

4　To complete the stretch operation:

- Click to select near the bottom corner of the wall and drag the cursor to the left 180 degrees.
- Enter **2000**. Press ENTER.
- Notice that the dimensions also update to reflect the new size.

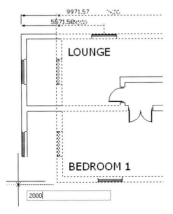

5　To use stretch with a Crossing Polygon selection:

- Press ENTER to repeat the Stretch command.
- Enter **CP** to specify a crossing polygon selection. Press ENTER.
- Define the crossing polygon by clicking points, as shown in the following image.

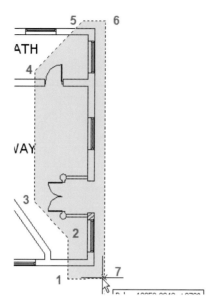

6   To add 2000 units to the right side of the structure:

  • Press ENTER to complete the crossing polygon selection.
  • Press ENTER to complete the object selection.
  • Click a point near the bottom corner of the wall.
  • Drag your cursor to the right at 0 degrees and enter **2000**. Press ENTER.

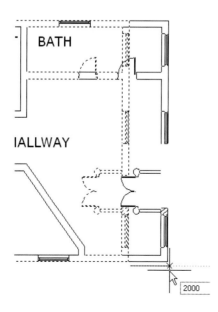

7   To use stretch with a crossing selection:

- Right-click anywhere in the drawing.
- Click Repeat Stretch.
- Enter **C**. Press ENTER for a crossing window.
- Click near point (1) and then point (2) to define the crossing window. Press ENTER.

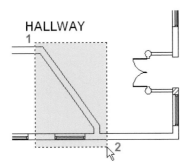

8   To slide an interior wall 1500 units to the right:

- Click a point below the floor plan, and then drag to the right at 0 degrees.
- Enter **1500**. Press ENTER.
  Notice how the window object moved with the stretch operation. This occurred because any geometry that is fully enclosed by the stretch window is moved rather than stretched.

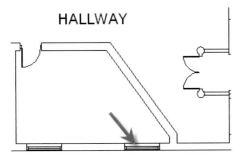

9   To select a window to move within a wall:

- Start Stretch.
- Click near point (1) and then point (2) to define the crossing window.
- Press ENTER.

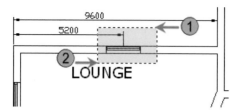

10   To complete the move:

- Click a point to the right of the window, and then drag to the right at 0 degrees.
- Enter **1000**. Press ENTER.
  Notice how the window object moved with the stretch operation and the dimension updated to reflect the new window location.

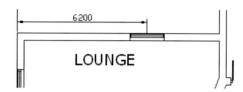

11   To select a door to relocate within a wall:

- Start the Stretch command.
- Click near point (1) and then point (2) to define the crossing window.
- Press ENTER.

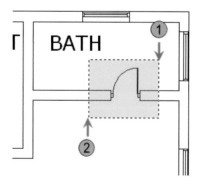

12   To relocate the door:

- Click a point to the right of the door, and then drag to the right at 0 degrees.
- Enter **1200**. Press ENTER.
  Notice how the door object moved, and the wall objects were stretched.

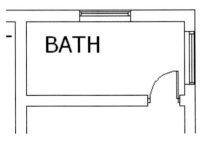

13 Close all files without saving.

Challenge Exercise | Architectural

In this exercise, you use what you learned about altering objects to modify the floor plan.

> **Note**
> You have the option of completing this exercise using either imperial or metric units. Select one version of the exercise to complete the steps.

The completed exercise

> **Completing the Exercise**
> To complete the exercise, follow the steps in this book or in the onscreen exercise. In the onscreen list of chapters and exercises, click *Chapter 5: Altering Objects*. Click *Challenge Exercise: Architectural Metric*.

Metric Units

1   Open the drawing you saved from the previous challenge exercise, or open *M_ARCH-Challenge- CHP05.dwg*.

2   Create the geometry to represent a wall 189 mm thick, working on the basis that the original lines you created represented the outside of the exterior and structural walls. The image shows the bottom stairwell. Note that the lines you drew for the stairwell in the Chapter 2 challenge exercise were dimensioned from the outside wall to the leading, or inside, edge of the wall. Add the door opening to the lower staircase to match the opening in the upper staircase.

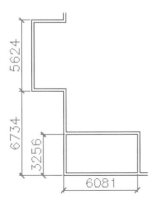

3   Add a 915 mm door opening in the right wall, positioned as shown in the image.

4   Add 15 window openings that are 914 mm wide and positioned as dimensioned. In the wall sections that jog out to the left toward the corners with the dimensions of 500, center the openings along that inside wall.

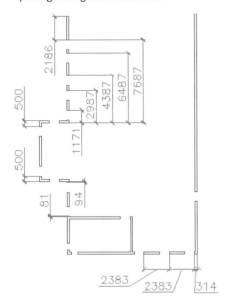

5   Add six window openings that are 610 mm wide and positioned as dimensioned.

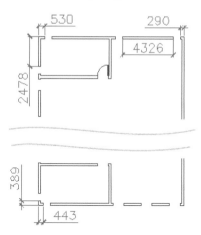

6   Create the interior walls 124 mm wide on the Wall-Interior layer. The 3 thicker walls are 336 mm. All interior door openings are 915 mm wide. Position the walls based on the dimensions shown in the image. For any geometry not specifically dimensioned, estimate its position and draw it as shown in the image.

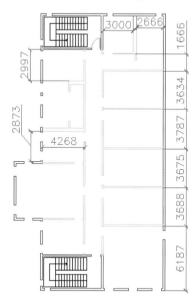

7   Save and close the drawing.

Chapter 5 | Altering Objects

Imperial Units

1   Open the drawing you saved from the previous challenge exercise, or open *I_ARCH-Challenge- CHP05.dwg.*

2   Create the geometry to represent a wall 7" thick, working on the basis that the original lines you created represented the outside of the exterior and structural walls. The image shows the bottom stairwell. Note that the lines you drew for the stairwell in the Chapter 2 challenge exercise were dimensioned from the outside wall to the leading, or inside, edge of the wall. Complete all of the exterior walls. Add the door opening to the lower staircase to match the opening in the upper staircase.

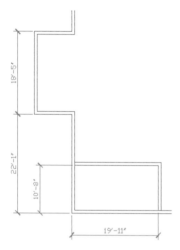

3   Add a 3'-0" door opening in the right wall, positioned as shown in the image.

4   Add 15 window openings that are 36" wide and positioned as dimensioned. In the wall sections that jog out to the left toward the corners with the dimensions of 1'-8", center the openings along that inside wall.

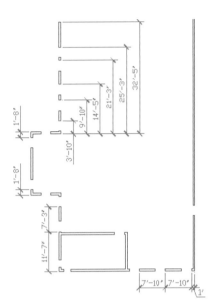

5   Add six window openings that are 24" wide and positioned as dimensioned.

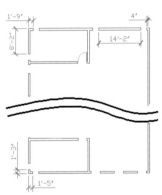

6   Create the interior walls 5" wide on the Wall-Interior layer. The three thicker walls are 13.5". All interior door openings are 3'-0" wide. Position the walls based on the dimensions shown in the image. For any geometry not specifically dimensioned, estimate its position and draw it as shown in the image.

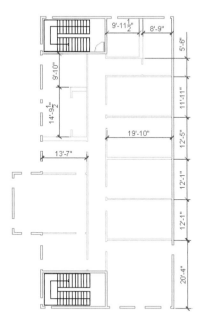

7   Save and close the drawing.

Challenge Exercise | Mechanical

In this exercise, you use what you learned about altering objects to edit geometry.

Note: In the following image, the views are closer together than they will appear in your drawing.

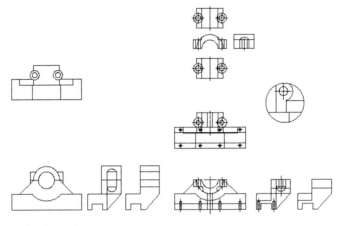

The completed exercise

> ### Completing the Exercise
> To complete the exercise, follow the steps in this book or in the onscreen exercise. In the onscreen list of chapters and exercises, click *Chapter 5: Altering Objects*. Click *Challenge Exercise: Mechanical*.

1   Open the drawing you saved from the previous challenge exercise, or open *M_MECH-Challenge- CHP05.dwg*.

2   Create and edit geometry so the views for the Rack Slider Top appear as shown.
    Note: The views in the image are closer together than they will appear in your drawing.

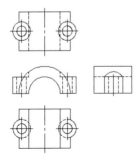

3 Create and edit geometry so the views for the Rack Slider Base appear as shown. Use Join to join the collinear lines that were created with Mirror in a previous challenge.
Note: The views in the image are closer together than they will appear in your drawing.

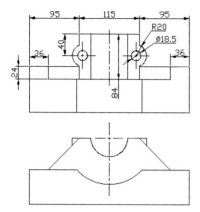

4 Create and edit geometry so the side view for the Rack Slider Base appears as shown. Note the 3mm radius fillets.

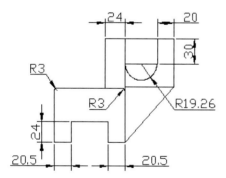

5 Copy geometry from the area indicated to the upper-right of the view.

- Scale the resulting geometry to twice its regular size.
- Draw a circle around the scaled geometry, then trim the geometry to the circle.

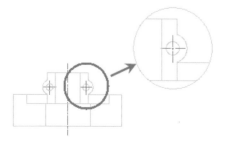

6   Copy geometry from the existing views to create the assembly views. You won't need the hidden and centerlines.

- Thaw the Start Points layer.
- Use the Assembly Start Point to locate the position of the assembly front view.
- Erase geometry as required if it would be hidden by other parts as it is assembled.

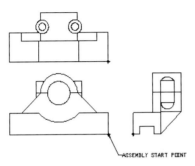

7   Delete the Assembly Start Point leader and text.

8   Create the centerlines for the detail view.

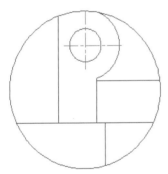

9   With the Hidden layer current, create the hidden geometry in these views using points in each view as references. Then create the centerline objects and place them on the Centerline layer. **Note**: In the following image, the views are closer together than they are in the drawing.

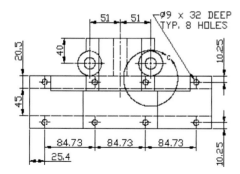

ⵉ⌀9 × 32 DEEP
TYP, 8 HOLES

51 51

20.5

40

10.25

45

84.73 84.73 84.73

25.4

10.25

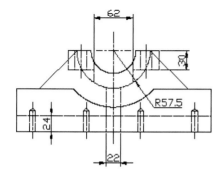

62

30

R57.5

24

22

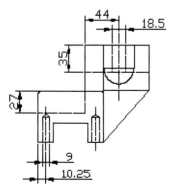

44

18.5

35

27

9

10.25

10 Copy the geometry for the side view to create a section (you will apply hatching in a later challenge exercise). Move the hidden geometry to the Visible layer, then delete and trim unnecessary geometry. Delete the hole geometry.

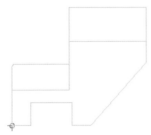

11 Copy the section view to the start point to the right of the side assembly view.
Copy the Rack Slide Top's side view and position it on top of the section view, then move hidden lines to the visible layer and remove the unnecessary geometry.

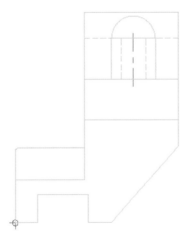

12 Save and close all files.

Chapter Summary

Every design you create begins with simple geometry. The procedures you use to edit these basic objects transform them into complex designs.

Having completed this chapter, you can:

- Change the length of objects using the Trim and Extend commands.
- Create parallel and offset geometry in your drawing by using the Offset command.
- Use the Join command to combine multiple objects into a single object.
- Break objects into two or more independent objects.
- Apply a radius corner to two objects in the drawing.
- Apply an angled corner to two objects in the drawing.
- Use the Stretch command to alter the shape of objects in the drawing.

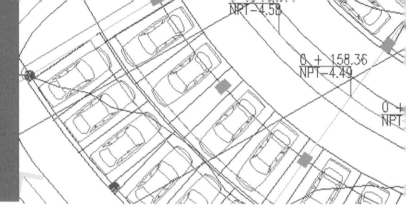

Chapter 06
Working with Layouts

Your design is only as good as your ability to communicate it to others. Your drawings can contain a lot of different information, and you need to be able to output a variety of aspects of the design.

Layouts and viewports help you to structure and focus your design and its supporting information for the final step of communicating it to others through both paper and electronic media.

You also need to understand how Layouts and Viewports work before you can add annotations, such as dimensions and text, to your drawings.

Objectives

After completing this chapter, you will be able to:

• Identify the environments in which you can plot data and create a new layout.

• Create and manipulate viewports.

Standard Object Snap and Status Bar Settings
Before completing the exercises in this chapter, refer to the "Settings for the Exercises" section in the Introduction.

Lesson 31 | Using Layouts

In this lesson, you learn how to create a layout, which is the environment you use to prepare your drawing for plotting. You also learn how to switch between layouts and layout viewports.

Plotting is a vital step in the process of communicating your design and the use of layouts is an important part of preparing for plotting.

The following illustration shows geometry that resides in model space and a plot preview from a corresponding layout.

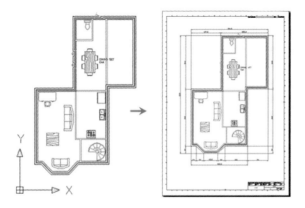

Objectives

After completing this lesson, you will be able to:

- Describe the purpose and key properties of layouts.
- Create a new layout.

About Layouts

A layout is an environment used to output your drawing data. That data can include model space geometry and geometry added to the layout to enhance a specific plotted sheet.

The following image shows an empty layout in a drawing. You can see the paper size, the printable area within the dashed lines, and the rectangular viewport for the selected layout.

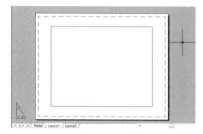

Defining the Layout

In a layout, you select what paper size you want to plot on. That paper size is then displayed at a visual full scale with a dashed rectangle indicating the area the selected plotter can plot within for that size paper. You also select paper orientation.

With the paper in the layout displaying at full scale, you insert your border and title block on the sheet at full scale. You can also create textual notes at full scale on the paper.

You display model space geometry on the paper in the layout by creating viewports. You can define multiple viewports and set their scale and location.

The following are some of the properties and settings that you can save in a layout:

- Printer/plotter
- Paper size
- Plot area
- Plot offset
- Plot style table
- Drawing orientation
- Plot scale

Example of Layouts

One advantage of using layouts is being able to plot using multiple scale factors on the same drawing sheet. For example, you can display an overall view of a floor plan at one scale, and right next to it two detail views, each at their own scales.

The following illustration shows a completed layout that includes the floor plan at a common scale; an elevation at a smaller scale; and a detail of the stairwell blown up at a larger scale.

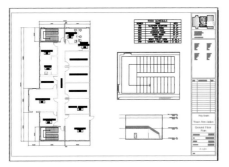

Creating a New Layout

You can add layouts to the current drawing based on a layout in a template file, by copying an existing layout in the drawing, or by adding a new one. To add a new layout, you use the Layout, New Layout, or Create Layout Wizard commands.

Command Access

Layout

Command Line: **Layout > New**
Status Bar: *Click view Layout; right-click to Display Layout and Model Tabs*

Layout tab or Model tab shortcut menu: *right-click to display options*

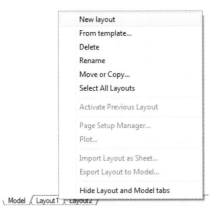

Note: Available only once Layout and Model tabs are displayed.
Menu Bar: **Insert > Layout > New Layout**

Procedure: Creating a New Layout

The following steps give an overview of creating a new layout in the drawing.

1   Right-click the Model tab or any layout tab.

2   Click New Layout.

3   Click the layout tab for the newly created layout.

Procedure: Creating a New Layout with the Layout Wizard

The following steps give an overview of creating a new layout in the drawing using the Create Layout Wizard.

1   On the command line, enter **LAYOUTWIZARD**.

2   Step through the wizard screen to:

  • Name the layout

  • Select a configured plotter

  • Select a paper size and its units of measurement

  • Select a paper orientation

  • Pick a standard title block if desired

  • Define the number of viewports and their scales

  • Set the location for the viewports on the paper

3   Click Finish.

Practice Exercise | Create a New Layout

In this practice exercise, you create a new layout from the Layout tab and from the Layout Wizard.

1   To create a new layout from the Layout or Model tab:

 • Right-click on the Layout or Model tab.

 • Click New Layout.

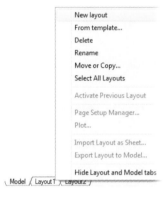

Note: If the tabs are not visible, right-click the Layout button on the status bar and click Display Layout and Model Tabs.

 • Select the new Layout tab.

 • The settings are based on the prior layout settings.

2   To create a new layout using the Layout Wizard:

 • On the command line, enter **LAYOUTWIZARD**.

 • Enter a name for the new layout. Enter **Floor Plan** and click Next.

 • For the Printer, select DWG to PDF.pc3 and click Next.

 • For the Paper Size, select ARCH D (36.00 x 24.00 Inches), Drawing units Inches, and click Next.

 • Select a Landscape orientation and click Next.

 • Select the *Architectural Title Block.dwg* and click Next.

- Select a Single Viewport setup with a Viewport scale of 1/8" = 1'-0" and click Next.

- To set a location on the layout page for the viewport, click Select location < and specify a viewport window clicking points (1) and (2) as indicated below.

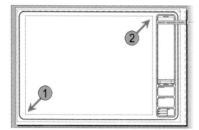

- Click Finish.

Exercise | Create Layouts

In this exercise, you activate different layouts and then create two additional layouts.

The completed exercise

Completing the Exercise

To complete the exercise, follow the steps in this book or in the onscreen exercise. In the onscreen list of chapters and exercises, click *Chapter 6: Working with Layouts*. Click *Exercise: Create Layouts*.

1   Open *M_Create-Layouts.dwg*.

2   To activate a layout:

- Click the Layout1 tab.

- Review the layout format and the information displayed.

Note: If the Layout tabs are not visible, right- click on the Layout button in the status bar and select *Display Layout and Model Tabs*.

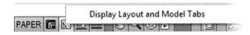

3 To activate another layout, click the Layout2 tab. Notice the differences in the model space geometry being displayed and the page size and orientation.

4 To create a new layout:

- Right-click the Layout tab.

- Click New Layout.

5 To review the newly created layout, click the new Layout3 tab. It includes a single viewport and the page configuration is based on the default Option settings in your installation of the software. You may or may not see any of your model space objects.

6 To insert a new layout, from the Menu Bar click Insert > Layout > Create Layout Wizard. If the Menu Bar is not visible, turn it on or enter LAYOUTWIZARD on the command line.

7 To specify a layout name:

- Enter **Wizard Layout** when prompted for the layout name.

- Click Next.

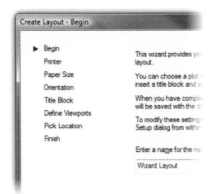

8   To choose a printer for the layout:

  • Select DWF6 ePlot.pc3 from the list of available printers.

  • Click Next.

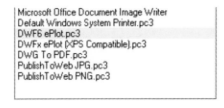

9   To set the paper size:

  • Select ISO A1 (841.00 x 594.00 MM) from the list of available paper sizes.

  • Click Next.

Select a paper size to be used for the layout. The paper sizes available are based on the plot device you selected.

Enter the paper units for layout "Layout3".

Drawing units	Paper size in units
◉ Millimeters	Width: 841.00 mm
○ Inches	
◉ Pixels	Height: 594.00 mm

10   Click Next to keep the paper orientation as Landscape.

11   To not include a title block:

  • Select None from the list of title blocks.

  • Click Next.

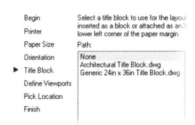

12 To specify a viewport scale:

- On the Define Viewports page, under Viewport Setup, verify that Single is selected.
- Under Viewport Scale, select 1:50 from the list.
- Click Next.

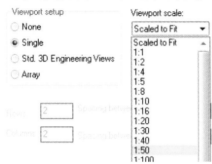

13 To set a location for the layout:

- Click Select Location.
- Click in the upper-left corner of the paper.
- Click the bottom of the page just past the halfway point as shown.
- Click Finish.

14 Close all files without saving.

Lesson 32 | Using Viewports

This lesson describes how to create a new rectangular viewport, set the viewport scale factor, and manipulate viewports.

Viewports are a key component in the ability to plot model space geometry from a layout. Each viewport acts as a display portal from the paper layout to the geometry in model space. By creating multiple viewports in a single layout, you can display different aspects of the model geometry at different scales on the same page.

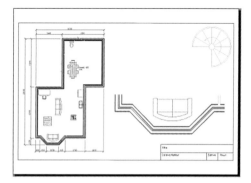

Objectives

After completing this lesson, you will be able to:

- Create a rectangular viewport.
- Modify the viewport scale factor.
- Move, copy, resize, rotate, and delete viewports.
- Rotate the view within a viewport.

Creating Rectangular Viewports

You create a rectangular viewport similar to the way you create a rectangle. However, a rectangular viewport created in a Layout is a kind of *window* that displays the geometry from the model space view into the current layout page.

You scale the view of the geometry displayed in each viewport and typically plot the overall layout 1:1. You can have more than one viewport on a single layout page showing different views of your drawing at different scales.

Typically the viewport is not plotted. You can create the viewport on a unique layer so that you can use the layer properties to prevent the viewport boundary from plotting.

Command Access

Single Viewport

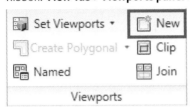

Command Line: **VPORTS**
Ribbon: **View Tab > Viewports panel > New > Viewports dialog box > Single**

Viewports dialog box:

Menu Bar: **View > Viewports > 1 Viewport**

Procedure: Creating Rectangular Viewports

The following steps give an overview of creating rectangular viewports. Though making a rectangular viewport is relatively simple, it is important to understand the overall setup.

1   If the layout tabs are not available, right-click the Layout button in the status bar and select *Display Layout and Model Tabs.*

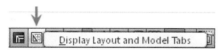

2   Activate the appropriate layout tab.

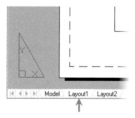

3   Confirm the paper size for the layout.

   • Right-click the layout tab and select the Page Setup Manager.

- Confirm that the Plot Size paper is correct (1).
- To change the paper size, select Modify (2).

4   Insert a title block if one is not already inserted.

5   Activate the viewports command.

- On the Viewports panel, click New (1).
- In the Viewports dialog box, on the New Viewports tab, under Standard Viewports, click Single (2).

6   Create the viewport.

- Specify the first corner (1).
- Specify the opposite corner (2).

7   Place the viewport on a layer that you will choose not to print.

- With the command line blank, select the viewport.
- From the Layer Control list, select the layer.
- Press ESC to deselect the viewport.

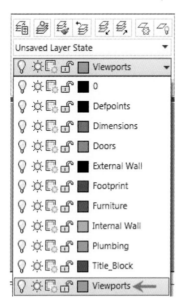

Guidelines for Creating Viewports

- You should always create viewports on their own layer.
- The viewports layer should be set to non-plotting.
- There is no practical limit to the number of viewports on a single drawing sheet.
- Each viewport can have its own plot scale factor.

Setting Viewport Scale Factor

Once you have created a layout viewport, you can set the display of the geometry within it to a specific scale compared to the paper units. This ensures that when you plot the layout at a scale of 1:1, the geometry in the viewport is at the desired scale on the paper.

In the following illustration, if 1:30 is selected, the geometry in model space will appear 30 times smaller on the paper. So if 1 unit on the paper is a millimeter, and the units in model space are millimeters, then a line 30 millimeters long in model space will be 1 millimeter long on paper. If the paper were in inches and 1 unit in model space represented a foot, then a line representing 30 feet in model space would be 1 inch long on the paper.

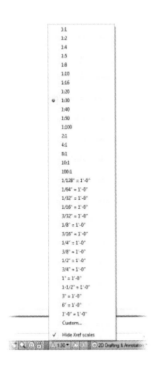

Viewport Scale Access

Viewport Scale

Status Bar: **Viewport Scale**

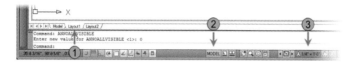

① Layout tab must be selected.

② The model or paper space button may be set to either mode:

- Model space on: Viewport can be active (bold).
- Paper space on: Viewport can be selected.

③ Viewport scale is accessible.

Procedure: Setting and Locking Viewport Scale

The following steps give an overview of setting a viewport scale and then locking the viewport so that it cannot be changed.

1   From the layout tab, select your viewport border.

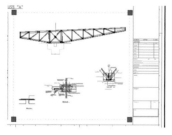

2   On the status bar, click the viewport scale list and select the scale to apply to the viewport.

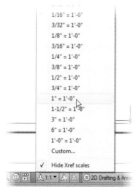

1/16" = 1'-0"
3/32" = 1'-0"
1/8" = 1'-0"
3/16" = 1'-0"
1/4" = 1'-0"
3/8" = 1'-0"
1/2" = 1'-0"
3/4" = 1'-0"
1" = 1'-0"
1-1/2" = 1'-0"
3" = 1'-0"
6" = 1'-0"
1'-0" = 1'-0"
Custom...

✓ Hide Xref scales

3   Double-click inside your viewport to activate model space and use pan to position your objects in the viewport.

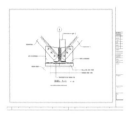

4   Double-click outside the viewport to activate paper space. Select the viewport border again. On the status bar, click Lock/Unlock Viewport. Now the viewport is locked at the scale you set.

5   With your viewport selected, the status line displays its current locked condition and scale.

Guidelines for Setting the Viewport Scale

- To set the scale for a layout viewport, select the viewport boundary. On the status bar, select the Viewport Scale list and pick the desired scale.

- It is a good habit to lock the viewport once the scale is set. Select the viewport boundary and then on the status bar, click Lock/Unlock Viewport.

- You must unlock the viewport before changing the scale. However, you may still pan the model data within the viewport.

- The viewport can be selected in Paper space mode or activated in Model space mode to set the Viewport Scale or Lock/Unlock the Viewport.

Practice Exercise | Setting Viewport Scale Factor

In this practice exercise, you draw some objects in model space, then create a rectangular viewport in a selected layout tab. From the layout, you Zoom the viewport in both the model space and paper space modes. Finally, you set the viewport to a specified scale.

1   Draw some geometry as shown below:
    - Begin a new blank drawing based on *acad.dwt*.
    - Create the objects in the drawing window without zooming the drawing area.

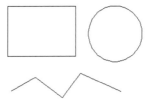

2   Select the layout tab. Notice that it already has a single viewport on it. You are going to erase this and create your own viewport.

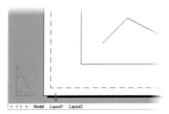

3   To practice making a single viewport, first delete the one that is already there.
    - With the Command line blank, click the viewport.
    - On the Modify panel, click Erase.

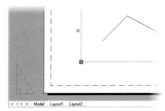

4   To create a single viewport:

  • At the Command line, enter **-vports** and press ENTER.
  • Specify the corner of the viewport (1).
  • Specify the opposite corner (2).

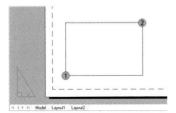

5   To zoom the geometry inside the viewport:

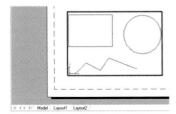

  • Double-click inside the viewport.
  • Notice that the viewport rectangle is bold, indicating it is active.

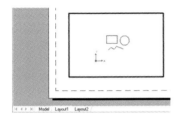

  • Use Zoom and Pan in real time to view your drawing in the viewport

6   To zoom the entire drawing layout:

  • Double-click outside the viewport.
  • Notice that the rectangular boundary is no longer bold.
  • Use the Zoom and Pan real-time commands to view your paper layout.

- Zoom to view your entire drawing in the Layout.

7   To set the viewport scale:

- Select the viewport.
- On the status bar, click Viewport Scale.

- In the list, select 1:2
- Press ESC to deselect the viewport.

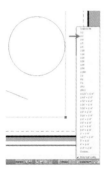

8   To change the Viewport Scale and lock the viewport:

- Select the viewport.
- On the status bar, click Viewport Scale.
- In the list, select 1:4.
- On the status bar, click Lock/Unlock Viewport.

- The icon should appear locked.
- Press ESC to deselect the viewport and view the results.

Manipulating Viewports

You can manipulate viewports in many ways. If you no longer want the viewport and the data it displays, you can use the Erase command to delete it. Since it only displays geometry from model space, deleting the viewport does not delete the model space geometry. You can use the Move command to change a viewport's position on the paper. You can also use the Copy command to duplicate the viewport and its display settings to another location on the layout. To resize a viewport, use the grips at its corners.

Another way of manipulating a viewport is to freeze the display of model space layers. By controlling the display of model space layers per viewport in this way, you can display the same area of model space in different ways in each viewport. To freeze or thaw the layer in the current viewport (1), the layout viewport must be active. To make a layout viewport active, you double-click inside the viewport boundary. You know when a viewport is active because the boundary is highlighted, as shown in the following illustration (2), and the crosshairs change to an arrow cursor when you pass over the viewport boundary.

You can override layer properties in each viewport to have them appear differently in a viewport than they do in model space. For example, you may want your layout to display the walls in a different color than they are displayed in the model. Property overrides are accessed from the Layer Properties Manager when opened with a layout tab current.

VP Freeze	VP Color	VP Linetype	VP Lineweight	VP Plot Style
	■ white	Continuous	—— Default	Color_7
	■ white	Continuous	—— Default	Color_7
	■ red	Continuous	—— 0.35 mm	Color_1
	□ 133	Continuous	—— Default	Color_133
	■ white	Continuous	▬▬ 0.50 mm	Color_7
	■ 32	Continuous	—— Default	Color_32
	□ 140	Continuous	—— Default	Color_140
	■ green	Continuous	—— Default	Color_3

Erasing Viewports

If after creating a viewport you no longer want the viewport and the data it displays, you can use the Erase command to delete it. Since it only displays a view of the geometry from model space, deleting the viewport does not delete the geometry. You can erase, move, or copy a viewport, and you can alter the way layers are displayed in a viewport, all without losing or changing the work you have done to the original model.

Moving, Copying, and Resizing Viewports

You can use the Move command to change a viewport's position on the paper. You can also use the Copy command to duplicate the viewport and its display settings to another location on the layout. To resize a viewport, use the grips at its corners.

Altering Layers in Viewports

You can freeze the display of a layer in a selected viewport. By controlling the display of model space layers per viewport, you can display the same area of model space in different ways in each viewport. Use the *freeze or thaw in current viewport* option in the Layer Control list or the VP Freeze option of a selected layer in the Layer Property Manager. You must do this when the layout viewport is active. To make a layout viewport active, you double-click inside the viewport boundary. You know when a viewport is active because the boundary is highlighted, as shown in the following illustration, and the crosshairs change to an arrow cursor when you pass over the viewport boundary.

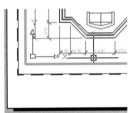

You can also override layer properties to have them appear differently in a viewport than they do in model space or other viewports. For example, you may want to display your walls at a different color in a layout than they are displayed in the model. Property overrides are accessed from the Layer Properties Manager when opened with a layout tab current. The four properties you can control are:

- VP Color
- VP Linetype
- VP Lineweight
- VP Plot Style

Procedure: Moving and Resizing a Viewport

The following steps give an overview of moving and resizing a viewport.

1   Start the Move command and pick your viewport border. Press ENTER to complete the selection process.

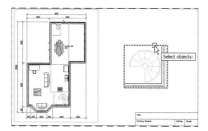

2   Pick a base point and then drag the viewport to a new position and pick your second point.

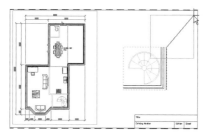

3   Select your viewport border. Click a corner grip to make it hot, then click and drag to increase or decrease the size of the viewport.

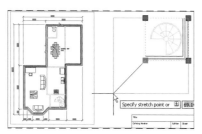

Guidelines for Manipulating Viewports

- Use grips to adjust the size of the viewport in a drawing layout.
- Copy a viewport to display the same objects then adjust the layer settings.
- Double-click inside a viewport to make it active.
- Only one viewport can be active at a time.
- Double-click outside the viewports to make the paper space layout active.
- To make multiple copies of viewports you can also use the Array command.
- Viewports can be rectangular or polygonal in shape.
- You can Clip a viewport with a polygonal shape.
- You can create a closed polyline or circle in a layout view and convert that object to a viewport.
- In AutoCAD LT®, you can create only rectangular viewports.
- Viewports created in the Model tab will display additional viewports of the drawing in the same workspace. Each viewport can display a different view of the drawing. You can switch between the viewports as you draw by clicking in the viewport first to make it active.

Practice Exercise | Manipulating Viewports

In this practice exercise, you create a simple drawing with geometry on several layers to practice freezing a layer in a selected viewport.

1   To create the practice drawing:
   - Begin a new drawing.
   - In the Layer Properties Manager, add the following layers with the following layer properties:
     - Layer name: **Center**
       Color: **Red**
       Linetype: **Center**
     - Layer name: **Hidden**
       Color: **Blue**
       Linetype: **Hidden**
     - Layer name: **Viewports**
       Color: **Cyan**
       Linetype: **Continuous**
   - Create a drawing similar to the one above, drawing the center line on the Center layer and the hidden lines on the Hidden layer.

2   Select the Layout1 tab.

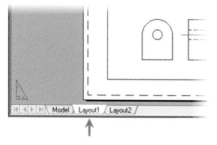

3   To adjust the viewport size:
   - With the command line blank, select the viewport.
   - Use the grips to adjust the size of the viewport as shown below.

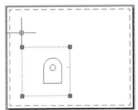

4   To adjust the view inside the viewport:

- Double-click inside the viewport.
- On the status bar, click the Viewport Scale list and select a scale of 1:2 (you may have to select a different scale to get your drawing to fit in the viewport).

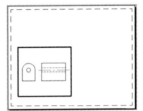

5   To move the viewport:

- Double-click outside the viewport.
- Begin the Move command.
- Select the viewport boundary and press ENTER.
- Specify a basepoint and a second point to move the viewport to the center left as indicated below.

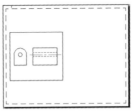

6   To copy the viewport

- Begin the Copy command.
- Select the viewport and press ENTER.
- Make a single copy of the viewport to the right, as indicated below.
- Press ENTER to complete the copy command.

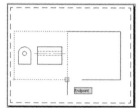

7   To freeze layers in a selected viewport:

- Double-click inside the viewport on the right.
- From the Layer Control list, select the icon indicated below to Freeze the Center and Hidden layers in the current viewport.
- Double-click outside the viewport so that neither viewport is selected.

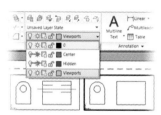

8   To change the viewports to the layer named Viewports:

- With the Command line blank, select the two viewports.
- In the Layer Control list, select the Viewports layer.
- Press ESC to deselect the viewports.

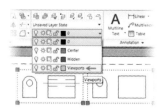

9   To keep the viewports from printing (Method 1):

- Select the Layer Control list and Freeze the Viewports layer.
- The viewports are not visible in the layout view and will not print.

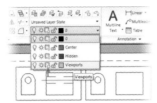

You can still double-click inside the viewport to make it active; however to adjust the viewport size, you have to Thaw the Viewports layer.

10 To keep the viewports from printing (Method 2):

- In the Layer Properties Manager, select the Viewports layer.
- Select the Plot icon to make the layer not plotting.

- Close the layers Properties Manager dialog box.
  The Viewports layer will be visible in the drawing layout, but will not plot.

Rotating Viewports

You rotate a viewport with the Rotate command or by using grips. You can also set the entire layout view to rotate with the viewport by setting the VPROTATEASSOC system variable.

The following image shows a viewport before and after it is rotated.

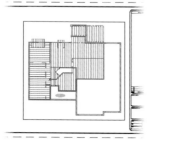

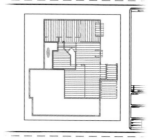

Before rotation   *After rotation*

Command Access

VPROTATEASSOC

Command Line: **VPROTATEASSOC**

VPROTATEASSOC System Variable

The VPROTATEASSOC system variable controls whether the view within a viewport is rotated with the viewport when the viewport is rotated. The VPROTATEASSOC system variable can be set to one of the following values.

Option	Description
0	When a viewport is rotated, the view inside is not rotated.
1	When a viewport is rotated, the view inside is rotated to match the rotation of the viewport.

Process: Rotating a View within a Viewport

The following steps give an overview of how to rotate a view within a viewport.

1   At the Command prompt, enter **VPROTATEASSOC**.

2   Set the value to 1.

3   On a layout tab, select the desired viewport.

4   Rotate the viewport to the desired angle.

5   Observe the entire view rotate within the viewport.

Exercise | Create and Manipulate Viewports

In this exercise, you change the scale factor of a viewport, move a viewport, freeze a layer in an active viewport, and create a new viewport.

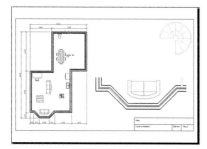

The completed exercise

> **Completing the Exercise**
> To complete the exercise, follow the steps in this book or in the onscreen exercise. In the onscreen list of chapters and exercises, click *Chapter 6: Working with Layouts*. Click *Exercise: Create and Manipulate Viewports*.

1   Open *M_Create-and-Manipulate- Viewports.dwg*.

2   In the Layout1 tab, click to select the green

3   To set the viewport scale:

   • On the status bar, click the Viewport Scale list and select 1:30.

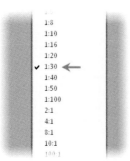

4   The floor plan should now appear smaller on the layout and you should be able to see all of the dimensions as shown.

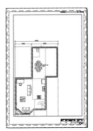

5   Click the Layout2 tab.

6   To move a viewport:
   • Start the Move command.
   • Select the green rectangular viewport that displays the circular staircase. Press ENTER.
   • Move it to the upper-right corner of the border, as shown.

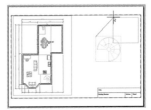

7   To activate model space in the layout:
   • Position the cursor inside the green rectangular viewport on the left side of the sheet.
   • Double-click to activate the model space environment through that viewport.
   • When the viewport is active, the crosshairs and UCS icon should appear as shown.

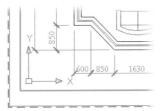

8   To freeze a layer in the current viewport:
   • Open the Layer Properties Manager.
   • Click the icon in the VP Freeze column for the layer Internal Wall to freeze that layer in the current viewport.
   • Click OK.
     Notice how the staircase is no longer displayed in the viewport on the left but it is in the viewport on the right.

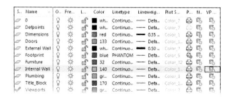

9   To change the color of a layer in the current viewport:

- Open the Layer Properties Manager.
- Click the icon in the VP Color column for the layer Furniture.
- Set the color to magenta.
- Click OK.

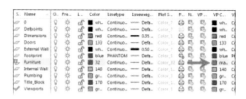

10   To verify that the Furniture color only changed in Layout2:

- Click the Model tab. Confirm that the furniture color remained brown.
- Click the Layout1 tab. Notice that the furniture color remained brown.
- Click the Layout2 tab. Confirm that the furniture color is still magenta in this layout.

11   To activate the layout environment:

- Position your cursor in the gray background outside the paper.
- Double-click to change the focus back to the layout environment.

12   To create a viewport:

- Type **-vports** on the command line
- Click and draw a rectangular viewport in the open area of the paper layout as shown.

13   To set the viewport scale:

- Double-click inside the new viewport to make it active.
- On the status bar, click the Viewport Scale list and click 1:30.

14 Pan the view in the viewport so you are viewing the bay walls and couch as shown.

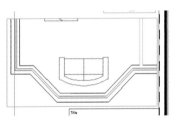

15 Double-click in the gray area outside the paper.

16 Grip edit the viewport from the upper-right corner to crop the display as shown.

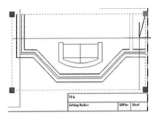

17 The green viewport borders are on the Viewports layer. To set that layer so it does not plot:

• Open the Layer Properties Manager.
• Click the printer icon in the Viewports layer row.
  With this setting, the viewport borders are not plotted when you output the drawing.

18 On the command line, enter VPROTATEASSOC. Enter **1**.

19 Select the viewport you created and then start the Rotate command on the command line:

• Select a corner of the viewport as the base point for the rotation.
• For the rotation angle, enter **90** and press ENTER.
  Note that when the rotation is complete, the view of the drawing rotates with the viewport. If the VPROTATEASSOC variable is set to zero the Rotate command only rotates the viewport and not the view within it.

20 Close all files without saving.

Challenge Exercise | Architectural

In this exercise, you use what you learned about working with layouts to configure a layout and a viewport for your design.

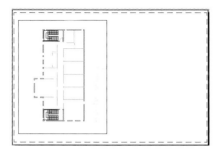

The completed exercise

Metric Units

1   Open the drawing you saved from the previous challenge exercise, or open *M_ARCH-Challenge- CHP06.dwg*.

2   Configure Layout1 to plot with the following settings:

- Orientation: Landscape
- Scale: 1:1
- Printer/Plotter: DWF6 ePlot.pc3
- Paper size: ISO A1 (841 x 594 mm) paper

3   Rename Layout1 to Plan View.

4   Add and configure the main viewport on the layout:

- A view of the main floor plan at a scale of 1:60.
- Lock the viewport when completed.

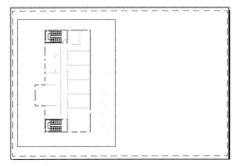

5   Save and close the drawing.

Imperial Units

1   Open the drawing you saved from the previous challenge exercise, or open *I_ARCH-Challenge- CHP06.dwg*.

2   Configure Layout1 to plot with the following settings:
   - Orientation: Landscape
   - Scale: 1:1
   - Printer/Plotter: DWF6 ePlot.pc3
   - Paper size: ARCH expand D (36.00 x 24.00 Inches)

3   Rename Layout1 to Plan View.

4   Add and configure the main viewport on the layout:
   - A view of the main floor plan at a scale of 3/16" = 1'.
   - Lock the viewport when complete.

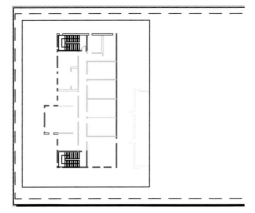

5   Save and close the drawing.

Challenge Exercise | Mechanical

In this exercise, you use what you learned about working with layouts to create and configure a layout with three viewports.

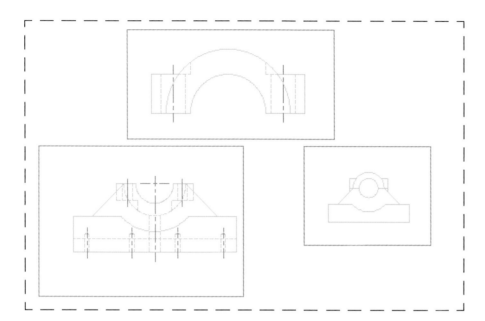

The completed exercise

Completing the Exercise

To complete the exercise, follow the steps in this book or in the onscreen exercise. In the onscreen list of chapters and exercises, click *Chapter 6: Working with Layouts*. Click *Challenge Exercise: Mechanical*.

1   Open the drawing you saved from the previous challenge exercise, or open *M_MECH-Challenge- CHP06.dwg*.

2   Create a new layout configuration with the following settings:

- DWF6 ePlot.pc3
- ISO A3 (420 x 297)
- Three viewports that do not show on the plot
- A scale factor for the view at the top of 1:1
- A scale factor for the view on the left of 1:2
- A scale factor for the view of the assembly on the right of 1:4

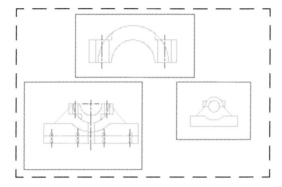

3   Perform a cleanup:

- Rename the layout Parts.
- Delete Layout2.
- Return to model space.

4   Save and close the drawing.

Chapter Summary

There are several ways you can prepare your design data for outputting to paper or to an electronic file. Layouts are an environment in which you select the paper size for printing on and then add borders, title blocks, and any textual notes for annotating the drawing. You display model space geometry on the paper in the layout by creating viewports, which can display various permutations of the data at different scales to help you to focus on what you are trying to communicate about your design.

Having completed this chapter, you can:

- Identify the environments in which you can plot data and create a new layout.
- Create and manipulate viewports.

Chapter 07
Annotating the Drawing

No drawing is complete without some kind of text to annotate the design. In this chapter, you learn to create and edit text objects. You also learn how to edit and scale text so that it appears consistently in your drawing and drawing layouts.

Objectives

After completing this chapter, you will be able to:

- Use the Mtext command to create multiline text.

- Create single line text.

- Use different methods to edit text.

- Create text styles to manage text.

Standard Object Snap and Status Bar Settings
Before completing the exercises in this chapter, refer to the "Settings for the Exercises" section in the Introduction.

Lesson 33 | Creating Multiline Text

This lesson describes how to create Multiline Text.

It is common practice to place paragraph style notes on drawings. These notes generally refer to the drawing as a whole rather than specific features, and often require more formatting options than standard single-line text objects.

The following illustration shows multiline a multiline text object being created.

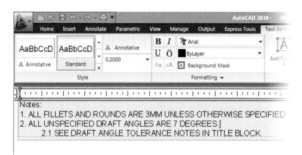

Objectives

After completing this lesson, you will be able to:

- Describe Multiline text.
- Use the Multiline Text command to create and format paragraphs of text.
- List the changes implemented to increase productivity when using Mtext.

About Multiline Text

You use the Multiline Text command to create paragraphs of text for notes and other information in your drawing or drawing Layout.

NOTES:
1. ALL FILLETS AND ROUNDS ARE 3MM UNLESS OTHERWISE SPECIFIED.
2. ALL UNSPECIFIED DRAFT ANGLES ARE 7°±1°.
   2.1. SEE DRAFT ANGLE TOLERANCE NOTES IN TITLE BLOCK.

Words and paragraphs remain intact and the width can be adjusted using grips.

Multiline Text Defined

Multiline Text is an assembly of words, symbols, and other textual information that can be written, formatted, and edited using the AutoCAD® built-in editor. You can create several paragraphs of text as a single multiline (mtext) object and format the text appearance which includes justification, italics, underline, bold, and inserting symbols.

The illustration below shows the editing options that are available within the multiline Text Editor when you right-click. These options also appear in the ribbon when the Multiline Text command is invoked or the text is selected for editing.

The options for the Text Editor appear within the AutoCAD drawing environment and are similar to other word programs.

Example of Multiline Text

This is an example of Multiline Text.

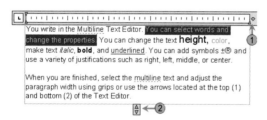

Example of Single Line Text

The text in single line text, which you will learn about in the next section, does not allow paragraph formatting.

This is single line text.
You will learn about single line text in the next section.
Each line is treated separately.
There is no paragraph formatting in single line text.

Creating Multiline Text

You use the Multiline Text command to create paragraph style text. You can create text in your drawing using formatting options found in most standard word processors, as well as functions that are specific to the software.

With the Multiline Text editor, you can:

- Create paragraph styled text.
- Create numbered and bulleted lists.
- Insert specific drafting and engineering symbols.
- Change the text justification.
- Create columns of text.
- Create Fields such as date, time and author.

Once the Multiline Text area is specified, the ribbon displays the Text Editor tool panels.

Command Access

 Multiline Text

Command Line: **MTEXT, MT, T**
Ribbon: **Annotate tab > Text Panel > Multiline Text**

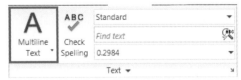

Ribbon: **Home tab > Annotation Panel > Multiline Text**

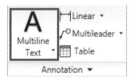

Menu Bar: **Draw > Text > Multiline Text**

Multiline Text Tab

When you use the Multiline Text command, the ribbon opens to the Multiline Text tab displaying the Text Editor. Use the options on the panels to control the text appearance, format your paragraphs, insert symbols, add fields, check spelling, and perform other functions specific to the annotation of your drawing.

① **Style** controls text style and text height.

② **Formatting** controls whether the text is bold, italic, underlined, or overlined. You can also choose to override the current text style font and color.

③ **Paragraph** controls the justification, line spacing, numbering, and bullets of selected text.

④ **Insert** allows you to insert symbols, columns, and fields (such as author and date).

⑤ **Spell Check** allows you to check spelling.

⑥ **Tools** contains the find and replace, import text, and change case options.

⑦ **Options** controls the display of text box rulers and changes the character set and editor settings.

⑧ **Close** enables you to close the Multiline Text Editor.

Editing Multiline Text

To edit existing multiline text, double-click the text. The Text Formatting toolbar appears so you can edit the text in the same way you created it.

Procedure: Creating Multiline Text

The following steps give an overview of creating multiline text.

1 Start the Multiline Text command.

2 Click two points to define the text area.

3 Confirm the text style (1) and text height (2) settings on the Style panel.

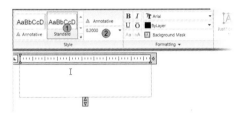

4 Begin creating text using the options as required for numbered or bulleted lists and symbols.

5 Use the ruler to adjust the width and height of the text area if necessary.

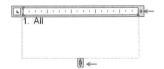

6 Double-click outside the Text Editor to accept the text and exit.

1. ALL OUTSIDE
    FILLETS .125
2. DRAFT ANGLES
    ARE 3°

Multiline Text Guidelines

- Keep the text window size relative to the area where you want the text to appear in the drawing. Use the grips to adjust the width and height.
- You can override the font in the current style by setting specific font options on the Formatting panel.
- To ensure that multiline text sentences maintain the ability to wrap within the text box, press ENTER only to begin a new line or paragraph.
- To format selected text, select the text first, then select the Formatting option. Single-clicking places the cursor in a new location, double-clicking selects the entire word and triple-clicking selects the entire paragraph.
- You can copy text from another location or program and paste it into the Text Editor. However it may retain the text format associated with its source. Paste the text first into Notepad then copy it again and past it into the Multiline Text Editor. This way it retains the text style you designate in AutoCAD.
- Multiline Text options may also be accessed by right-clicking in the Text Editor window.
- If you Explode multiline text, it becomes single lines of text.
- You can type **MTEXT** or simply **T** and press ENTER to begin the Multiline Text command.
- It is good practice to always place text on its own layer.

MText Columns and Grips

When you use Mtext objects in your drawings, you have the ability to format the text into columns. You can also edit the text using grips in a similar manner to tables.

Placing Mtext

When you place Mtext, the Text Editor tab activates on the ribbon. Additionally, you can specify that you want the text to be formatted with columns using the Column option on the Insert panel.

Column options on the Ribbon

Column Settings dialog box

Option	Description
Dynamic Column	Sets the dynamic columns mode to the current Mtext object. Dynamic columns are text driven. Adjusting the columns affects the text flow and the text flow causes columns to be added or removed. Automatic or manual height options are available.
Static Column	Sets the static columns mode to the current Mtext object. You can specify the total width and height of the Mtext object and the number of columns. All of the columns share the same height and are aligned at both sides.
No Column	Specifies no columns for the current Mtext object.

Note
You can also insert a manual column break from the ribbon. This option is disabled when No Columns is selected.

Editing Mtext with Grips

Grip editing mtext is the ability to adjust column width and height using grips.

1 Location Grip

2 Column Width

3 Mtext Width

4 Mtext Width and Mtext Height

5 Mtext Height

Exercise | Create Multiline Text

In this exercise, you use the Multiline Text command to create multiline text in the drawing.

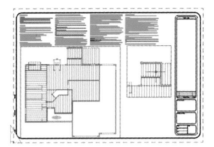

The completed exercise

Completing the Exercise
To complete the exercise, follow the steps in this book or in the onscreen exercise. In the onscreen list of chapters and exercises, click *Chapter 7: Annotating the Drawing.* Click *Exercise: Create Multiline Text.*

1   Open *C_Create-Mtext.dwg.*

2   Zoom into the upper-right corner of the title block.

3   On the status bar, click Object Snap to turn it off.

4   To place an address on the title block:

- Start the Multiline Text command.
- Click two points to define the multiline text box as shown.

5   To set the text height and enter the address:

- On the Style panel, in the text size list, enter **6**.
- Enter the text as shown.
- Press ENTER after the last line.

6   To change the text height and enter the phone and fax numbers:

   - In the Text Height list, enter **3**.
   - Press ENTER.
     Note: You can enter values or select values in this list.
   - Enter the text for the telephone and fax numbers as shown.
   - Click on the Close Text Editor on the Close panel or double-click outside the Text Editor.

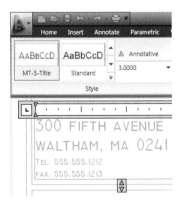

7   Zoom to the extents of the drawing.

8   Zoom a window around the view label text.

9   Repeat the Multiline Text command. Click two points to define the multiline text box as shown.

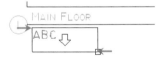

10 On the Style panel, select ViewLabel from the text style list.

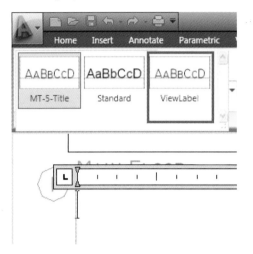

11 Enter the text as shown below.

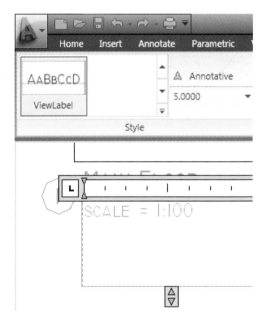

12 Double-click outside the Text Editor to close it.

13 Zoom to the extents of the drawing.

14 Close all files without saving.

Edit Mtext to Display Columns

In this exercise, you adjust existing text from a single column to a more orderly column layout.

1   Open *I_Mtext-Columns and Grips.dwg* .

2   Change to the Title Block layout.

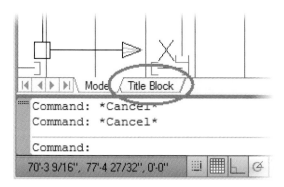

3   Select the Mtext object.

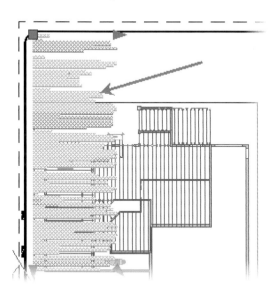

4   Open the Properties palette from the command line. Under Text, for Columns, click [...].

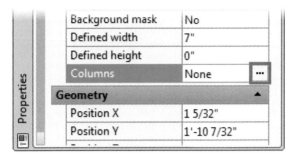

5   In the Column Settings dialog box:
- Under Column Type, select Dynamic Columns.
- For Height, enter **6"**.
- Under Width, for Column, enter **6".**
- For Gutter, enter **7/16".**
- Click OK.

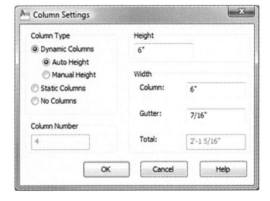

The Mtext object is displayed with four columns.

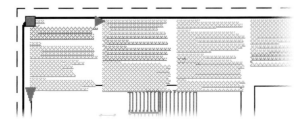

6 On the Mtext object, click the Mtext Height grip.

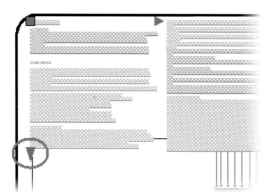

7 Drag the cursor up and select a point above the viewport as shown.

8 Move the same grip back down as shown. The fifth column is removed.

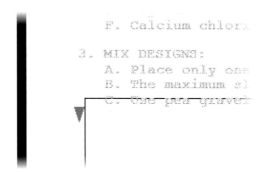

9 Press ESC to clear grips

10 Close all files. Do not save.

Lesson 34 | Creating Single Line Text

This lesson describes how to use the Text command to create single line text in your drawings. With Single line text, each line of text or textual object that is created can be edited independently. This distinguishes single line text from multiline text created with the Mtext command, because a single Mtext object can contain multiple lines of text.

Where Mtext is very robust and feature rich, single line text enables you to quickly create and locate small text objects. The most common use for single line text is to place a number or letter inside a circle.

In the following illustration, single line text of varying heights, justification, and rotation angle is used in a title block.

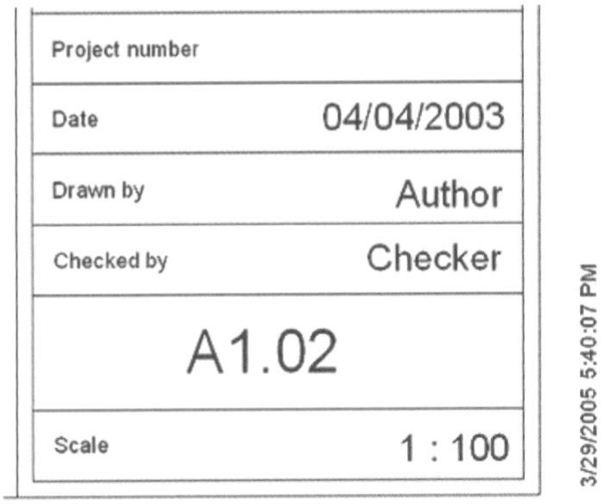

Project number	
Date	04/04/2003
Drawn by	Author
Checked by	Checker
	A1.02
Scale	1 : 100

3/29/2005 5:40:07 PM

Objectives

After completing this lesson, you will be able to:

- Describe Single Line text.
- Use the Text command to create single line text. Make single line text associative.

About Single Line Text

Single line text is used for information that is usually a single word, a letter or a short sentence or phrase. The options available to single line text are different than those available with Multiline text and there are fewer formatting options. An example of a typical use for single line text is to center a letter or number in a circle.

If you explode Multiline text, it would be converted to single lines of text. When you type using the single line Text command, pressing ENTER begins a new line of text.

THIS IS LINE ONE
THIS IS LINE TWO

Pressing ENTER twice will exit the Text command.
When you select a single line of text with the Command line blank, only one grip is displayed.

THIS IS LINE ONE
THIS IS LINE TWO

When you select Multiline text, four grips are displayed.

THIS IS MULTILINE TEXT.
YOU CAN FORMAT THE
PARAGRAPHS SIMPLY BY
STRETCHING THE GRIPS.

Single Line Text Defined

The Text command creates a single line of text. When you begin the command, you are prompted for a single insertion point for the text location.

Once you pick that point, you are prompted to specify a height and a rotation angle. Other options include Justify and Style which can be initiated by pressing the DOWN ARROW on the keyboard or right-clicking to access the shortcut menu.

Below are some examples of the Justify options.

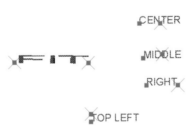

Creating Single Line Text

You use the Text command to create single line text objects. When you start the Text command, you are first shown the current text style and height. You are then prompted to select a start point for the text, followed by the text height and rotation angle.

While the term *single line text* is used when referring to the Text command, it does not mean that you can only create a single line of text at a time. To create the next line of text, press ENTER and begin typing the next line. If you press ENTER on a blank line, the command ends. Each line of text you create in this way is a separate object. If you use the Text command to create four lines of text, it results in four separate text objects, each representing a single line of text, and each capable of being edited independently of the others.

You can create single line text objects that are associative. For example, you could link a single line text object representing the drafter's name in a title block to the drawing file's Author property. Then, if a different person took over the drawing and changed the drawing file's Author property to their name, the text would update to the new person's name in the title block.

The text in the following image was created using the Text command. Even though all lines of text were created at the same time, you can select and edit them individually.

EPDM ROOF CONSTRUCTION:
EPDM ROOFING MEMBRANE
3/4"[19] T & G PLYWOOD SHEATHING
TJI ROOF JOISTS
VAPOUR BARRIER
1/2"[12.5] GYPSUM BOARD
SUSPENDED ACOUSTIC TILE

Command Access

Single Line Text

Command Line: **TEXT, DTEXT, DT**
Ribbon: **Annotate tab › Text Panel › Single Line Text**

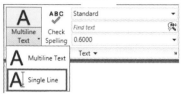

Menu Bar: **Draw › Text › Single Line Text**

Command Options

Once you begin the Single Line Text command, you choose justification or style options by pressing the DOWN ARROW on the keyboard or right-clicking anywhere in the drawing to access the shortcut menu.

Justify: Use this option to specify a justification for the text. Once you select Justify, a list of options appears as shown on the right.

Style: Use this option to specify a text style other than the current text style.

Note: It is easier to select the current text style from the Text panel before you start the Text command. Using this option requires you to enter the text style name on the command line.

The following image illustrates the various justification options.

> **Text Style Height Setting**
> If the current text style uses a height of 0, when you create single line text you are prompted for the text height. If the current text style has a height specified, you are not prompted for the text height.

Procedure: Creating Single Line Text

The following steps give an overview of creating single line text.

1   Start the Text command.

2   To set the justification options, right-click anywhere in the drawing. Click Justify and enter a justification option on the command line, or right-click and select the justification on the shortcut menu.

3   Specify a start point for the text.

4   Specify a height and rotation angle.

5   Begin entering the lines of text.

6   Each time you press ENTER, a new line of text and therefore a new text object is created. Press ENTER on a blank line to complete the command.

Single Line Text Guidelines

- When you create single line text, each line is a separate text object.
- Pressing ENTER begins another line of text that is aligned with the previous line of text.
- Picking a point in the drawing window specifies a new location for the next line of text.
- Pressing ENTER twice ends the single line text command.
- Single line text is created in the current text style unless you specify another style when you start the command. It is easiest to chose another text style from the list located in the Text panel *before* you begin the single line text command.
- When creating single line text, follow the Command line prompts.
- You can specify the text height and rotation angle by picking points in the drawing window.
- To edit single line text, double-click it.
- To change the justification, style, or height of a single line text object, select it and right-click. Select the Properties or Quick properties palette from the shortcut menu.
- You can copy text from another location such as the Command line or Text Window (F2) and paste it into the single line text typing area.
- If you Explode multiline text, it will become single lines of text objects.
- If you type **T** and press ENTER at the Command line you will begin the Multiline Text command. If you enter **text** and press ENTER, you will begin the Single Line Text command.
- It is good practice to always place text on its own layer.

Exercise | Create Single Line Text

In this exercise, you create Single Line Text in the drawing Layout and in model space. You will size the text accordingly so that it appears at the proper height.

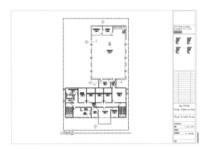

The completed exercise

1   Open *C_Create-Single-Line-Text.dwg.*

2   Zoom into the lower-right area of the title block.

3   Use Single Line Text to place your name in the Checked By area of the title block.

   • Start the Single Line Text command.
   • Right-click anywhere in the drawing. Click Justify. Click Right.
   • Click the point indicated by the arrow in the following image to specify the right justification of the text.
     Note: You may need to zoom in closer to prevent Object Snap from selecting the endpoint of that nearby line.

- Press ENTER to use default text size.
- Press ENTER to confirm the default rotation angle of 0.
- Enter your name and press ENTER twice.

4   To check the Viewport Scale:

- Zoom Extents to view the entire drawing.
- With the Command line blank, select the viewport (1).
- Note the Viewport Scale of 1:100 (2).

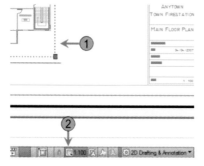

- Press ESC to cancel the viewport selection.

5   Click the Model tab to switch to model space.

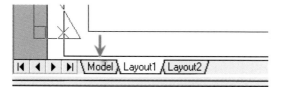

6   Start the Zoom Window command. Click two points approximately as shown by the arrows in
     the following image.

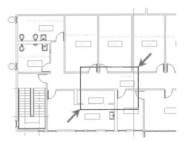

7   On the Layers panel, click Make Object's Layer Current (1) and select the Corridor
     (2) text object.

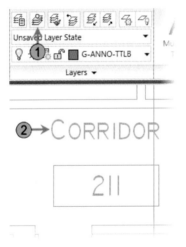

8   To check the status bar settings:
     • Make sure Polar Tracking, Object Snap, Object Snap Tracking and
       Dynamic Input are on.
     • Right-click Object Snap. Click Settings and confirm that the Midpoint
       object snap mode is checked.

9   Select the text style list from the Text panel and click Standard.

10 To center text above a rectangular object:

- Zoom in closer to the rectangle to the lower left side of the word "Corridor".
- Start the Single Line Text command.
- Right-click anywhere in the drawing. Click Justify.
- Click Center.
- Hover over the midpoint of the rectangle as shown (do not select) and track slightly above it. Click.

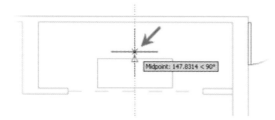

- Specify a text height of 300.
  Note: Since the Viewport Scale in the Layout is set to 1:100, setting your text height to 300 in model space will result in a text height of 3 when viewed through the layout viewport.
- Specify a rotation angle of (0).
- Enter **kitchen** and press ENTER twice.

11 To place text in the middle of the rectangle:
- Begin the Single Line Text command.
- Right-click. Click Justify.
- Select Middle from the next menu.
- Track the midpoints of two adjacent lines of the rectangle and select the point where they intersect in the middle of the rectangle. Click.

- Press ENTER twice to accept the default height of 300 and the default rotation angle of 0.
- Enter **210** and press ENTER twice.

12 Repeat the previous steps to label each room with text as shown below:

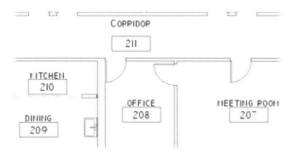

13 To view the results:

   • Zoom to display the entire drawing in model space.
   • Select the Layout tab to view the text in the drawing layout.

14 Close all files without saving.

Lesson 35 | Editing Text

This lesson describes how to edit both multiline and single line text.

Most drawings include at least some text objects. You need to be able to make edits to existing text quickly and efficiently. It is often easier to make a copy of an existing text object and then edit the copy than it would be to create the text from scratch.

In the following illustration, text editing commands were used to modify the title block text and create a numbered list in the notes.

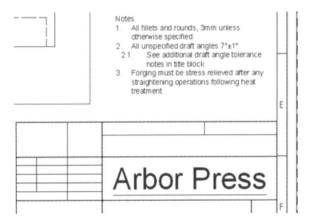

Objectives

After completing this lesson, you will be able to:

- Edit text using a variety of commands and methods.

Editing Text

There are five tools that you can use to edit text. These are:

- Multiline Text Editor ribbon
- In-place text editor
- Properties palette
- Quick Properties
- Grips

The quickest way to edit text is to double-click the text object. If you double-click a multiline text object, the Multiline Text Editor is displayed in the ribbon along with the In-Place Text Editor. If you double-click a single line text object, the In-Place Text Editor opens where you can edit the text in the same way you created it.

You can use the Quick Properties or the Properties palette to edit the properties associated with text as well as the content of the text object. You can also use grips to edit the text's position and width. When you select text once, grips are displayed. You can grip edit text objects using the same methods as grip editing geometry.

In addition to the Multiline Text Editor, the in-place text editor offers real-time spell checking.

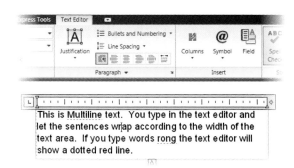

Command Access

Multiline Text Edit

Double-click Multiline Text
Command Line: **MTEDIT, DDEDIT, ED**
Ribbon: *double-click Multiline Text* **Multiline Text tab > Text Editor Panel**

Menu Bar: **Modify > Object > Text > Edit**

Command Access

Single Line Text Edit
Double-click Single Line Text
Command Line: **DDEDIT, ED**
Menu Browser: **Modify > Object > Text > Edit**

Spell Check the Entire Drawing
You can check for spelling errors in the entire drawing or selected text objects. Type **spell** at the command line and use the options in the dialog box.

Procedure: Editing Multiline Text

The following steps give an overview of editing multiline text.

1   Double-click the Multiline Text.

2   Use the in-place text editor to edit text content or select text to format using the options located on the ribbon.

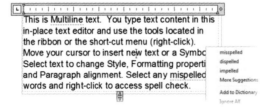

3   Use the Text Editor options found on the ribbon to format text selected from the in-place text editor to insert symbols, line spacing, numbering, bullets, or change paragraph justification in the selected text.

4   Double-click outside the text editor window to end the editing operation.

Editing Multiline Text with the Quick Properties Palette

Another option for editing text objects is to use the Quick Properties palette. You can modify most of the properties associated with the text as well as the text content.

In the example on the right, the text justification option is being changed to Middle center using the Quick Properties palette.

Procedure: Editing Single Line Text

The following steps give an overview of editing single line text.

1   Double-click the Single Line Text.

2   Use the in-place text editor to edit the content in each single line of text. You can right-click to check and correct misspelled words.

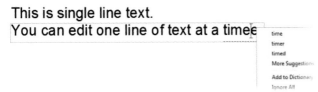

3   Click outside the text editor window to end the editing operation.

Editing Single Line Text with the Quick Properties Palette

You can use the Quick Properties palette to modify most of the properties associated with single line text as well as the text content.

In the example on the right, the text rotation option has been changed to 30 degrees using the Quick Properties palette.

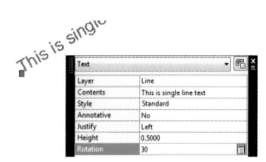

Chapter 7 | Annotating the Drawing

Exercise | Edit Text

In this exercise, you edit single line text and multiline text to change the properties and create a numbered list.

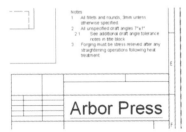

The completed exercise

Completing the Exercise
To complete the exercise, follow the steps in this book or in the onscreen exercise. In the onscreen list of chapters and exercises, click *Chapter 7: Annotating the Drawing.* Click *Exercise: Edit Text.*

1   Open *M_Edit-Text.dwg*.

2   Zoom into the title block area of the drawing.

3   Select the Arbor Press text to display the grip. Note the location of the grip, indicating that the text is left justified.

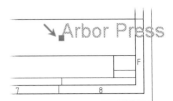

4   If the Quick Properties palette is not open, select it from the status bar or right-click to access it from the shortcut menu:

   • Under Text, enter **%%uArbor Press** in the Contents field.
     Note: These are the ASCII characters for underlining the text. If this were Multiline Text you would be able to use the Formatting options from the ribbon.
   • In the Justify list, select Middle.
   • In the Height field, enter **10.**

5 Press ESC to clear the selection. Note the new appearance of the text.

6 Zoom into the notes above the title block.

7 Double-click the notes text. The Text Formatting toolbar is displayed with the In- Place Text Editor.

Click the beginning of each line and press DEL to remove the numbers.

8 Highlight all of the text beneath the word Notes. On the ribbon, in the Paragraph panel, click Numbering. Click Numbered.

The text should now appear as shown.

9   Place the cursor at the beginning of line 3 and press TAB.

The line is automatically renumbered as a subnote and the numbers are reordered.

10   Click Close Text Editor on the Close panel.

11   Zoom to the extents of the drawing.

12   Close all files without saving.

Lesson 36 | Using Text Styles

This lesson describes how you can use text styles to control text appearance.

In a typical design environment, there can be several designers creating drawings. If each designer were to choose their own text fonts for annotation, the resulting drawings would lack a uniform appearance. Using text styles can help to create a consistent appearance across drawings by providing predefined text formats.

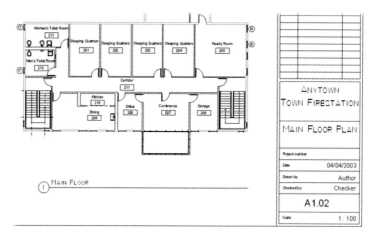

Objectives

After completing this lesson, you will be able to:

- Explain the purpose of text styles.
- Create and use text styles.

Text Styles

Text styles provide an easy way for you to control the default appearance of text. Each text object contains properties such as font, height, width factor and oblique angle. Using text styles, you can predefine each of these properties, resulting in a uniform appearance of text objects that use the same style.

Another benefit of using text styles is that you can update all text in the drawing that uses a certain style simply by changing the style.

The following image illustrates the effect of changing a text style when it is being referenced by text objects. In the floor plan on the right, the text style uses a smaller font so that the text objects better fit the space.

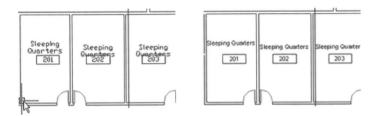

Text Styles Defined

A text style is a collection of common text properties used by one or more text objects in the drawing. You generally create several text styles. For example, you could have a text style for dimensions, another for view labels, and another for title blocks or general drawing annotation.

$$|40,57 \qquad \langle 14 \rangle$$

Example of Text Styles

On a typical drawing, you might have one style defined for all of your general notes, text and dimensions, another style for object labels, and another style for the title block information.

Text Style Key Points

- A text style is a collection of predefined text properties such as font, height, width factor, and oblique angle.
- You create text styles to keep a uniform appearance of text objects in the drawing.
- You can update all text in the drawing that uses a certain style simply by changing the style.
- You generally create several text styles for objects such as dimensions, view labels, your title block or general drawing annotation.

Creating and Using Text Styles

You use the Style command to create and manage text styles. By default, all new drawings contain two text styles, one named Standard and one named Annotative. Standard is the current text style for all new drawings, unless you base a new drawing on a template that has another style set as the current style.

Creating and Using Text Styles

Text styles are similar to layers in that they are used to organize objects in the drawing. You create a Text Style and make it current so that the text you enter appears in that style. You can also change the Text Style of selected text after it was placed in the drawing.

To create text styles, you use the Text Style dialog box. To switch from the current text style to another, you can select a text style from the list on the Text panel the same way you can make a Layer current from the Layer Control list. Similarly, you can assign a text style to selected text from the text style list.

Command Access

Style

Command Line: **STYLE, ST**

Ribbon: **Annotate tab > Text panel > Text Style**

Menu Bar: **Format > Text Style**

Text Style Dialog Box

You use the Text Style dialog box to create and manage text styles.

① Use this area to view your current text Styles. You can also edit a selected style or rename it.

② Select a Font Name from the list of available fonts. Apply a Font Style such as Bold or Italic if required.

③ Specify the size of your text in this section. If you choose to make your text Size *Annotative*, the Height field changes to *Paper Text Height*. Enter the Paper Text Height you want to appear in all your layout viewports for text created with this style regardless of the viewport scale.

④ Select any Effects to apply to the text such as Width Factor and Oblique Angle. A Width Factor of 1 is normal. Less than 1 would make the text narrow and greater than 1 would make the text wide.

> **Applying Height to the Text Style**
> When you set the text height, it becomes the default value for text created with that style. If this value is 0, you will be prompted to specify the text height each time you create Single Line Text. When using the Multiline Text command, the text height can be chosen or typed from the list in the Text panel.

Annotative Property

You can choose the Annotative Style (1) or assign the Annotative property (2) to a text style when you want the text height to display and plot the same size in the drawing layout, regardless of the viewport scale.

You can Match the text orientation to the layout (3) so that the text objects display horizontal if the view is, for instance, isometric.

When Annotative is selected, the Height property changes to Paper Text Height (4). Enter a value other than zero to set the height for all the text that utilizes this style. The text in the viewports is automatically scaled to the paper height size in the drawing layout.

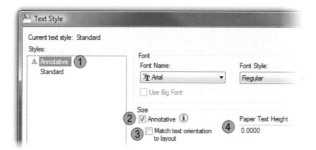

Example of Text Oriented to Layout

In the following images, two views are shown on the layout. In the first view, the text appears in the same orientation that it was created, which is normal to the plan view and layout. In the second image, the view was changed to isometric, but the text remains oriented to the layout.

Plan View   *Isometric View*

Setting Height in the Text Style
When you set a value for Height (Paper Text Height for annotative styles) in the text style, it becomes the default value for all text created with that style. Then, when you create a single line text object using the Text or Dtext commands, you are not prompted for a paper height. Leave this option set to o if you want to be prompted for the paper height when using the Text or Dtext commands.

Procedure: Creating and Using Text Styles

The following steps give an overview of creating and using text styles.

1   Start the Style command.

2   Select New (1) and enter a New Text Style Name (2).Click OK.

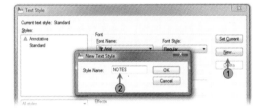

3   Select the new style (1), assign a Font Name (2), a Height (3), Apply (4) and Set Current (5). Then Close the dialog box.

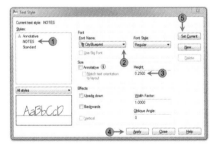

4   Begin the Text command.

5   To change from one text style to another, choose the Text style from the list.

6   To assign a Text Style to existing text objects:

- With the Command Line blank, select the objects.
- Select the text style from the list.
- Press ESC to deselect the text objects.

Redefining Styles

If you redefine a style to be annotative or nonannotative, the objects that used that style are not automatically updated. You can use the Annoupdate command to update the objects to the new style, or change them using the Properties palette.

Text Style Guidelines

- The default text style for all new drawings is Standard unless the new drawing is based on a template with a different default style.
- All text is assigned to a text style. If you do not create any new text styles, all text is assigned to the Standard text style.
- The default font for the Standard style is Arial.
- You cannot delete or rename the Standard text style.
- If you copy and paste text from another drawing or insert a block into a drawing that has the same Text Style name with different properties, the text properties of the host drawing will take precedence.
- Changes made to a text style affect all text objects using the style.
- The software uses two types of fonts: Line fonts (*.shx) and True Type fonts (*.ttf).
- Create only the number of text styles necessary to keep the text properties in a drawing consistent.
- Delete text styles that are not being used in the drawing.

Exercise | Use Text Styles

In this exercise, you modify the Standard text style to automatically update all text in the drawing. You then create new text styles and assign text objects to the new styles.

The completed exercise

Completing the Exercise
To complete the exercise, follow the steps in this book or in the onscreen exercise. In the onscreen list of chapters and exercises, click *Chapter 7: Annotating the Drawing*. Click *Exercise: Use Text Styles*.

1   Open *C_Text-Styles.dwg*.

2   Using the Zoom command, zoom into various areas of the drawing to see the text. Note the appearance and font used.

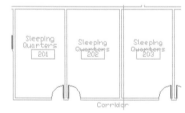

3   To change the font of the Standard style:

- On the Text panel, click Text Style.
- In the Text Style dialog box, select Arial in the Font Name list.
  Tip: Enter **A** to scroll the list to the fonts starting with the letter A.
- For Height, enter **0**.
- Click Apply.
- Click Close.

4   View the text in the drawing again. With a simple change to the text style, all text using the modified style is updated.

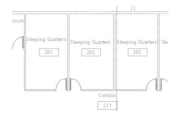

5   Zoom to display the entire drawing.

6   To create new text styles to be used in the drawing:
    - Start the Text Style command.
    - In the Text Style dialog box, click New.
    - In the New Text Style dialog box, enter **MT-5-Title**.
    - Click OK.
    - From the Font Name list, select Technic.
    - For Height, enter **8**.
    - Click Apply.
    - Click New.
    - In the New Text Style dialog box, enter **ViewLabel**.
    - Click OK.
    - For Height, enter **5**.
    - Click Apply.
    - Click Close.
      Note: As you create each new text style, it becomes the current text style.

7   Select the view label *Main Floor* and the number tag located near the bottom of the view.

8   On the Text panel, select ViewLabel in the Text Style list.

9   Press ESC to clear the selection. The new text style is assigned to the view label text.

10   Adjust the view in the drawing to see the title block text. Select the text as shown.

11   To change the style of the text:

- On the Text panel, select MT-5-Title in the Text Styles list.
- Press ESC to clear the selection.
- The new text style is applied to the selected text.

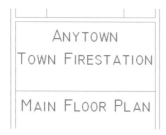

12   Close all files without saving.

Challenge Exercise | Architectural

In this exercise, you use what you learned about annotation to create a text style and add annotation to your floor plan.

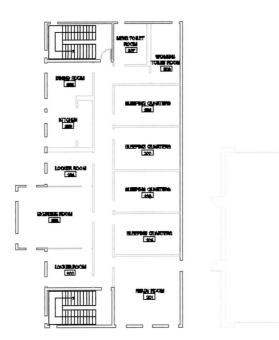

The completed exercise

1   Open the drawing you saved from the previous challenge exercise, or open *M_ARCH-Challenge- CHP07.dwg.*

2   Make initial settings:
   - Return to Model Space.
   - Set the Annotation layer as current.

3   Create a new text style with the following characteristics:
   - Style Name: Labels
   - Font Name: Arial
   - Height: 0
   - Width Factor: 0.9000

4   Add room labels and room ID numbers that are 300 mm tall as shown in the illustration:
   - 221 through 224 - SLEEPING QUARTERS
   - 201 - READY ROOM
   - 202 & 204 - LOCKER ROOM
   - 203 - EXERCISE ROOM
   - 205 - DINING ROOM
   - 206 - KITCHEN
   - 207 - MEN'S TOILET ROOM
   - 208 - WOMEN'S TOILET ROOM

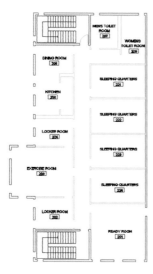

5   Save and close the drawing.

Imperial Units

1   Open the drawing you saved from the previous challenge exercise, or open *I_ARCH-Challenge- CHP07.dwg*.

2   Make initial settings:
   - Return to Model Space.
   - Set the Annotation layer as current.

3   Create a new text style with the following characteristics:
   - Style Name: Labels
   - Font Name: Arial
   - Height: 0
   - Width Factor: 0.9000

4   Add room labels and room ID numbers that are 1' tall as shown in the illustration:
   - 221 through 224 - SLEEPING QUARTERS
   - 201 - READY ROOM
   - 202 & 204 - LOCKER ROOM
   - 203 - EXERCISE ROOM
   - 205 - DINING ROOM
   - 206 - KITCHEN
   - 207 - MEN'S TOILET ROOM
   - 208 - WOMEN'S TOILET ROOM

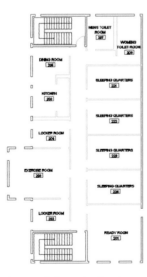

5   Save and close the drawing.

Challenge Exercise | Mechanical

In this exercise, you use what you learned about annotation to add annotation
to the drawing views.

Note: The following illustration depicts only some of the views that require annotation.

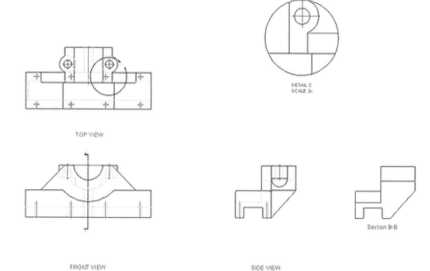

The completed exercise

Completing the Exercise

To complete the exercise, follow the steps in this book or in the onscreen exercise. In
the onscreen list of chapters and exercises, click *Chapter 7: Annotating the Drawing*. Click
Challenge Exercise: Mechanical.

1   Open the drawing you saved from the previous challenge exercise, or open *M_MECH-Challenge- CHP07.dwg*.

2   Make initial settings:
  •   Make the Annotation layer current.
  •   Thaw the Section Line layer.

3   Create a new text style with the following characteristics:
  •   Style Name: Labels
  •   Font Name: Arial
  •   Height: 0
  •   Width Factor: 0.9000

4   Annotate the drawing views by adding view labels that are 8.0 mm tall as shown in the following illustrations. Note that the annotation indicated on the left side of the view reads Outfeed Side and needs to be 4.0 mm in height.

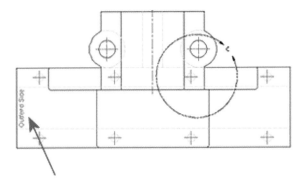

TOP VIEW

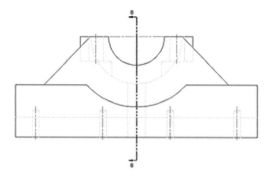

FRONT VIEW

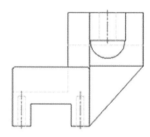

SIDE VIEW

5   More views

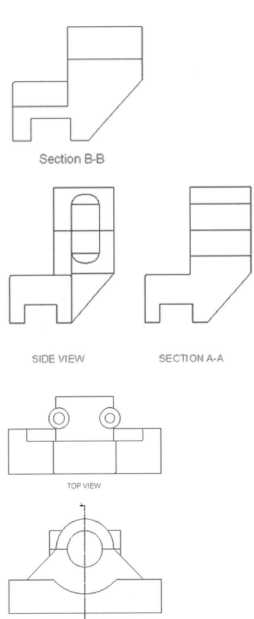

Section B-B

SIDE VIEW   SECTION A-A

TOP VIEW

FRONT VIEW

6   Save and close all files.

Chapter Summary

Using the annotation commands, you can create and edit the annotation that is typically required in drawings. By using the annotative properties of your annotations, you can create annotations that get reused in many viewports at any desired scale.

Having completed this chapter, you can:

- Use the Mtext command to create multiline text.
- Create single line text.
- Use different methods to edit text.
- Create text styles to manage text.

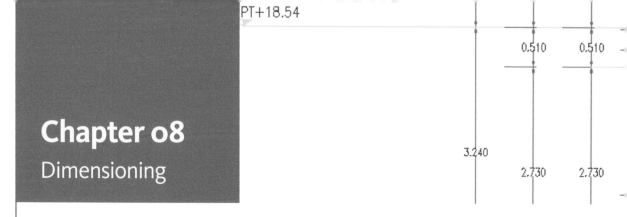

Chapter 08
Dimensioning

You use dimensions on drawings to convey size and specifications. Most drawings are not complete until you have added dimensions.

When dimensioning a drawing, you need to consider the final output scale of the drawing, the placement of dimensions, and how the dimensions should appear.

In this chapter, you learn how to create, edit, and manage dimensions in a typical design environment.

Objectives

After completing this chapter, you will be able to:

- Create dimensions.

- Use dimension styles to manage dimensions.

- Create and edit multileader styles and multileaders.

- Use different commands and methods to edit dimensions.

Standard Object Snap and Status Bar Settings
Before completing the exercises in this chapter, refer to the "Settings for the Exercises" section in the Introduction.

Lesson 37 | Creating Dimensions

This lesson describes how to use the various dimension commands to place dimensions on your drawings.

Dimensions are a vital element of annotation. They display measurements and illustrate how your drawings meet specifications.

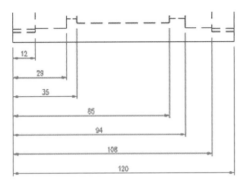

Objectives

After completing this lesson, you will be able to:

- Create different types of dimensions on linear objects.
- Create different types of dimensions on curved objects.
- Enhance dimensions for clarity of purpose.

Creating Dimensions on Linear Objects

Placing dimensions on objects in the drawing is a straightforward process. Your dimensions will be as accurate as your drawing, provided you use the object snaps correctly. Dimension commands are located on the Annotate tab of the Ribbon. Pay attention to the Command line prompts as they guide you to the required selections.

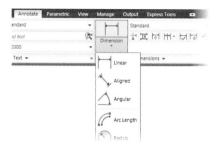

The following illustration shows a variety of dimensions for linear objects.

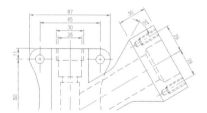

Procedure: Creating a Linear Dimension

Use the following command to create horizontal or vertical Linear dimensions:

Command Line: **DIMLINEAR, DIMLIN**
Ribbon: **Annotate tab > Dimensions panel > Linear**

The following steps give an overview of creating a Linear dimension:

1   Start the Dimlinear command.

2   Press ENTER to select the object or, using object snap, select the first extension line origin (1) and the second extension line origin (2).

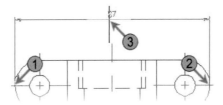

3   Click to position the dimension (3).

Practice Exercise | Linear Dimensions

In this practice exercise, you create the object below, and apply linear dimensions as shown.

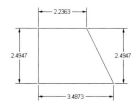

1   To draw your object to dimension:

   • Begin with a blank drawing.
   • Draw a simple rectangle (any size).
   • Use the Grips to stretch one corner of the rectangle.
   • Press ESC to deselect the object.

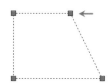

2   To create a Linear dimension by selecting two points on the object:

   • Begin Linear dimension.
   • Using object snap, click to specify the first extension line origin (1).
   • Click to specify the second extension line origin (2).
   • Click to specify the dimension line location as shown (3).

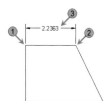

3   To create a Linear dimension by selecting the object:

- Begin Linear dimension.
- Press ENTER to select the object.
- Select the object where indicated (1).
- Drag and place the dimension as shown (2).
- Repeat the Linear dimension command.
- Create dimensions (3) and (4).

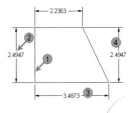

Note: When you dimension the angled line (4), you have the option to create a horizontal or vertical Linear dimension, depending on the direction you drag the dimension.

Procedure: Creating an Aligned Dimension

Use the following command to create a dimension that is aligned to an object or two points:

Command Line: **DIMALIGNED**
Ribbon: **Annotate tab > Dimensions panel > Align**

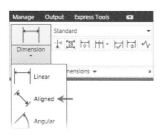

Note: Once you select a dimension type from the list, it becomes the predominant button in the Dimensions panel.

The following steps give an overview of creating an aligned dimension:

1   Start the Dimaligned command.

2   Press ENTER to select the object or, using object snap, select the first extension line origin (1) and the second extension line origin (2).

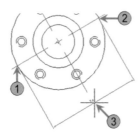

3   Click to position the dimension (3).

Practice Exercise | Linear Dimensions

In this practice exercise, you create the object below and apply aligned dimensions as shown.

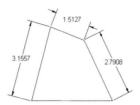

1   To draw your object to dimension:

- Begin with a blank drawing.
- Draw a simple rectangle (any size).
- Use the Grips to stretch the corners of the rectangle.
- Press ESC to deselect the object.

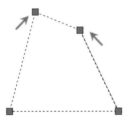

2   To create an Aligned dimension by selecting two points on the object:

- Begin the Aligned dimension command.
- Using object snap, click to specify the first extension line origin (1).
- Click to specify the second extension line origin (2).
- Click to specify the dimension line location as shown (3).

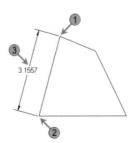

3   To create an Aligned dimension by selecting the object:

- Begin the Aligned dimension command.
- Press ENTER to select the object.
- Select the object where indicated (1).
- Drag and place the dimension as shown (2).
- Repeat to create dimension (3).

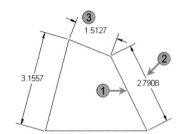

Procedure: Creating an Angular Dimension

Use the following command to create an angular dimension between two lines. The Angular dimension command can also be used to measure the angle between two points on a circle, the angle of an arc, or the angle between three points.

Command Line: **DIMANGULAR, DIMANG**
Ribbon: **Annotate tab > Dimensions panel > Angular**

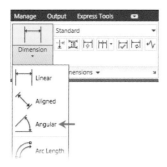

Note: Once you select a dimension type from the list, it becomes the predominant button in the Dimensions panel.

The following steps give an overview of creating an angular dimension:

1   Start the Dimangular command.

2   Select the first line segment (1).

3   Select the second line segment (2).

4   Click to position the dimension (3).

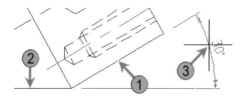

Practice Exercise | Angular Dimensions

In this practice exercise, you create the object below and apply angular dimensions as shown.

1   To draw your object to dimension:

- Begin with a blank drawing.
- Draw a simple rectangle (any size).
- Use the Grips to stretch the corners of the rectangle.
- Press ESC to deselect the object.

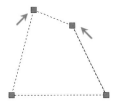

2   To create an Angular dimension by selecting two lines:

- Begin the Angular dimension command.
- Select the first line (1).
- Select the second line (2).
- Specify the dimension arc line location as shown (3).

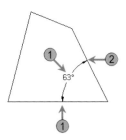

Note: You can drag the arc dimension to inside or outside the arc angle.

3   Repeat to dimension the remaining angles.

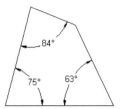

Procedure: Creating Baseline Dimensions

Use the following command to create baseline dimensions. Create a Linear, Aligned or Angular dimension first to use the base dimension. By default, the baseline dimension is built off of the last dimensioned line selected.

Command Line: **DIMBASELINE, DIMBASE**
Ribbon: **Annotate tab > Dimensions panel > Baseline**

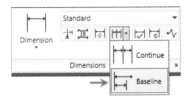

The following steps give an overview of creating baseline dimensions:

1 To use the Baseline dimension, begin by creating the base dimension.
   Note that by default, the last linear, aligned or angular dimension created is used as the base dimension, or you are prompted to select a base dimension.

2 For the baseline dimension, begin the Linear dimension and select the first extension line origin (1) and the second extension line origin (2).
   Note that the baseline will be built off of the first extension line origin.

3 Click to position the Linear dimension (3).

4 Start the Dimbaseline command. Select the next extension line (4).

5 Continue selecting points (5 and 6) for as many baseline dimensions as you require.

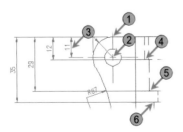

6 Press ENTER to end the Baseline command.

Practice Exercise | Baseline Dimensions

In this practice exercise, you create the object below and apply baseline dimensions as shown.

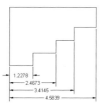

1   To create your base dimension using the Linear dimension command:

- Begin Linear dimension.
- Specify the first extension line (1).
- Specify the second extension line (2).
- Specify the dimension location.

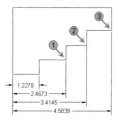

Note: Baseline dimensions build off of the first extension line origin.

2   To add the Baseline dimensions:

- Continue with the Baseline command.
- Specify a second extension line at (1), (2) and (3).
- Press ENTER twice to complete the command.

Note: If you choose to select a base dimension that was already created, be sure to select it towards the extension line that you want to be the baseline. In this example, it would be the left side of the Linear dimension you created.

Procedure: Creating Continuous Dimensions

Use the following command to continue placing dimensions based on a Linear, Aligned or Angular dimension. Select or create the base dimension. The continued dimensions are built from the last dimension origin point.

Command Line: **DIMCONTINUE, DIMCONT**
Ribbon: **Annotate tab > Dimensions panel > Continuous**

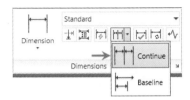

The following steps give an overview of creating continuous dimensions:

1 To use the Continue dimension, begin by creating the base dimension.
Note that by default, the last linear, aligned or angular dimension created is used as the base dimension, or you are prompted to select a base dimension.

2 For the base dimension, begin the Linear dimension. Use object snaps to select the first extension line origin (1) and the second extension line origin (2).
Note that the continuous dimensions will be built off of the second extension line origin.

3 Click to position the Linear dimension (3).

4 Start the Dimcontinuous command. Select the next extension line (4).

5 Using object snap, continue selecting points (5 and 6) or objects for as many continuous dimensions as you require.

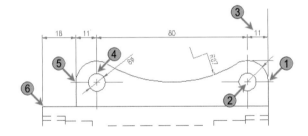

Practice Exercise | Continuous Dimensions

In this practice exercise, you create the object below and apply continuous dimensions as shown.

1   To create your base dimension using the Linear dimension command:

- Begin Linear dimension.
- Specify the first extension line (1).
- Specify the second extension line (2).
- Specify the dimension location.

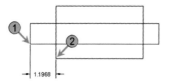

> **Note**: Continuous dimensions build off of the second extension line origin.
> **Note**: When you choose the dimension origin points as indicated, the gap between the dimension extension lines and the object is visible.

2   To add the Continuous dimensions:

- Begin the Continuous dimension command.
- Specify a second extension line at (1) and (2).
- Press ENTER twice to complete the command.

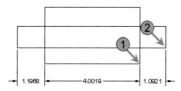

> **Note**: If you choose to select a base dimension that was already created, be sure to select it towards the extension line you want the Continuous dimension to follow. In this example, it would be the side of the Linear dimension you created.

Dimensions for Linear Objects Guidelines

- Always use Object Snaps to select the dimension origin points.
- Depending on the geometry you are dimensioning you may select objects to dimension rather than specifying the endpoints.
- A Linear dimension will be horizontal or vertical depending on the direction you drag the dimension line from the object.
- An Angular dimension may be located inside or outside the angle depending on where you drag the arc line location.
- To ensure that Continuous and Baseline dimensions build correctly, create the base Linear, Aligned, or Angular dimension choosing the first and second origin points accordingly. Baseline dimensions are built from the first origin point. Continuous dimensions are built from the second origin point.
- When you select the base dimension for your Continuous or Baseline dimensions, select the dimension towards the side that you want the continued or baseline dimension to reference.
- Adjust the location of the dimension using Grips when necessary.
- If the origin point you selected is incorrect, zoom in closer to the object and use the grips to relocate the origin point to the object.

Tip

The Dimlinear and Dimaligned commands prompt you for two points or to select an object. Press ENTER to select the object to dimension. This is often quicker than selecting two points.

Creating Dimensions on Curved Objects

Using commands to place dimensions on curved objects in the drawing is a straightforward process. Pay attention to the command prompts as they guide you through the required selections. These dimensions can be selected from the list on the Dimensions panel.

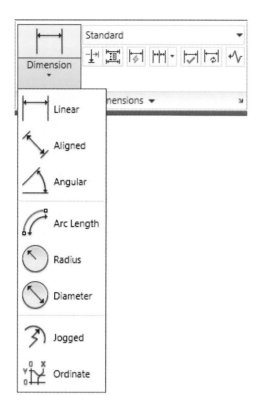

The following illustration shows a variety of dimensions for curved objects.

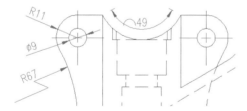

Chapter 8 | Dimensioning

Procedure: Creating an Arc Length Dimension

Use the following command to dimension the length of an arc.

Command Line: **DIMARC**
Ribbon: **Annotate tab > Dimensions panel > Arc Length**

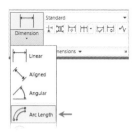

The following steps give an overview of creating an arc length dimension:

1   Start the Dimarc dimension command.

2   Select an arc (1).

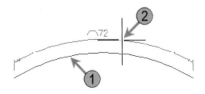

3   Click to position the arc length dimension (2).

Practice Exercise | Arc Length Dimensions

In this practice exercise, you draw several arcs, then use the Arc Length command to dimension the arcs.

1   To create Arc Length dimensions on the arcs you have drawn:
   - Begin the Arc Length command.
   - Select the arc (1).
   - Specify the arc length dimension location (2).

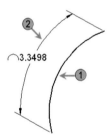

2   Repeat the Arc Length command to dimension the remaining arcs.

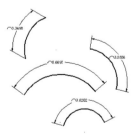

Note: The arc length symbol can precede the dimension text, be above the dimension text, or be turned off. This symbol can be controlled using the DIMSTYLE command. Select: Modify > Symbols and Arrows > Arc Length Symbol.

Procedure: Creating a Radius Dimension

Use the following command to dimension the radius of a circle or arc.

Command Line: **DIMRADIUS, DIMRAD, DRA**
Ribbon: **Annotate tab > Dimensions panel > Radius**

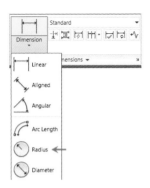

The following steps give an overview of creating a radius dimension:

1   Start the Dimradius command.

2   Select an arc or circle (1).

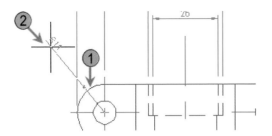

3   Click to position the dimension (2).

Practice Exercise | Radius Dimensions

In this practice exercise you use the Radius Dimension command; first, create a drawing that resembles the object shown below.

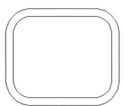

Note: To ensure a manageably sized drawing, begin with a blank drawing based on the *acad.dwg* template.

1   To create the object to dimension:

- Draw a rectangle.
- Begin the Fillet command and set the fillet radius to .25 or .5.
- Use the Polyline option of the Fillet command to fillet all 4 corners of the rectangle.
  Note: A rectangle is a polyline meaning all the lines are connected and recognized as a single object.
- Begin the Offset command.
- Specify an offset distance of .15.
- Offset the polyline.

2   To dimension the outside fillet:

- Begin the Radius command.
- Select the arc (1).
- Specify the dimension line location (2).

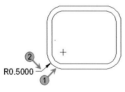

3   Repeat the command to dimension the inside radius (3).

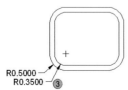

Procedure: Creating a Jogged Radius Dimension

Use the following command to dimension a radius where you want to override the center origin point of the dimension to another location. This will create a jogged radial dimension.

Command Line: **DIMJOGGED**
Ribbon: **Annotate tab > Dimensions panel > Jogged**

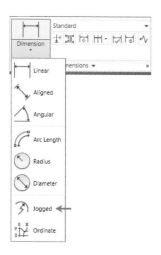

The following steps give an overview of creating a jogged radius dimension:

1   Start the Dimjogged command.

2   Select an arc or circle (1).

3   Specify a center location override (2).

4   Specify a dimension line location (3).

5   Specify the jog location (4).

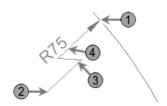

Practice Exercise | Jogged Radius Dimensions

In this practice exercise you draw an arc and use the Jogged radius dimension command.

1   Draw an arc.

2   To create a jogged radius:

- Enter **DIMJOGGED** and press ENTER.
- Select the arc (1).
- Specify the center point location override (2).
- Specify the dimension line location (3).
- Specify the jog location.

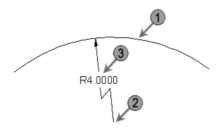

Procedure: Creating a Diameter Dimension

Use the following command to dimension the diameter of a circle or arc:.

Command Line: **DIMDIAMETER, DIMDIA**
Ribbon: **Annotate tab > Dimensions panel > Baseline**

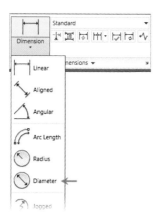

The following steps give an overview of creating a diameter dimension:

1   Start the Dimdiameter command.

2   Select an arc or circle (1).

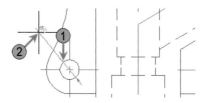

3   Click to position the dimension (2).

Practice Exercise | Diameter Dimensions

In this practice exercise you draw several circles and use the Diameter dimension command.

1   To dimension the diameter of a circle:
   • Begin the Diameter dimension command.
   • Select the circle (1).
   • Specify the dimension line location (2).

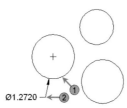

2   Repeat the Diameter command to dimension the remaining circles.

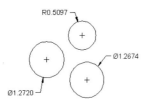

Procedure: Creating Center Marks

Use the following command to create a center mark.

Command Line: **DIMCENTER**
Ribbon: **Annotate tab > extended Dimensions panel > Center Mark**

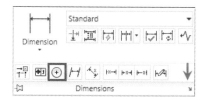

Note: You can type DIMCEN to change the value (size) of the Center Marks.

The following steps give an overview of creating center marks:

1   Start the DIMCENTER command.
2   Select an arc or circle (1).

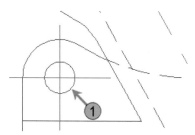

Note: The Center Mark size and appearance is set in the Dimension Style or you can change the size by typing DIMCEN.

Practice Exercise | Create Center Marks

In this practice exercise you draw several circles and arcs and place a Center Mark in each one.

1   Draw several circles and arcs.

2   To place center marks in the circles and arcs:
   - Begin the Center Mark dimension command.
   - Select a circle or arc.
   - Repeat and continue to place a center mark within each object.

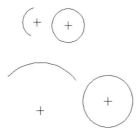

Note: The Center Mark appearance and size is controlled using the DIMSTYLE command (select: Modify > Symbols and Arrows > Center marks).

Enhancing Dimensions

Placing dimensions on objects in the drawing is a straightforward process, however you may need to use some additional tools to produce drawings to your desired standard. Pay attention to the command prompts; they guide you through the required selections.

The following illustration shows a variety of dimensions that have been enhanced for adherence to a drafting standard.

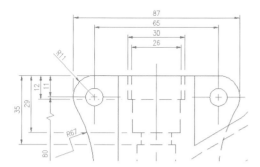

Procedure: Placing a String of Quick Dimensions

Use the following command for placement of a semi-automated string of *quick* dimensions:

Command Line: **QDIM**
Ribbon: **Annotate tab > Dimensions panel > Quick Dimension**

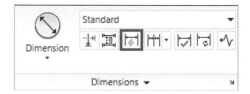

The following steps give an overview of the Quick Dimension command. This command only works for model space dimensioning.

1   Start the Qdim command.

2   Select the geometry to dimension using standard selection methods.

3   By default, a series of continuous dimensions is previewed. Right-click anywhere in the drawing to change the dimension types or options. Available options are: Continuous, Staggered, Baseline, Ordinate, Radius, Diameter, Datumpoint, Edit, and Settings.

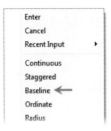

4   Click to position the dimensions.

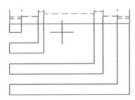

The dimensions are created.

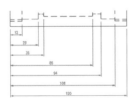

Warning
QDIM is not available in AutoCAD LT®.

Procedure: Ordinate Dimensions

Use the following command to create Ordinate dimensions.

Command Line: **DIMORDINATE, DIMORD**
Ribbon: **Annotate tab > Dimensions panel > Ordinate**

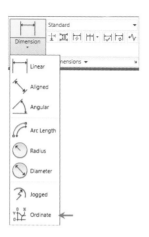

The following steps give an overview of creating Ordinate Dimensions. To dimension using Ordinate Dimensions, you must first change the Origin point.

1. Enter **UCS** and press ENTER. Specify the origin point on the object for the Ordinate dimensions to reference. Accept your selection by pressing ENTER.

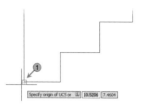

2. Start the Dimordinate command.
3. Use object snap to specify the feature location (2), then specify the leader endpoint (3).

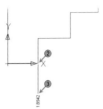

4   Repeat Dimordinate and continue to select the next feature location and leader endpoint.
    Then return the UCS origin back to World.
    Note you can use the Ordinate option with the Quick Dimension command.

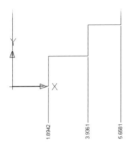

Procedure: Breaking Dimensions

Use the following command to break dimension or extension lines where they overlap other lines:

Command Line: **DIMBREAK**
Ribbon: **Annotate tab > Dimensions panel > Break**

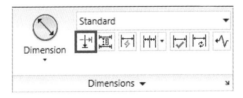

The following steps give an overview for breaking dimensions:

1   Start the Dimbreak command.

2 Select the dimension to break (1).
  Note: Use the Multiple option to break multiple dimensions.

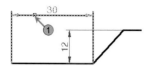

3 Select objects to break the dimension (2) and press ENTER.
  Note: Simply press ENTER to break the dimension automatically wherever it intersects with other objects or dimensions.

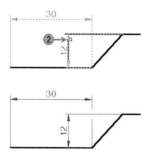

Procedure: Creating Jogged Linear Dimensions

Use the following to command to add a jog line to a dimension line.
Command Line: **DIMJOGLINE**
Ribbon: **Annotate tab > Dimensions panel > Jog Line**

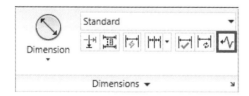

The following steps give an overview for adding a Jog Line to a dimension:

1 Create a linear dimension between two points and enter the text override value to represent the stated value

2   Start the Dimjogline command and select a linear dimension.

3   Click a point on the dimension to place the jog line symbol.

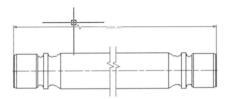

Removing a Linear Jog from a Dimension

To remove the jog symbol from a jogged linear dimension, use the Remove option of the Dimjogline command.

Procedure: Spacing Dimensions

Use the following command to adjust the space between parallel linear dimensions.

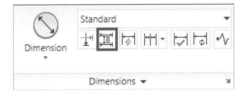

Command Line: **DIMSPACE**
Ribbon: **Annotate tab > Dimensions panel > Adjust Space**

The following steps give an overview for spacing dimensions uniformly after they have been placed in the drawing:

Chapter 8 | Dimensioning

1 Start the Dimspace command and select the base dimension.

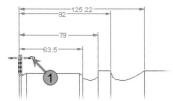

2 Select the dimensions to be spaced from the base dimension, and press ENTER.

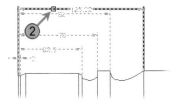

3 Enter a value for spacing the dimensions, or press ENTER to use the automatic method.

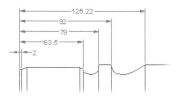

Dimensions Are Associative

When you create dimensions, they are associative to the geometry or points you select. If the geometry changes size, the dimension updates accordingly.

Procedure: Adding Tolerances

Use the following command to add a dimension Tolerance to your drawing:

Command Line: **TOLERANCE, TOL**
Ribbon: **Annotate tab > Dimensions panel > Tolerance**

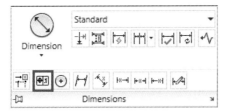

The following steps give an overview of adding a dimension Tolerance:

1   Start the Tolerance command.

2   From the Geometric Tolerance dialog box, select the desired Symbol, Tolerance and Datum. Click OK.

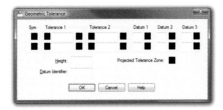

3   Click to place the Tolerance in the drawing.

Procedure: Inspecting Dimensions

Use the following command to add an inspection label to a selected dimension:

Command Line: **DIMINSPECT**
Ribbon: **Annotate tab > Dimensions panel > Inspect**

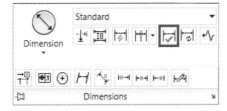

The following steps give an overview of creating an inspection label.

1   Start the Diminspect command.

2   From the Inspection Dimension dialog box, select a Shape and a Label and/or Inspection rate.

3   Select the dimension(s) and click OK.

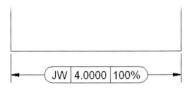

Exercise | Create Dimensions

In this exercise, you create several types of dimensions using the appropriate dimension commands.

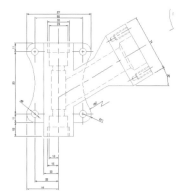

The completed exercise

Completing the Exercise

To complete the exercise, follow the steps in this book or in the onscreen exercise. In the onscreen list of chapters and exercises, click *Chapter 8: Dimensioning*. Click *Exercise: Create Dimensions*.

1   Open *M_Create-Dimensions.dwg*.

2   To create a linear dimension:

- On the Dimensions panel, click Linear.
- Click the points indicated in the following image and position the dimension as shown.

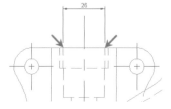

3   Repeat the Linear Dimension command and place dimensions as shown.
    Note: You correct the spacing in the next step.

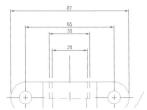

4   To correct the dimension spacing.

   - On the Dimensions panel, click Dimspace.
   - Select the inner most dimension for the base.
   - Click the remaining three dimensions from bottom to top.
   - Press ENTER. Press ENTER again to accept Auto spacing.

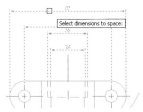

The dimensions are equally spaced.

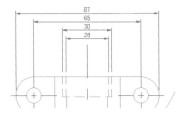

5   To create an aligned dimension

   - On the Dimensions panel, click Aligned.
   - Select point (1) as shown.
   - Select point (2).
   - Position the dimension as shown.

6   To create a radial dimension:

  - On the Dimensions panel, click Radius.
  - Select the arc indicated and position the dimension as shown.

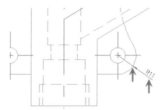

7   To create a jogged dimension:

  - On the Dimensions panel, click Jogged.
  - Select the arc at point (1).
  - Specify the center location override at point (2).
  - Specify the dimension line location at point (3).
  - Specify the jog location at point (4).

8   To create a diameter dimension:

  - On the Dimensions panel, click Diameter.
  - Select the circle indicated (1) and position the dimension as shown (2).

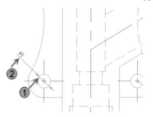

9   To create an angular dimension:

  - On the Dimensions panel, click Angular.
  - Select the line at point (1).
  - Select the line at point (2).
  - Position the dimension as shown.

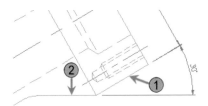

10 To create a linear dimension

- On the Dimensions panel, click Linear.
- Select point (1).
- Select point (2).
- Position the dimension as shown.

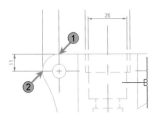

11 To create continuous dimensions on the left side:

- On the Dimensions panel, click Continue.
- The last dimension created is automatically used as the continue dimension.
- Select point (1), point (2), and point (3) in order.
- Press ENTER to finish continuous dimensioning.
- Press ENTER to exit dimensioning.

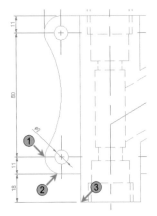

12   To create a linear dimension:

- On the Dimensions panel, click Linear.
- Select point (1).
- Select point (2).
- Position the dimension as shown.

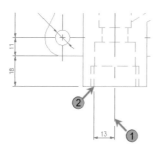

13   To create baseline dimensions:

- On the Dimension toolbar, click Baseline.
- The last dimension created is automatically used as the base dimension.
- Select point (1), point (2), point (3), and point (4) in order.
- Press ENTER to complete the baseline command.
- Press ENTER to complete the dimension command.

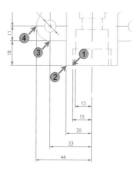

14   To clean up the overlapping extension lines:

- On the Dimensions panel, click Dimbreak.
- Right-click. Click Multiple.
- Select the left end extension line 1 and 2 as shown.
- Right-click. Click Break.
  The selected extension lines break whenever they cross another extension line.

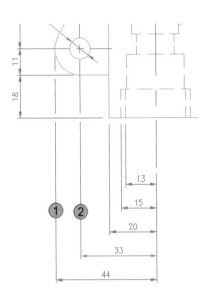

15 Zoom to the drawing extents.

16 Close all files without saving.

Lesson 38 | Using Dimension Styles

This lesson explains dimension styles, how to create and format dimension styles, and how you can use them to manage dimensions.

You use dimension styles to manage dimensions in much the same way you use text styles to maintain uniformity in your drawing annotations. Dimension styles organize your dimensions.

In the following illustration, two dimensions are placed, each using a different dimension style. Note the difference in the arrowheads and the display of units.

Objectives

After completing this lesson, you will be able to:

- Describe dimension styles and how they are used.
- Create and modify dimension styles to control the appearance of dimensions.

About Dimension Styles

Dimension styles control dimension appearance. Each dimension object contains a number of features, such as extension lines, arrows or symbols, text, and tolerances. Dimension styles control whether these features appear, and if they do, what they look like. For example, the dimension style might specify what type of arrowhead to use or what color the dimension lines or text should be.

The following image illustrates some of the dimension features you can control with dimension styles.

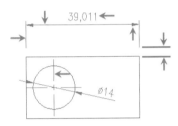

Definition of Dimension Styles

A dimension style is a group of dimension settings or variables that control how dimensions appear. You name this group of variables and then assign it to specific dimensions, which simplifies the determination of how dimensions look in the drawing. You can use more than one dimension style in a drawing.

Annotative Property

You assign the Annotative property to a Dimension Style when you want dimension features in objects created with that style to be displayed with the same plotted size in multiple viewports with different viewport scales. To make a dimension style annotative, you select the Annotative option on the Fit tab in the New Dimension Style or the Modify Dimension Style dialog boxes.

Dimension Style Facts

- Every drawing must contain at least one dimension style, but you can create multiple dimension styles.
- Every new imperial unit drawing contains a dimension style called Standard and another called Annotative. Standard is set as the current dimension style.
- Every new metric unit drawing contains a dimension style called ISO-25 and another called Annotative. ISO-25 is set as the current dimension style.

Example of Dimension Styles

The dimension style controls the type and size of the arrow, the placement and size of the dimension text, the offset of the extension line from the part, and many other variables as shown in the following image.

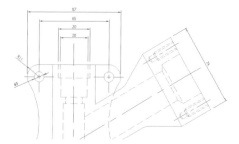

Creating and Modifying Dimension Styles

You use the Dimension Style command to create and manage dimension styles. Each drawing can have multiple dimension styles, but only one dimension style can be current at a time.

As you create dimensions in the drawing, they are assigned the current dimension style and inherit its properties. Use the dimension style list on the Dimensions panel to quickly switch the current dimension style.

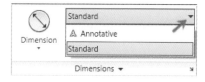

Command Access

Dimension Style

Command Line: **DIMSTYLE**
Ribbon: **Annotate tab > Dimensions Panel > Dimension Style**

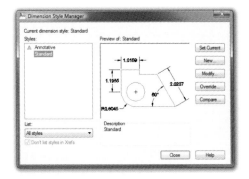

Menu Bar: **Format > Dimension Style**

Dimension Style Manager

The Dimension Style Manager displays all dimension styles available in the drawing. Use the options in the Dimension Style Manager to create a New dimension style, Modify an existing style, Override a style, Compare styles or set a style Current.

Create New Dimension Style Dialog Box

In the Dimension Style Manager, select New (1) to access the Create a New Dimension Style Dialog box. Enter a new style name (2) based on an existing dimension style that you choose from the list (3). A new dimension style is typically used for all dimensions (4), or you can create a substyle that applies to a specific dimension type (5). Check Annotative (6) to make the dimensions appear in a consistent size when you have multiple viewports in the drawing layout.

Note: Select Modify from the Dimension Style Manager to access the same dimension style options that could be assigned to any new dimension style.

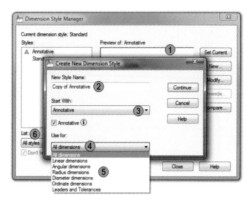

New Dimension Style Dialog Box - Lines Tab

Use the Lines tab to adjust properties for the dimension and extension lines. The preview window will display the effect of your changes. These dimension line settings are based on common drafting standards and typically are not changed.

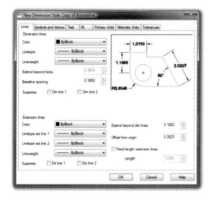

New Dimension Style Dialog Box - Symbols and Arrows Tab

Use the Symbols and Arrows tab to adjust the arrowheads, center mark features, dimension break size, the location of the arc length symbol, the radius jog angle, and linear jog dimension height. Typically the most common feature to change in this tab is the arrowheads for the first and second extension lines, such as changing them from closed filled to oblique.

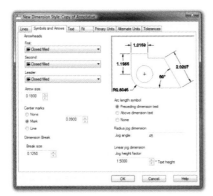

New Dimension Style Dialog Box - Text Tab

Use the Text tab to adjust text appearance, text placement, and text alignment options. The most typical changes made in this tab are to specify a text style, to specify the text alignment such as align with dimension line, and to change text placement for vertical and horizontal dimensions.

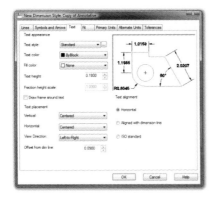

New Dimension Style Dialog Box - Fit Tab

Use the Fit tab to specify an overall scale for the dimension features. If the Annotative dimension style was selected, this area will be grayed out. Other options you can change are the Fit option for text and arrows, text placement for dimension, and fine tuning features such as whether to draw dimension lines between extension lines or not.

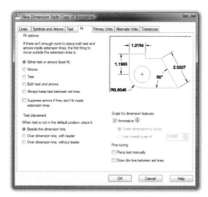

Scale for Dimension Features

When not using Annotative, you control dimension feature scale by clicking the Use Overall Scale Of option and entering a value. The value entered here is stored as the DIMSCALE system variable. You could also change this value by entering **DIMSCALE** on the command line.

A simple way to remember how to set DIMSCALE is that it should always be equal to the plot scale factor of your drawing. When the drawing is scaled to fit on a sheet of paper, the dimensions must undergo the same scaling. Setting DIMSCALE equal to your plot scale factor ensures that the dimension features start out at the correct size before they are scaled with the rest of the drawing prior to being plotted or placed on a layout.

For example, for metric units, if your final plot scale is 1:40, set DIMSCALE to 40. For imperial units, if your final plot scale is 1/4"=1', set DIMSCALE to 48 (12 / .25 = 48). DIMSCALE will multiply the dimension values by the overall scale, but does not change those values.

New Dimension Style Dialog Box - Primary Units Tab

Use the Primary Units tab to set options for the primary units displayed on the dimensions. You can set the unit format for linear and angular dimensions, adjust the precision settings, use zero suppression for the beginning and end of dimensions, and adjust the measurement scale factor for dimensioning geometry that was not drawn at full scale. The primary units are always displayed and they reflect the current drawing units setting.

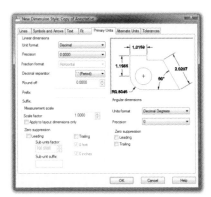

New Dimension Style Dialog Box - Alternate Units Tab

Alternate units are used when you need to show two measurement units, metric and imperial.

Use the Alternate Units tab to display and format alternate units on your dimensions. Select the Display Alternate Units option to turn on alternate units. The remaining options are only available after you select this option. You can adjust the unit format, precision, zero suppression, and placement. The multiplier for alternate units is preset to convert from millimeters to inches in a metric unit drawing or inches to millimeters in an imperial unit drawing.

By default, the Display alternate units option is turned off in the Standard and ISO-25 dimension styles.

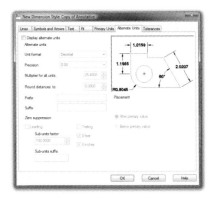

New Dimension Style Dialog Box - Tolerances Tab

Use the Tolerances tab to add tolerances to your dimensions. By adding tolerances to your dimensions, you are setting a valid range in which the as-built measurement of the feature must be maintained in order to ensure functionality.

You can select a method, set the tolerance precision, choose upper and lower values, scale the tolerance text height, set the vertical position, and control zero suppression. If you are including alternate units in your dimensions, set the alternate unit tolerance precision value and zero suppression options here.

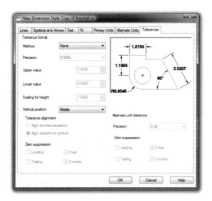

Procedure: Creating and Modifying Dimension Styles

The following steps give an overview of creating and modifying dimension styles.

1   Start the Dimension Style command.

2   In the Dimension Style Manager, click New or Modify.

3   For a new dimension style, enter a name and click Continue. If you are modifying an existing dimension style, proceed to the next step.

4   Select the appropriate tabs in the Modify Dimension Style dialog box, depending on the features you need to adjust. Select dimension style options as required. Click OK.

5   In the Dimension Style Manager, click Close.

Key Points

- Dimension styles control the appearance of dimension features.
- Dimension style options are based on general drafting standards.
- Only one dimension style can be current at a time.
- If you modify a dimension style, all dimensions using that style in the drawing update automatically.
- To set a dimension style current or to rename or delete a dimension style, select the name in the Dimension Style Manager and right-click to access these options.
- You cannot delete a dimension style if it is current or if it is being referenced in the drawing.
- The quickest way to make a new dimension style current is to select it from the list in the Dimensions panel.
- A blank drawing based on the ACAD drawing template will contain a Standard style and an Annotative style.
- The Annotative dimension style will display dimensions that are equal in size regardless of the viewport scale in the drawing Layout.
- For non-annotative dimensions, you must set the dimension scale equal to your plot scale.

Exercise | Modify a Dimension Style

In this exercise, you modify the existing dimension style to allow the dimensions to appear correctly on the sheet. You also change the dimension style to display architectural ticks instead of arrows, and alternate units.

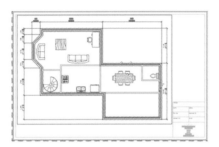

The completed exercise

Completing the Exercise
To complete the exercise, follow the steps in this book or in the onscreen exercise. In the onscreen list of chapters and exercises, click *Chapter 8: Dimensioning.* Click *Exercise: Modify a Dimension Style.*

1   Open *M_Dimension-Styles.dwg.*
    Note: The red lines around the floor plan indicate objects that are actually dimensions, but the annotative scale is not currently set for the dimension text or other features to be visible.

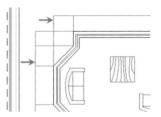

2   Click the Paper button on the status bar to change the display to Model space.

3   To modify the current dimension style's arrowhead:

- Select the Annotate tab on the ribbon. On the Dimensions panel, click Dimension Style. The current dimension style is ISO-25.
- In the Dimension Style Manager, click Modify.
- In the Modify Dimension Style dialog box, Symbols and Arrows tab, under Arrowheads, select Architectural Tick from the First list.
  Note: the Second arrowhead will automatically default to the same selection.

4   To modify the current dimension style's text style setting:

- Click the Text tab.
- In the Text style list, select TECH.
  Note: The text height for the dimensions is set to 2.5.

5   To modify the dimension style to be annotative:

- Click the Fit tab.
- Under Scale for Dimension Features, click Annotative.
- Click OK.

6   In the Dimension Style Manager, click Close. Note that no changes in the drawing are visible.

7   To set the model space annotation scale:

- On the status bar, Annotation Scale list, click 1:50.

8   To update the dimensions with the new annotation scale:
    - On the Dimensions panel, click Dimension
    - Update.
    - Enter **ALL**.
    - Press ENTER to complete the selection.
    - Press ENTER.
      Notice the effect that changing the annotation scale has on the dimensions in the drawing.

9   To change the dimension style to display alternate units:
    - On the Dimensions panel, click Dimension Style.
    - In the Dimension Style Manager, click Modify.
    - In the Modify Dimension Style dialog box, Alternate Units tab, click Display Alternate Units.
    - In the Unit Format list, select Architectural Stacked.

10 Under Placement, select Below Primary Value. Click OK.

Placement

○ After primary value

○ Below primary value

11 In the Dimension Style Manager, click Close to exit the dialog box.

12 To update the layout annotative scale:
    - Click the layout tab to return to the drawing layout.
    - Click to select the viewport border.

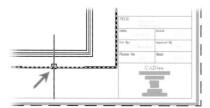

- On the status bar, Annotation Scale list, click 1:50.
  Note: You may need to click another scale then click 1:50 to get the viewport scale to reset.
- On the status bar, VP Scale, click to lock the viewport.

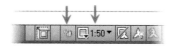

The dimensions now appear at the correct size in relation to the size of the sheet and the viewport.
Note: The dimension update may take several seconds to appear.

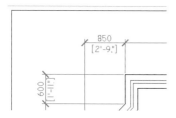

13 Zoom to the drawing extents.

14 Close all files without saving.

Lesson 39 | Using Multileaders

This lesson describes multileaders, multileader styles, and the options available for placing multileaders in the drawing.

You use multileader objects for leader-based annotation. Leaders are important because they enable you to connect features on the geometry to notes, balloon callouts, or other objects. Using multileaders as leader objects provides greater flexibility and control than standard leader objects.

The following illustration shows multileader objects used for balloon callouts.

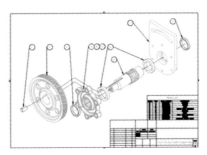

Objectives

After completing this lesson, you will be able to:

- Describe multileaders.
- Describe multileader styles.
- Create and edit multileaders.

About Multileaders

Using multileaders, you can create associative leader-based annotation objects that behave intelligently as a single object. Similar to associative dimensions, multileaders are treated as single objects with specific object properties.

In the addition to this associativity, multileaders have additional options for placing, editing, and managing leader-based annotation objects.

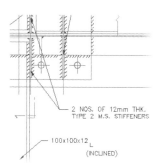

Definition of a Multileader

A leader is an annotation that includes an arrow, a leader line, a landing, and some form of text or other object. A multileader is a style-based associative leader object that combines several different common elements such as lines and text into a single associative object. When you select a multileader object, grips are displayed at several points on the object. You can edit any of these points; you select the grip and move it to a different location.

If you double-click a multileader, the Properties palette is displayed showing properties specific to the multileader object. The initial property settings originate from the current multileader style, but can be overridden just like properties on other objects.

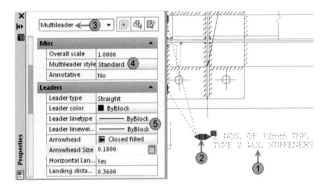

1. Selected multileader object

2. Multileader grips

3. Multileader object type identified in the

4. Properties palette Properties specific to multileader objects

5. Properties specific to multileader objects

Example of Multileaders

In the following illustration, two multileader objects are used to identify six different areas on the drawing. Because the objects are style based and associative, if you need to make changes, you can do so easily.

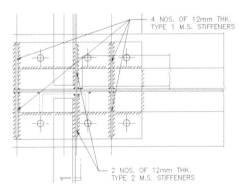

If standard leader objects were used in the drawing above, a change, such as print scale, would require that you redraw all of the leaders and change the text height for each text note.

About Multileader Styles

Multileader objects are style-based, which means that the properties for the individual elements originate from the current multileader style.

In the following illustration, a typical multileader object is shown. While there are several properties associated with a multileader, they can be organized into three main categories.

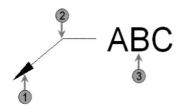

① The Leader Format properties enable you to specify arrowhead type and size, as well as the leader type, straight or spline.

② The Leader Structure properties enable you to specify constraints on the leader line such as segment angles, landing settings, and the overall leader scale or annotative property.

③ The Content properties enable you to specify the type of content that will be attached to the leader.

Command Access

Multileader Style

Command Line: **MLEADERSTYLE**
Ribbon: **Annotate tab > Leaders panel > Multileader Style Manager**

Menu Bar: **Format > Multileader Style**

Multileader Style Manager

You use the Multileader Style Manager to manage and edit multileader styles. The dialog box and options work almost identically to the Dimension Style Manager. You use this dialog box to create, edit, delete, and set current multileader styles.

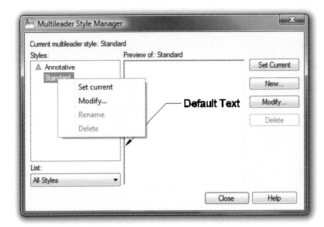

Modify Multileader Style

You use the Modify Multileader Style dialog box to edit the properties associated with the multileader style. Style properties are organized on three tabs with each tab containing specific types of properties. As soon as you exit the Multileader Style Manager, changes you made to an existing style are reflected automatically on any multileaders that are using the style.

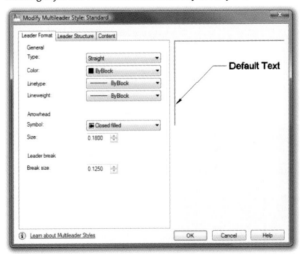

Multileader Content Types

You can specify three different content types for multileader objects. On the Content tab of the Modify Multileader Style dialog box, you can select from the following:

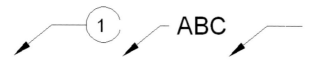

Block
Several default blocks are available such as circle, slot, and triangle. The default block options contain attributes. You can also specify your own block. You are prompted for values when you create the multileader.

Mtext
This is the default multileader type and consists of mtext objects.

None
This multileader object contains a leader only.

Using Multileaders

Using multileaders involves several tasks. These include creating and managing multileader styles, placing multileaders, adding leaders, and aligning and collecting multileaders.

With the exception of creating and managing multileader styles, which should generally be done first, there is no prescribed order for creating and editing multileaders or for using any of the multileader tools.

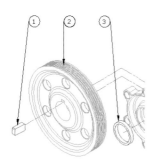

Multileaders Ribbon Panel

You use the Multileaders panel to access tools specific to creating and editing multileaders. The panel contains the standard buttons for accessing commands as well as a multileader style list that you use to set the active multileader style. You can also use the list to change the style of a selected multileader object.

The following commands are found on the Leader panel in the Annotate tab.

Icon	Command	Description
⌐O	**Multileader**	Creates a single multileader object.
+O	**Add Leader**	Adds leader lines to existing multileader objects.
✗O	**Remove Leader**	Removes leader lines from existing multileader objects.
⊞8	**Align Multileaders**	Aligns multileaders horizontally or vertically in the drawing.
⌐8	**Collect Multileaders**	Collects multiple multileaders and combines them into a single multileader object with multiple content elements.

Process: Using Multileaders

The following steps describe the overall process for using multileaders.

1   Determine the multileader style you want to use: Depending on your needs, you may need to create a new style or edit an existing one. The product provides two default styles. You can use them as is, modify them, or create new ones.

2   Use the Mleader command to create multileaders.

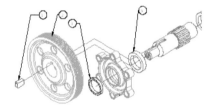

3   Use the Add Leader or Remove Leader tools to modify existing multileaders.

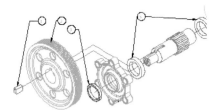

4   Use the Align Multileaders and Collect Multileader tools to further modify the appearance of
     multileaders on the drawing.

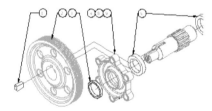

Guidelines

- Use Annotative scaling or the Annotative style for your multileader. This makes the
  multileaders in drawings that have multiple views the same size.
- You do not need a style for small or individual changes to a multileader. You can
  use the Properties palette to change individual properties for selected multileader
  objects.
- After you have placed a multileader, you can adjust its location using grips.

Using Dimension Break
You can use the Dimbreak command to break multileader objects at intersections of
objects or dimensions in the drawing..

Exercise | Use Multileaders

In this exercise, you create a multileader style to add callouts to an exploded view drawing. You then add multileaders to the drawing using different options associated with multileaders.

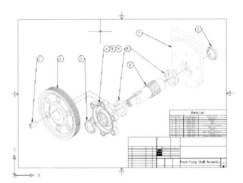

The completed exercise

Completing the Exercise
To complete the exercise, follow the steps in this book or in the onscreen exercise. In the onscreen list of chapters and exercises, click *Chapter 8: Dimensioning.* Click *Exercise: Use Multileaders.*

1   Open *c_Front-Pump-Assembly.dwg.*

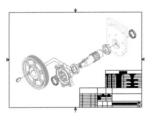

2   To create a new multileader style:
- On the Leaders panel, click the Multileader Style Manager dialog box launcher.
- In the Multileader Style Manager dialog box, click New.
- In the Create New Multileader Style dialog box, New Style Name, enter **Balloon_ Callout.** Click Continue.

3   To assign the Content type:

- Click the Content tab.
- In Multileader Type, select Block from the list.
- Under Block Options, select Circle from the list. Click OK.

4   In the Multileader Style Manager, verify that Balloon_Callout is the current multileader style. Click Close.

5   Check the Object Snap Settings to ensure that Endpoint, Midpoint, and Intersection snap modes are selected.

6   To place a Multileader:

- On the Leaders panel, click Multileader.
- Using Object Snap, select the Midpoint of the top line of the keyway (1).
- Move the cursor above the pulley and click a location (2).
- Notice the command line. An attribute has been assigned to this block. Enter 1 (3).

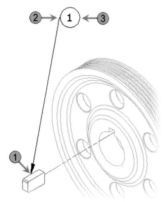

7   Using the same steps, place a multileader for the pulley and seal as shown. Enter **2** for the pulley and **3** for the seal.

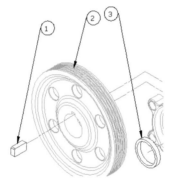

8   To align multileaders:

- On the Leaders panel, click Align.
- Use a crossing window to select all three multileaders. Press ENTER.
- Right-click to access the shortcut menu. Click Options. Click Distribute.
- Select a point on the highest multileader (1).
- Move the cursor horizontally with Polar Tracking, indicating that the motion is straight (2). Try not to select an object snap because this may override the horizontal direction.

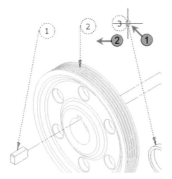

- Click to align the multileaders.

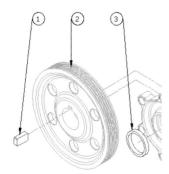

9   Place a multileader on the bearing as shown. Enter **5.**

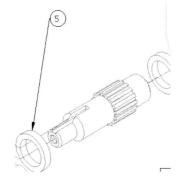

10   To add a multileader to an existing multileader:

- On the Leaders panel, click Add Leader.
- Select the number 5 multileader.
- For the second leader arrowhead location, select the bearing at the other end of the shaft. Press ENTER.

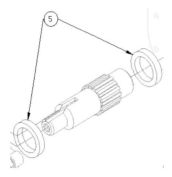

11   Add multileaders 4, 8, and 9 to the front pump housing.

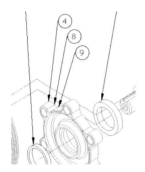

12   To collect multileaders:

- On the Leaders panel, click Collect.
- Individually select multileaders 4, 8, and 9 in order. Press ENTER.
- Verify in the Command line that Horizontal is the current option. If not, right-click and select it from the shortcut menu.
- Click to place the collected multileaders.

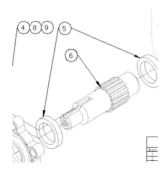

13   To add a multileader specifying content first:
- On the ribbon, Leaders panel, click Multileader.
- Right-click. Click Options.
- Select Content type.
- Click a location below the number 5 callout. Enter **6.**
- Locate the arrowhead of the multileader to the shaft.

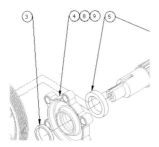

14   To add a multileader specifying the landing first:
- On the Leaders panel, click Multileader. Enter **L**. Press ENTER.
  Note: You can right-click in the Command line or enter the capitalized letter of the command options.
- Click a point to the left of the rear housing to locate the callout.
- Click the rear housing to locate the arrowhead. Enter **7.**

15   Using the options of your choice, add a multileader to the last part in the exploded view. Enter **3.**

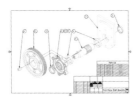

16   Close all files without saving.

Lesson 40 | Editing Dimensions

This lesson describes how to edit dimensions, but mainly how to edit dimension text. There are a variety of ways to edit dimensions depending on what kind of editing you need to do. You can reposition dimensions using grips. You can edit dimension features that override the dimension style, you change dimensions from one style to another, and you can edit the dimension text.

Inevitably, once you place dimensions in the drawing, you will need to edit them either by repositioning or adding additional information to the dimension.

In the following illustration, a string of continuous dimensions is being moved to a new position using grips.

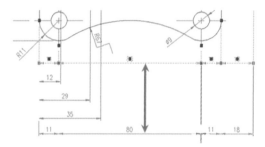

Objectives

After completing this lesson, you will be able to:

- Edit dimensions using grips and the Dimedit and Dimtedit commands.

Editing Dimensions

You can use the Dimedit command to edit or override the dimension text measurement. You can use the Dimtedit command to edit the position of the dimension text. You can also right-click a selected dimension to access the Quick Properties or the Properties palette where you can edit any of the dimension style features for the selected dimension. Any global changes that you make to the dimension style do not affect the changes that you have made to the individual dimensions unless you change the selected dimension from one dimension style to another.

In addition to editing the dimension style features from the Properties palette, you can also edit dimension text.

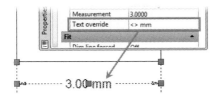

Note: The arrows (<>) keep the original text measurement that is associated to the object dimensioned.

Command Access

Dimension Edit - Edit Text

Command Line: **DDEDIT**
Pointing Device: Double-click a text object.

Dimension Edit - Justify Text

Command Line: **DIMTEDIT**

Dimension Edit - Justify Text
Ribbon: **Annotate tab > extended Dimensions panel > Text Angle (1), Left Justify (2), Center Justify (3), Right Justify (4)**

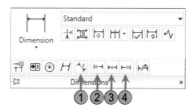

Dimension Edit - Oblique Angle
Command Line: **DIMEDIT**
Home, New, and Rotate are also DIMEDIT options when entered at the command line.
Note: Home, New, and Rotate are also DIMEDIT options when entered at the command line.
Ribbon: **Annotate tab > extended Dimensions panel > Oblique**

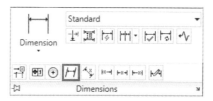

Note
The quickest way to edit the dimension text measurement is with the DDEDIT command. When you type over the text it will override the associative feature of the dimension text measurement. If you type <> before or after the associative dimension text, the associative measurement continues to be displayed.

Procedure: Adding Text to a Dimension with DDEDIT

The following steps give an overview of how to add text to a dimension using the Dimedit command.

1   On the command line, enter **ddedit** to start the DDEDIT command.

2   Select the dimension text to Edit.

3   The In-Place Text Editor appears. The highlighted number represents the true dimension
     value associated with the part being dimensioned. Click after the associative dimension (1)
     and type any additional notations (2).

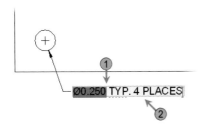

4   Click outside the Text Editor to Exit.

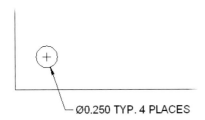

Procedure: Justifying Dimension Text with DIMTEDIT

The following steps give an overview of how to justify text on a dimension using the Dimtedit
command.

1   Click Annotate tab > Dimension panel > Dimensions drop-down > Left Justify(1).

2   Select a dimension (2).

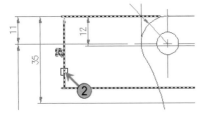

3   The text is justified (3).

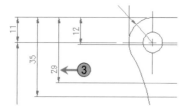

Procedure: Creating an Oblique Dimension Angle with DIMEDIT

The following steps give an overview of how to give a dimension an oblique angle with the Dimedit command.

1   On the ribbon, click Annotate tab > Dimensions panel > Dimensions drop-down > Oblique (1).

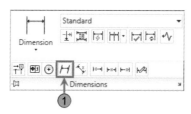

2   Select a dimension (2). Press ENTER.

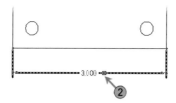

3   Enter an oblique angle (i.e. 80).

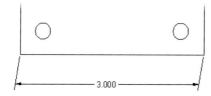

Exercise | Edit Dimensions

In this exercise, you edit dimensions by adjusting their placement, adding text to the default dimension value, and creating a new dimension substyle for diameter dimensions.

The completed exercise

Completing the Exercise
To complete the exercise, follow the steps in this book or in the onscreen exercise. In the onscreen list of chapters and exercises, click *Chapter 8: Dimensioning*. Click *Exercise: Edit Dimensions*.

1   Open *M_Edit-Dimensions.dwg*.

2   To use grip editing to move a string of dimensions:

   • Select the string of continuous dimensions in the left view of the drawing.
   • Press SHIFT+select on the five grips indicated (1), (2), (3), (4), and (5). They turn red.
   • Click one of the selected grips (6) and drag the dimensions to the left.
   • Press ESC to clear the selection.

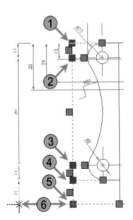

3   To move dimension text to a new location with the right justify Dimtedit command:
- On the command line, enter **dimtedit**. Press ENTER.
- Select the 29mm linear dimension indicated (1).
- Right-click anywhere in the drawing. For justification, select Right.

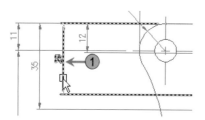

- Repeat the previous step on the 35 mm linear dimension.
- The dimensions should appear as shown.

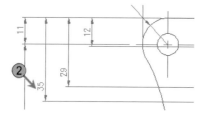

4   To relocate dimension text with grips:
- Select the jogged radial dimension.
- Select the grip (1) and drag it to a new
- location as shown (2).
- Press ESC to clear the selection.

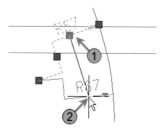

5   To flip the arrow of a dimension:
- Select the radial dimension on the upper left corner of the part.
- Right-click anywhere in the drawing. Click Flip Arrow.

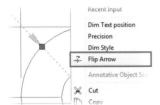

- The arrow should now be on the inside of the radius.

6   Locate and view the diameter dimension in the lower left corner of the part.

7   To create a diameter dimension substyle:

- On the Annotate tab, click Dimensions panel > Dimension, Dimension Style.

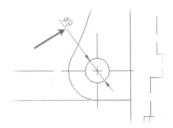

- In the Dimension Style Manager, click New.
- In the Create New Dimension Style dialog box, select Diameter Dimensions from the Use For list.

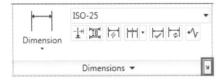

- Click Continue.
  This creates a dimension substyle of ISO-25 in which modifications only apply to the diameter dimensions.

8   To set the text alignment for the substyle:

• In the New Dimension Style dialog box, Text tab, under Text Alignment, select ISO Standard.

• Click OK.

The new dimension substyle appears under the ISO-25 dimension style.

9   Click Close to exit the Dimension Style Manager. The dimension value is now horizontal as a result of the new dimension substyle.

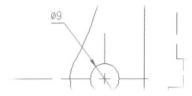

10   Close all files. Do not save.

Challenge Exercise | Architectural

In this exercise, you use what you learned about dimensioning to create a dimension style and add dimensions to your floor plan.

> **Note**
> You have the option of completing this exercise using either imperial or metric units. Select one version of the exercise to complete the steps.

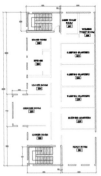

The completed exercise

> **Completing the Exercise**
> To complete the exercise, follow the steps in this book or in the onscreen exercise. In the onscreen list of chapters and exercises, click *Chapter 8: Dimensioning.* Click *Challenge Exercise: Architectural Metric.*

Metric Units

1   Open the drawing you saved from the previous challenge exercise, or open *M_ARCH-Challenge- CHP08.dwg*.

2   Set layer Dimension current.

3   Create a new dimension style called Architecture with the following settings:

• Arrowheads = Architectural tick
• Arrow size = 3
• Text Style = Labels
• Text height = 3
• Text Alignment = Horizontal
• Overall Dimension Scale = **60**
• Primary Unit Precision = **0**

4   Add dimensions to the floor plan on the appropriate layer to show the lengths of the walls and their position relative to each other as shown. Create additional dimensions as desired to meet your specific requirements.

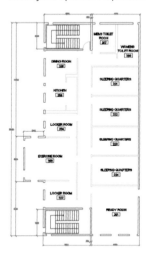

5   Save and close the drawing.

Imperial Units

1   Open the drawing you saved from the previous challenge exercise, or open *I_ARCH-Challenge- CHP08.dwg*.

2   Set layer Dimension current.

3   Create a new dimension style called Architecture with the following settings:

   • Arrowheads = Architectural tick
   • Text Style = Labels
   • Text height = 1/8 (.125)
   • Text Alignment = Horizontal
   • Overall dimension scale = **38.4**
   • Unit format = Architectural
   • Primary Unit Precision = **0'-0"**

4   Add dimensions to the floor plan on the appropriate layer to show the lengths of the walls and their position relative to each other as shown. Create additional dimensions as desired to meet your specific requirements.

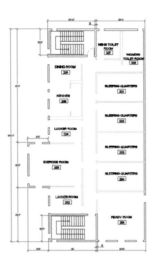

5   Save and close the drawing.

Challenge Exercise | Mechanical

In this exercise, you use what you learned about dimensioning to add dimensions to the drawing.

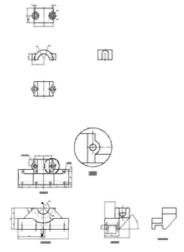

The completed exercise

Completing the Exercise

To complete the exercise, follow the steps in this book or in the onscreen exercise. In the onscreen list of chapters and exercises, click *Chapter 8: Dimensioning.* Click *Challenge Exercise: Mechanical.*

1   Open the drawing you saved from the previous challenge exercise, or open *M_MECH-Challenge- CHP08.dwg.*

2   Make the Dimension layer current.

3   Create a new dimension style called Mech-2 with the following settings:

  • Arrow size = 2
  • Center Marks = None
  • Text Style = Labels
  • Text height = 2
  • Overall dimension scale = **2**
  • Primary Unit Precision = **0.0**

4   To create two dimension substyles for Diameter and Radial dimensions, set the Text Alignment for these substyles to ISO Standard.

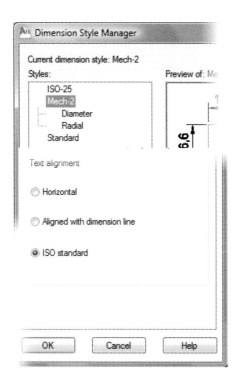

5   Place dimensions on the part views as shown in the following images.

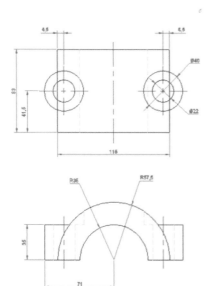

6 More views.

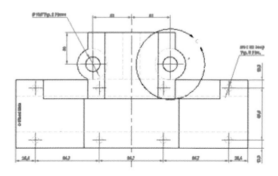

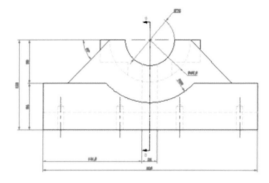

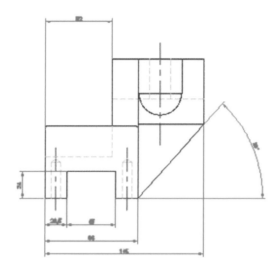

7 Save and close all files.

Chapter Summary

Dimensions are vital annotations used on most drawings to convey important design size and position specifications. You can create a variety of dimension types. You control dimension placement and appearance using dimension styles. Once placed, you can edit dimensions by using grips to move the dimensions or text to new locations or by double-clicking the dimensions and modifying their properties in the Properties palette. You can also use the Dimedit, Dimtedit, and Ddedit commands to modify dimensions and dimension text.

Having completed this chapter, you can:

- Create dimensions.
- Use dimension styles to manage dimensions.
- Create and edit multileader styles and multileaders.
- Use different commands and methods to edit dimensions.

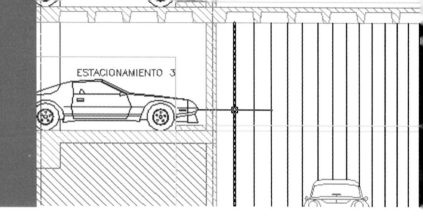

Chapter 09
Hatching Objects

You can use hatch patterns and gradient fills on the drawing to bring focus or call attention to certain areas. Once you have created hatch patterns and fills, you can edit them using similar methods.

Objectives

After completing this chapter, you will be able to:

- Create hatch and gradient fill patterns on objects in the drawing.

- Edit hatch and gradient fills that have been placed in the drawing.

Lesson 41 | Hatching Objects

This lesson describes how to hatch and fill objects in your drawing using the Hatch and Gradient commands. In the following illustration, the roof has a roof tile hatch pattern and the walls a brick pattern. The background is composed of two gradient fills.

Hatching is used across all design disciplines to enhance drawing views, to clarify design features, and to show areas that were modified in drawings when you communicate with your clients. For example, you can add hatching when you draft roof or floor tiles or create section views of manufactured parts. You can also use hatching in construction, steelwork, or road design..

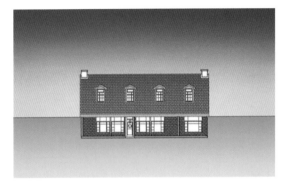

Warning!
Gradient Fills cannot be created with AutoCAD LT®.

Objectives

After completing this lesson, you will be able to:

- Describe the characteristics of hatch and fill patterns.
- Describe the characteristics of associative hatch patterns.
- Create hatch patterns and fills.

Introduction to Hatch Patterns and Gradient Fills

You may want to add patterns that represent materials, special regions, or textures to your drawing to help communicate your ideas. Applying hatch patterns to areas of your drawing can quickly augment their appearance and help to convey design intent. You can use the provided solids, gradients, and predefined hatch patterns or define your own.

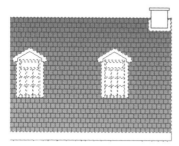

Definition of Hatch and Fill Boundaries

Hatch patterns are graphical elements that are often used to represent materials, special regions, or textures in a drawing. In addition to using a pattern to define an area, you can use gradient or solid fill.

In the following image, the Hatch command was used to create hatch patterns and gradients on several areas of the elevation. The highlighted edges around the bricks illustrate the boundaries that were used to create the pattern. A boundary for a hatch or fill is any combination of selected objects, such as lines, polylines, circles, and arcs, that create an enclosed area.

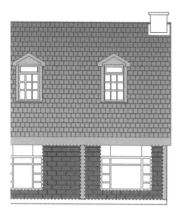

Hatch Boundaries

When you click an area within a drawing to hatch, the boundaries in the drawing are automatically evaluated to determine how to place the hatch based on the specifications you set in the Hatch and Gradient dialog box.

When a hatch boundary cannot be determined, it may be because the specified internal point is not within a fully enclosed area. Red circles are displayed around unconnected endpoints of the boundary to identify any gaps in the hatch boundary.

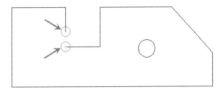

The red circles remain displayed even after you exit the Hatch command. They are removed when you select another internal point for the hatch or when you use the Redraw, Regen, or Regenall commands.

Example of Hatch and Fill Patterns

Using hatch patterns and fills is like coloring in an area, but with more sophistication. For instance, you might select blue to color an ocean. This color alone represents water, but with hatch and fill, you can go beyond color and add patterns and textures, such as waves or ripples.

The following illustration shows that in addition to a brick color on the building front, a hatch has also been applied to better represent how brick would appear in real life.

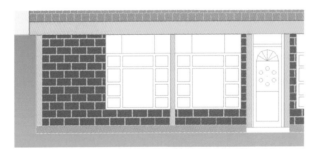

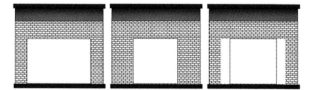

Key Points for Hatch and Gradient Fill

Consider the following when using hatch and gradient fills:

- Hatch patterns are graphic elements that are often used to represent materials, special regions, or textures in a drawing.
- You can use the provided solids, gradients, and predefined hatch patterns, or define your own.
- Boundaries define which area of your drawing can be hatched or filled.
- A boundary for a hatch or fill is any combination of selected objects, such as lines, polylines, circles, and arcs, that create an enclosed area.

Associative Hatch Patterns

By default, hatch patterns are associated with the space they fill, which means that when the hatched object is edited, the hatch adjusts to the new shape. This feature eliminates the rework of recreating the hatch every time you edit a hatched object or area within your drawing.

Removing Associativity

You can elect not to associate a hatch with the object or area. To do this, clear the Associative option under Options in the Hatch and Gradient dialog box.

Nonassociative Hatch Patterns

Hatches made using the Gap Tolerance feature are nonassociative. This means that after you modify the unclosed area containing the hatch, you will need to rehatch it.

When you use the Gap Tolerance feature, all subsequent hatches are also nonassociative. To make hatches associative again, select Associative in the Hatch and Gradient dialog box under Options.

Example of an Associative Hatch Pattern

Suppose you need to alter the opening in a brick fireplace. If your hatch is associative, the brick pattern adjusts to the new space. If your hatch is not associative, it does not adjust and you need to delete it and rehatch the area.

Associative Hatch Key Points

Consider the following points when using hatches:

- By default, hatch patterns are associated with the space they fill, which means that when the hatched object is edited, the hatch adjusts to the new shape.
- Hatches made using the Gap Tolerance feature are nonassociative. This means that after you modify the unclosed area containing the hatch, you will need to rehatch it.
- When you use the Gap Tolerance feature, all subsequent hatches are also nonassociative. To make hatches associative again, select Associative in the Hatch and Gradient dialog box under Options.

Creating Hatched Objects

With the Hatch command, you can fill selected areas of your drawing with patterns, colors, or gradients. You fill these areas by defining boundaries based on points or objects in the drawing.

When you start the Hatch command, the Hatch and Gradient dialog box is displayed. Using this dialog box, you select the type and pattern for the hatch, adjust the angle, scale, and hatch origin, and then define the boundaries that will contain your hatch.

After adjusting the hatch properties and defining the hatch boundaries, you can use the Preview button to preview the hatch pattern before you create it.

Note: Gradient fills are not supported by AutoCAD LT, so the Hatch and Gradient dialog box is just called the Hatch dialog box in AutoCAD LT.

In the following image, hatch and gradient objects are used to create a quarter-section view of the part. The hatch patterns indicate the area sectioned while the gradient patterns are used to add color to the drawing view.

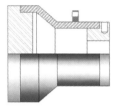

Command Access

Hatch

Command Line: **HATCH, H**
Ribbon: **Home tab > Draw panel > Hatch**

Hatch and Gradient Dialog Box: Hatch Tab

Click the arrow at the bottom-right of the Hatch and Gradient dialog boxes to access the advanced hatching options.

Type and Pattern

You use the Type and Pattern area of the Hatch and Gradient dialog box to select the hatch pattern. You can select patterns from the Pattern list or click the browse button or Swatch area to open the Hatch Pattern Palette dialog box. Using this dialog box, you can select patterns based on a visual swatch.

Hatch Pattern Palette Dialog Box

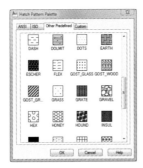

Angle and Scale

You use the Angle and Scale area to adjust the angle and scale of the pattern. When you enter an angle, it is relative to the default angle of the hatch. For example, the ANSI 31 hatch pattern has a default angle of 45 degrees built into the hatch definition. If you enter 45 degrees in the angle field, it is added to the default angle and the pattern lines are drawn vertically at 90 degrees.

Hatch Origin

Some hatching situations may require that you adjust the hatch origin for better placement of the hatch pattern. Using the Hatch Origin options, you can create a more realistic pattern by controlling where the pattern begins.

Command Access

Gradient

Command Line: **GRADIENT**
Ribbon: **Home tab > extended Draw panel > Gradient**

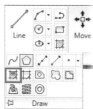

Hatch and Gradient Dialog Box: Gradient Tab

In the Hatch and Gradient dialog box, click the Gradient tab to create gradients in your drawing. You can choose between a one color gradient with adjustments to mimic shading or tint and a two color option in which you specify two colors for the gradient.

Select the gradient pattern from nine predefined choices.

In the Orientation area, you can choose to have the gradient centered within the boundary and adjust the angle of the gradient.

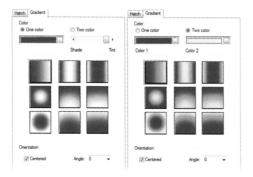

Hatch and Gradient - Boundaries and Advanced Options

The following interface options and descriptions apply to both hatches and gradients.

Boundaries

Every hatch or gradient you create is based on a boundary you define. Use the options in this area of the dialog box to create boundaries by selecting points inside a boundary or objects that define a boundary.

Options

When the Associative option is selected, the resulting hatch is associative with the boundary. When you are creating hatch patterns in multiple boundaries at once, you can use the Create Separate Hatches option to create a separate hatch for each boundary defined. Using this option, you can change any of the resulting hatch patterns independently of the others.

Use the Draw Order list to adjust the draw order of the hatch pattern. The draw order determines the pattern or gradient's position behind or in front of other objects. Use this option to create multiple pattern fills that include both a hatch and a solid fill or a hatch and a gradient.

Inherit Properties

When you edit drawings that already contain hatch patterns, use this option to retrieve the properties of an existing hatch pattern. Using this feature, you can easily match the properties of other hatch patterns or gradients.

Islands

Select Island Detection to detect boundaries that are inside the boundary you define. Choose between Normal, Outer, or Ignore. This is extremely useful when hatching areas that contain text. The text is treated as a boundary and, unless you choose the Ignore option, the pattern or gradient does not overrun the text.

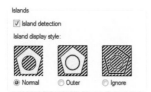

Boundary Retention

If you select the Retain Boundaries option, a new object is created representing the defined boundary. You can choose between a Region or Polyline object.

Boundary Set

Use this option to determine how the drawing is analyzed for boundaries. On large drawings, this can speed up boundary analysis by limiting the objects that are considered.

Gap Tolerance

If the boundary has gaps, you can set the gap tolerance to allow any gap that is equal to or smaller than the tolerance to be ignored.
Note: If a gap exists in the boundary, the hatch pattern will not be associative.

Inherit Options

If you use the Inherit Properties option to create the hatch, you can use the Inherit options to control the location of the hatch origin.

Procedure: Creating a Hatch Pattern

The following steps give an overview of creating a hatch or gradient in the drawing.

1   On the ribbon, click Home tab > Draw panel > Hatch.

2   Select the hatch pattern type and define its properties.

3   Click Add: Pick Points or Add: Select Objects and select points internal to a boundary or objects that define a boundary.

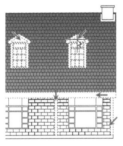

4   Adjust other options as required in the Hatch and Gradient dialog box.

5   Click Preview to preview the hatch.

6   When the hatch is previewed, click anywhere in the drawing to return to the Hatch and Gradient dialog box or right-click to accept the hatch pattern as it is previewed.

Layers for Hatch and Gradient
It is good practice to create all of your hatches on one layer and all gradients on another.

Hatch Guidelines

Consider the following guidelines when creating hatched objects:

- All hatch and gradient patterns must fill a boundary. A boundary is an enclosed area that can consist of lines, polylines, circles, and arcs.
- The easiest way to specify a boundary is to zoom into the area you want to hatch and select a point inside that area using the Add: Pick points Boundaries option.
- You can delete the boundary without deleting the hatch or gradient fill.
- Do not use a densely hatched pattern to create the effect of a solid fill. Instead use the Solid hatch pattern provided by the software. The Solid hatch pattern is located at the top of the Pattern list.
- Click the Expand button in the lower-right corner of the Hatch and Gradient dialog box to access advanced options.
- Most of the time you will want the Associative Option checked when creating a hatched object.
- If you are placing the hatch or gradient fill within more than one boundary area, it will be treated as a single hatch unless you choose Create separate Hatches located in the advanced options.
- Scaling a hatch pattern is similar to scaling Text and Dimensions. It should be scaled proportionate to the display scale of the object it is filling. For instance if the object will be displayed to plot at a scale of & #188;" = 1", then the hatch scale should be 48 (4 x 12).
- Select the Annotative Option when there will be multiple views of the object at multiple scales in the drawing layout. This will keep the hatch scale consistent in all the viewports.
- If you enter an angle for the hatch, it is added to the angle already defined in the pattern.
- Use the Hatch Origin options to fine tune hatch placement.
- Use draw order to create multiple pattern fills containing both hatch patterns and gradients or solid colors.
- Create separate layers for hatch patterns in your drawing.
- An exploded hatch pattern will result in thousands of separate objects and increase the size of your drawing.
- You can set the hatch pattern scale factor to a desired default scale that will appear in the dialog box by typing HPSCALE at the command line and entering a new value.

Practice Exercise | Create Hatched Objects

In this practice exercise you create a drawing similar to the one below and use the Hatch and Gradient commands.

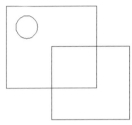

1   Begin a blank drawing and create the objects to hatch and gradient fill. Make two overlapping rectangles and place a circle in one of them.

2   To create a solid hatch pattern in a selected object:

- On the Home tab, click Draw panel > Hatch.
- In the Hatch and Gradient dialog box, select ANSI31 from the Pattern list.
- Select 0 from the Angle list.
- Select 1.000 from the Scale list.
- Under Boundaries, click Add: Select Objects.
- Click the overlapping rectangle as indicated.

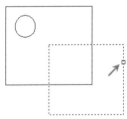

- Right-click the selected object. Click Preview.
- Right-click to accept the hatch.

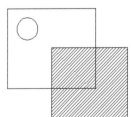

3   To create a gradient fill using two colors:

- On the Home tab, click Draw panel > Hatch.
- In the Hatch and Gradient dialog box, click the Gradient tab.
- Under Color, click Two color.
- Choose any of the gradient patterns.
- Under Boundaries, click Add: Pick points.
- Click inside the part of the other overlapping rectangle as indicated below. The boundary is detected and highlighted.

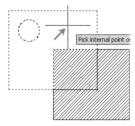

- Right-click the selected object. Click Preview.
- Click inside the drawing window to return to the dialog box.
- Select another gradient pattern.
- Click Preview.
- Right-click to accept the gradient.

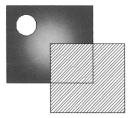

4   To create a Solid fill hatch pattern:

- On the Home tab, click Draw panel > Hatch.
- In the Hatch and Gradient dialog box, Pattern list, select Solid.
- From the Swatch list, select Select Color.
- In the Select Color dialog box, click the Color Books tab.
- Select a color from one of the Color book guides. Click OK to return to the Hatch and Gradient dialog box.

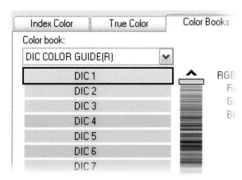

- Under Boundaries, click Add: Pick points.
- Click inside the circle. Notice the boundary is highlighted.
- Right-click to Preview.
- Press ENTER to accept the hatch.

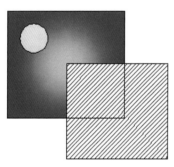

5   To modify an associative hatched object:

- With the command line blank, select the hatched objects.

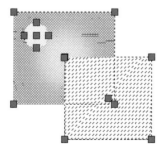

- Select the grips to adjust the shape of the objects.

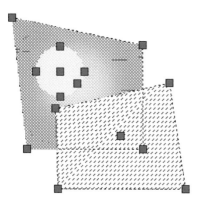

- Press ESC to deselect the objects.

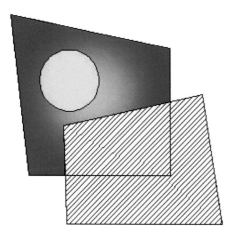

The hatch and gradient fills adjusted to the modified shapes of the objects because the Associative option in the Hatch and Gradient dialog box was selected.

Exercise | Create Hatch

In this exercise, you use the Hatch command to create hatch patterns on the elevation drawing. You use the Create Separate Hatch option to see how it affects a multiple boundary pattern.

The completed exercise

Completing the Exercise

To complete the exercise, follow the steps in this book or in the onscreen exercise. In the onscreen list of chapters and exercises, click *Chapter 9: Hatching Objects*. Click *Exercise: Create Hatches*.

1   Open *M_Hatch-Objects.dwg*.

2   Zoom into the left area of the elevation as shown.

3   Use the Hatch command to place separate hatches on the front of the building:

- On the Home tab, click Draw panel > Hatch.
- In the Hatch and Gradient dialog box, select AR-B816C from the Pattern list.
- In the Scale field, enter **1**.
- Place a check mark in the box next to the Create Separate Hatches option.
- Click Add: Pick Points.
- Click two points (1) and (2) define the boundary as shown.

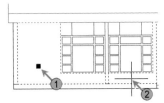

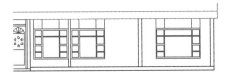

4   To complete the hatch:
   - Press ENTER.
   - In the Hatch and Gradient dialog box, click Preview to preview the hatch.
   - If the hatch pattern appears correct, press ENTER to accept the hatch.

5   Pan to the right side of the elevation.

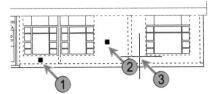

6   To place a single hatch on the three areas on the right side of the elevation:
   - On the Home tab, click Draw panel > Hatch.
   - Clear the Create Separate Hatches option.
   - Click Add: Pick Points.
   - Click three points (1), (2), and (3) to define the boundaries as shown.

7   To complete the hatch:
   - Press ENTER to return to the Hatch and Gradient dialog box.
   - Click Specified Origin.
   - Click the Click to Set New Origin button.
   - Select the endpoint as shown.
   - In the Hatch and Gradient dialog box, click OK.

8   Select the previously created hatch. Notice all boundaries are treated as a single hatch object.

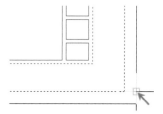

9   Zoom to display the entire drawing.

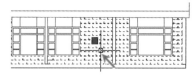

10   On the View tab, click Navigate panel > Extents drop-down > Window. Window zoom into the area shown in the following image. Make certain only part of the roof area is visible.

11   On the command line, enter **Regen**.

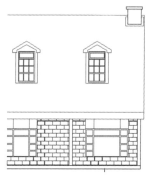

12   To expand the Hatch dialog box:
   • On the Home tab, click Draw panel > Hatch.
   • Expand the Hatch and Gradient dialog box.

13   To specify the island detection type, under Islands, click Outer.

14   To apply a hatch pattern to the roof even though the entire area is not displayed:

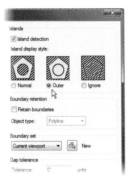

- In the Pattern list, select AR-B88.
- Click Add: Pick Points.
- Select a point on the roof.
- Press ENTER.
- Click Preview.
- Press ENTER to accept the hatch pattern.

15 Zoom to display your entire drawing.

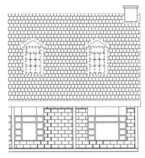

16 Close all files. Do not save.

Exercise | Create Fills and Gradients

In this exercise, you create solid fills and gradients. You use draw order to place the gradients and fills behind existing patterns, and you use the Inherit Properties options to copy gradient and fill patterns.

> **Warning!**
> Gradient fills are not supported by AutoCAD LT. If you attempt this exercise in AutoCAD LT, you will need to use solid fills instead of gradient fills. The Hatch and Gradient dialog box is named the Hatch dialog box in AutoCAD LT.

The completed exercise

> **Completing the Exercise**
> To complete the exercise, follow the steps in this book or in the onscreen exercise. In the onscreen list of chapters and exercises, click *Chapter 9: Hatching Objects*. Click *Exercise: Create Fills and Gradients*.

1   Open *M_Create-Fills-Gradients.dwg*.

2   Apply a gradient to the elevation roof:

- On the Home tab, click Draw panel > Gradient.
- Click Inherit Properties.
- Select the gradient pattern in the top block.

3   Select a point on the roof as shown.

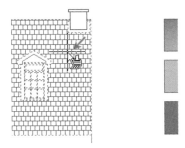

4   Right-click anywhere in the drawing. Click Preview. Notice how the gradient pattern hides the roof hatch pattern.

5   To move the gradient fill behind the roof hatch:
   • Press ESC to return to the Hatch and Gradient dialog box.
   • Under Options, select Send to Back in the Draw Order list.
   • Under Islands, make certain Outer is selected.
   • Under Options, select Send to Back from the Draw Order list.
   • Click Preview. The gradient should appear behind the roof hatch pattern.
   • Right-click anywhere in the drawing to accept the gradient fill.

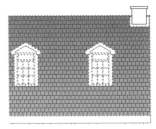

6   To add a gradient fill to the fascia and columns area of the elevation:
   • On the Home tab, click Draw panel > Gradient.
   • Click Inherit Properties. Select the second swatch.

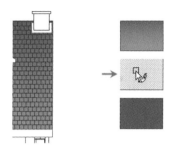

7   Press ESC to return to the Hatch and Gradient dialog box.

The fill is detected as a solid color, and the Hatch tab of the dialog box is displayed again.

8   Under Options, select Send to Back in the Draw Order list:

- Click Add: Pick Points.
- Select points inside the fascia area, columns, and outer areas of the upper floor windows.

  Note: The following image reflects the selections only on the right side of the drawing.
- Press ENTER.
- Click Preview.

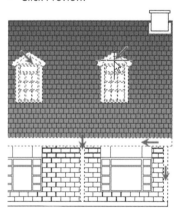

9   If the fills look correct, right-click anywhere in the drawing to accept the hatch.

Chapter 9 | Hatching Objects

10 Repeat the Gradient command. Use the Inherit Properties option to assign the gradient on the lower swatch to the bricks on the front elevation.

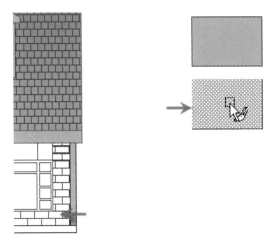

Once applied, the elevation should appear as shown.

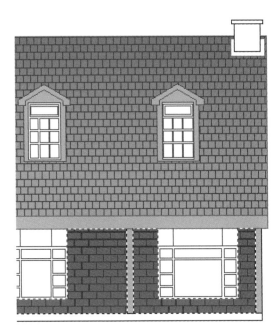

11   To add a solid hatch to the foundation area or the elevation:

- On the Home tab, click Draw panel > Hatch.
- In the Pattern list, make sure SOLID is selected.
- In the Swatch list, choose Select Color.
- In the Select Color dialog box, Index Color tab, under Color, enter **254**.
- Click OK.

12   Click Add: Pick Points. Select the foundation area of the elevation.

- Preview the hatch.
- Right-click anywhere in the drawing to accept the hatch.
  Note: Make sure you select the foundation area on both sides of the door.

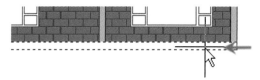

13   On the Layers panel, freeze the Hatch_Swatch layer.

14   On the Layers panel, thaw the Background- Frame layer.

15   Zoom to display the entire drawing. Note: To save time, lines were drawn to use as a boundary for the background and foreground fills.

16   Add a gradient fill to the upper background representing the sky:

- On the Home tab, click Draw panel > Gradient.
- Under Color, click One Color.
- Click the Color button and select Blue on the Index Color tab of the Select Color dialog box.
- Click OK.
- Adjust the Shade - Tint slider as shown. Click the middle right gradient swatch.

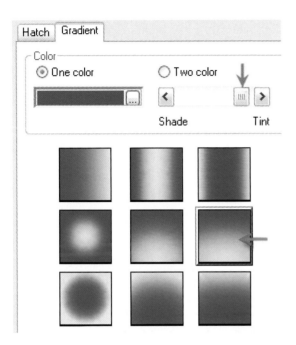

17   Click Add: Pick Points. Select the upper area above the elevation.
   • Right-click anywhere in the drawing. Click Preview.
   • Right-click anywhere in the drawing to accept the gradient fill.

18   Repeat the Gradient command, this time using a green color on the lower area of the elevation.
   Tip: Use the True Color tab of the Select Color dialog box, and enter **109, 184, 71** for Color.

19   Close all files. Do not save.

Lesson 42 | Editing Hatch Objects

This lesson describes how to edit hatch and gradient patterns with the Hatchedit command.

Most projects are subject to design changes, so the ability to easily modify an existing hatch is important to remaining productive. The change can be as simple as changing the scale of a hatch object or as complex as altering the boundary or adding or removing islands.

Warning!
The name of the Hatch and Gradient dialog box in AutoCAD LT is the Hatch dialog box.

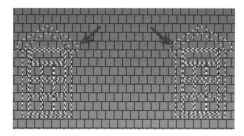

Objectives

After completing this lesson, you will be able to:

- Describe which edits maintain associative properties and which destroy the associativity.
- Use the Hatchedit command to edit hatches and fills.

Maintaining Associative Properties when Editing Hatches

Understanding when a hatch might lose its associativity, and thus not fill a newly edited object or area, is critical in learning how to effectively edit hatched objects and maintain a high productivity rate. Failure to understand this may result in unnecessary rework.

Hatch Associativity Guidelines

Consider the following guidelines for associative and nonassociative hatches:

- If a hatch's associativity is lost, it cannot be restored. You have to delete and recreate the hatch pattern.
- If you do not close a hatch boundary, the hatch properties change from associative to nonassociative.

Gaps in Hatch Boundaries Remove Hatch Associativity

When you are editing an object or area containing a hatch and you create a gap in the boundary, the hatch pattern loses its associativity. If this occurs, a message on the Command line indicating the hatch boundary associativity has been removed is displayed, and the hatch pattern does not fill the object or area, as shown in the following illustration.

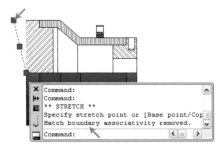

Editing Hatches

The options and functionality in the Hatch Edit dialog box are identical to those found in the Hatch and Gradient dialog box. When you edit a hatch pattern or fill, you can use the same options you used when you created the hatch or fill.

When you start the Hatchedit command, you are prompted to select a hatch pattern. After you select the hatch pattern, the Hatch Edit dialog box is displayed and shows the properties of the selected hatch pattern or fill. You can adjust any of the properties used to create the hatch pattern and apply those changes immediately.

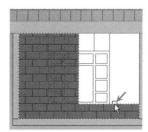

You can also edit a nonassociative hatch using grips.

Command Access

Edit Hatch

Command Line: **HATCHEDIT**
Ribbon: **Home tab › Modify panel › Edit Hatch**

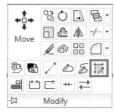

Note: You can also double-click a hatch pattern in the drawing to access the Hatch Edit dialog box.

Hatch Edit Dialog Box

Except for a slight wording difference in the Options area (Separate Hatches versus Create Separate Hatches), the Hatch Edit and Hatch and Gradient dialog boxes are identical.

Hatch Boundary Grips

The following grips are available for a nonassociative hatch.

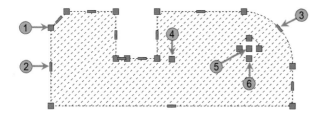

1. **Select a Vertex**: Moves or removes the selected point.

2. **Select an Edge**: Add a new point to the line segment or convert the line segment to an arc.

3. **Select an Edge**: Add a new point to the arc segment, stretch the arc, or convert the arc segment to a line.

4. **Location Grip**: Move the entire hatch object to a new location using the selected grip point as the base point.

5. **Island Location**: Move the island to a new location.

6. **Island Stretch:** Stretch the specified edge.

When you hover over a grip, the tooltip that displays shows the editing options for the grip. You can cycle through the options by selecting a grip and pressing CTRL. The following grips are available for a nonassociative hatch.

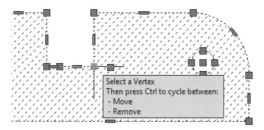

Procedure: Editing Hatch Patterns and Fills

The following steps give an overview of editing hatch patterns and fills.

1   Double-click a hatch pattern or gradient fill.

2   Make the appropriate changes to the pattern in the Hatch Edit dialog box and click Preview.

3   Right-click anywhere in the drawing to accept the changes or left-click anywhere in the drawing to return to the dialog box.

Hatch Editing Guidelines

Consider the following guidelines when editing hatches:

- The Hatch Edit and Hatch and Gradient dialog boxes are almost identical.
- You edit hatches with the same options you used to create them.
- Double-click a hatch pattern or gradient fill to start the Hatchedit command. This saves you the step of having to start the command, then select the hatch pattern.

Exercise | Edit Hatch Patterns and Fills

In this exercise, you edit existing hatch patterns and fills. You erase geometry and view how the hatch pattern and fills update accordingly. You remove boundaries that are no longer needed and create new boundaries.

> **Warning!**
> Gradient fills are not supported by AutoCAD LT.

The completed exercise

> **Completing the Exercise**
> To complete the exercise, follow the steps in this book or in the onscreen exercise. In the onscreen list of chapters and exercises, click *Chapter 9: Hatching Objects*. Click *Exercise: Edit Hatch Patterns and Fills*.

1   Open *M_Edit-Hatches-Fills.dwg*.

2   Zoom to display the elevation as shown.

3   Erase two of the dormers from the roof:

   • Start the Erase command.
   • Enter **w** and press ENTER to create a window selection.
   • Create a window selection around the two center windows as shown.
   • Press ENTER.

4   Verify that the roof pattern and gradient are updated automatically.

5   Double-click the fill applied to the front fascia of the elevation to start the Hatchedit command.

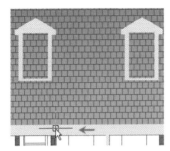

6   To remove the boundaries associated with the erased dormers:
    • In the Hatch Edit dialog box, click Remove Boundaries.
    • Select the highlighted boundaries to remove them. As you select the boundaries, they disappear.
    • Continue selecting the boundaries until they are all removed.

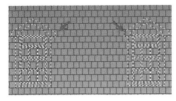

7   Press ENTER to return to the Hatch Edit dialog box. Click OK.

8   Change the pattern and scale of the roof hatch:
    • Double-click the roof hatch to start Hatchedit.
    • Under Type and Pattern, select the Pattern list.
    • Click AR-RSHKE.
    • Under Angle and Scale, enter **1.5** in the Scale list.
    • Click OK.

9   Zoom in to the left side of the elevation.

10 Move a window:

- Start the Move command.
- Enter **w** and press ENTER to use a window selection.
- Click two points to define the selection window as shown.
- Press ENTER.

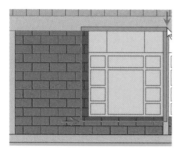

11 Make sure either PolarSnap or ortho is turned on and do the following:

- Click anywhere on your drawing for the base point.
- Drag your cursor to the left at 180 degrees.
- Click to move the window to the left any amount as shown.

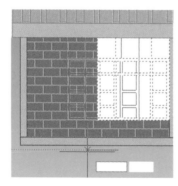

12 Because the move generated a gap in the boundary, the hatch boundary associativity is removed. To correct this, remove the old boundary and create a new boundary for both the hatch and the fill:

- Double-click the fill area to begin the Hatchedit command.
- In the Hatch Edit dialog box, click Remove Boundaries.
- Select the boundary as shown.

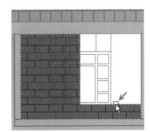

13   To add the new boundary:
- Right-click anywhere in the drawing.
- Click Add Boundaries.
- Select a point as shown.
- Press ENTER.

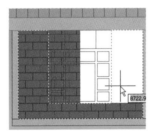

14   In the Hatch Edit dialog box, click OK.

15   Double-click the hatch pattern and repeat the previous process to remove and add a new boundary. When complete, the area should appear as shown.
Note: The preceding steps do not reassociate the hatch and fill with the geometry. Once associativity is removed from the hatch pattern, you would need to recreate the hatch pattern to achieve associativity. This lesson focuses on editing hatch patterns, but in some cases it could be quicker to delete the hatch and recreate it.

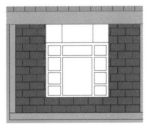

16   Zoom to display the entire drawing.

17   Close all files. Do not save.

Chapter 9 | Hatching Objects

Challenge Exercise | Architectural

In this exercise, you edit existing hatch patterns and fills. You erase geometry and view how the hatch pattern and fills update accordingly. You remove boundaries that are no longer needed and create new boundaries.

Note
You have the option of completing this exercise using either imperial or metric units. Select one version of the exercise to complete the steps.

Warning!
If completing this exercise in AutoCAD LT, in step 2, use a solid fill with a grey color (color 9).

The completed exercise

Completing the Exercise
To complete the exercise, follow the steps in this book or in the onscreen exercise. In the onscreen list of chapters and exercises, click *Chapter 9: Hatching Objects*. Click *Challenge Exercise: Architectural Metric*.

Metric Units

1 Open the drawing you saved from the previous challenge exercise, or open *M_ARCH-Challenge- CHP09.dwg*.

2 Set up the layers and add a gradient fill.

   • Thaw the existing layer, Site - Concrete, and make it the current layer.
   • Freeze the Dimension layer.
   • Add a gradient hatch to the geometry as shown.

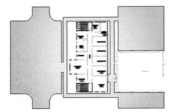

3   Add additional hatching to the drawing as desired. For example, you could hatch the area between the wall lines or hatch different rooms.

4   Save and close the file.

Imperial Units

1   Open the drawing you saved from the previous challenge exercise, or open *I_ARCH-Challenge- CHP09.dwg.*

2   Set up the layers and add a gradient fill.

- Thaw the existing layer, Site - Concrete, and make it the current layer.
- Freeze the Dimension layer and add a gradient hatch to the geometry on as shown.

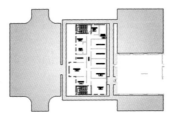

3   Add additional hatching to the drawing as desired. For example, you could hatch the area between the wall lines or hatch different rooms.

4   Save and close the file.

Challenge Exercise | Mechanical

In this exercise, you use what you learned about hatching objects to add hatch patterns and fills to the drawing.

> **Warning!**
> If completing this exercise in AutoCAD LT, in step 5, use a solid fill instead of a gradient fill.

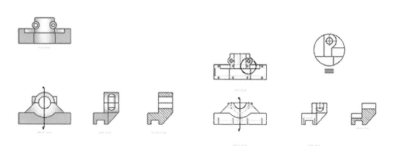

The completed exercise

> **Completing the Exercise**
> To complete the exercise, follow the steps in this book or in the onscreen exercise. In the onscreen list of chapters and exercises, click *Chapter 9: Hatching Objects*. Click *Challenge Exercise: Mechanical*.

1   Open the drawing you saved from the previous challenge exercise, or open *M_MECH- Challenge- CHP09.dwg.*

2   Make the Hatch layer current.

3   Apply an ANSI32 hatch pattern to the view as shown. Adjust the scale and angle accordingly.

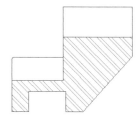

Section B-B

4   Apply the same hatch pattern to the assembly section view as shown.

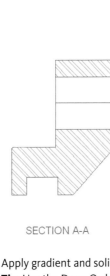

SECTION A-A

5   Apply gradient and solid fills to the assembly views as shown. Use your own choice of colors. **Tip**: Use the Draw Order option to prevent the patterns from covering the lines.

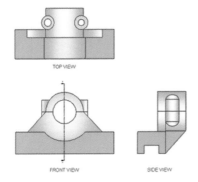

TOP VIEW

FRONT VIEW   SIDE VIEW

6   Save and close all files.

Chapter Summary

You use hatch patterns to create sections and other types of views. As you have seen in this chapter, hatch patterns and gradient fills can be used to enhance the entire drawing.

Having completed this chapter, you can:

- Create hatch and gradient fill patterns on objects in the drawing.
- Edit hatch and gradient fills that have been placed in the drawing.

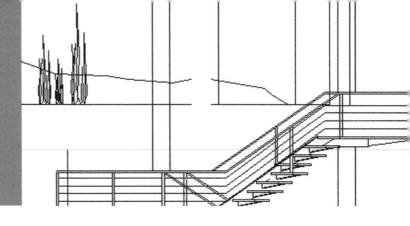

Chapter 10
Working with Reusable Content

When you create a drawing file, you are creating and interacting with a special database file through a graphical interface. In some cases, you need to define a number of individual objects as a single object for greater ease of use. That single object is referred to as a *block*.

Once you have grouped objects together into a block, you can reuse that data in other locations in the same drawing or in other drawings. Leveraging existing data in your drawings helps you to work more efficiently and keeps your design data consistent. In addition to blocks, there are other types of information that you can reformat and reuse in your drawing files.

Use DesignCenter to drag specific content, or even an entire drawing, from one drawing file into another. You can also use tool palettes to organize and share data such as blocks, hatches, and even commands.

In this chapter, you are introduced to these methods for leveraging existing drawing information.

Objectives

After completing this chapter, you will be able to:

- Create a block definition and insert a block definition or file into a drawing to place block references.

- Use DesignCenter to reuse the data in a drawing.

- Access tool palettes and use their tools.

Standard Object Snap and Status Bar Settings
Before completing the exercises in this chapter, refer to the "Settings for the Exercises" section in the Introduction.

Lesson 43 | Using Blocks

This lesson describes how to create a block definition and insert a block definition or file into a drawing. For example, in the following illustration, the single block object on the left was created from all of the geometry on the right. The block object keeps all of the geometry tied together. The chair on the right is made of individual lines, arcs, and polylines while the objects on the left are a block definition; you can insert them into a drawing as a single object.

Using groups of objects to create block definitions that act as a single object can help you work more efficiently. Multiple objects that are defined as a block increase the reusability of that geometry when you or others use the block in other drawings or locations. Creating blocks to use in other drawings vastly improves overall efficiency and helps you to maintain consistency in your designs.

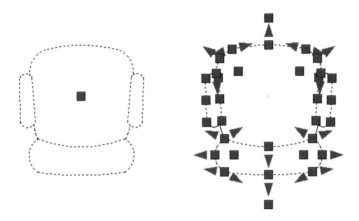

Objectives

After completing this lesson, you will be able to:

- Describe blocks and how they are used to group objects together.
- Describe the properties that affect block behavior in the drawing.
- Use the Block command to create a block definition.
- Use the Insert command to insert a block reference in a drawing.

About Blocks

Blocks provide an efficient way to group a set of objects together and reuse them throughout all of your drawings and projects. You can create your own blocks or use some of the thousands available from others via the Internet.

The following illustration shows an example of typical blocks you might use to create an office or home layout drawing.

The following illustration shows an example of typical blocks you might use to create a mechanical or electrical drawing.

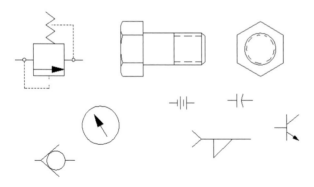

Mechanical symbols

Blocks Defined

Blocks are often referred to as symbols. These symbols are made up from a collection of objects grouped together into a block definition. A block definition can be made from a single object in your drawing or from multiple objects. You only need to draw a symbol once; then, whenever you need that symbol in any drawing, you simply insert it.

One symbol found in most drawings is a title block and border.

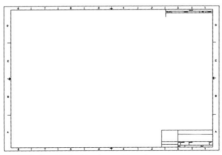

"D" sized title block and border

Tracing Analogy

In the days of manual drafting, draftsman used cardboard or plastic templates to trace common items onto their drawing. Some of the most simple were circles and ellipse templates, but mechanical engineers also used templates for arrowheads, bolts, and hydraulic cylinders. Architects traced common fixtures such as sinks, bath tubs, or lavatories. By tracing these templates, draftsmen were able to produce common objects consistently throughout their drawings.

Example: Blocks used for Architectural Drafting

In architectural drafting, blocks are used for common objects, including doors, windows, case goods, plumbing fixtures, and furniture. The following drawing shows a simple floor plan that is made from many blocks.

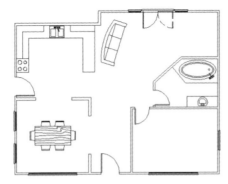

How Blocks Behave

Blocks behave exactly as you want them to, provided you follow the rules for creating them. When you insert a block, the color, linetype, and lineweight of objects in the block retain their original settings regardless of the current settings in the drawings. However, you can create blocks with objects that inherit the current color, linetype, and lineweight settings.

In this image, both blocks were inserted with the Visual layer current. Each block was created on a different layer with different properties. On the left, the original block geometry is created on layer 0. On the right, the original block geometry is created on a layer other than 0 and has different linetype and color properties.

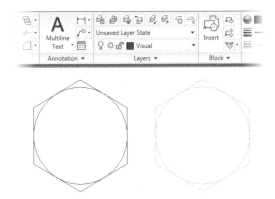

Definition of Block Behavior

When a Block is inserted into a drawing, there are three possible ways the block can behave in regards to its Properties (Color, Layer, Linetype, and Lineweight): (1) It can retain its original properties; (2) It can inherit its properties from the current Layer on which it is inserted; (3) It can inherit its properties from the current Property settings:

- **Retain Original Properties** (1): Objects in the block do not inherit color, linetype, and lineweight properties. The properties of the object in the block do not change regardless of the current settings. For this choice, it is recommended that you set the color, linetype, and lineweight properties individually for each object before you create the block definition. *Do not use BYBLOCK or BYLAYER for the properties of these objects.*
- **Inherit Properties from current Layer** (2): Objects in the block inherit color, linetype, and lineweight properties from the color, linetype, and lineweight assigned to the current layer. For this choice, before you create objects to be included in the block definition, set the current layer to 0 and set the current color, linetype, and lineweight to BYLAYER when you create the geometry for your block.

- **Inherit Properties from current Property Settings** (3): Objects in the block inherit color, linetype, and lineweight from the current color, linetype, and lineweight. This is like setting an override by not assigning the property from the current layer. For this choice, before you create objects to be included in the block definition, set the current color, linetype, and lineweight to BYBLOCK.

In summary, a block takes on the properties of the current layer when inserted, provided it has either been created on layer 0 or with the properties of its objects set to BYLAYER. A block retains its original properties from the layer it was created on when the properties of the objects contained in the block have been set to BYLAYER.

Example of Block Behavior

Assume that you want to create a sink block and you want the sink to take on the properties of the current layer when inserted. First, you should make layer 0 current and set the color, layer, linetype, and lineweight properties to BYLAYER. Then create your geometry and make a block out of it. When you insert your sink block, it inherits the color, linetype, and lineweight from the current layer.

Creating Blocks

The Block command creates a single object out of multiple objects so they appear and behave like a single piece of geometry. The definition for the block is stored in the drawing database and referred to as a *block definition*. A visible block definition in a drawing is called a *block reference*. A block definition can exist in the drawing file database and not have a block reference in the drawing.

You define the block through the options in the Block Definition dialog box. You define items such as the name of the block, what objects will be in the block definition, the base point for the block, what units the geometry is drawn in, if it has to be scaled uniformly, whether it can be exploded, and a general description.

The base point you specify for the block defines the point you will use to position the block when inserting it in a drawing. This point also becomes the grip point for the block. The following illustration demonstrates the importance of selecting a proper base point. When creating a bi-fold door block and specifying the base point, you should snap to an object endpoint (1) so that when you insert the bi- fold door block in your drawing you can accurately place it at the end of the closet wall (2).

Command Access

Block

Command Line: **BLOCK, B**
Ribbon: **Insert tab > Block panel > Create**

Insert | Create | Block Editor

Block ▾

Block Definition Dialog Box

For each block you create, you specify the name and the insertion base point; you also select the objects to include in your block definition. You can also choose among various other settings as needed.

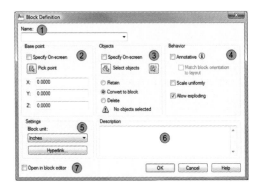

① Specify the name of the block.

② Define the base point. Click Pick Point to snap to a location on your objects and return the X, Y, and Z values; or enter the absolute X, Y, and Z values.

③ Click Select Objects and select the geometry to include in this block. Under Objects, select the option to define what happens to the selected geometry after you click OK to create the block. The objects are either left as individual objects (retained), converted to a block reference, or deleted.

④ Select your Annotative behavior and whether to scale the block uniformly and allow it to be exploded based on your requirements.

⑤ Select the units the geometry was drawn with. Enter a description for the block.

⑥ Check this box to open the block editor after clicking OK.

Procedure: Creating a Block

The following steps give an overview of creating a block with the Block command.

1   On the ribbon, click Insert tab > Block panel > Create (1).

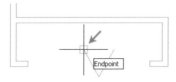

2   In the Block Definition dialog box, enter a name for the block (2) and click Pick Point (3).

3   Use an object snap to select a location on your object for the pick point.

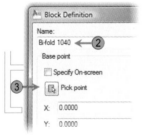

4   Under Objects, click Select Objects (4).

5   Select the geometry to include in this block.

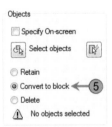

6   Under Objects, select the option to define what happens to the selected geometry (5). Then click OK.

Note: Other options to enhance your block definitions include choosing whether the block is annotative or not, setting the block units, and giving the block a description.

Guidelines for Creating Blocks

- Name the blocks in a logical order, for example Door32, Door36, Window28, etc.
- Use the Purge command to purge unreferenced blocks that you will not be using in your drawing.
- Use the WBLOCK command to write the blocks in your drawing to individual drawing files. Type W to access the Write Block dialog box. Choose the block from your drawing and the Destination folder. Keep a folder for all of your block symbols to use in other drawings.
- You can nest blocks, meaning you can create a block that has other blocks within it. There is no limit to how many blocks can be nested in another block.

- If a block definition exists in a drawing and it is referencing a layer, you will not be able to delete the layer unless the block is purged.
- You cannot purge a reference if there is an instance of the block in the drawing.
- To make changes to a block, Explode it and re-create the block. If you re-create a block with the same name as a previously defined block, it will change all of the blocks in the drawing with that name.
- If you create a block and do not specify a Base point, the default base point will be 0,0,0.
- To Rename a block, use the Rename command. Select the old block name from the list and Rename it.

Practice Exercise | Create Blocks

In this practice exercise, you draw a simple object, create a block out of it, and name the block.

1   Begin a blank drawing and create some simple geometry.

2   To create a block:

- On the Insert tab, click Block panel > Create.
- In the Block Definition dialog box, for the block name, enter **widget** (1).
- For the block base point, click Pick Point (2).
- Using object snap, select a point on the object (3).
- Click Select Objects (4) and select the geometry you have created. Press ENTER to return to the dialog box.
- Click the Convert to Block option (5).
- Select OK to exit the dialog box.

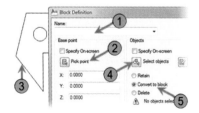

3   To check that the geometry was converted to a block:

- With the command line blank, select the object.
- The object should be highlighted with one grip visible at the base point you selected for the block.

4   Save this drawing to practice the Insert command in the next section.

Inserting Blocks

You use the Insert command to select a block definition or a file so you can place a block reference in your drawing. After selecting the block definition or file, you specify the insertion point, scale factor, and rotation angle for that block in the Insert dialog box or in the drawing window.

When you use Insert and select a file, a block definition of that entire file is added to the drawing database. So in a sense, the Insert command creates a block from a file on the fly.

Command Access

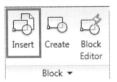

Insert

Command Line: **INSERT, I**
Ribbon: **Insert tab > Block panel > Insert**

Insert Dialog Box

For each block you insert, you provide the block name, insertion point, scale, and rotation when you place the block in your drawing.

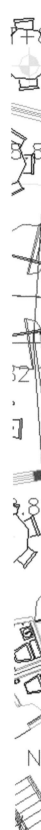

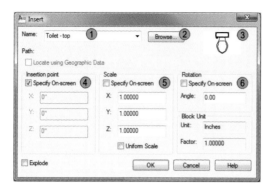

① Specify the name of a block to insert or the name of a file to insert as a block.

② Opens the select file dialog box allowing you to select a drawing file to insert as a block into your current drawing.

③ Preview of the selected block when a preview image is available.

④ Specify the insertion point of the block in your drawing. Decide whether the insertion point should be defined in the dialog box or on screen in the drawing area. If on screen, then select the Specify On- Screen option. If not, clear this option and enter the X, Y, and Z values. You will most often specify this point on screen.

⑤ Specify the scale factor for the block. Decide whether the scale factor should be defined in the dialog box or on screen in the drawing area. If on screen, then select the Specify On- Screen option. If not, clear the option and enter the X, Y, and Z scaling factors.

⑥ Specify the rotation angle of the block. Decide whether the rotation angle should be defined in the dialog box or on screen in the drawing area. If on screen, then select the Specify On- Screen option. If not, clear the option and enter a rotation angle. You can also change this on screen while placing the block.

Procedure: Inserting a Block

The following steps give an overview of inserting a block into a drawing.

1   On the ribbon, click Insert tab > Block panel > Insert.

2   In the Insert dialog box, select the block name from the list of blocks or click Browse and select a file.

3   Select the Specify On-Screen option (1), set your scale factor (2), and your rotation angle (3). The default rotation direction is CCW.

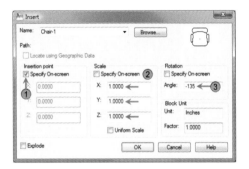

4   Click OK.

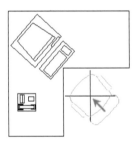

5   Drag the block to the desired location and click to place it. You can use object snaps for an exact placement if desired.

Your block is placed in the drawing based on the parameters you specified.

Guidelines for Inserting Blocks

- When creating a Title block, you typically want the insertion point to be at 0,0. Otherwise, select the insertion point in the drawing.
- You can specify the X,Y scale and rotation angle at the command line when you insert the block if you uncheck Specify On-screen for Scale and Rotation.
- You can specify different X and Y scales. The block will be scaled proportionately.
- Browse to select a drawing file or a wblock that is located outside of the drawing.
- Once a drawing file is inserted into the current drawing, everything that the drawing geometry references will come with it such as blocks, layers, linetypes, text styles, and dimension styles.
- Use the Purge command to purge your drawing of unreferenced information that you will not need in your drawing. This will result in a more efficient drawing size.
- Once a block is inserted into a drawing you can move, copy, rotate, scale, mirror, or handle it like any other geometry.
- When you Explode a block, the geometry returns to its original properties.
- When you Explode a block that has another block nested in it, you can then Explode the nested block.

Practice Exercise | Inserting Blocks

In this practice exercise, you create and insert a block. You also draw a simple object then create a block out of it, called a widget. After you create the widget, you insert it into your drawing.

1   Begin a blank drawing and create some simple geometry.

2   To create a block:
   - On the Insert tab, click Block panel › Create.
   - In the Block Definition dialog box, for the block Name, enter **widget** (1).
   - For the block base point, click Pick Point (2).
   - Using object snap, select a point on the object (3).
   - Click Select Objects (4) and select the geometry you have created. Press ENTER to return to the dialog box.
   - Click the Convert to Block option (5).
   - Select OK to exit the dialog box.

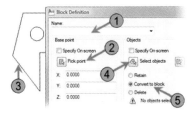

3   To check that the geometry was converted to a block:
   - With the command line blank, select the object.
   - The object should be highlighted with one grip visible at the basepoint you selected for the block.

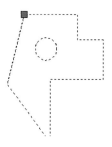

4   To insert the block into the drawing:

- On the insert tab, click Block panel > Insert.
- Select the block name from the list (1).
- For the insertion point, place a check mark in the box next to the Specify on-screen option (2).
- Clear Scale (3). X, Y, and Z should be 1.000.
- Clear Rotation (4). The Rotation angle should be 0.
- Click OK.

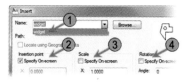

5   Specify the insertion point on the screen.

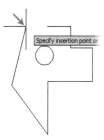

6   On the Insert tab, click Block panel > Insert. Insert the block again, change the scale, and rotate the angle.

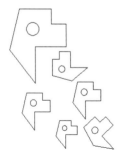

Exercise | Create and Insert Blocks

In this exercise, you create a block from individual lines that represent a phone. You then insert another instance of the phone in the drawing. You then save the drawing file and insert it into a new drawing.

> ### Warning!
> If completing the exercise with AutoCAD LT®, in step 9 you will need to use the *acadltiso.dwt* file.

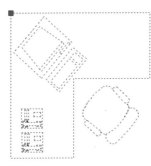

The completed exercise

Completing the Exercise
To complete the exercise, follow the steps in this book or in the onscreen exercise. In the onscreen list of chapters and exercises, click *Chapter 10: Working with Reusable Content*. Click *Exercise: Create and Insert Blocks*.

1   Open *C_Workstation.dwg*.

2   To view an object's information:

- On the command line, enter list to start the **List** command.
- Select the bottom horizontal line on the phone.
- Press ENTER.
- Notice that the object listed is a line object.

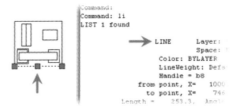

- Press **F2** to close the AutoCAD® text window.

3　On the Insert tab, click Block panel > Create.

4　To define the block using the Block Definition dialog box:

- For Name, enter **Phone** (1).
- For the base point, click Pick Point (2).
- Snap to the lower right endpoint of the phone (3).
- Under Objects, click Select Objects (4).

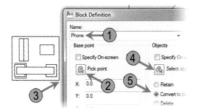

- Select the phone geometry with a window selection.

- Press ENTER to return to the dialog box.
- Under Objects, click Convert to Block (5).
- Verify the setting in the Block Definition dialog box. Click OK.

5　To view the object information:

- On the command line, enter **list** to start the List command.
- Select the line on the phone that you previously selected.
- Press ENTER.
- Notice that the object is now listed as a block reference with the name Phone.

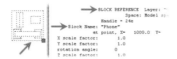

- Press **F2** to close the AutoCAD text window.

6　To insert the block into the drawing:

- On the Insert tab, click Block panel > Insert.
- In the Insert dialog box, select the phone block from the list (1).

- Specify the insertion point in the screen (2). The default scale should be 1.0 and the rotation angle should be 0.
- Click OK.

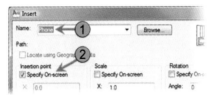

7   Click to place the phone just below the original phone.

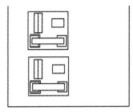

8   Save this file. On the title bar, notice the path where *C_Workstation.dwg* is saved.

9   To start a new file using a template:
- On the ribbon, click Application Menu > New.
- In the Select Template dialog box, select the *acadiso.dwt* file.
- Click Open.

10   On the Insert tab, click Block panel > Insert.

11   To insert the file into the current drawing:
- In the Insert dialog box, click Browse.
- In the Select Drawing File dialog box, navigate to and select *C_Workstation.dwg*.
- Click Open.
- With C_Workstation now listed in the Insert dialog box, click OK to insert the C_Workstation block into the drawing. Insert the block anywhere in the drawing window, or if you clear the option to specify the insertion point on -screen, it inserts the block at 0,0.

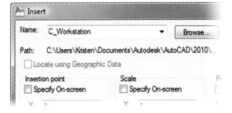

12 To view the block in the drawing:

- Zoom out to view the block.
- On the Insert tab, click Block panel > Insert.
- Select the list and notice that the C_Workstation drawing is now inserted as a block into the current drawing along with all of the blocks that belonged to that drawing. Each of these blocks is now part of the current drawing database.
- Click Cancel to close the Insert dialog box.

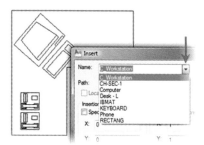

13 To view other properties in the drawing:

- On the Home tab, click Layers panel > Layer Control.
- Notice that the layer A-EQPM-IDEN is now part of the current drawing database. This layer was brought into the drawing along with the C_Workstation block.

14 Close all files. Do not save.

Lesson 44 | Working with DesignCenter

This lesson describes how to use DesignCenter to reuse data from another drawing in the active drawing.

Reusing data saves you valuable design time and helps ensure consistency across your designs and among designers.

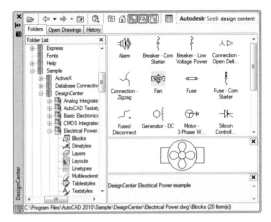

Objectives

After completing this lesson, you will be able to:

- Use DesignCenter to add data to a drawing.

Using DesignCenter

You use DesignCenter to view existing content in other drawings and drag it into the current drawing. You can drag an entire drawing file or any of the following named objects within a drawing file: blocks, dimension styles, layers, layouts, linetypes, table styles, text styles, or xrefs. You can also drag drawing files and blocks from DesignCenter onto a tool palette.

The DesignCenter interface is split between a tree view and a content pane. The four tabs, Folders, Open Drawings, History, and DC Online, determine what you see in the tree view. When you select an item in the tree view, its contents are displayed in the content pane, and you can drag it into the current drawing.

The following image shows an expanded tree view (1) of the Open Drawings tab (2). The Blocks category is selected (3) and its contents are displayed in the upper right pane. You can turn the Preview (4) and Description (5) options on so that you can view the details of a selected block (6) in the lower right panes.

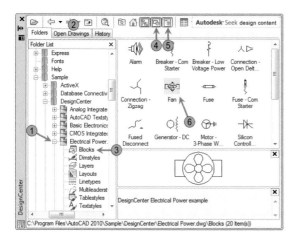

Since DesignCenter is a palette, you can adjust its display to match the way you work. For example, you can resize it, dock it, anchor it, or set it to roll up into the title bar when you pass the cursor over the title bar.

Use the following tabs in DesignCenter to locate content.

Tab	Description
Folders	Displays a standard Windows-like tree view so that you can navigate easily to content files.
Open Drawing	Displays only drawings currently open in the software.
History	Displays drawing accessed during the current session of the application.
DC Online	Accesses content on manufacturers' web pages.

Command Access

 Design Center

Command Line: **ADCENTER**
Ribbon: **Insert tab > Content panel**

Ribbon: **View tab > Palettes panel > DesignCenter**

Procedure: Reusing Content with DesignCenter

The following steps give an overview of using DesignCenter to insert content from another drawing into the current drawing.

1   On the ribbon, click View tab > Palettes panel > DesignCenter.

2   Click the Folders, Open Drawings, or History tab to populate the tree view with a place to search for content.

3   Navigate and expand the tree view to display the desired folder or drawing file and category.

4   In the tree view, click the folder or category to display its contents in the content pane.

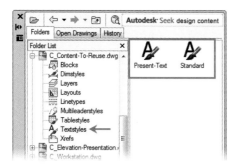

5   In the content pane, insert the item into the current drawing in one of three ways:

- Drop it in the drawing.
- Double-click it.
- Right-click it and select the appropriate option.

Exercise | Using DesignCenter

In this exercise, you use DesignCenter to insert two blocks that reside in another file into the current drawing. You also insert a text style from that file.

The completed exercise

Completing the Exercise

To complete the exercise, follow the steps in this book or in the onscreen exercise. In the onscreen list of chapters and exercises, click *Chapter 10: Working with Reusable Content*. Click *Exercise: Use DesignCenter*.

1   Open *C_Content-To-Reuse.dwg* and *C_Elevation-Presentation.dwg*.

2   On the View tab, click Palettes panel > DesignCenter.

3   In DesignCenter:

- Click the Open Drawings tab.
- In the tree view, expand and show the categories under C_Content-To-Reuse.dwg and C_Elevation-Presentation.dwg.

4   In the tree view under C_Content-To- Reuse.dwg, click Blocks.

5   Drag and drop the block elev-conifer from the content pane to the front right area of the house as shown.

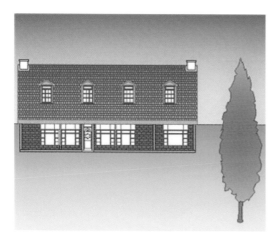

6   In the content pane of DesignCenter, double-click elev-deciduous.

7   In the Insert dialog box:

- Under Scale, enter **2** for the X scale factor.
- Under Scale, enter **4** for the Y scale factor.
- Under Insertion Point, select Specify-On-Screen.
- Click OK.

8   Click to position the tree to the left and down from the house as shown.

9   In the tree pane of DesignCenter, under C_Elevation-Presentation.dwg, click the Textstyles category. The only text styles currently in the drawing are Annotative and Standard.

10   Under C_Content-To-Reuse.dwg, click the Textstyles category.

11   In the content pane of DesignCenter, drag and drop the Present-Text style into the drawing area.

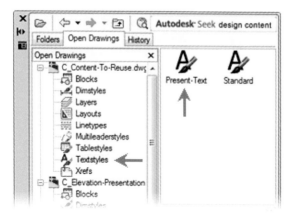

12   In the tree pane, under C_Elevation- Presentation.dwg, click Textstyles. The Present-Text style now exists and is available for use in this drawing file.

13   Close all files. Do not save.

Lesson 45 | Using Tool Palettes

This lesson describes how to access tool palettes and use the tools in your drawings.

Using tool palettes, you can organize and access the tools you use most often, which helps you to work more efficiently.

The following illustration shows the Tool Palettes window and some of the tools on the Architectural and Civil tool palettes.

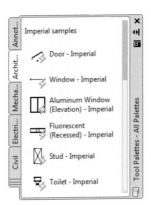 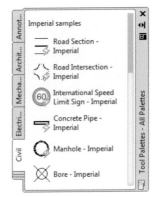

Objectives

After completing this lesson, you will be able to:

- Use a customized tool palette to add geometry to your drawing.

Using Tool Palette Tools

The Tool Palettes window contains a tab for each tool palette. You use these tool palettes to organize and share frequently used commands and objects, such as blocks and hatches, so that you can access and use them more efficiently.

You can create, delete, and rename palettes using the shortcut menu. By right-clicking a tool, you can change its properties to make the tool even more efficient. For example, you might have a block automatically explode after insertion, create text with a specified text style, or create geometry on a specific layer every time.

You can add tools to a palette in the following ways:

- Drag blocks or drawing files from DesignCenter.
- Right-click and drag a single piece of geometry from the drawing window to a palette.

When you add geometry to a palette in this manner, blocks create block instances when reinserted, standard geometry adds the command, and hatches add the command plus the hatch settings.

You can adjust the display of the Tool Palettes window to match the way you work. You can resize it, dock it, or set it to roll up into the title bar.

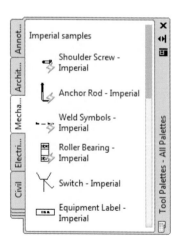

The Mechanical Tool Palette

Command Access

Tool Palettes

Command Line: **TOOLPALETTES**
Ribbon: **View tab > Palettes panel > Tool Palettes**

Tip

When you insert a block from a tool palette, if the block has defined units, it scales to the defined insertion scale units of the target drawing.

Procedure: Adding Geometry to a Drawing Using the Tool Palettes

The following steps give an overview of using tool palette tools to add geometry to a drawing.

1   On the ribbon, click View tab > Palettes panel > Tool Palettes.

2   Click the tool palette tab that contains the desired item.

3   In the tool palette, click the icon of the desired item.

4   Click in the drawing area to create the item.

Exercise | Add Content from Tool Palettes

In this exercise, you use tool palette tools to add a block, a hatch, and text to a drawing.

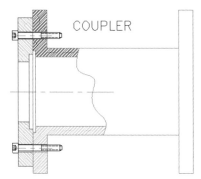

The completed exercise

Completing the Exercise

To complete the exercise, follow the steps in this book or in the onscreen exercise. In the onscreen list of chapters and exercises, click *Chapter 10: Working with Reusable Content*. Click *Exercise: Add Content from Tool Palettes*.

1   Open *M_Tool-Palettes.dwg*.

2   On the View tab, click Palettes panel > Tool Palettes.

3   On the Tool Palettes window, click the Mechanical tab.

4   To insert a bolt into the drawing:

     • Click the icon for Hex Socket Bolt (Side) - Metric.

     • Click the intersection of the top centerline and the far left line. The drawing should look like the following illustration.

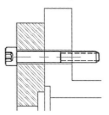

5   In the Tool Palettes window, click the Hatches and Fills tab.

6   Make layer 3 current.

7   To apply a steel hatch pattern to the cutaway section:

- Under ISO Hatches, click the icon for the Steel hatch pattern.

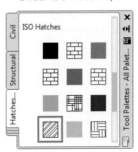

- Position the cursor in the open rectangular area just above the recently placed bolt, as shown.
- Click to create the hatch.

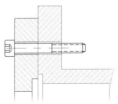

8   Insert the same hatch pattern in the area below the bolt, as shown.

9   In the Tool Palettes window, click the Draw tab.

10   To add a text note to the drawing:

- Make the text layer current.
- Click the icon for MText.
- Create the text window to the right of the bolt and hatch, as shown.
- Enter **12** for the text height in the Style panel of the Text editor shown in the ribbon.
- Enter **COUPLER**.
- Click Close Text Editor.

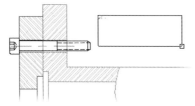

11   Close all files. Do not save.

Challenge Exercise | Architectural

In this exercise, you use what you learned about reusable content to create a block definition and reuse existing content.

Tip
You have the option of completing this exercise using either imperial or metric units. Select one version of the exercise to complete the steps.

Completing the Exercise
To complete the exercise, follow the steps in this book or in the onscreen exercise. In the onscreen list of chapters and exercises, click *Chapter 10: Working with Reusable Content*. Click *Challenge Exercise: Architectural Metric*.

Metric Units

1   Open the drawing you saved from the previous challenge exercise, or open *M_ARCH-Challenge- CHP10.dwg.*

2   Define a block from the door geometry you created in Chapter 2. Name it **Door-Typical.**

3   Set the appropriate layer current before inserting each block.

4   Insert and position Door_Glass-915 for each of the locations labeled (1) as shown. Insert and position Door-Typical in all the remaining door openings.

5   Insert the block Elevation-Exterior from the file *M_ARCH-Challenge-Supporting-Details.dwg.*

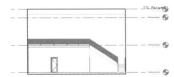

6   Insert and position the two different-sized windows in the openings.

7   Insert and position plumbing fixtures in the floor plan.

8   Close and save all files.

Imperial Units

1   Open the drawing you saved from the previous challenge exercise, or open *I_ARCH-Challenge- CHP10.dwg.*

2   Define a block from the door geometry you created in Chapter 2. Name it **Door-Typical.**

3   Set the appropriate layer current before inserting each block.

4   Insert and position Door_Glass-3-0 for each of the locations labeled (1) as shown. Insert and position Door-Typical in all the remaining door openings.

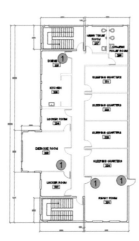

5   Insert the block Elevation-Exterior from the file *I_ARCH-Challenge-Supporting-Details.dwg*.

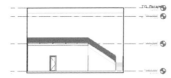

6   Insert and position the two different-sized windows in the openings.

7   Insert and position plumbing fixtures in the floor plan.

8   Close and save all files.

Challenge Exercise | Mechanical

In this exercise, you use what you learned about reusable content to create a block and reuse content.

> **Warning!**
> If completing this exercise with AutoCAD LT, in step 3, you will need to locate the block at
> ...\Program Files\AutoCAD LT 2010\Sample\DesignCenter\Fasteners - Metric.dwg.

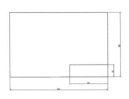

The completed exercise

> **Completing the Exercise**
> To complete the exercise, follow the steps in this book or in the onscreen exercise. In the onscreen list of chapters and exercises, click *Chapter 10: Working with Reusable Content*. Click *Challenge Exercise: Mechanical*.

1   Open the drawing you saved from the previous challenge exercise, or open *M_MECH-Challenge- CHP10.dwg.*

2   In model space, draw the following border and title block (without the dimensions). Define it as a block with the name Titleblock. Use the lower-left corner of the border as the base point. **Note**: You will use this block in a later challenge exercise.

3   Insert the block Hex Flange Screw - 10 mm top from the file ...*Program Files\AutoCAD 2009*
    Sample \DesignCenter\Fasteners - Metric.dwg. Scale it up (Uniform Scale) 1.6 times and position
    the screws in the top view of the assembly as shown.

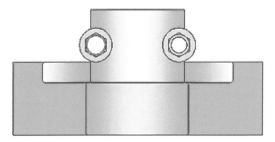

4   Insert, size, and position the block definition Hex Bolt Head (10mm) -side view that exists in
    this drawing. Scale the block to 1.6 times its original size.

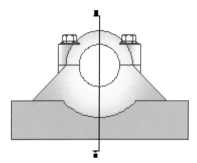

5   Save and close the drawing.

Chapter 10 | Working with Reusable Content

Chapter Summary

Reusing the data in a drawing file helps you to work more efficiently and maintains consistency in the design data. Making geometry into blocks that behave like a single object encourages the reuse of design geometry. Using DesignCenter and tool palettes makes it easy to organize and locate frequently used design data.

Having completed this chapter, you can:

- Create a block definition and insert a block definition or file into a drawing to place block references.
- Use DesignCenter to reuse the data in a drawing.
- Access tool palettes and use their tools.

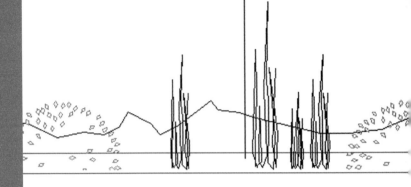

Chapter 11
Creating Additional Drawing Objects

Depending on your design requirements, you might need to have connected line and arc segments defined as a single continuous object or you might need to create smooth curves in a free-form shape or on a specific elliptical path. You might also need to add tabular information to your drawing. Each one of these needs can be easily met using the right command.

Objectives

After completing this chapter, you will be able to:

- Create and edit polylines with the Polyline command.

- Create smooth curves with the Spline command.

- Create ellipses and elliptical arcs with the Ellipse command.

- Create and edit basic tables and use table styles to control their appearance.

Standard Object Snap and Status Bar Settings
Before completing the exercises in this chapter, refer to the "Settings for the Exercises" section in the Introduction.

Lesson 46 | Working with Polylines

This lesson describes how to create and edit polylines. The following illustration shows polyline segments in a lot boundary line and an arrow created with a polyline.

With polylines you can create geometry and return information much more quickly than with other methods. When you use polylines, you can easily calculate a perimeter distance or the area of an irregular shape. By offsetting polylines, you do not spend time trimming or extending geometry at the corners. Sharp corners are maintained in the offset.

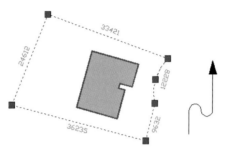

Objectives

After completing this lesson, you will be able to:

- Describe polylines and how they differ from standard objects.
- Use the Polyline command to create polylines.
- Use the Edit Polyline command to edit polylines.

About Polylines

Polylines enable you to create more complex geometry while at the same time, in some cases, simplifying the creation process. Object selection is also simplified because several objects can be combined into a single editable object.

In the following illustration, several objects are shown and each of them represents a single polyline that was created using different methods.

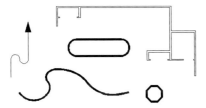

Definition of Polylines

Polylines are special types of entities that incorporate segments of common entities such as lines and arcs into a single object. Polylines also have special properties that are not available on other objects. These properties include:

- Global Width Start
- Segment Width End
- Segment Width

In addition to the properties mentioned above, polylines also provide significantly more choices for controlling their shape during object creation as well as specific tools and options for editing the objects after you create them.

In the following illustration, a polyline containing 6 segments is shown. Segments (1) and (6) have varying start segment widths and end segment widths. Segments (2) and (5) are constant widths segments. Segments (3) and (4) are varying width arc segments.

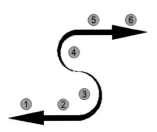

Example of Polylines Being Used in a Drawing

In the following illustration, polylines are used to represent the lot boundary and proposed building footprint. Using the polyline objects enables the designer to quickly determine properties such as area or perimeter and also to add a global width to emphasize the polylines.

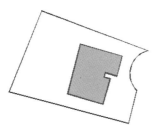

Creating Polylines

You use the Polyline command to create line and arc segments as a continuous single object. Each segment of a polyline is connected at its endpoint to the next segment in the object. When creating polylines, you can switch back and forth between straight line segments and arc segments. You can also set a single width for all segments of the polyline, or you can vary the width of a segment from its beginning to its end.

The following illustration shows examples of polylines. You can calculate the area of the lot with the Area command when the boundary is one object. The footprint of the structure stands out in the design when you add width to its polyline outline. You can create straight and arcing arrows from two segments of a polyline by varying the width of the arrowhead segment from beginning to end.

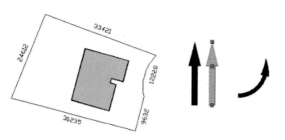

Command Access

Polyline

Command Line: **PLINE, PL**

Ribbon: **Home tab > Draw panel > Polyline**

Command Options

These command options are for creating or changing polylines.

Option	Description
Arc	Use this option to draw arc segments within the polyline.
Close	Use this option to automatically create an arc or line segment from the last point entered to the first point of the polyline.
Undo	Use this option to remove the previous segment when you want to either exclude it or create a new segment with a different appearance.
Width	Use this option to set the width of a polyline in drawing units from the first vertex to the second vertex.
Line	Use this option to resume drawing straight line segments within the polyline after creating arc segments.

Procedure: Creating a Custom Arrowhead

The following is an overview of creating a custom arrowhead using the Pline command.

1 On the ribbon, click Home tab > Draw panel ‹ Polyline.

2 Pick your start point.

3 Drag your cursor to the right at o degrees. Enter the length of the arrow.

4   Right-click. Click Width.

5   Enter the starting width which should be larger then the ending width.

6   Enter the ending width which is usually 0.

7   Drag your cursor to the right at 0 degrees. Enter a value or click a point to define the length of the arrowhead.

8   Press ENTER.

Editing Polylines

You modify polylines using the same commands you use to modify a line or circle. Commands like Copy, Erase, Move, Offset, and Array can all be used to modify a polyline. When you use the Fillet or Chamfer command and at least one of the segments you select is a polyline, the other selected segments become part of the polyline object. However, you cannot fillet or chamfer the first segment of a polyline with the last segment of the same polyline. To create a fillet or chamfer in that situation, you must first use the Explode command to break the polyline into individual line and arc objects.

Polyline Edit

You use the Pedit command to change certain characteristics of a polyline or to convert a line or arc into a polyline.

Command Access

    Edit Polyline

Command Line: **PEDIT, PE**
Shortcut menu for selected polyline: **Polyline Edit**
Ribbon: **Home tab > Modify panel > Edit Polyline**

Option	Description
Open	This option is used to edit a closed polyline. Open either opens a closed polyline or removes the last segment created by the Close option when the polyline was created.
Close	The Close option is used to edit an open polyline. Close connects the last segment with the first by either joining the first and last vertex or by adding a closing segment between the first and last vertex.
Join	This option is used to add polylines, lines, and arcs to the polyline being edited. The endpoints of the segments must match perfectly in order to be joined, and only two segments can be joined at the vertex.
Reverse	This reverses the order of the vertices for the selected polyline. from the first vertex to the second vertex.
Width	This option sets the same width value for all segments in the polyline.

Exploding Polylines

You use the Explode command to convert a polyline into its most basic shapes such as lines and arcs. When you explode a polyline, all the attributes associated with polylines, such as width, are lost and a separate object is created for each segment of the polyline.

Command Access

Explode

Command Line: **EXPLODE, X**
Ribbon: **Home tab › Modify panel › Explode**

Procedure: Joining Lines and Arcs into a Polyline

The following is an overview of using the Join option of the Pedit command to combine a series of lines and arcs into a single polyline.

1   On the ribbon, click Home tab > Modify panel > Edit Polyline.

2   Select any one of the lines or arcs that you are going to join into a polyline.

3   If the selected object is already a polyline, you will not be prompted for this step. If the selected object is not a polyline, press ENTER at the prompt asking you to make it one.

4   Click Join.

5   Select all the objects that you want to join into a polyline. Press ENTER.
    Note: Use a window or crossing selection for the best results. It does not matter if extra objects are selected.

6   Press ENTER to complete the polyline edit. The object now highlights as a single object when selected as shown in the following image.

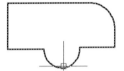

Procedure: Exploding a Polyline

The following is an overview of using the Explode command to break a polyline into individual lines and arcs.

1   On the ribbon, click Home tab > Modify panel > Explode.

2   Select one or more polylines in your drawing.

3   Press ENTER to complete the explode. Your profile highlights as individual objects as shown in the following image.

Exercise | Create and Modify Polylines

In this exercise, you create a polyline that includes lines and arcs of varying widths. You also change the width for all segments of a polyline and then fillet the polyline and list its properties.

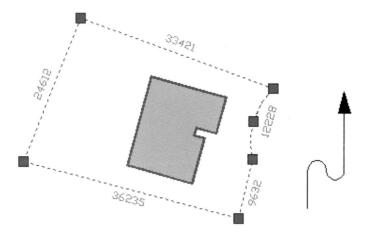

The completed exercise

Completing the Exercise

To complete the exercise, follow the steps in this book or in the onscreen exercise. In the onscreen list of chapters and exercises, click *Chapter 11: Creating Additional Drawing Objects*. Click *Exercise: Create and Modify Polylines*.

1   Open *M_Polylines.dwg*.

2   In the next few steps, you create a custom arrow:
   • On the Home tab, click Modify panel > Polyline.
   • To set the start position, click anywhere to the right of the existing geometry.
   • Move the cursor straight up.
   • Enter **6000**. Press ENTER.

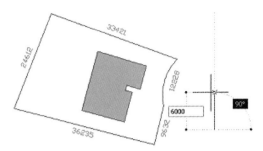

3 To create polyline arc segments:

- Right-click. Click Arc.
- Move the cursor directly to the right.
- Enter **3000**. Press ENTER.
- Move the cursor farther to the right.
- Enter **3000**. Press ENTER.

4 To switch back to polyline line segments:

- Right-click. Click Line.
- Move the cursor straight up.
- Enter **9000**. Press ENTER.

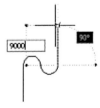

5 To add width for the arrowhead:

- Right-click. Click Width.
- For starting width, enter **2000**. Press ENTER.
- For ending width, enter **0**. Press ENTER.

Chapter 11 | Creating Additional Drawing Objects

6   To finish the polyline:

- Move the cursor straight up.
- Enter **3500**. Press ENTER.
- Press ENTER to complete the object .

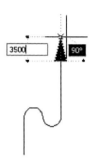

7   To edit the polyline:

- Select and right-click the blue outline of the structure.
- On the shortcut menu, click Properties.
- On the Properties palette, for the Global Width, enter **200**.

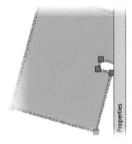

Geometry	
Vertex	1
Vertex X	95752.345
Vertex Y	35457.069
Start segment width	200.0000
End segment width	200.0000
Global width	200.0000
Elevation	0.0000
Area	167797728.9
Length	57988.200
Misc	
Closed	No

- Press ESC to clear the selection.

8   Click the arc in the dark green lot boundary. The grips are displayed, showing the arc as part of a polyline. Notice that the far left green line is not part of the polyline.

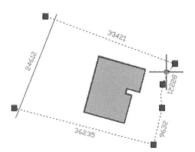

9   Press ESC.

10   To add a line to the polyline using the Fillet command:

   - On the Home tab, click Modify panel > Fillet.
   - Click the bottom polyline (1) as shown.
   - Press SHIFT and click the far left line (2) as shown.

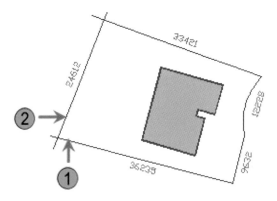

11   Click the far left line.
     Notice that it is now part of the original polyline.

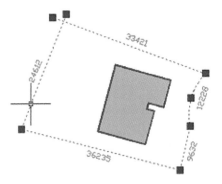

12   Grip edit the top left ends of the polyline to form a corner as shown.

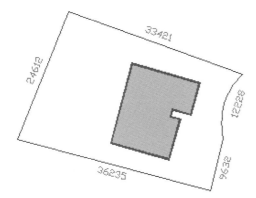

13   To determine the area and perimeter of the new polyline:

- On the command line, enter list to start the List command.
- Click the top green line.
- Press ENTER.

14   In the AutoCAD® Text Window, take note of the area and perimeter values for this closed polyline.

15   Close all files. Do not save.

Lesson 47 | Creating Splines

This lesson describes how to create splines with the Spline command.

In many designs you need to show a smooth free-form line or edge that cannot be defined with straight lines and arcs, such as the curved edge shown here. Creating smooth curves with splines provides the look you want while creating an efficient object in the drawing file.

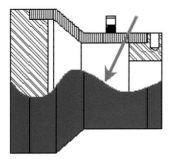

Objectives

After completing this lesson, you will be able to:

- Describe splines.
- Describe the procedure for creating a spline.

About Splines

Splines are smooth curves that pass through specified points. The curve elements of splines are not true arcs nor polylines, therefore splines must be handled differently from arcs or polylines with arc segments. The simplest way to modify the shape of a spline is to use its grips.

Spline Definition

Splines are curves which fit through control points using nonuniform rational B-splines (NURBS). Splines are specified in the drawing through fit points with a fit tolerance that permits a smooth curvature. Splines can be edited using grips or using the spline edit options. Polylines edited with the Spline option may resemble a spline, but will still be a polyline unless converted to a spline using the Spline edit object option. While a splined polyline can be converted to a spline, a spline cannot be converted to a polyline using basic AutoCAD commands.

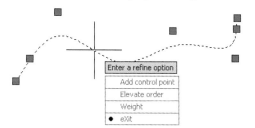

You create a spline similar to the way you draw a polyline, specifying each consecutive point or vertex to determine the shape of the object. Below is an example of a polyline. Each grip highlights a vertex point.

When creating a spline, a smooth curve is fit through the control points instead of line segments and the tangency of each endpoint must be specified. Below is an example of a spline passing through exactly the same points as the polyline shown above.

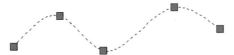

Spline Examples

You can create a spline and close it using the spline edit command. Below is an example of a closed spline.

You can create a polyline and use the polyline edit command to create a splined polyline. Then you can convert it to a spline using the spline edit command with the Object option. Both a splined polyline and a splined polyline converted to a spline would appear identical, as shown below, however both would behave differently because they are inherently different objects. It is the tangency of the endpoints and the tolerances of the control points that keep the curvature smooth and makes a spline behave a particular way.

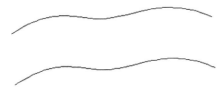

The following example shows the same polyline object splined, converted to a spline object, and closed using the spline edit command. This object is a closed spline.

A polyline splined using the Polyline edit option and closed produces a different result. The object below is a closed polyline.

Chapter 11 | Creating Additional Drawing Objects

All of the objects in these examples were created using exactly the same control points. One was created using the spline command the other was created using the polyline command.

Creating Splines

Using the Spline command, you create smooth curves that pass through or near the points you specify. The spline passes through the points by default because the initial tolerance value for the spline is zero.

Each spline is a single object in the drawing with all of the defining points, tolerances, and tangencies stored as part of that spline. The software creates these smooth splines based on nonuniform rational B-spline (NURBS) curves.

The following image shows two spline objects. The lower half of the image shows the points that define the spline.

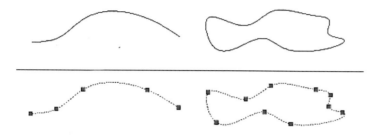

Command Access

Spline

Command Line: **SPLINE**
Ribbon: **Home tab > Draw extended panel > Spline**

Command Access

Edit Spline

Command Line: **SPLINEDIT**
Ribbon: **Home tab › Modify panel › Edit Spline**

Note: Grip editing is the easiest way to modify the shape of a spline.

Spline Key Terms

- **Open Spline:** A spline in which the first and last points are not joined together to create a single continuous flowing spline.
- **Closed Spline:** A spline that has the same first and last point and was created with the Close option of the Spline command.
- **Fit Points:** The points in the drawing that you specify when you create the spline.
- **Control Points:**
  Note: After you refine a spline through its control points, the fit point data is lost.
- **Fit Point Tolerance:** A maximum value in drawing units for how closely you must draw the spline to the fit points you specify. The default value of zero means that the spline must be drawn directly through the fit point.
- **Start or End Tangencies:** For open splines, you can define a vector direction through the first or last fit point to which the spline must be tangent. For closed splines, the tangency controls the transition between the first and last defined segments.

Procedure: Creating a Spline

The following steps give an overview of creating a spline in a drawing.

1   On the ribbon, click Home tab › Draw panel › Spline.

2   Click in consecutive order the locations that the spline must be drawn through.

3   Right-click. Click Enter.

Chapter 11 | Creating Additional Drawing Objects

4   Do one of the following:

- Right-click to accept the default tangency through the first point.
- Move the cursor to define a direction to which the first part of the spline must be tangent. Click. The dashed magenta spline shows the path if you accept the default tangency.

5   Do one of the following:

- Right-click to accept the default tangency through the last point.
- Move the cursor to define a direction to which the last part of the spline must be tangent. Click. The dashed magenta spline shows the path if you accept the default tangencies.

Procedure: Editing a Spline

The following steps give an overview of editing a spline in a drawing using grips.

1   With the Command line blank, select the spline.

2   Select a grip control point (1) and drag it to a new location (2) and click.

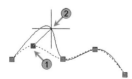

3   When finished adjusting the spline using grips, press ESC.

Procedure: Convert Spline to Polyline

The following steps give an overview of converting a spline into a polyline.

1   With the command line blank, select the spline.

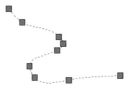

2   Right-click in an open area of the drawing and click Spline.

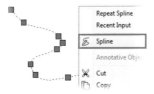

3   If Dynamic Input is turned off, right-click in an open area of the drawing and click Convert to Polyline. If Dynamic Input is turned on, the menu automatically appears.

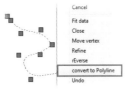

4   On the command line, enter a precision value or press ENTER to accept the default value. The spline is converted to a polyline.

5   Select the polyline to view or edit it.

Exercise | Create a Spline

In this exercise, you create a spline through given points.

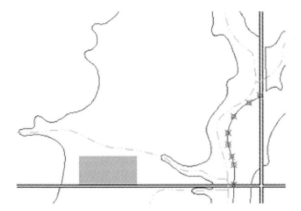

The completed exercise

> **Completing the Exercise**
> To complete the exercise, follow the steps in this book or in the onscreen exercise. In the onscreen list of chapters and exercises, click *Chapter 11: Creating Additional Drawing Objects*. Click *Exercise: Create a Spline*.

1   Open *C_Spline.dwg*.
2   Set Node as the only running object snap.

3   Zoom into the area shown.

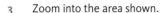

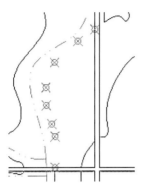

4   On the Home tab, click Draw panel > Spline.

5   To create the spline:

- Click to start the spline at the bottom magenta point.
- Click each of the remaining seven points, moving from the bottom to the top.
- After selecting all the points, right-click.
- Click Enter.

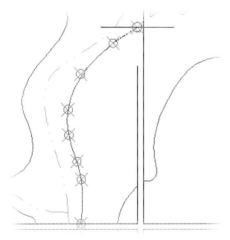

6   Right-click when prompted to specify the start tangent.

7   To specify the end tangent:

- Move the cursor up and to the right to set the tangency through the last point as shown.
- Click in the drawing area to complete the spline.

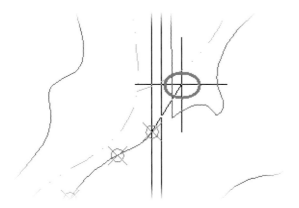

8   Close all files. Do not save.

Lesson 48 | Creating Ellipses

This lesson describes how to create ellipses and elliptical arcs with the Ellipse command. The following image shows examples of ellipses and elliptical arcs in drawings.

When your design requires an elliptical shape, you can create ellipses and elliptical arcs as easily as you can create geometry such as lines and circles.

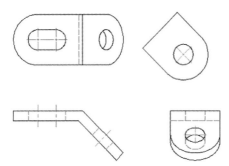

Objectives

After completing this lesson, you will be able to:

- Describes ellipses.
- Create an ellipse.

About Ellipses

The Ellipse command creates a closed ellipse. The Ellipse Arc command creates a section of an ellipse. Both objects can be modified in the same way as other drawing objects.

Definition of Ellipse

An ellipse is a closed curve generated by four fixed points defining major and minor axes and crossing at right angles through the center point.

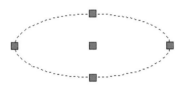

Each axes endpoint is recognized as a quadrant when using object snap. But notice that an ellipse quadrant is relative to the axes endpoint, regardless of the angle.

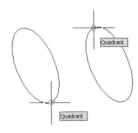

Creating an Ellipse Arc

You can create an ellipse arc the same way you create an ellipse with parameters that define the portion of the arc that displays. You could also create an ellipse arc by creating an ellipse and trimming out a portion of it. You can create an ellipse arc with the Ellipse Arc command using the arc option, or you can create an ellipse arc using the ellipse arc command. An ellipse arc is still recognized as an ellipse.

An ellipse, or oval shape, is a circle tilted on a plane at a specified rotation angle.

Example of Ellipses

Ellipses and arcs are particularly useful when drawing an isometric view of an object.

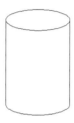

Creating Ellipses

You use the Ellipse command to create an ellipse object. An ellipse is a smooth curve shape defined by a major axis and a minor axis that intersect at their midpoints and are perpendicular to each other. You can create a full ellipse or an elliptical arc. To create an ellipse, you can either define the start point and endpoint of one axis and then the endpoint of the other axis, or you can first define the center of the ellipse and then define the location of the axis endpoints relative to the center.

The following image shows an ellipse at the top left and the same ellipse at the bottom left with lines indicating the major axis and minor axis. The major axis is the longer of the two axes. The image also shows an elliptical arc with half of the major and half of the minor axis lines.

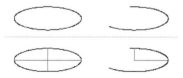

There are three procedures you can follow to create an ellipse or elliptical arc. The procedure you use depends on what you want to create and the data you have available.

Command Access

Ellipse/ Ellipse Arc

Command Line: **ELLIPSE**
Ribbon: **Home tab > Draw panel > Center/Axis, End/Elliptical Arc**

Option	Description
Center	Use this option to create an ellipse by defining the center point of the ellipse and then one endpoint for each axis.
Arc	Use this option to add additional prompts to the command sequence to create an elliptical arc or a full continuous ellipse.
Axis, End	Use this option to create and ellipse or an elliptical arc. The first two points of the ellipse determine the location and length of the first axis. The third point determines the distance between the center of the ellipse and the end point of the second axis.

Procedure: Creating an Ellipse

The following steps give an overview of creating an ellipse by defining the axis endpoints.

1   On the ribbon, click Home tab > Draw panel > Ellipse.

2   Click to specify the first axis endpoint (1) and the other axis endpoint (2).

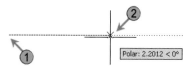

3   Click to specify the distance to the other axis endpoint (3).

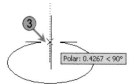

The completed ellipse.

Note: To use the other Ellipse options, follow the command line prompts. Right-click to specify the options from the shortcut menu or enter the capitalized letter on the command line.

Procedure: Creating an Elliptical Arc

The following steps give an overview of creating an elliptical arc. The first few steps are identical to creating a ellipse.

1   On the ribbon, click Home tab > Draw panel > Ellipse Arc.

2   Click to specify the first axis endpoint (1) and the other axis endpoint (2).

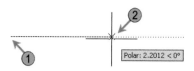

3   Click to specify the distance to the other axis endpoint (3).

Chapter 11 | Creating Additional Drawing Objects

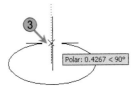

The completed ellipse.

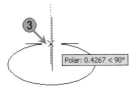

Note: To use the other Ellipse options, follow the command line prompts. Right-click to specify the options from the shortcut menu or enter the capitalized letter on the command line.

Procedure: Creating an Elliptical Arc

The following steps give an overview of creating an elliptical arc. The first few steps are identical to creating a ellipse.

1   On the ribbon, click Home tab > Draw panel > Ellipse Arc.

2   Click to specify the first axis endpoint (1) and the other axis endpoint (2).

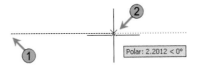

3   Click to specify the distance to the other axis endpoint (3).

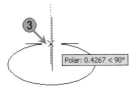

4   Move the cursor to specify the start angle position (4).

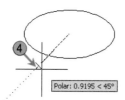

Polar: 0.9195 < 45°

5   Move the cursor to specify the end angle (5). Notice that the polar angle is set to 45 degrees.

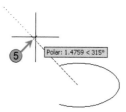

Polar: 1.4759 < 315°

Note: The order in which the start and end angle are specified will determine which part of the ellipse is removed.

Exercise | Create Ellipses

In this exercise, you use the Ellipse command to create two full ellipses using two different techniques, trim one of the ellipses so that it becomes an elliptical arc, and then create an elliptical arc with the Ellipse command.

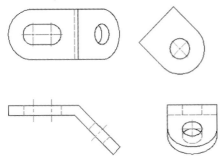

The completed exercise

Completing the Exercise

To complete the exercise, follow the steps in this book or in the onscreen exercise. In the onscreen list of chapters and exercises, click *Chapter 11: Creating Additional Drawing Objects*. Click *Exercise: Create Ellipses*.

1   Open *C_Ellipse.dwg*.

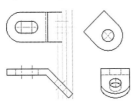

2   Zoom into the unfinished area of the top view.

3   To create an ellipse to represent the top of a hole from the inclined surface:

- On the Home tab, click Draw panel > Ellipse.
- Click the first point at the bottom intersection, as indicated by the bottom arrow in the following image.
- Click the second point at the top intersection, as indicated by the top arrow in the image.
- Click the third point at the right intersection, as indicated by the right arrow in the image.

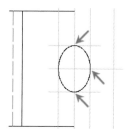

4   To create an ellipse to represent the bottom of the hole from the inclined plane:
    - On the Home tab, click Draw panel > Ellipse.
    - Right-click. Click Center.
    - Click the intersection on the left of the previous ellipse, as shown.

5   Move the cursor straight up and click at the intersection.

6   Click at the center of the first ellipse.

7   To trim part of the second ellipse:
    - Start the Trim command.
    - Click the first ellipse as the cutting edge.
    - Click the far left side of the second ellipse as the object to trim.
      The left ellipse is trimmed to an elliptical arc, as shown.

8   To create an ellipse in the top view to represent the outer edge of the inclined surface:

 - On the Home tab, click Draw panel > Ellipse.
 - Right-click. Click Arc.
 - Right-click. Click Center.

9   Click the center of the first ellipse.

10   To define the endpoint of the first axis, snap to the end of the horizontal line.

11   To define the endpoint of the second axis, snap to the intersection on the right.

12   To specify the start angle, snap to the end of the horizontal line.

13   To specify the end angle position, snap to the end of the horizontal line on the top.

14   Freeze layer construction. Zoom to display your completed drawing.

15   Close all files. Do not save.

Lesson 49 | Using Tables

This lesson describes how to create and modify table styles, and how to create tables using the Tablestyle and Table commands.

You can use tables in your drawings to meet a number of needs. For example, you might use them to show revisions in the drawing, or to create tabulated dimensions, as shown.

The following illustration represents a tabular dimension table.

PART NAME	A	B	C
B762	762	686	305
B838	838	762	343
B914	914	838	381
B991	991	915	419
B1067	1067	991	457

Objectives

After completing this lesson, you will be able to:

- Describe tables.
- Use the Tablestyle command to create table styles.
- Create tables and enter values in the table cells.

About Tables

You can use tables to organize data into columns and rows. Data can be entered in the table or extracted from objects including blocks that contain special attributes. When you place information into tables, you can format rows and columns and apply formulas.

DOOR	COST	QTY	TOTAL
A1	$175.00	3	$525.00
A2	$207.00	6	$1242.00
A3	$125.00	4	$500.00
A4	$787.00	2	$1454.00
A5	$1345.00	1	$1345.00
			$5066.00

Definition of a Table

Tables contain rows and columns which create an array of individual cells that are designated by the row number and column letter in which the cell resides.

A table is a database that exists within the AutoCAD program.

Example of Using Tables

You use the Table command to insert a table into your drawing. You specify the number of rows and columns, the heading style, and other parameters. You can create a variety of table styles to use within your drawing. The Table and Table Style commands insert and create a database that is unique to this program.

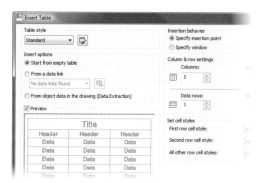

This is not the same as inserting an external database from another program using OLE Objects (Object Linking and Embedding), which is not covered in this course.

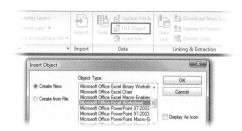

Creating Table Styles

Table styles are similar to the concept of dimension styles because they set the format for tables in the drawing. You create and manage them with the Tablestyle command.

You can have more than one table style, but each new drawing you create contains only one table style called Standard. If you create additional table styles, use the Table Styles list on the Styles toolbar to set the current table style.

Like dimension styles, if you make a change to a table style, any table using that style in the drawing updates to reflect the changes.

The following illustration demonstrates the effect of modifying a table style.

PART NAME	A	B	C
B762	762	686	305
B838	838	762	343

PART NAME	A	B	C
B762	762	686	305
B838	838	762	343
B914	914	838	381
B991	991	915	419
B1067	1067	991	457

Command Access

Table Styles

Command Line: **TABLESTYLE**

Ribbon: **Home tab > Annotation extended panel > Table Style**

Ribbon: **Annotate tab > Tables panel > Table Style**

Table Style Dialog Box

You use the Table Style dialog box to create, modify, and manage table styles.

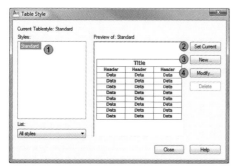

① Select the table style to set it as current, to base a new style on, or to modify.

② Click to make the selected style current.

③ Click to create a new style based on the selected style.

④ Click to edit the selected style.

New Table Style Dialog Box

Use the New Table Style dialog box to set the properties for a new table style.

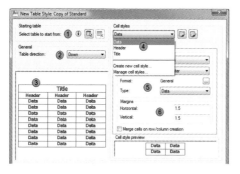

① Use the default table style or one of your own as the basis for the new style.

② Select the table direction: up or down.

③ Refer to the preview as you make modifications to the style.

④ Create and save your styles for the Data, Header, and Title cells.

⑤ Set the properties for Data, Header, and Title cell styles.

⑥ Set your margins for the chosen cell style. Different margins can be set for the Data, Header, and Title cells.

Procedure: Creating Table Styles

The following steps give an overview of creating table styles.

1 Start the Tablestyle command.

2 In the Table Style dialog box, click New.

3 Enter a name for the new table style. Select an existing style in the Start With list. Click Continue.

4 In the New Table Style dialog box, adjust the general, text, and borders properties in the Cell styles area for the Data, Header, and Title cells. Click OK.

5 In the Table Style dialog box, double-click the new table style to make it the current style.

Table Style Key Points

- Table styles control the appearance of tables.
- You can have more than one table style, but only one table style can be current.
- Each new drawing contains a table style called Standard.
- If you make a change to a table style, existing tables using that style update to reflect the changes.

Creating Tables and Entering Table Data

There are three main steps to inserting a table. First, select the table style; second, place the table in the drawing; and third, enter data in the appropriate cells. When you select the style in the Insert Table dialog box, you can also set the number and size of the columns and data rows.

You double-click a cell to enter data using the In-Place Text Editor, similar to the way you edit multiline text. To navigate the cells, use standard keyboard navigation techniques such as the TAB or ARROW keys.

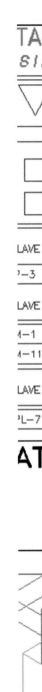

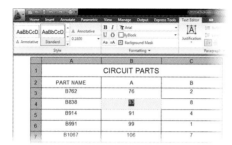

Single-click a cell to access the table formatting options.

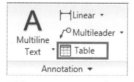

Command Access

Table

Command Line: **TABLE**

Ribbon: **Home tab > Annotation panel > Table**

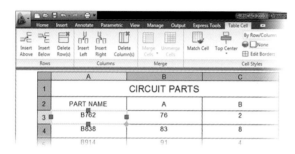

Ribbon: **Annotate tab > Tables panel > Table**

Insert Table Dialog Box

To insert a table, you first select the table style to use for the new table and then select whether the table should be inserted at a specific point or by using a window. Under Column & Row Settings, you adjust the options for the number of columns, column width, number of data rows, and row height.

① Select your desired table style or click to create a new style.

② Select your insert option.

- Start from an empty table.
- From a data link. Use this option to select an existing spreadsheet to link to as a table.
- From object data in the drawing. Use this option to extract data from an existing object in your drawing.

③ Choose to insert your table by a corner point or by selecting a windowed area to fit into.

④ Choose the number of columns and rows, the column width, and the row spacing.

⑤ Select a cell style for the first row cell, the second row cell, and all remaining cells.

⑥ Observe your preview window to verify your settings.

Note
Using the Specify Window option, you can dynamically adjust the number of cells in the table based on the size of the table window you specify. When you select this option, the options for the number of columns and the row height are set to Auto and you can specify the column width and number of rows.

Warning!
In the Insert Options area, the From Object Data In The Drawing (Data Extraction)
option is not available in AutoCAD LT®.

Procedure: Inserting a Table

The following steps give an overview of inserting a table.

1 Start the Table command.

2 In the Insert Table dialog box, select the table style. Set the Insert Behavior and Column and
   Row Settings options. Click OK.

3 Specify an insertion point for the table. If you used the Specify Window option, click two
   points to define the table size.

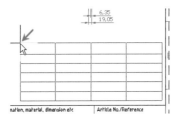

The first cell in the table is automatically activated for editing.

Procedure: Navigating and Entering Table Data

The following steps give an overview of navigating and entering data in a table.

1 Double-click a cell in the table to start the In-Place Text Editor. Enter the required values in
   the cell.

2 To navigate to other cells, you can use the TAB key to move to the right, SHIFT+TAB to move
   to the left, or the ARROW keys to navigate in any direction.

3 You can enter standard spreadsheet-style formulas in the cells to reference other cells
   in the table.

	A	B	C	D
1	PART NAME	A	B	C
2	B762	762	686	305
3	B838	838	762	343
4	B914	914	838	381
5	B991	991	915	419
6	B1067	1067	=B6-76	457
7				

4   You can copy a formula or value from one cell to multiple cells using the Auto-Fill grip. Click the cell to be copied and then click the cell's Auto-Fill grip (1). Drag your mouse up or down over the cells to copy and click in the last cell to complete the copy (2).

	A	B	C	D
1	PART NAME	A	B	C
2	B762	762		305
3	B838	838	991	343
4	B914	914		381
5	B991	991		419
6	B1067	1067	991	457
7				

5   To finish editing the table, press ESC.

PART NAME	A	B	C
B762	762	686	305
B838	838	762	343
B914	914	838	381
B991	991	915	419
B1067	1067	991	457

Table Data Guidelines

- You can enter formulas in table cells.
- Cell formulas can range from simple math formulas to formulas referencing other cells, even cells in other tables in the drawing.
- Use fields to extract data from objects in your drawing. For example, you can place the area of a closed polygon into a cell.
- Use the Auto-Fill grip to copy a formula or value from one cell to multiple cells.
- Use standard Windows Cut, Copy, and Paste commands to efficiently populate your cells.

Exercise | Create a Dimension Table

In this exercise, you create a new table style using the Tablestyle command. You create a new table containing tabulated dimensions for the design. You enter static values in the table as well as a formula that you copy to other cells.

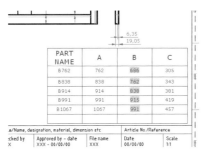

PART NAME	A	B	C
B762	762	686	305
B838	838	762	343
B914	914	838	381
B991	991	915	419
B1067	1067	991	457

The completed exercise

Completing the Exercise

To complete the exercise, follow the steps in this book or in the onscreen exercise. In the onscreen list of chapters and exercises, click *Chapter 11: Creating Additional Drawing Objects*. Click *Exercise: Create a Dimension Table*.

1   Open *M_Create-Table.dwg.*

2   To create a new table style and make it current:
   - On the Annotation panel (or Annotate tab > Tables panel), click Table Style.
   - In the Table Style dialog box, click New.
   - In the Create New Table Style dialog box, enter **NT-2.5**.
   - Click Continue.

3   To specify text height for data cells:
   - Click the Data Cell style.
   - Click the Text tab.
   - For Text Height, enter **2.5.**

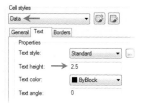

4   To specify the text height for column cells:

- Click the Header cell style.
- Click the Text tab.
- For Text Height, enter **3.5**.
- Click OK.

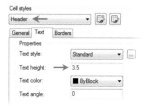

5   To make the new table style current:

- In the Table Style dialog box, double-click the new style.
- Click Close.

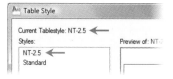

6   To place a table in the drawing:

- Start the Table command.
- In the Insert Table dialog box, under Insertion Behavior, click Specify Insertion Point.
- Under Column & Row Settings, adjust the options as shown.
- Under Set Cell Styles, adjust the options as shown to create a table with no title row.
- Click OK.

7   Specify an insertion point for the table as shown.

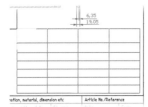

8   The In-Place Text Editor appears with the first cell in the table ready for editing:

     • Enter **PART NAME** and press TAB. Tip: Press ALT+ENTER to create a second line in
       the cell.
     • Enter **A** and press TAB.
     • Enter **B** and press TAB.
     • Enter **C** and press TAB. Your table should appear as shown.

     Note: If you need to move the table, select the table, and then move it by selecting
     the top corner grip.

9   Zoom in to the table.

10   To add additional data to the table cells:

     • Double-click the empty cell under PART NAME.

- Enter **B762**, and then press DOWN ARROW.
- Continue entering values in the cells as shown, pressing DOWN ARROW to move to the cell below.

11   Continue entering values in the table:

- After entering the data in the last row, press TAB to move to the next column.
- Press UP ARROW to move to the top of the table.
- Enter the values as shown for Column A.
  Tip: The numbers are the same as the PART NAME column without the B prefix.

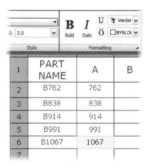

12   Enter a formula in a cell:

- Press TAB to move to the last row in the next column.
- Enter **=B6-76**. This subtracts 76 from the value of cell B:6.
  Note: Do not confuse the labels in the table with the actual cell letter or number. Functions must reference the actual cell location.
- Click OK to close the In-Place Text Editor.

A	B ←	C
PART NAME	A	B
B762	762	
B838	838	
B914	914	
B991	991	↓
B1067	1067	=B6-76

13 To copy the contents of one cell to others:

- Click the cell containing the formula to highlight it.
- Click the Auto-Fill grip (1).
- Move your cursor upward (2).
- Click anywhere in the top cell (3).
  The copied formula is pasted into the other cells, maintaining reference to relative cell numbers.

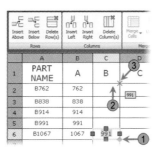

- Press ESC to clear the selection.

14 To add the remaining data to column C:

- Double-click the first cell in the last column.
- Enter the values as shown.

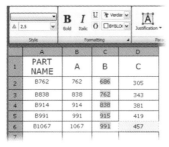

15 Compare the values in your table to the values shown.

Chapter 11 | Creating Additional Drawing Objects

PART NAME	A	B	C
B762	762	686	305
B838	838	762	343
B914	914	838	381
B991	991	915	419
B1067	1067	991	457

16   Zoom to the drawing extents.

17   Close all files without saving.

Challenge Exercise | Architectural

In this exercise, you use what you learned about creating drawing objects to create a table, a closed polyline for calculating an area, and spline topographic lines.

> **Tip**
> You have the option of completing this exercise using either imperial or metric units. Select one version of the exercise to complete the steps.

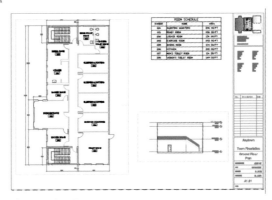

The completed exercise

> **Completing the Exercise**
> To complete the exercise, follow the steps in this book or in the onscreen exercise. In the onscreen list of chapters and exercises, click *Chapter 11: Creating Additional Drawing Objects*. Click *Challenge Exercise: Architectural Metric*.

Metric Units

1   Open the drawing you saved from the previous challenge exercise, or open *M_ARCH-Challenge- CHP11.dwg*.

2   Set layers and create contours.

   • Thaw and set current the existing layer, Topo.
   • Draw smooth curved contours from node to node as shown.

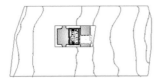

3　　Calculate the square area of the lot this fire station sits on. The lot is shown with the blue grips active in the following image.

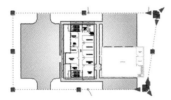

4　　Place a title block on the layout.

- Activate the Plan View layout.
- Insert the block Titleblock centered on the layout.
- Add text to the title block as shown.

5　　Add and configure two viewports.

- A view of the elevation detail at a scale of 1:100.
- The key plan in the upper-right corner of the title block, zoomed to fit. For each of the viewport configurations, adjust the layer display to achieve the results shown.

6　　Create a table showing the following Room Schedule data:

- NUMBER - NAME - AREA
- 221 - SLEEPING QUARTERS - 21 m2
- 201-READYROOM-36m2

- 202 - LOCKER ROOM - 14 m2
- 203 - EXERCISE ROOM - 23 m2
- 205 - DINING ROOM - 24 m2
- 206-KITCHEN-6m2
- 207 - MEN'S TOILET ROOM - 11 m2
- 208 - WOMEN'S TOILET ROOM - 14 m2

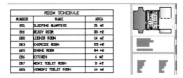

7   Save and close the drawing.

Imperial Units

1   Open the drawing you saved from the previous challenge exercise, or open *I_ARCH-Challenge- CHP11.dwg.*

2   Set layers and create contours.
- Thaw and set current the existing layer, Topo.
- Thaw the layer, Site - Concrete.
- Draw smooth curved contours from node to node as shown.

3   Calculate the square area of the lot this fire station sits on. The lot is shown with the blue grips active in the following image.

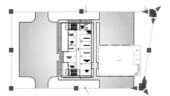

4   Place a title block on the layout.
- Activate the Plan View layout.
- Insert the block Titleblock centered on the layout.
- Add text to the title block as shown.

Anytown

Town Firestation

Ground Floor
Plan

Project number	2008-65
Date	02/25/2008
Drawn by	M. Andrews
Checked by	R. Olding

A1.01

Scale

5   Add and configure two viewports.

- A view of the elevation detail at a scale of 1/8" = 1'.
- The key plan in the upper-right corner of the title block, zoomed to fit.
  For each of the viewport configurations, adjust the layer display to achieve the results shown.

6   Create a table showing the following Room Schedule data:

- NUMBER - NAME - AREA
- 221 - SLEEPING QUARTERS - 236 SQ/FT
- 201 - READY ROOM - 386 SQ/FT
- 202 - LOCKER ROOM - 150 SQ/FT
- 203 - EXERCISE ROOM - 383 SQ/FT
- 205 - DINING ROOM - 134 SQ/FT
- 206 - KITCHEN - 200 SQ /FT
- 207 - MEN'S TOILET ROOM - 114 SQ/FT
- 208 - WOMEN'S TOILET ROOM - 149 SQ/FT

7   Save and close the drawing.

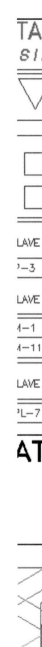

Challenge Exercise | Mechanical

In this exercise, you use what you learned about creating drawing objects to represent an edge on a part, create a border around a view, and create a closed loop to calculate area. You will also update your layout including a titleblock.

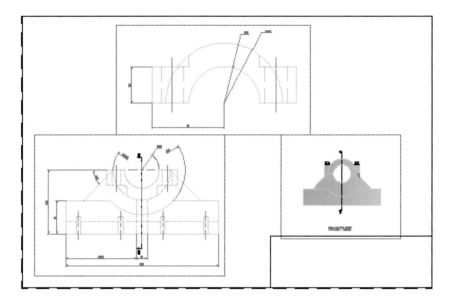

The completed exercise

Completing the Exercise

To complete the exercise, follow the steps in this book or in the onscreen exercise. In the onscreen list of chapters and exercises, click *Chapter 11: Creating Additional Drawing Objects*. Click *Challenge Exercise: Mechanical*.

1   Open the drawing you saved from the previous challenge exercise, or open *M_MECH-
    Challenge- CHP11.dwg.*

2   In the side views for both the base part and assembly, the cut for the hole is too high with an
    arc. Draw the representation correctly using an ellipse.

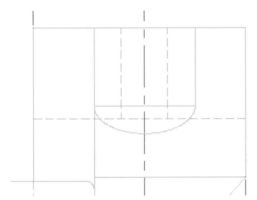

3   Change the border around the detail view from a circle to a spline shape.

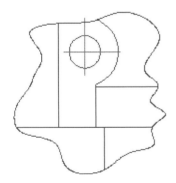

4   Calculate the square millimeter area of the two flat surfaces in the front view of the base part.

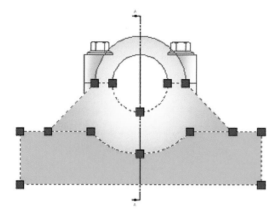

(Value Check: The area of the lower face = 17185.9487)

5   Update the Parts layout.
   - Switch to the Parts layout.
   - Insert the Titleblock block.

6   Save and close the drawing.

Chapter Summary

To meet your design needs, you can create multiple segments of lines and arcs as a single polyline, you can create smooth curved geometry as splines or ellipses, and you can add tables to your drawings.

Having completed this chapter, you can:

- Create and edit polylines with the Polyline command.
- Create smooth curves with the Spline command.
- Create ellipses and elliptical arcs with the Ellipse command.
- Create and edit basic tables and use table styles to control their appearance.

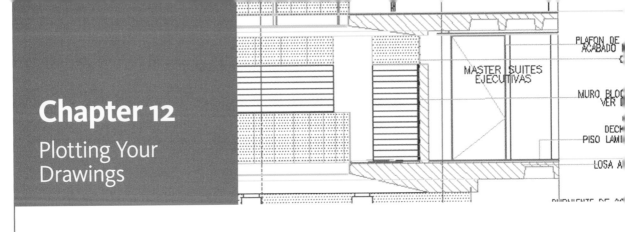

Chapter 12
Plotting Your Drawings

The final step of the drawing process is to communicate the design to others through both paper and electronic media.

Objectives

After completing this chapter, you will be able to:

- Create and activate page setups.

- Plot design geometry from model space or from a layout.

Standard Object Snap and Status Bar Settings
Before completing the exercises in this chapter, refer to the "Settings for the Exercises" section in the Introduction.

Lesson 50 | Using Page Setups

This lesson describes how to activate and save page setups in the layout environment.

Since you may need to output data to a variety of devices and in different forms at different times, using saved page setups can save you valuable time. You can also save time by selecting saved page setups when outputting multiple sheets from a number of files at once with the Publish command. However, the Publish command is not covered in this lesson.

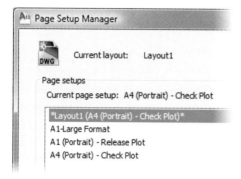

Objectives

After completing this lesson, you will be able to:

- Apply a page setup to an existing layout.
- Create and modify a page setup.

Applying Page Setups to Layouts

Named page setups are useful for easily plotting a layout in different ways and for quickly configuring a layout. Each time you create a layout or execute the Plot command, you can set various configuration options and save these settings as a named page setup. Using Page Setup Manager, you can then activate a page setup for a layout or modify your page setups. When you create a page setup in the layout environment, you can only make that page setup current for layouts, not for model space. However, you can also create page setups for your model space plotting needs.

Command Access

Page Setup

Command Line: **PAGESETUP**
Application Menu: **Print > Page Setup**
Shortcut Menu: **Right-click the Model or Layout tab, click Page Setup Manager**

Shortcut Menu: **Right-click the Model or Layout tab, click Page Setup Manager**

Page Setup Manager Dialog Box

In the Page Setup Manager, you can make an existing page setup current, modify page setups, create new page setups, and import a page setup from a different drawing file. The current page setup is the one that takes effect when you execute the Plot command.

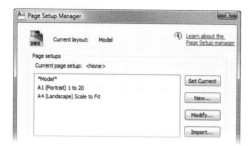

Page Setup Manager Access Options

When you click the Page Setup Manager from the ribbon you will be creating settings for the current drawing layout or model space. To access the Page Setup Manager from a selected layout or model space, there are two options.

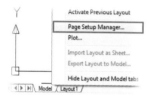

Option #1: Make the Layout and Model Space tabs visible:

- Right-click in the drawing window or Command line area and select Options.

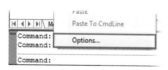

- In the Options dialog box, select the Display tab.
- Click to place a checkmark before Display Layout and Model Tabs.

- Select Apply and Close the Options dialog box.
- Select the desired layout or model tab.
- Right-click to access Page Setup Manager.

Option #2: Activate Page Setup from the Quick View Layouts or Quick view Drawings button on the status bar:

- Double-click the Quick View Layouts, or click Drawings.
- Select the desired Layout (2) and right-click.
- Select the Page Setup Manager (3)

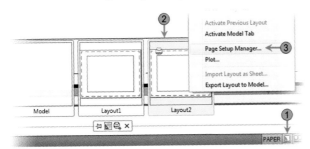

Procedure: Applying a Saved Page Setup to a Layout

The following is an overview of making a saved page setup current in an existing layout.

1   Select the layout tab.

2   Right-click the tab. Click Page Setup Manager.

3   In the list of saved page setups in Page Setup Manager, double-click the name of the page setup.

4   Click Close.

Practice Exercise | Applying Page Setups to Layouts

In this practice exercise, you create a simple Page Setup based on some very simple settings in the Page Setup Manager, then you apply that new setup to your drawing. In the next section, you learn more about creating and modifying page setups using the Page Setup Manager.

1   Open a new drawing using the *acad.dwt template*.

2   Create some simple geometry.

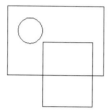

3   To Access the Page Setup Manager for the Model Tab:

- Select the Model tab and right-click (1).
- Click Page Setup Manager.

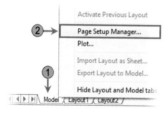

> Note: If the Model tab is not visible, right-click in the Command line area. Click Options. In the Options dialog box on the Display tab, under Layout elements, select the Display Layout and Model tabs check box.

4   To Create a New Page Setup:

- In the Page Setup Manager, select New (1).
- For the New page setup name, enter **TEST_PRINT** (2).
- Click OK.

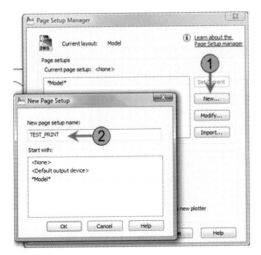

5   To create some simple settings in the Page Setup dialog box:

• Under Printer/Plotter, select a printer from the Name list.
• Select a common paper size from the Paper Size list.
• Under Plot area, select Extents from the What to Plot list.
• Under Plot Offset, select Center the Plot.
• Under Plot Scale, select Fit to Paper.
• Select Landscape for the Drawing Orientation.
• Click Preview. Confirm that the drawing is displayed in the preview window. Press to exit the preview window.
• Click OK to exit the Page Setup dialog box.

6   To make the New Page Setup current:

• In the Page Setup Manager, select TEST_PRINT.
• Click Set Current.
• Close the dialog box.
  Now when you print from the Model tab, the drawing prints according to the current page setup.

Creating Page Setups

Once your layouts are created, you should assign a page setup to them. You can import page setups from your template files or other drawings. If necessary, either modify an existing setup or create a new one. When creating a new page setup, you need to know the printer/plotter device, paper size, plot scale, and many other plot properties.

New Page Setup

In Page Setup Manager, click New. The New Page Setup dialog box opens. Here, you can start with an existing setup or create a new one from the default <None>.

Page Setup Dialog Box

The Page Setup dialog box is displayed when you are creating a new page setup or when you click Modify in the Page Setup Manager.

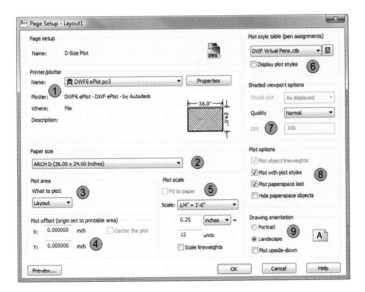

The Page Setup dialog box is almost identical to the Plot dialog box. Use the Page Setup dialog box to select and define the following items:

1. Select the plotter or plotter configuration file to use.

2. Select the paper size to output to.

3. Select the area of the file that should be plotted. You can select to plot the current display, drawing extents, or specify a window. When you create a page setup on the model tab, you can also specify to plot the limits of the drawing. When you create a page setup on the layout tab, you can specify to plot the entire layout.

4. Select where the geometry is positioned on the paper relative to the paper's origin point.

5. Select the scale factor to use when outputting the geometry.

6. Select the plot style table to use to further control the appearance of the geometry on the paper or in the output file.

7. Determine whether a viewport should be shaded and, if so, the quality of that shading.

8. Select additional plot options, such as whether to plot using plot styles, and the order for calculation when outputting the geometry.

9. Select the orientation of the geometry on the paper.

Procedure: Creating and Saving a Page Setup

The following steps give an overview of creating and saving a page setup.

1   Select the model space or a layout.

2   On the Application Menu, click Print > Page Setup Manager.

3   In the Page Setup Manager dialog box, click New.

4   In the New Page Setup dialog box, enter a name for the new page setup. Click OK.

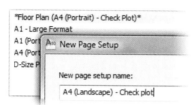

5   Set the options in the Page Setup dialog box as required. Click OK. You can now make the page setup current in any layout.

Exercise | Create and Activate Page Setups

In this exercise, you activate a saved page setup for an existing layout, then create another page setup that you can use in any layout.

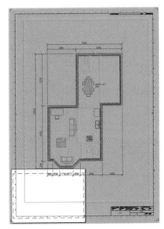

The completed exercise

Completing the Exercise
To complete the exercise, follow the steps in this book or in the onscreen exercise. In the onscreen list of chapters and exercises, click *Chapter 12: Plotting Your Drawings*. Click *Exercise: Create and Activate Page Setups*.

1   Open *M_Page-Setup.dwg*.

2   To access the Page Setup Manager:
   - Right-click the Layout2 tab.
   - Click Page Setup Manager.
     In the Page Setup Manager, under Selected Page Setup Details, notice that the layout has no plotter selected and has a plot paper size of 420 x 594 mm.

3   To make a page setup current:
   - Double-click For Book of Examples.
     This page setup is set to current and specifies to use the DWF6 ePlot.pc3 plotter configuration and a paper size of 297 x 210 mm. The paper size is reflected in the layout display.
   - Click Close.

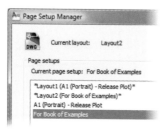

4   Click the Layout1 tab to make that layout active.

5   On the ribbon, click Output tab > Plot panel > Page Setup Manager.

6   To start creating a new layout:
    - In the Page Setup Manager, click New.
    - For the New Page Setup Name, enter **A4 (Portrait) - Check Plot.**
    - Click OK.

7   To specify a paper size:
    - Select ISO A4 (210.00 x 297.00 MM) from the Paper Size list.
    - Click OK.

8   To set a current page setup:
    - In the list of page setups, double-click A4 (Portrait) - Check Plot.
    - Click Close.

9   Zoom to the extents of the drawing to see all the geometry in the layout.
    This layout was originally set to plot at 1:1 on an A1 size sheet of paper. It will not fit on A4 paper at 1:1. Therefore, you need to change the scale factor for this page setup.

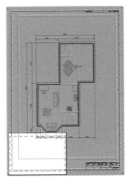

10 To access the Page Setup Manager:
   - Right-click Layout1.
   - Click Page Setup Manager.

11 To modify an existing page setup:
   - Select A4 (Portrait) - Check Plot from the Page Setups List
   - Click Modify

12 To specify plot options:
   - Under Plot Area, select Extents from the What To Plot list.
   - Under Plot Scale, select the Fit to Paper option.
   - Click OK.
   - Click Yes, when prompted to update the page setup.

13 Click Close.

14 Close all files without saving.

Lesson 51 | Plotting Drawings

In this lesson, you learn how to plot from a layout or model space to paper or to an electronic file. Outputting your drawings is a crucial step in communicating your design ideas to others.

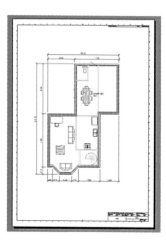

Objectives

After completing this lesson, you will be able to:

- Identify the environments from which you can output data.
- Explain the reason for and characteristics of plotting from model space.
- State the characteristics of plotting from layouts.
- Plot drawings from model space or from a layout.
- Use the Preview command to view what you plot.

About Plotting Environments

You create drawings to store design data and to communicate it to others. The communication occurs when you output the data on paper or to an electronic file. The terms *print* or *plot* are used interchangeably to describe the process of outputting the data stored in a drawing file. Design Web Format (DWF) is the most common and versatile electronic file format you can use to output and distribute your drawings.

There are two methods for outputting data. One is to plot from model space and the other is to plot from layouts. Each method has its own list of items to configure and control to achieve the desired output. No matter which method you use, your design data is created in model space and remains at full scale, also referred to as real world size.

Plotting from the drawing Layout or from the drawing Model

The following illustration shows the drawing Layout. You select a layout tab (1) to activate the drawing layout. The Layout displays the paper (2), the plot area designated by the a dashed line (3), the drawing viewports (4) and the scaled view of the drawings in those viewports. The paperspace icon is visible in the left corner (5).

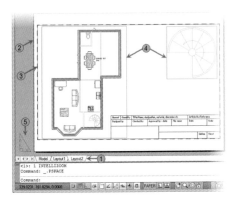

The illustration below shows the drawing model. You select the Model tab (1) to activate model space. This is the environment where you create your drawing. If the UCS icon is on, it is displayed, typically in the left corner (2).

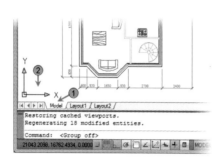

Plot or Publish

When you output data from a single layout in a drawing file, you usually use the Plot command. When you need to output data from multiple layouts within one or more drawings, you can use the Publish command. Publishing gives you the ability to create a list of drawings to plot, select what to plot from multiple files, and save that selected information as a Drawing Set Descriptions (DSD) file. Using a DSD file, you can easily open and plot the data from the drawing list without having to reiterate what and how to plot.

Key Terms

Defined Below are some key terms associated with plotting.

Term	Description
Plot	The act of outputting the active drawing file to a plotter, printer, or file.
Model Space	The area of the file where you draw your model at full scale after you decide what one unit in the drawing represents in the real world (millimeters, centimeters, inches, feet, and so on).
Layout	An environment used to set up your data for output. You can specify the paper size, add a title block, display multiple views of the drawing at multiple scales, and add notes specific to that plotted sheet.
DWF	A highly compressed file that contains the output data for others to view electronically.

Example of When to Plot

While the design industry is migrating toward a paperless process, we still require design output to paper and compressed image files. You use the Plot command to create this output. As you work on your design, you may need to send a check plot to the laser printer in your work area. You can use this printed output to discuss the design with others or fax it to a colleague to review. You may want to post the same data to your Web site for others to view electronically. In this case, you would plot the file to DWF format for posting to your Web site.

Plotting from Model Space

The main reason to plot from model space is to have a paper printout of a specific area of your design so that you can review it. The following image is an example of geometry in model space that can be plotted.

When you plot from model space, all the geometry that resides in the model space environment can be printed. If you want to print a specific part of your drawing, you have to specify the area to plot. If you want to print your drawing at a specific scale, you have to specify the plot scale. If you want to have a border and title block around the geometry in model space, you have to scale it up or down based on the plot scale you are using.

For example, a drawing that will plot at a scale of 1:20 requires a border and title block that are created scaled up 20 times. When you plot your drawing at a scale of 1:20, the border, title block and drawing will be scaled down to fit the paper.

To plot text and dimension objects at a specific size from model space, choose the annotative property for each style and set the Annotative scale for the drawing. The images below show the details of the Text Style and Dimension Style dialog box (Fit tab) where you can choose the Annotative property.

The following image shows where you can access the Annotative Scale list on the status bar.

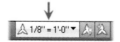

Plotting Annotations

When you plot from model space, all objects appear with the same relative scale as they appear on screen. Objects that have the annotative property assigned to them display and plot using the annotative scale that is currently set on the status bar. So, for annotative objects, you need to adjust the annotation scale to a value that provides a legible annotation size on screen before plotting your drawing.

If you do not assign the annotative property to objects such as Text Style and Dimension Style, you have to create the text and dimension at a height and fit that are proportionate to the plot scale in order for them to be legible.

Procedure: Plotting from Model Space

The following steps give an overview of plotting a windowed area of your drawing from model space.

1   Start the Plot command. In the Plot dialog box under Plot Area, select Window from the What to Plot list.

2   When prompted to specify a window for printing, drag a window around an area to be plotted, as shown.

3   When prompted to specify a window for printing, drag a window around an area to be plotted, as shown.

4   Adjust Paper size, Plot scale, and other parameters as needed in the Plot - Model dialog box. Click Preview to view and plot your selected area.

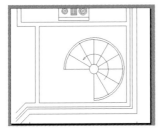

Guidelines for Plotting from Model Space

- Use the annotative property for text and dimension styles and choose the annotation scale for your plot. Annotations automatically scale themselves in the drawing according to the annotation scale you select.
- When creating a text style using the Annotative property, you can specify the paper text height. This height is multiplied by a scale factor that is determined by the annotation scale.
- You can create different text styles with different text heights and fonts for your annotations; for example, you could create one style for notes and dimensions and another style for titles.
- The most common plot areas you use when plotting from Model space are Extents and Window.
- Use the Center plot option to keep uniform white space around your plotted output.
- The plot area varies according to the printer/plotter selected.
- Choose the Fit to Paper plot scale option to check your drawing when creating a plot from model space.
- If your title block or border is drawn full scale, and your plot scale is not 1:1, you must scale the title block according to the plot scale. For example, if the annotation scale is 1:10 your scale factor is 10. If the annotation scale is & #188;" – 1'0", your scale factor is 48 (4 x 12").
- You can retain the Plot settings in the Page Setup Manager. Right-click the Model tab to access the Page Setup Manager.

Plotting from Layouts

Use layouts to set up the information you want to output. For each layout, you select the size of paper you want and set the plot scale to 1:1. In the paper layout, one unit represents the paper distance on a plotted sheet and the units are either millimeters or inches.

Since the geometry is not scaled during the plot process, you can add the border and any textual notes on the layout at the desired output size. For example, if drawing notes are supposed to be 1/8" tall, you set the text height to 1/8".

Another advantage of layouts is that you can create multiple views of model geometry on the same sheet and display them at different scales or create multiple layouts to display different views of the model space geometry. Additionally, one instance of annotative objects, such as text or dimensions, can be displayed at the same size in several views of different scales.

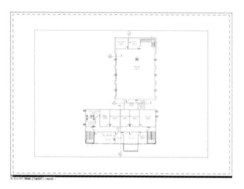

Procedure: Plotting from a Layout

The following steps give an overview of plotting a layout.

1   Start the Plot command and verify that the Plot area is set to Layout. Also, verify that your plot scale is set to 1:1. Your paper size was also set while creating the layout so it should not need to be changed.

2   Your layout should have a page setup, and the plotter should already be assigned using the Page Setup Manager from the Layout tab. Verify that these settings are as you want them. Click Preview to review your output. If your preview looks correct, right-click, and click Plot. If you need to make a change, right-click, click Exit to return to the plot dialog box and make your changes.

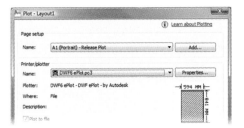

Guidelines for Plotting from a Layout

- Create the design geometry in the model environment at full scale.
- Set the paper size for the layout and a plot scale of 1:1 for the paper using the Page Setup Manager.
- The scale factor of the model geometry on the layout is determined by the scale factor that you set for each viewport.
- For text and dimensions created in model space, you should use Annotative styles. The Annotative styles scale according to the selected viewport scale. Annotations plot at the text size you choose when you set up your Annotative styles.
- You can create multiple viewports to display different sections of the model geometry or show it at different scales.
- On a layout with multiple viewports, you can freeze layers in selected viewports independently to create different displays of the same geometry.
- Insert the border and title block on the layout at full scale.
- When plotting from the Layout, make sure the Paper space is active and not the Model in the viewport.

Plot Command

The Plot command prints data from the active drawing to a plotter, printer, or file using the settings in the Plot dialog box.

Command Access

Plot

Command Line: **PLOT, PRINT**
Application Menu: **Print** or **Print > Plot**
Quick Access Toolbar: **Plot**

Ribbon: **Output tab > Plot panel > Plot**

Plot Dialog Box

Click the Expand button at the bottom-right of the Plot dialog box to access more options.

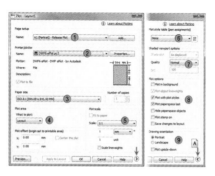

① Use this option to select a saved page setup with plot options already set or to add the current configuration as a saved page setup.

(2) Select a printer from this list to specify where to send the plot. You can select system printers or application-specific plotter configuration (PC3) files.

(3) Select a paper size from the list available for the selected plotting device.

(4) Specifies where the plot geometry will come from. When plotting from a layout, area options include Display, Extents, Window, View, and Layout. When plotting from model space, you can choose the Limits option.

(5) Use this to set the ratio of printed units to geometry units. By plotting at a specific scale, you can use a scale to measure distances on the printed copy. If your drawings do not need to be at a set scale, select Fit To Paper.

(6) The selected table controls the appearance of the plotted geometry. Based on settings in the table, the output of geometry could be different than what is displayed in the software. For example, the geometry could be plotted in a different color, it could be plotted wider than it shows, or it could have a different line type.

(7) Specifies how shaded and rendered viewports are plotted including their resolution level and the dpi (dots per inch).

(8) Use this area to specify options for line weights, plot styles, plot stamp, and the order in which objects are plotted.

(9) Use to specify how the geometry is oriented on the sheet.

Warning!
The Plot Options shown in area 8 are not all available in AutoCAD LT®.

Plotter Configurations

All of the settings you specify in the Plot dialog box can be saved and imported to use with other drawings or on different workstations. A saved plot configuration is a PC3 file. Earlier versions of AutoCAD® plotter configurations are PCP or PC2 files. Click Properties (1) in the Plot dialog box to access the Plot Configuration Editor to access the Save (2) and Import (3) options.

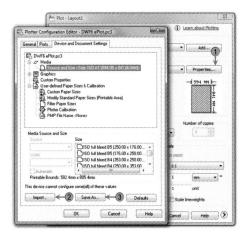

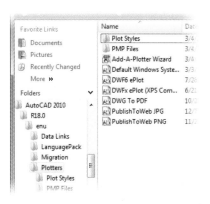

You can also add or edit a plotter configuration using the Plotter Manager.

Command Access

Plotter Manager

Command Line: **PLOTMANAGER**
Application Menu: **Print > Manager Plotters**
Ribbon: **Output tab > Plot panel > Plot**

Chapter 12 | Plotting Your Drawings

The Plot Style Manager command opens the folder of existing plot styles where you can choose a plot style to edit or add a new plot style.

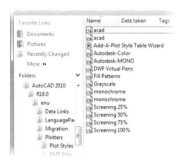

Command Access

Plot Styles Manager

Command Line: **STYLESMANAGER**
Application Menu: **Print › Manager Plot Styles**

Guidelines for the Plot Command

- Plot and Print are the same command. There is not a separate Print command. To print a drawing, use the Plot command.
- Plot settings can be saved in the Page Setup Manager for the Model tab or for each Layout.
- You can override the settings in the Page Setup Manager from the Plot dialog box.
- You can save a Plot setup from the Plot dialog box by clicking Add and naming the page setup. Named plot setups appear in the list for later reuse.
- To save changes to a plot setup, click Add and enter the original name for the new page setup. This redefines the previously named setup.
- You must select a printer or plotter in order to Preview the plot settings.
- You can use CTRL+P to initiate the Plot dialog box.
- You can save a plotter configuration and import it into another drawing. A saved plot configuration is a PC3 file. Earlier versions of AutoCAD plotter configurations are PCP or PC2 files. Click Properties in the Plot dialog box to access the Save and Import options.
- Save Plotter configurations and Plot Style Tables for later reuse when plotting your drawings or when using other computer workstations to plot your drawings.
- If you do not specify a plot style table, the drawing plots according to the default printer settings.

Preview Command

Previewing gives you an opportunity to review a full-page version of how the final plot will appear on the printed sheet or in the electronic file. Within the Preview window, you can pan and zoom the display to assist you in your review. You can click the Plot button to directly plot what is displayed, or you can close the Preview window. If you initiated the preview from within the Plot dialog box, closing the Preview window returns you to the Plot dialog box.

Command Access

 Preview

Command Line: **PREVIEW**
Application Menu: **Print > Plot Preview**
Plot Dialog Box: **Preview**
Ribbon: **Output tab > Plot panel > Preview**

Preview Command Guidelines

- Preview enables you to view your drawing before plotting it, which is a good idea.
- Start the preview from the Plot dialog box or by using the Plot Preview button on the Plot panel.
- You can plot from the Preview window, without returning to the Plot dialog box.
- Closing the Preview window does not close the drawing.
- If there is no plotter assigned to the layout, you cannot preview the drawing.

Chapter 12 | Plotting Your Drawings

Exercise | Plot a Drawing

In this exercise, you preview what you are going to plot, then you plot to a DWF file and to the default Windows system printer.

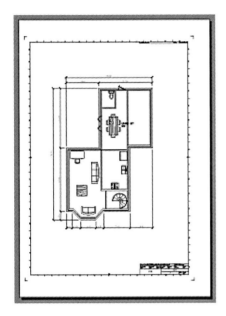

The completed exercise

Completing the Exercise

To complete the exercise, follow the steps in this book or in the onscreen exercise. In the onscreen list of chapters and exercises, click *Chapter 12: Plotting Your Drawings*. Click *Exercise: Plot a Drawing*.

1 Open *M_Plotting.dwg*.

2 To preview the plot, click Output tab > Plot panel > Preview.
Notice that the green rectangular viewport shown on the layout is not shown in the preview. This is because the layer on which the viewport resides has its layer property set to No Plot.

3 Click Close Preview Window or press ESC to close the preview window.

4 On the Plot panel, click Plot.

5 To create the DWF plot:
- In the Plot dialog box, click OK.
- In the Browse for Plot File dialog box, click Save.
  This accepts the default file name and location, and plots the layout to the file as a DWF file.

6 To specify a page setup when plotting:
- Click Plot.
- In the Plot dialog box, under Page Setup, select Check Plot - Monochrome from the Name list.

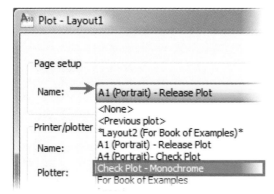

7   To preview the plot, click Preview in the Plot dialog box.
     Notice that this plot outputs the geometry in shades of black on a smaller sheet of paper.

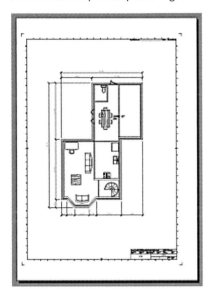

8   To create the plot:
     • In the Preview window, click Plot.
     • When prompted, add **-B** to the file name to create a DWF file called
       M_Plotting- Layout1-B.dwf.
     • Click Save.
9   Click the Model tab.

10   Click Plot.

11   To specify the printer/plotter, select DWF6 ePlot.pc3 from the Name list.

12   To define the plot area:
   • Select Window from the What To Plot list.
   • Specify a window that encompasses the kitchen area as shown.

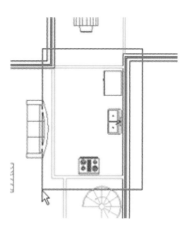

13   Click OK.

14   Click Save to create a DWF file called *M_Plotting-Model.dwf*. Take note of the location in which the file is being created in.

15   Close all files without saving.
   Note: You can now view the plots you created in the DWF Viewer by navigating to the location the files were created, and then double-clicking on them.

Chapter Summary

Depending on your business environment, you will produce a variety of completed design specifications. In this chapter you learned how to output your design data from both Model and Layout views. Saving layout configurations as page setups makes it easier and more efficient to set the configuration values for a layout and to quickly plot the information in different ways including output to paper and electronically.

Having completed this chapter, you can:

- Create and activate page setups.
- Plot design geometry from model space or from a layout.

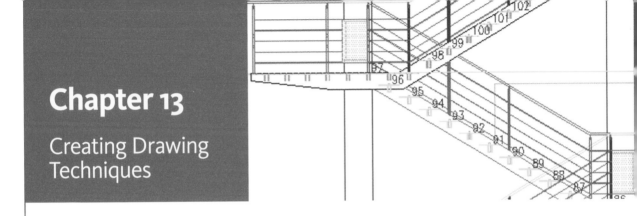

Chapter 13

Creating Drawing Techniques

Most companies have some kind of standard or guidelines for their drawings to ensure a consistent look and functionality. You can create drawing templates to store these standards or guidelines in the form of drawing properties and other settings. When you use the templates to create new drawings, you ensure consistency with these standards.

Objectives

After completing this chapter, you will be able to:

- Create drawing templates.

Lesson 52 | Creating Drawing Templates

This lesson describes how to create drawing templates.

By creating drawing templates, you save time with every new drawing that you create. The settings in the drawing template are carried over to each new drawing that is created by using the template.

The following illustration shows the Template Options dialog box with measurement units, description, and new layer notification.

Objectives

After completing this lesson, you will be able to:

- Describe drawing templates.
- Identify various options of drawing templates.
- Create drawing templates.

About Drawing Templates

Drawing templates are extremely helpful in situations where you need to create your drawings with predefined drawing standards, such as layers and text styles. Using drawing templates enables you to save the time that you would have to otherwise spend in setting the required standards every time you begin a drawing. Many organizations have CAD Managers who create template drawings and make them available for their team.

The software provides various drawing templates for creating new drawings. Most of the predefined drawing templates are suitable for creating basic drawings. However, you can use these predefined drawing templates to create your own set of templates specific to your drawing requirements.

Definition of Drawing Templates

A drawing template is a collection of standard predefined settings, such as units, title blocks, layers, text styles, and dimension styles, which can be used for creating many drawings. Drawing template files have a *.dwt* file extension.

Drawing Templates and CAD Standards

When you work in a project where many people are involved in creating a design, there is a possibility that all team members do not consistently follow the same drawing settings. Therefore, to maintain consistency across drawings, you can establish CAD standards by sharing and using DWT files.

To create a DWT file, you define the required drawing settings and save the file as a drawing template. You can also save a DWT file as a drawing standard (DWS) file. You can then use a DWS file to check and map a drawing with a drawing template for any violation of the set standards.

> **Tip**
> After creating a drawing which is based on a DWT file, if you modify the new drawing, the changes do not affect the DWT file.

Example of Drawing Templates

The following illustrations show various examples of drawing templates.

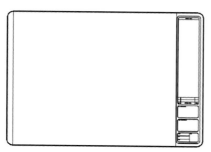

An architectural template title block

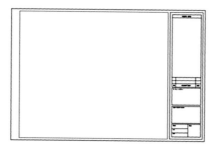

A drawing template with D-size title block settings

Drawing Template Options

When creating drawing templates, you can save all or some of the template properties and settings, based on the type of drawings that can be created with a new template. You can modify these properties later, if required.

Chapter 13 | Creating Drawing Templates

Template Properties and Settings

You use drawing templates to provide a starting point for all the new drawings that you create. In most design environments, your drawings share some common properties and settings. When you save a drawing template, you can save all the drawing commonalities, eliminating the need to create or adjust properties and settings each time you create a new drawing.

The following are some of the properties and settings that you can save in a drawing template:

- Unit settings
- Layers
- Snap, grid, and ortho mode settings
- Limits
- Dimension styles
- Text styles
- Linetypes
- Table styles
- Layouts
- Page setups for all layouts and model space
- Title blocks and borders
- Blocks, such as symbols or other objects, that you commonly use in your drawings

Template File Location

Before you create your drawing templates, you need to specify their storage location.

You specify where template files are stored on the Files tab of the Options dialog box. By default, this path is set to a subfolder of the current user folder. This path might work if you are working in a single user environment, but if you are working as part of a design team, you should set the path to a network location where all project drawing templates can be consolidated.

The path that you select controls the default location that appears when you select the Drawing Template (*.dwt) format in the Files of Type list in the Save Drawing As, Select Template, and Select File dialog boxes.

Template Options Dialog Box

By using the Template Options dialog box, you can set the drawing units to either imperial or metric, provide a description for the template, and control new layer notification.

To access the Template Options dialog box, you select the AutoCAD Drawing Template (*.dwt) option from the Files of Type list in the Save As dialog box.

Command Access

Save As
Command Line: **SAVEAS**
Application Menu: **Save As > AutoCAD Drawing Templates**

The following illustration shows the Template Options dialog box.

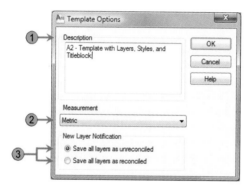

① **Description** - Specifies a description for the DWT file. This description is displayed in the Create New Drawing dialog box.

② **Measurement** - Determines whether drawings based on this template use English or Metric units.

③ **New Layer Notification** - All the layers in a DWT file are saved as unreconciled by default. Saves all layers as unreconciled or reconciled. When you save a DWT file with unreconciled layers, the layer baseline is not created; therefore the new layer notification is not displayed. When you save a template with reconciled layers, layer baseline is created; therefore the software notifies you of any new layers in the drawing.

Creating Drawing Templates

Creating drawing templates saves time. It enables you to start a drawing with the required predefined settings of layers, linetypes, and dimension styles. You can also import settings from other templates into the current drawing to create a new template.

Procedure: Creating Drawing Templates

The following steps describe how to create a drawing template:

1   Create a new drawing by using an existing template, or by using the no template options.

2   Modify the drawing to include the required layers, styles, layout settings, and title blocks.

3   Adjust the Drawing Template File Location path in the Options dialog box, if required.

4   Save the drawing.

5   In the Template Description dialog box, enter a description, specify the measurement unit, and specify the new layer notification.

6   Open the newly created template and verify that the resulting drawing contains the settings that you created.

> **Tip**
> Store the DWT files that you create at the location that is specified under Template Settings in the Options dialog box. Storing the DWT files at this location helps you easily access the templates you create.

Exercise | Create a Drawing Template

In this exercise, you create a drawing template that contains text styles, dimension styles, drawing units, layers, layouts, and a title block.

Scenario

You do the following:

- Set units, styles, layer properties, and page setup.
- Create a drawing template.
- Open a drawing based on a new template file.

The completed exercise

Completing the Exercise
To complete the exercise, follow the steps in this book or in the onscreen exercise. In the onscreen list of chapters and exercises, click *Chapter 13: Template Drawing Creation*. Click *Exercise: Create a Drawing Template*.

Set Units, Styles, Layer Properties, and Page Setup

1   Open *c_create_drawing_template.dwg*.

2   On the Annotate tab, Text panel, click Text Style.
    You are creating architectural drawings and need to have the layer settings that correspond to AIA standards. You decide to specify the required layer settings in a template that you can use for all the typical architectural drawings.

3   In the Text Style dialog box:

  - Select Arial from the Font Name list.
  - Click Apply to save the changes.

4   In the Text Style dialog box, click New.

  - In the New Text Style dialog box:
  - For Style Name, enter **3.5 Gen Notes**.
  - Click OK.

5   In the Text Style dialog box:

  - Select Tahoma from the Font Name list.
  - For Height, enter **3.5.**
  - Click Apply to save the changes.
  - Click Close.

6   On the Annotate tab, Text panel, select Standard in the Text Styles list.

7   On the Annotate tab, Dimension panel, click Dimension Style.

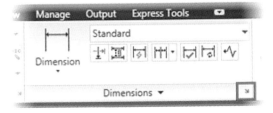

8   In the Dimension Style Manager dialog box, click Modify.

9   In the Modify Dimension Style dialog box:

   • On the Primary Units tab, select '.' (Period) from the Decimal Separator list.
   • On the Text tab, under Text Alignment, click the ISO standard.
   • Click OK.

10   Click Close to exit the Dimension Style Manager.

11   On the Home tab, Layers panel, click Layer Properties to display the Layer Properties Manager.

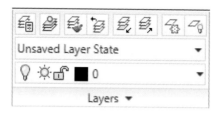

12   In the Layer Properties Manager:

   • Create new layers and assign layer properties, as shown.
   • Set the Objects layer current.
   • Close the Layer Properties Manager.
     Note: Color assignments are not critical. Use your own color preferences.

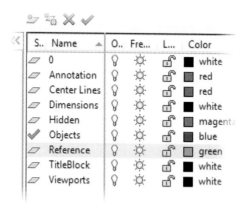

13   On the status bar, click Layout1 to activate Layout1.

- Select the predefined viewport.
- Right-click anywhere in the drawing. Click Display Viewport Objects > No.
- On the application menu, click Print > Page Setup.

14   In the Page Setup Manager, click New.

- In the New Page Setup dialog box:
- For New page setup name, enter **A2-ePlot.**
- Click OK.

15   In the Page Setup - Layout1 dialog box:

- Select DWF6 ePlot.pc3 from the Name list as the printer/plotter device.
- Select ISO A2 (594.00 x 420.00 MM) from the Paper size list.
- Ensure that 1:1 is selected from the Scale list.
- Click OK.

16   In the Page Setup Manager dialog box, double- click the A2-ePlot page setup to assign it to Layout1 and click Close.

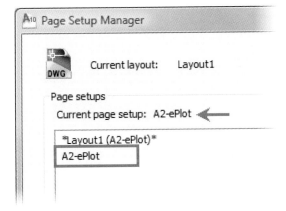

17   Continue to the next exercise or close all files without saving.

Create a Drawing Template

1　On the Home tab, Layers panel, select TitleBlock in the Layers list.

2　On the Insert tab, Block panel, click Insert.

- In the Insert dialog box, click Browse.
- In the Select Drawing File dialog box, navigate to *A2-Title.dwg*.
- Click Open.
- Make sure Specify On-screen is not checked, enter **0,0,0** for the insertion point, and complete the block insertion procedure.
- Click OK

3　To delete the extra layout:

- On the status bar. click Ouick View Layouts

- Right-click the Layout2 preview, and click Delete.
- In the AutoCAD dialog box, click OK.

4　Click the Model tab to activate model space.

5　On the Home tab, Layers panel, select Objects in the Layer list.

6　Right-click anywhere in the drawing. Click Options.

- In the Options dialog box, Files tab, expand Template Settings > Drawing Template File Location.
- Double-click the existing path.
- In the Browse for Folder dialog box, navigate to the location where the exercise datasets are installed and click OK.
- Click OK to close the Options dialog box.
  Note: In a real world situation, these *.dwt* files would probably be stored on a network where all users would have access to them.

7   On the Application menu, click Save As > AutoCAD Drawing Template.

- In the Save Drawing As dialog box:
- Verify AutoCAD Drawing Template (*.dwt) is selected from the Files of Type list.
- Verify that the Save In folder switches to the location specified in the Options dialog box.
- For File name, enter **A2-Template.**
- Click Save.

8   In the Template Options dialog box, enter the description as shown and click OK.

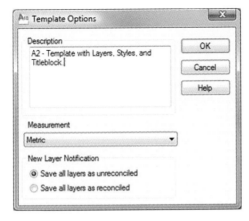

9   Close all drawings. Do not save.

Open a Drawing Based on New Template File

1   To start a new drawing using the new template:

   • In the Application menu, click New > Drawing.
   • In the Select Template dialog box, select the template and click Open.

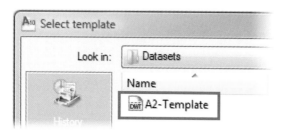

2   Check the units, layers, text styles, dimension styles, Layout1 settings, and title block of the new drawing.

3   Right-click anywhere in the drawing. Click Options.

4   Return the configuration settings to their default settings. In the Options dialog box, Files tab:

   • Expand Template Settings > Drawing Template File Location.
   • Double-click the existing path.
   • Navigate to the default location for the template file *C:Users<user name>AppDataLocal AutodeskAutoCAD 2010R18enuTemplate*.
     Note: For AutoCAD LT® users, navigate to *C:Users<user name>AppDataLocalAutodeskA utoCAD LT 2010R15enuTemplate*
   • Click OK in the Browse for Folder dialog box.
   • Click OK to close the Options dialog box.

5   Close all files without saving.

Chapter Summary

Because drawing templates serve as the basis for all new drawings you create, you should spend time creating and maintaining the required templates. If you are working in a multi-user design environment, this process becomes even more critical, as the time saved by using templates can be multiplied by the number of people creating new drawings.

Having completed this chapter, you can:

- Create drawing templates.

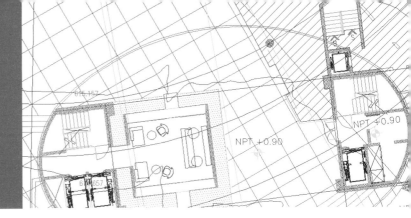

Appendix A

Additional Resources

Additional Resources

A variety of resources are available to help you get the most from your Autodesk® software. Whether you prefer instructor-led, self-paced, or online training, Autodesk has you covered.

For additional information please refer to the disc that accompanies this training guide.

- Learning Tools from Autodesk
- Autodesk Certification
- Autodesk Authorized Training Centers (ATC®)
- Autodesk Subscription
- Autodesk Communities

Learning Tools from Autodesk

Use your Autodesk software to its full potential. Whether you are a novice or advanced user, Autodesk offers a robust portfolio of learning tools to help you perform ahead of the curve.

- Get hands-on experience with job-related exercises based on industry scenarios from Autodesk Official Training Guides, e-books, self-paced learning, and training videos.
- All materials are developed by Autodesk subject-matter experts.
- Get exactly the training you need with learning tools designed to fit a wide range of skill levels and subject matter—from basic essentials to specialized, in-depth training on the capabilities of the latest Autodesk products.
- Access the most comprehensive set of Autodesk learning tools available anywhere: from your authorized partner, online, or at your local bookstore.
- To find out more, visit *http://www.autodesk.com/learningtools*.

Autodesk Certification

Demonstrate your experience with Autodesk software. Autodesk certifications are a reliable validation of your skills and knowledge. Demonstrate your software skills to prospective employers, accelerate your professional development, and enhance your reputation in your field.

Certification Benefits

- Rapid diagnostic feedback to assess your strengths, and identify areas for improvement.
- An electronic certificate with a unique serial number.
- The right to use an official Autodesk Certification logo.
- The option to display your certification status in the Autodesk Certified Professionals database.

For more information:

Visit *www.autodesk.com/certification* to learn more and to take the next steps to get certified.

Autodesk Authorized Training Centers

Enhance your productivity and learn how to realize your ideas faster with Autodesk software. Get trained at an Autodesk Authorized Training Center (ATC) with hands-on, instructor-led classes to help you get the most from your Autodesk products. Autodesk has a global network of Authorized Training Centers which are carefully selected and monitored to ensure you receive high-quality, results- oriented learning. ATCs provide the best way for beginners and experts alike to get up to speed. The training helps you get the greatest return on your investment, faster; by building your knowledge in the areas you need the most. Many organizations provide training on our software, but only the educational institutions and private training providers recognized as ATC sites have met Autodesk's rigorous standards of excellence.

Find an Authorized Training Center

With over 2000 ATCs in more than 90 countries around the world, there is probably one close to you. Visit the ATC locator at *www.autodesk.com/atc* to find an Autodesk Authorized Training Center near you. Look for ATC courses offered at *www.autodesk.com/atcevents*.

Many ATCs also offer end-user Certification testing. Locate a testing center near you at *www. autodesk.starttest.com.*

Autodesk Subscription

Autodesk® Subscription is a maintenance and support program that helps you minimize costs, increase productivity, and make the most of your Autodesk software investment. For an attractive annual fee, you receive any upgrades released during your Subscription term, as well as early access to product enhancements. Subscription also gives you flexible license terms, so you can run both current and previous versions (under certain conditions) and use the software on both home and office computers. In addition, Subscription gives you access to a variety of tools and information that save time and increase productivity, including web support direct from Autodesk, self-paced learning, and online license management.

- Autodesk Subscription offers a way to make software costs predictable. Whether a customer opts for a one-year subscription or a multiyear contract, the costs are known for the entire term of the contract.
- A complete library of interactive learning tools and high-quality, self-paced lessons help users increase their productivity and master new skills. These short lessons are available on-demand and complement more in-depth training provided through Autodesk Authorized Training Centers.
- Autodesk Subscription makes managing software licenses easier. Customers have added flexibility to allow their employees to use their Subscription software—in the office or at home. Better yet, designers are entitled to run previous versions of the software concurrently with the latest release under certain conditions.
- Get what you need to stay productive. With web support Autodesk support technicians provide answers to your installation, configuration, and troubleshooting questions. Web and email communications deliver support straight to your desktop.
- For more information visit *www.autodesk.com/subscription.*

Autodesk User Communities

Autodesk customers can take advantage of free Autodesk software, self-paced tutorials, worldwide discussion groups and forums, job postings, and more. Become a member of an Autodesk Community today!

Note
Free products are subject to the terms and conditions of the end-user license agreement that accompanies download of the software.

Feedback

Autodesk understands the importance of offering you the best learning experience possible. If you have comments, suggestions, or general inquiries about Autodesk Learning, please contact us at *learningtools@autodesk.com*.

As a result of the feedback we receive from you, we hope to validate and append to our current research on how to create a better learning experience for our customers.

Useful Links

Learning Tools - *www.autodesk.com/learningtools*

Certification - *www.autodesk.com/certification*

Find an Authorized Training Center - *www.autodesk.com/atc*

Find an Authorized Training Center Course - *www.autodesk.com/atcevents*

Autodesk Store - *www.store.autodesk.com*

Communities - *www.autodesk.com/community*

Student Community - *www.students.autodesk.com*

Blogs - *www.autodesk.com/blogs*

Discussion Groups - *www.discussion.autodesk.com*

Index

Notes

Notes

Notes

Notes

Notes

Notes

Notes

Notes

Notes

Notes

Notes

Notes

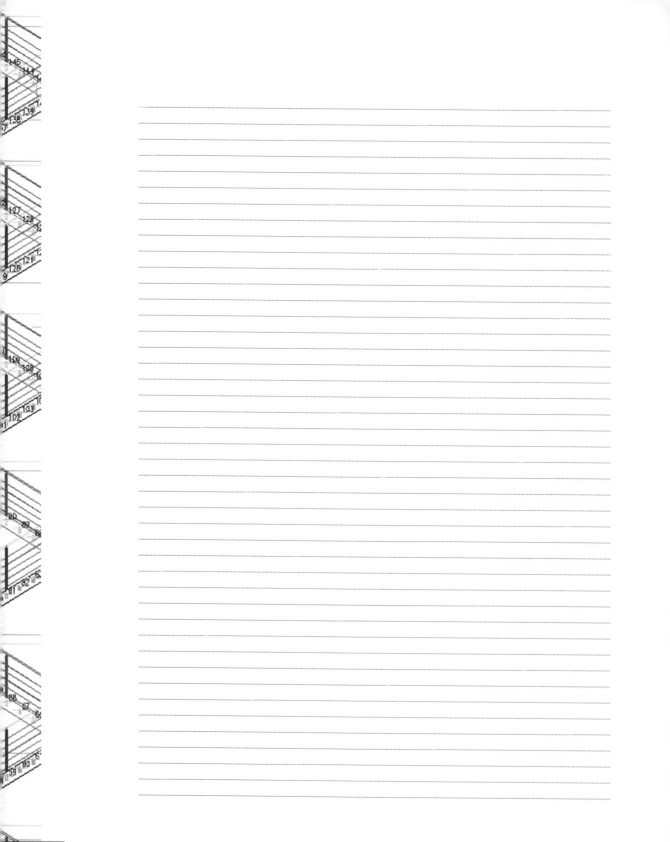

Notes

Notes

Notes